HOLLYWOOD ENDING

ALSO BY KEN AULETTA

HOLLYWOOD ENDING

HARVEY WEINSTEIN AND
THE CULTURE OF SILENCE

Ken Auletta

PENGUIN PRESS

NEW YORK

2022

For Binky

CONTENTS

HOLLYWOOD ENDING

PROLOGUE
The Gray Concrete Carpet

Once, he exuded power. Films he produced and distributed garnered 81 Academy Awards and 341 Oscar nominations. Only Steven Spielberg was thanked more often from the awards stage. He boasted of his friendships with Presidents Clinton and Obama, and of the famous actresses he claimed to have bedded. Inside the office, he terrified the four assistants who serviced his needs, and he bellowed at most of his executives. Outside the office, he flashed a dazzling, capped-toothed smile while strolling hundreds of red carpets, trailed by clicking cameras, often accompanied by his second wife, fashion designer Georgina Chapman, who dressed some of the stars lit by the paparazzi flashes. He was that rare Hollywood figure known instantly by his first name: Harvey.

The gray concrete sidewalk Harvey Weinstein crossed daily in the winter of 2020 was not a red carpet, but a gauntlet. Waiting for him to arrive at the criminal court building at 100 Centre Street were armed police officers and metal police barricades corralling a throng of reporters who did not adhere to the respectful protocols of a Hollywood opening. Because of his recent back surgery, when his black Cadillac Escalade braked in front of the New York State Supreme Court building, Harvey had to be helped out of the back seat by two burly men. He slowly shuffled in black orthopedic shoes toward the building's entrance a hundred or so feet away on a four-wheel walker, trailed by his team of lawyers and public relations advisers. Harvey did not pause and rarely looked up to respond to shouted questions or to smile for the cameras. Once inside the building, he dutifully emptied his pockets and passed through a metal detector. An elevator whisked Harvey and his entourage to the fifteenth floor, where he passed a second gauntlet of cameras and reporters before entering courtroom 1530 for his criminal trial for predatory rape and sexual assault.

Harvey's world—the world in which he was in charge—was upended forever over a few days in early October 2017, when *The New York Times* and *The New Yorker* publicly proclaimed that he was a sexual beast, and the Weinstein Company fired him. Seven months later, Harvey was indicted by a grand jury convened by the Manhattan district attorney. Now as he entered the courtroom, he faced a criminal trial that threatened to place him behind bars for the rest of his life. For eight weeks, beginning on January 6, 2020, Harvey walked this concrete carpet Monday through Friday.

He now dressed more like a midwestern businessman out of a Sinclair Lewis novel than a Hollywood power broker—drab, boxy suits; white shirts with crumpled collars; and dull, slightly askew ties. He looked miserable. He had lost at least seventy-five pounds, his pallor was gray, and his scruffy stubble beard failed to camouflage the crevices and lines of his swollen face.

In court, Harvey would settle into a low-backed leather chair, flanked by his five lawyers at a table facing Judge James M. Burke on his elevated platform. His prosecutors, assistant district attorney and Special Counsel to the D.A. Joan Illuzzi and her deputy, Meghan Hast, deputy chief of the Violent Criminal Enterprises Unit, were seated at a table to his right, close to the twelve-member jury box. Every day, about one hundred twenty-five journalists and spectators crammed into the courtroom; more reporters and spectators often waited outside to enter or for a chance to verbally assail Harvey and his lawyers.

Assistant district attorney Illuzzi would say more than once that Harvey's walker was "a prop" to elicit sympathy, a view widely shared by his detractors and not a few members of the press. In truth, Harvey Weinstein was not well. After a car accident in 2019, he had been dragging his right foot for a solid year, and his back was operated on days before the trial began to ease pain and correct spinal stenosis and drop foot. The operation was not successful. He also suffered from high blood pressure, elevated cholesterol, chronic diabetes, a weak heart, and he was receiving what his lawyer described as "shots in his eyes" to treat macular degeneration. In all, Harvey had prescriptions for twenty different medications.

Harvey had been indicted on five counts of assault and rape of three women: Miriam Haley (formerly Haleyi), a production assistant at the Weinstein Company; aspiring actress Jessica Mann; and established actress Annabella Sciorra. Woven throughout the prosecution case was the assertion that Weinstein abused his power as head of Miramax, and later the Weinstein Company, to entrap aspiring actresses, models, and women on his staff. After he coerced sexual access, sometimes brutally, they kept silent, shamed or fearful he would sabotage their careers. They wanted to be in the movie business, and he was not only their biggest but often their only connection.

Harvey's team believed their defense was formidable. Sex with these women was consensual, his lawyers insisted. They pounded the jury with evidence that both Haley and Mann, on whose testimony the case pivoted, kept in touch with Harvey after his alleged assaults, sending him emails, asking for jobs and favors, and eventually engaging in voluntary sex with him. Sciorra did not maintain contact, but the defense hit back hard at her for being unable to identify the year—1993 or 1994—in which the rape occurred, suggesting that she had lied. Two of the three other female witnesses who would testify also sought favors from Harvey after he allegedly abused them. And given the flood of negative publicity about Harvey over the two years since the stories broke, the defense claimed he was robbed of a presumption of innocence because it was not easy to locate jurors who did not have an opinion about Harvey Weinstein. Just over one third of the approximately six hundred potential jurors screened by Judge Burke in the courtroom prior to the trial were excused when they said they could not be "impartial."

This was understood by all to be a watershed trial. Typically in sex-crime cases, law enforcement chooses not to prosecute if there is no forensic evidence and no contemporaneous police reports. This case was even more challenging because there was email evidence that the victims not only kept in touch with their abuser but in some cases had consensual sex with him after being assaulted. By pursuing this case, District Attorney Cyrus Vance was seeking to enlarge opportunities to prosecute sex crimes. To the #MeToo movement and many others enraged by the abusive behavior of powerful men—Harvey Weinstein, Roger Ailes, Bill Cosby, Les Moonves, Bill O'Reilly, Matt Lauer, Russell Simmons, Kevin Spacey, USA Gymnastics doctor Larry Nassar, R. Kelly, among many others—the trial was seen as a reckoning, a call to justice for victims of sexual assault everywhere.

On February 25, after a trial that lasted twenty-two days over two months and was followed by twenty-six hours of jury deliberation over five days, the jury foreman rose and declared that his colleagues found Weinstein guilty of two of the five counts.

The packed courtroom went silent, then it abruptly flooded with two dozen armed court officers, four of whom stood directly behind Harvey at the defense table. The officers inched closer to him as Judge Burke announced that he was remanding the defendant to the prison on Rikers Island. Before Harvey was lifted by his arms and taken by two court officers out a side door, the judge set sentencing for two and a half weeks later, on March 11.

On that day, Judge Burke announced that he was sentencing Weinstein to twenty-three years in prison. Harvey's head dropped to his chest. He did not unleash his famous temper. Instead, he feebly responded, as if he could not believe this was happening to him, "But I'm innocent." He said this to his lawyers three times.

It was a long, dark road to this point. *Innocent* is a word few others would use to describe Harvey Weinstein, in this or any other context. Championing good movies and exhibiting good behavior did not always overlap in Hollywood, but Harvey broadened the chasm between the two. How extreme that divide was in the motion picture industry is one of the questions this book explores. The pressing question is how, and why, he was enabled, decade after decade, by the silence or shuttered eyes of so many in Hollywood, including so many of those who worked for him, to get away with sexually abusing women. To understand this culture of silence, it's necessary to take a close look at the architecture of collusion, both intentional and unwitting, that he built at his companies.

Those who worked for Harvey were daunted by his talent yet terrorized by his volcanic personality. After a long day in the office, staff members would sometimes repair to a bar for a recuperative drink to ponder the source of Harvey's frightening rage. As Amanda Lundberg, who started working at Miramax in 1988 and in her ten years there rose to worldwide head of public relations, put it, "We used to say of his home, 'They must have done a number on those kids.'" Shocked by Harvey's behavior, a former intimate confided, "He's like someone who's been raised by wolves."

But upbringing can only explain so much. Harvey's life offers confirmation of the Greek philosopher's adage popularized by George Eliot, "Character is destiny." Just as Richard Nixon or Donald Trump drowned in the currents of malice and paranoia that overwhelmed their judgment, Harvey Weinstein was unable to tame the demons that warped his behavior and will shape his legacy: One, his ferocious rage, which erupted without warning, alienating colleagues and competitors. Two, his predatory sexual compulsions, which he indulged and successfully masked for decades. Three, his promiscuous spending on films and expense accounts, nearly bankrupting his companies. And four, his unhinged, Shakespeare-worthy relationship with his younger brother, Bob Weinstein, which gyrated from an impregnable partnership to screaming matches, stony estrangements, and, at least once, bloody blows.

Harvey Weinstein was found guilty of crimes prompted by his raging impulses and his unquenchable need to dominate. But the question
his staff asked still lingers, rooted in one of the great films Harvey loved
and hoped to emulate. Orson Welles spoke of his creation, Charles
Foster Kane, as being burdened by an "enraged conviction that no one
exists but himself, his refusal to admit the existence of other people with
whom one must compromise, whose feelings one must take into account."

What is Harvey Weinstein's Rosebud—a loss, a lack, that explains
what came after? *Is* there an explanation for a life lived as he has? Any
such search begins in the Flushing, Queens, home where Harvey was
raised.

YOUNG WEINSTEIN

(1952–1969)

Ear-piercing screams were as common in Harvey and Bob's childhood home in Flushing as they later were in their company offices. In Queens, the screams usually emanated from Harvey's mother, Miriam, who by all accounts constantly berated Harvey and never seemed satisfied—with his grades, his eating habits, his weight.

Two years after Harvey was born in 1952, Miriam and Max Weinstein, with Harvey and infant brother, Bob, in tow, moved from Brooklyn to a six-story brick building in Queens, a rent-controlled working-class housing project known as Electchester, built by Local 3 of the electrical workers union, the IBEW.

The Weinsteins' two-bedroom ground-floor apartment lacked air-conditioning until Harvey was a teenager, and the brothers shared a bedroom. The apartment contained just one bathroom and a tiny kitchen; a slim dining room table was jammed into an alcove, and the only furniture in the living room was a couch and two chairs. But their Flushing neighborhood was safe, the subway was near, and trees and playgrounds were plentiful among the thirty-eight buildings on Electchester's 103 acres, located between Forest Hills and Fresh Meadows. Miriam's older sister,

Shirley Greenblatt, and her husband, Shimmy, lived in the apartment next door. Max was employed as a diamond cutter in Manhattan, working out of a small stall. "In a good year," Harvey would remember, "we went away to the Catskill Mountains. In a bad year, Bob and I got shipped up to Grandma's bungalow" in Monticello, New York. In those bad stretches, Miriam traded being a housewife for a secretarial job in Manhattan. Rather than dreary, Harvey recalled those summers away from the Weinstein household as fun.

One of ten children born to parents who immigrated from Poland, Max grew up in what Bob Weinstein describes as "a cold household. Nobody was close, and that bothered him. I remember him telling me that his father actually left in the will different amounts of money for different kids. So it was in his head that he wanted his sons to be close." Max was a heavyset, physically imposing man who smoked cigars but was quiet and withdrawn, leaving for work in the wee hours and usually returning after the family had eaten dinner. He dreamed of starting his own diamond-cutting business and raised the money to open a small booth in one of the crowded jewel bazaars, many of them Jewish run, on Manhattan's West Forty-Seventh Street. "In his head he's going, 'I'm a worker. I don't want to be a worker. I want to be a somebody,'" recalled Bob Weinstein, who was closer to his father than Harvey was. He did well at first by pairing jade with diamonds, and the boys followed his sales avidly. Left to monitor the counter one day, thirteen-year-old Harvey managed to sell a diamond ring for twelve hundred dollars. But lack of capital and copycat vendors led to the collapse of the business, and Max headed back to the grinding workshop.

In good years or bad, Miriam ruled the house. She was one of two daughters of Sarah and Joseph Postel, Polish immigrants who ran a small egg-and-dairy store in Brooklyn, but Miriam's modest background did not circumscribe her ambitions. Her hair was fire-engine red, and she always made herself up and dressed as if she were going out. She had a loud, shrill, New York–accented voice, recalled Harvey's childhood friend Alan Brewer. "She was dominant, overbearing, a somewhat nagging mother. She put constant pressure on the boys. Harvey called her 'Momma Portnoy.'"

In Philip Roth's novel *Portnoy's Complaint*, Alexander Portnoy's mother is always waiting for him when he comes home from school, always adoring and solicitous of her boy—until her will is thwarted and a gorgon emerges. Tormented by her constant complaints, he wonders, "How can she rise with me on the crest of my genius during those dusky beautiful hours after school, and then at night, because I will not eat some string beans and a baked potato, point a bread knife at my heart?"

Roth adds a bleak kicker: "And why doesn't my father stop her?"

Since Max rarely got home from work before 8:00 p.m., the boys usually ate dinner with Miriam, solidifying her dominant role in the home. Regularly, Harvey once told me, she would "kick our ass," like the "quintessential Jewish mommy." Though the daughter of working-class immigrants, she nonetheless had a much keener sense of the wider social landscape than her husband. She devoutly read the gossip columns, and at dinner she would quote from Earl Wilson's *New York Post* column: "Sinatra's in town performing at the Copa." The implication, which Harvey found alluring and Bob thought ridiculous, was that they should all go.

"She had style," said Bob Weinstein, marveling at her coiffed hair and always neat attire. He once asked her, "'Mom, where did you get that?'" "And she said that as a little girl she used to ask her mother to buy what was called the fancy magazines, like *Vogue*, and she'd look at these pictures and she was enamored of the glamorous people and the lifestyle depicted in these magazines and wanted to be part of that." Glamour held little appeal for Bob, who had an early feeling for numbers and preferred playing basketball and baseball. He drew closer to his father, but Harvey was under the spell of Miriam and her tales. "Certainly, Harvey's first passion was in making movies," Bob recalled. "However, like my mom he was attracted to the glamour and lifestyle that came along with being in the movie business. At some point, they became intertwined."

In their room, the brothers stayed up late to surreptitiously listen to Yankee games on their transistor radio. Before going to sleep, their dad sometimes read Damon Runyon stories to them, stories that celebrated New York characters who had inspired the musical *Guys and Dolls*, outrageous characters who were always on the make.

Max shared two basic pieces of advice with his sons. He counseled his boys to be tough, "to take no shit from anybody." And, recalled Harvey, "he also talked about John and Bobby Kennedy, and how loyal they were as brothers. So, he said, 'You always have to be loyal to your brother.' And he used them as an example."

The brothers would become known for locking shields against common foes—real or perceived—but Harvey showed early signs that his loyalty could shift depending on the risks to himself. One night, Harvey, who was not yet fat but had a lust for sweets and was sly, poked Bob awake to say there was a bounty of ice cream, cake, and candy in the refrigerator from the company Miriam and Max had had over. "Why don't you sneak in there, get it, and we'll have a little party," Harvey said.

"Why am I the one going?" asked Bob.

"You're smaller than me. There's less chance of you getting caught. And if you do, I promise I'll take the blame," Harvey said.

Bob came back with the goodies and they had a raucous time, laughing so loud that it woke Max. Bob explained to Max that it was Harvey's idea, but "Harvey feigned ignorance—a big double cross—and said he didn't know what I was talking about."

Bob was the younger brother, and Harvey's friends called him "little Bobby," when he wasn't beneath their notice. Bob was also less visible to Harvey's friends since he was two years younger, and years later as a teenager he attended a different high school. Bob did find ways of torturing his older brother and briefly gaining the upper hand. When Aunt Shirley gave them each a bag of M&M's, Harvey rapidly gobbled his up. Bob laid his on the table, slowly separating them by color, tormenting Harvey, who begged Bob to share. Later in life, Harvey demanded M&M's be available at all times and would consume them by the handful, berating assistants if they weren't peanut filled.

Harvey had a terrible accident soon after he turned ten. He and his friends were playing Davy Crockett, King of the Wild Frontier, after a favorite TV show, when a friend's toy musket slammed into his eye; he would require surgery and six months' recovery at home. It was, Harvey recalled, "just one of those rare moments in your life when things changed for me." A next-door neighbor, Francis Goldstein, a librarian, brought him books to read, and in the little room he shared with Bob, he devoured them one-eyed, the other covered by an eye patch. "I read *Gone with the Wind*, I read *War and Peace*. I mean, I started to read everything. . . . That's where the love of reading started." It's also where, after reading *Mila 18* and *Exodus*, he said, "I realized Jews could be tough like John Wayne."

The tough guy was a bit of a nerd. When he entered Campbell Junior High School, Harvey became a member of the Color Guard and the Cafeteria Squad. His school picture showed a teenager with a cap of short, dark-reddish hair, big ears, and a cherubic smile on a slightly chubby face. The eye injury did not affect his appearance, and the long absence did not affect Harvey's academic standing: he made the honor roll and was selected as one of a few dozen students chosen to skip the eighth grade (as his brother later would be too).

An early glimpse of Harvey-brand entrepreneurialism came in the seventh grade, when he and a friend pretended to be Boy Scouts selling cookies to raise funds for their troop. They purchased old uniforms and bought hundreds of boxes of cookies for thirty-nine cents each, going door-to-door selling each box for a dollar and pocketing the difference.

When Harvey entered his teen years, Miriam pushed Max Weinstein to get the boys out of the house on Saturdays. "It was Miriam's beauty parlor day," Bob remembered, and Miriam's red hair always had to be perfectly styled. At first the Weinstein men tried fishing. "We were bored to death," Bob said, so they started going to the Saturday matinees. Max, who was bent over the facet-grinding wheel all week, sometimes closed his eyes for a snooze during the action-adventure flicks while the boys stared, rapt. "There was magic in the theater. We felt close to our dad."

Harvey does not hold a vivid place in the memories of many of his classmates, and those who do remember him often say they ignored him because he wasn't part of a "cool" crowd. Movies became his escape, and then his obsession.

Perhaps the first film that showed him the real power of the medium was François Truffaut's unsparing autobiographical masterpiece *The 400 Blows*, a founding film of the French New Wave that hit the fourteen-year-old Harvey with the force of an epiphany. "It was a story about alienation," he recognized immediately, and it was "exactly what I was feeling."

The movie wasn't like anything either of the boys had seen before. Harvey recalled, "We'd seen every movie in the neighborhood—all the spear, sword, and sandal movies." One day, "We read that a movie called *The 400 Blows* is playing at the Mayfair movie theater—it's Truffaut, but we don't know this at the time. And we think, OK, here it is—you know, sex movie, *The 400 Blows*." They induced six friends to play hooky, walking two miles to the theater. By the end of the black-and-white film, the only ones left in their seats were Harvey and Bob. His friends had walked out, declaring, "This is shit, this isn't what we were supposed to see. Harvey, you're an idiot."

The brothers were mesmerized by the tale of the troubled Antoine Doinel growing up misunderstood in a decidedly gritty Paris and getting on the wrong side of the law, and by the raw, harsh, truth-telling quality of the cinematography, which ends with an arresting close-up of the runaway as he glimpses the sea for the first time. "The day I saw Francois Truffaut's *400 Blows* was the day I wanted to make movies. . . . I didn't know that you could make movies like that," Harvey said. "I thought all movies were Hercules and James Bond and *The Ten Commandments*, so instead here's the Mayfair movie theater, and the Mayfair movie theater is paradise. . . . Every week. Anytime I could go. Fellini. Visconti. I mean, my eyes were falling out of my head." He decided he had to learn everything he could about how films were made, and who got to make them. He read every book on Hollywood he could find, and developed an encyclopedic knowledge, a mental card file of the directors, stars, scriptwriters, cinematographers, even the casting directors of important movies. Harvey later recalled a time in high school when, riding the subway back from Manhattan, proud brother Bob quizzed him on movie trivia before an audience of college students. Intent on deflating him, one asked, "Who directed the Russian version of *Napoleon*? Of *War and Peace*?"

"I knew that it was Sergei Bondarchuk, and that was it," recalled Harvey. "These guys went fucking out of their minds."

The forgettable kid was suddenly someone to remember.

Inside, Harvey may have felt as alienated as Truffaut's Antoine Doinel, but he was a fairly ordinary classmate at John Bowne High School, a stone's throw from Queens College. Until the rule was changed in his senior year, boys were required to wear ties and girls skirts. It was a turbulent time. Anti–Vietnam War protests were surging. Harvey and many fellow students believed the war was morally wrong, and the military draft felt like an imminent threat to every male teenager. Like his small circle of friends, Harvey was skeptical of mainstream society but didn't find an outlet to do anything about it; he felt inspired by the protests and the hippie promise of freedom and self-expression, but at home under Miriam's rule, his red hair stayed short. His nerd status was easing, though, and he was finding places where he could make his voice heard; he served as an editor on the school newspaper and a member of the student council. Still, as he later recalled, he was "not part of the in-crowd."

Classmates could not recall Harvey having a girlfriend. Classmate Michael Ellenberg, an attorney, said, "Harvey was not particularly attractive to the opposite sex." And because he had skipped a grade, he was a year younger than the girls in his class and might have seemed emotionally immature. Cari Best, who became a children's book author, remembered him as "sullen" with "bad skin," and "not confident with girls," not bothering to flirt or perhaps being afraid to try. Margaret Bishop, a fellow senior, thought he had disdain for girls, and for most boys. "I don't remember him looking at anybody. His eyes darted about whoever he was talking to. He never seemed to be interested in what you were saying." Bob Weinstein insisted that Harvey had a girlfriend in high school, who he once introduced to the family at a dinner, but it could not have been a deep relationship since Bob does not recall her name or meeting her more than once.

Few classmates predicted great success for Harvey. Michael Fox, who sometimes hung out with Harvey and went on to become a lawyer and start a theater company in Washington, D.C., remembered that he was loud and "schlubby," and "not somebody you'd think would end up rich and famous. He just didn't stand out in any way in high school." His former close friend, Alan Brewer, who became a movie producer, agreed that "Harvey was not an impresario. He wanted to be cool." But he did see traces of what Harvey would become: "He volunteered to manage our band. He paid for our first recorded demo, and later on, during our college years, he got us work. When he was a successful music promoter in Buffalo, he got us booked as the opening act for Bruce Springsteen in Niagara Falls. He would hustle, get on the phone with people. Even in high school he had the idea to be an organizer of some kind in the entertainment business."

Childhood friend Peter Adler, a retired college professor, glimpsed the take-charge Harvey: "He was the kind of guy who was always getting people together." Although he was unathletic, Harvey organized their softball games. In their senior year, recalls Adler, they took a class together that combined English literature and social studies. It consisted of sixty students, two back-to-back classes, and dual teachers. The students were enraptured by the work of Padraic Colum, an Irish poet, who was then ninety years old. "I don't know how, but Harvey got the guy to come to John Bowne High School to his class and he read poetry to us. Harvey arranged that. He was very, very close to one of the teachers, Mr. Vidachuvich, and he would hang out with him a lot, talk with him a lot, and I would think he was an intellectual inspiration."

A female classmate who worked on the student newspaper and asked to remain incognito saw another Harvey: "He was a bully. He had a temper. He was arrogant. He took great pride and pleasure in being a jerk." It's likely the rudeness camouflaged an awkward teenager's insecurity, but the bombast and aggression would become a Harvey trademark, both a useful tool of domination and a habit he could not escape.

It might have been something he learned at home. Like Portnoy, Harvey discovered that his father was not King Kong. That role was played by his mother. Each weekend his group of friends played poker at a different house, but the one house they avoided was the Weinsteins'. Miriam yelled at such a high decibel level and fanned such tension in the house that they stopped playing there, said Peter Adler, who knew Harvey from age three because Miriam's sister, Shirley, was his mother's best friend. "Miriam would hover and she would natter, and she wasn't nice." She would scream, "'Harvey, do you really need to eat that bagel? You're fat. Don't eat that!' in front of his friends. It was embarrassing." How did Harvey respond? "He was afraid of her," Adler said. Alan Brewer also recalled Miriam as verbally abusive, "always comparing Harvey to the other kids."

It's likely she was also vituperative toward Max, with his cycles of success and failure, and the way he would empty out their savings on a dream. Even small incidents in the house were greeted with shrieks. Bob, in what was intended to be an affectionate and comic portrait of his parents, wrote of a trip to the beauty parlor gone terribly wrong. Tearful Miriam badgered Max for hours to tell her the truth about her hair, and at last he did. "The sound of horror that emanated from my mother will be remembered forever by those who heard it. Of course, Max was ordered to seek retribution: 'Have the hairstylist fired and sue the beauty parlor for everything they've got!'"

"It's hurtful to admit," Bob Weinstein said, "but it's true that there was a lot of screaming in the household, which was initiated by my mother. She could be gracious, but there was a volatility to her that was tough to understand as kids. . . . One moment she could be charming and make you feel good about yourself. The next moment, she could turn on you and be very belittling and degrading."

Experts on aberrant sexual behavior believe that what occurred in a child's home often critically shapes adult behavior. Dr. Glen Gabbard, a professor of psychiatry at the Baylor College of Medicine in Houston, who made clear he was not commenting on the Weinstein home, says, "In the home, one of the things you would look for is a mother or a father who has a sadistic streak and enjoys humiliating the child, making the child feel, in some way, that they acted horribly and deserved to be punished for it." The other thing to look for in the home "would be a child that felt totally unloved and has a deep wound from that and is sort of desperate to be loved as an adult—which is how so many narcissists are. They're desperate for validation and love from mothers."

Bob expressed love for both parents, but acknowledged, "My mother was the tougher one," the disciplinarian. Miriam's temper might well have been fueled by frustration with the limited options of the era, and with what Max could provide. She would pass that hunger for a bigger world beyond Electchester onto her sons. "Miriam was born out of time. She could have been Sheryl Sandberg or one of these CEOs of a company. She had that kind of smarts," Bob said. And she had a fighter's instincts. Reportedly, the quote she selected for her high school yearbook was "Don't scratch until you see the red of their cheeks." In the early days of Miramax, people used to ask Bob, "'Do you get scared meeting these guys at HBO?' I'd go, 'Are you kidding me? After living with Miriam and getting through high school, that was easy.'"

Bob described Max as "softer," a "gentler soul," someone he thought of as "a moral man." Asked what he saw of his dad in Harvey, Bob said simply, "I see my mother in my brother."

Bob describes Max as having "a real sense of integrity and doing the right thing." Harvey tried his best to craft a myth about Max, once asserting that after serving as a supply sergeant in Cairo in World War II, Max stayed in the Middle East after the war to secretly supply arms to the Jewish underground in Palestine, which was pure fiction. The real male authority figure for Harvey, thought Peter Adler, was Uncle Shimmy Greenblatt, husband of Aunt Shirley. Where Max receded, often retreating to watch TV or fall asleep in the living room, Shimmy loomed over every room he entered, a tall, heavyset, charming man with a prominent mustache, usually accompanied by a cigar and a story to tell. "He was a character," said Adler. "It's my contention that where Harvey got his business acumen from . . . was from Shimmy, who my father used to call a Damon Runyon character. He was larger than life. He was funny. He was great with kids. He would always give us candy." Shimmy owned an appliance store in Brooklyn and was said to brag that he tricked his customers into overpaying. Shimmy was a clever, innovative businessman. For poorer customers who could not qualify for bank loans, he offered free credit. "His attitude," Bob Weinstein recalls, "was, 'Sure, some will not pay back. But that's the cost of doing business.' He also introduced an installment plan where customers could pay five dollars per week. His business took risks. His mindset stuck with me, and with Harvey." Dressing up as a Boy Scout to sell each box of cookies for two and a half times what he paid for sounded to Adler like a classic Shimmy hustle.

On graduation day from John Bowne, Harvey's class of a thousand students was too large for the school auditorium, so the ceremony was moved to a seedy Jamaica theater that featured porn movies, its marquee announcing DEBBIE DOES DALLAS, and below that, JOHN BOWNE GRADUATION. The graduating class was predominantly Jewish, with just 5 percent of the students Black, Hispanic, or Asian. The commencement program contained a "heartiest congratulations" letter from President Nixon. Harvey did not smile for his 1969 yearbook picture; at this start of the freewheeling Summer of Love, he was dressed in a suit and tie, perhaps at the insistence of Miriam, and had a tense and somewhat unfocused gaze, as if a little unsure of who he was, or where he was going.

2

BECOMING HARVEY

(1969–1978)

I got accepted to five of the state universities," Harvey later remembered. "I didn't have tuition to apply anywhere else. We didn't have the money." There would be no Ivy League for him, but New York has a good system of public universities, and tuition was cheap for state residents. Before making up his mind where to go, the seventeen-year-old hitchhiked four hundred miles to have a look around the State University of New York at Buffalo, sandwiched between Lake Erie and Lake Ontario. A student told him that he could take courses on the history of blues music and grade himself.

"What do you mean?" he asked.

"You listen to Eric Clapton records and John Lee Hooker records and you decide whether you get an A or a B," the student explained. That cinched it for Harvey.

How true that claim proved to be has gone unrecorded, but it certainly fit the spirit of the moment. The year Harvey entered SUNY Buffalo as a freshman was the year of Woodstock, of revulsion at the swearing in of Nixon and Agnew, of the Stonewall riots, and above all of antiwar rage that was now splitting the country in two and dominating the discourse on college campuses, as the draft lottery hung over a generation's head. When Howard Kurtz, now a Fox News media analyst, arrived on the Buffalo campus in the fall of 1970, he remembered, "Many students regarded it as the 'Berkeley of the East.'" There had been a firebombing of the school library, faculty sit-ins, and student clashes with the police. Harvey was aligned with his peers in his love of music and abhorrence of the war in Vietnam. To Harvey's delight, even Max Weinstein supported the stick-a-finger-in-your-eye New York City mayoral candidacy of Norman Mailer and his running mate, Jimmy Breslin, in the fall of 1969 against incumbent reform mayor John Lindsay.

At Buffalo, Harvey slowly became more assertive, revealing hints of a money-obsessed entrepreneur and trickster in the making. In his freshman year he roomed with William Currao, who became a lifelong friend, and also struck up a friendship with Horace "Corky" Burger, a Buffalo native, who remembered visiting Harvey in New York the summer after freshman year and going to see *Hair*. At intermission, he once said, "Harvey was outside selling flowers. He bought them from someone on the street and was reselling them for a profit." Harvey's upbringing had teetered between middle and working class, depending on Max's fortunes, but like Miriam, he longed to make enough dough to see Sinatra at the Copa.

In Buffalo, Harvey thirsted to be known. He wrote for *The Spectrum*, the student newspaper, usually about music—the Stones, the Beatles, Fleetwood Mac, Sinatra. He adpoted a swaggering pose, and sometimes aimed to shock. He shared a byline with Corky on a piece about "Denny the Hustler," a fictive character who chased women in Buffalo bars and "did not take no for an answer." Denny's pickup line veered closer to intimidation than seduction: "Look, baby, I'm probably the best-looking and most exciting person you'll ever want to meet— and if you refuse to dance with me, I'll probably crack this bottle of Schmidt's over your skull. . . . Raw energy. Power. She cannot refuse. Another success for Denny the Hustler, who underneath all is one of the most ethical people you'll ever want to know." Decades later, Corky denied writing "one word of this."

Harvey and Corky also spent time selling ads for the student newspaper. They were terminated by the newspaper for unethical behavior, two former *Spectrum* editors said. "One day they gave me a two-page positive review of a restaurant," former features editor Christina Metzler recalled. "It was an ad." Concluding that they were not acting as independent journalists, she rejected it. "They went around me to the typesetters and said, 'Do this.'" Metzler went to the newspaper's editor, who investigated and "found irregularities in how they were getting ads. They were getting under-the-table payments" for writing glowing reviews. The "one word" that sums up the Harvey she knew in college was "operator," said classmate Jo-Ann Armao, today an editor at *The Washington Post*, who confirmed Metzler's account.

Asked about this recently, Harvey vehemently denied the story to me, calling it "complete BS." In his version of events, "no one was giving up anything under the table. We went from *The Spectrum* to another student magazine called *Ethos*, which was more interesting. And it was our decision." The *Spectrum* controversy and Harvey's response fit a pattern that would recur throughout his career: get called out for misbehavior, defiantly deny all accusations, then insist that severed relationships were by his choice.

In his adult years, Harvey would have few intimate friends, but he made three enduring ones in college. In addition to Currao, in his sophomore and junior years he roomed in an off-campus house with two local students, Eugene M. Fahey and Dennis E. Ward, who were active in Democratic politics. Through Fahey and Ward he got to know Buffalo mayor Frank Sedita and Erie County Democratic Party chairman Joseph Crangle; Harvey and his roommates served as foot soldiers in campaigns for local office seekers. Together they opposed Richard Nixon and participated in antiwar demonstrations. But when protestors screamed that cops were "pigs," Harvey drew the line: "The idea of calling these guys pigs made me throw up." Gene Fahey's father was a captain in the Buffalo Police Department and his mother, Barbara, Harvey said, "was like a second mother to me," offering meals and a

free couch where he could sleep on weekends. Fahey would affection-
ately remember Harvey playing football and blocking when blocks
weren't entirely necessary.

Throughout his adult life, Harvey remained close with Fahey and
Ward, their families convening every year for the July Fourth holiday.
Fahey was appointed by the governor as an associate judge on New York
State's highest court, the Court of Appeals, in 2015, and Ward served as
an elected State Supreme Court judge in Buffalo. Both retired at the end
of 2021. Harvey's closest lifelong friend would be William Currao, who
went on to become a pediatrician and, almost a half century later, would
be described by Harvey as "my best friend," frequently accompanying
him to court for his 2020 criminal trial for rape and sexual assault.

Harvey's first taste of the concert business came at the end of his
sophomore year, in June 1971. Miriam Weinstein, who, despite
her demanding manner at home, was sociable and an easy collector of
friends, in 1968 prevailed on a contact at Apple Records to give Harvey
a summer job at the label founded by the Beatles. She told her friend
that Harvey knew and loved music, which was true. Harvey moved
back home to Electchester while working the Apple job and was assigned a minor role helping out on George Harrison's August 1 benefit
concert to relieve famine in Bangladesh. One of the first all-star rock
charity concerts, it was held in Madison Square Garden. A limousine
arrived to ferry him to the concert. "We never saw a limousine where I
grew up in Queens," Harvey exclaimed. "I was excited. I was wearing
cool clothes. I had my pass to get into the Garden." The driver knocked
on the front door to escort Harvey to the limo. Always anxious about
her son's often slovenly ways, Miriam, Harvey recalled, "opens up the
window so the whole neighborhood could hear it and she barked, 'Did
you brush your teeth and wash your face?'"

The years of public and private shaming left scars, though Harvey
would eventually try to turn his resentment of Miriam's fastidiousness

into a banner of outsider cred in an industry that was reverential about personal grooming and unforgiving about excess weight. He would maintain a flat stomach only briefly, while in Buffalo.

Harvey was elected to the student council at the university, and, playing on his Apple Records experience, headed up its music committee and coordinated school concerts with an assist from Corky. Beryl Handler, the student union leader, worked with another student group to lure performers to the university, and she actively disliked Harvey. "There was a lot of resistance" to him, she said. "He wasn't popular because he would try to bully his way into concert situations."

Harvey's critics failed to deter him. A Stephen Stills concert had been scheduled for May 1972, but the university had exhausted its budget. Harvey, a college junior, flew down to New York City to meet with Stills's agent "and somehow," he said, "we convinced him that we could do the concert ourselves." Harvey promised to rent an appropriate hall and to pay them twenty thousand dollars. This, too, established a pattern followed throughout his life: Harvey made daringly bold promises, yet usually pulled a rabbit out of his hat. For their first concert, Harvey and Corky raised the money locally and made a six-thousand-dollar profit.

This success prompted them to skip final exams, drop out of school in junior year, and form Harvey & Corky Presents. With rock and roll ascendant, and with Harvey exhibiting early traces of his fabled moxie and salesmanship, Harvey and Corky almost instantly became Buffalo's preeminent popular concert promoters, luring the Grateful Dead, the Rolling Stones, Billy Joel, Diana Ross, Elton John, Fleetwood Mac, Bette Midler, Chuck Berry, the Police, Bonnie Raitt, Jimmy Buffett, and a highlight for Harvey, Ol' Blue Eyes, Frank Sinatra. A few of the acts, like Sinatra on September 4, 1974, performed at the seventeen-thousand-seat Buffalo Memorial Auditorium. Another venue they reserved was the old three-thousand-seat Century movie theater, which Harvey & Corky Presents would eventually buy. They also welcomed up-and-coming performers at the five-hundred-seat Stage One nightclub, which they would ultimately buy and remodel after New York's famed Bottom Line.

"Harvey seemed to be able to develop the right contacts in Buffalo," recalled Bronx-born Mickey Osterreicher, a fellow student who became the official photographer for Harvey & Corky. "He was politically connected here. But he also had music connections outside of Buffalo." They were not exactly celebrities, recalled Harvey's classmate Jo-Ann Armao, "but people in Buffalo knew Harvey and Corky . . . by their first names."

Buffalo's scrappy political scene offered some of his first tutorials on the art of publicity. Fahey and Ward persuaded him to campaign for the election of an establishment Democrat, Buffalo mayor Frank Sedita, and Harvey vividly remembered the story the mayor once told him about when he first ran for the city council. To get noticed, Sedita said, "What we used to do is throw a smoke bomb in the middle of the street. Everybody would come out of their houses and see the smoke. And then I'd jump on a soapbox and I'd say, I'm Frank Sedita, and this kind of crime—we won't permit these random acts of violence and crime if I'm elected councilman." Publicity, Harvey learned, often involved throwing virtual smoke bombs and turning them to your advantage.

People began to see the qualities in Harvey that would become familiar traits. He was cunning, brash, loud, and volatile, often screaming at those who worked with him. Dave Channon, a high school classmate who had always thought Harvey "didn't stand out in any way," also attended SUNY Buffalo. An artist, he crafted posters for some of Harvey's concerts, and was "shocked" at how Harvey's prominence and new power had transformed him. "He made a reputation for himself as the Godfather. He started to talk like Marlon Brando in *The Godfather.*"

Harvey had catapulted himself from being an undergrad intern to being at the helm of a company, and for the rest of his forty-plus-year career he would remain there. In the early days of Harvey & Corky, some of his management peculiarities and explosive habits were already taking shape. While he would nominally one day have corporate bosses to answer to at Disney, he mostly defied them. Harvey would never put in the years of apprenticeship common in the film industry, years that

might have taught him what it was like to be at the bottom of a hierarchy, or to be on the receiving end of a harangue from a boss who had
the power to elevate or destroy you, or to experience the pressure from
superiors to learn how to build teamwork and a harmonious corporate
culture, or to interact with fellow workers who were underlings or peers.
John Wolf, who was employed by Harvey & Corky, remembered Harvey's tirades about inconsequential things, like an order of jumbo shrimp
that wasn't jumbo enough. "As a boss, Harvey could be pretty demanding. But I learned everything about the concert business from him. He
could yell and scream at you, but the next day he would take you out
to dinner. If he was bad to you, he made it up in spades."

Harvey would occasionally mentor people he thought showed promise,
and he was shrewd enough to know when to be charming. But the tool
he seemed to reach for most often was a hammer. Negotiations were usually a zero-sum game for Harvey: only one side won. He felt compelled
to establish how tough he was in every exchange. Recalled a CBS Records
executive who negotiated with him, "He would push and push. He was a
very impressive and tough marketer. When other promoters were in town,
he would not seek alliances. He sought to kill the other guy."

By contrast, Osterreicher said, Corky "was very calm. He never got
ruffled, whereas Harvey was volatile." While Harvey displayed the bold
drive and moxie of an entrepreneur, Corky was an affable but grounded
businessman, playing good cop to tempestuous Harvey's bad cop and
keeping careful watch over the finances. Corky cultivated a neatly
trimmed mustache and usually wore a tie and patterned, wide-lapel
jackets; a bearded Harvey, still sporting a relatively flat stomach, favored
shirtsleeves—except when they persuaded Sinatra to appear at the Memorial Auditorium. Osterreicher's backstage picture of the trio shows a
tuxedoed Sinatra flanked by Corky and a freshly shaved, smiling Harvey wearing a wide-lapel three-piece beige suit. Max traveled to Buffalo
to witness his son's triumph.

There was little time for private life. "I never saw Harvey with a
woman in a social sense," said Osterreicher. "I never saw him with a date.

He was always working." And while Harvey lost his teen softness, he was still far from confident about his looks. A doctor who lived next door to Harvey and who became an investor in the Century treated him for severe cystic acne over his chest and back; he recalled Harvey nick-named himself "the Gru," short for Gruesome, when horsing around with his kids. Hope d'Amore, a student who worked for Harvey & Corky part time as an intern and would have a shattering encounter with Harvey, said he did have "a girlfriend at the time," though she doesn't recall her name. Harvey insisted much later, "I had many steady girlfriends in Buffalo. Two in particular."

It wasn't that Harvey was uninterested in women. At Stage One, Harvey & Corky's nightclub, Harvey was renowned for yelling at buxom waitresses to "bend over more." Harvey's predaceous reputation spread. Kauri Githens, a young disc jockey, years later told *The Washington Post* there were several unwritten rules in the Buffalo music world: "Don't mention the competition on the air. Don't put two car ads in the same segment. And, if you're a young woman, don't be alone with Harvey Weinstein."

Harvey was not the most confiding soul, but someone he totally trusted was brother Bob, who chose to enroll in 1971 at another nearby state university, Fredonia. The older brother was very much in command, and Bob was still Bobby, gladly performing as Harvey's San-cho Panza. By 1973 the brothers had both dropped out of college and had moved together into a rented house in Buffalo. Bob became an employee of, though not a partner in, Harvey & Corky Presents, whose dumpy headquarters were above the downtown Century Theatre. "Bob kept to himself. I don't know what his job was. I saw him at the end of the day once," Hope d'Amore recalled. Harvey physically dwarfed his shorter brother, who was just five foot nine. He had trim, curly dark hair that was already thinning, leaving him with a prominent forehead. He wore square, rimless glasses, but behind them his eyes were larger than Harvey's and more expressive, shaded by bushy, dark eyebrows. Unlike his more flamboyant older brother, Bob was more tightly coiled, a nearly constant scowl on his face. When Harvey smiled, it was a fulsome smile, mouth wide open. When Bob smiled, his lips usually stayed together, as if he were suppressing gaiety. The brothers were both quick with a quip, though Harvey's were more bombastic. Bob was often as invisible to Harvey's friends as he was in Queens, which annoyed him—they called him "Bobby," which he interpreted as a deliberate slight—but Bob knew what his mission was. It was to steer the brothers into the movie business they had lusted to join since devouring movies at the Mayfair Theater in Queens.

The company had acquired the decrepit Century Theatre mainly for Friday night rock concerts. The balcony of the Century had begun to sway noticeably during concerts, and Harvey and Bob, fearing that it would collapse, switched to showing movies instead. In the movie business, the kid brother who'd sat beside him through all those matinees was a full partner. Harvey would boast about how Bob came up with the idea to show three movies for the price of one on Saturday nights. "Bob had a formula," Harvey recalled. "At eight o'clock, he'd show a good movie," and then two less well-known films. He charged $1.50 if moviegoers bought their ticket in advance, and $2.00 if they purchased them on Saturday. They learned a lot about the way the audience responded to movies—and it wasn't always the way the brothers intended.

"What we did," Harvey said, "was we programmed a twenty-four-hour Goodbye Movie Festival. I mean all the hits that kids had loved over the years: *2001*, Frank Zappa's movie, you name it. The wildest movies. And in the middle of it, I put my favorite movie at the time, *And Now My Love*, by Claude Lelouch. And I put that in the middle of the festival." This 1974 film by the French director of *A Man and a Woman* meanders through the tragedies of two world wars and the ordinary passions of three generations, until finally the two lovers that fate intended for each other meet at the end of the film. Ten minutes into the movie, members of the audience started screaming, "Fuck this movie! Fuck French subtitles!"

Harvey came onstage. "Listen, you fuckers. I've given you so many movies. . . . This is my favorite movie. Those of you who don't want to watch this movie, go outside." A hundred or so took him up on the invitation, but the rest of the marathoners stayed and applauded the film, enthralled, he said. Harvey was beginning to feel that there could be an audience for the kinds of movies he prized. "That," he recalled, "is how Miramax started."

The 1970s were a period of fertile transition in American cinema. In the '60s the avant garde was associated predominantly with so-called world cinema—with the French New Wave directors, with Kurosawa, and with contemporaries such as carnivalesque Federico Fellini and dour Ingmar Bergman. Harvey and Bob championed these and other foreign films. But by the late 1960s and into the '70s, serious American filmmakers who had grown up watching the European films began making adventurous, risk-taking movies of their own, films like *Bonnie and Clyde*, *Harold and Maude*, and *Mean Streets*. The replacement of the restrictive Hays Production Code in 1968 with the more liberal Motion Picture Association of America rating system we know today (PG, R, etc.) let filmmakers push more boundaries. A network of independent distributors like United Artists and New Line, and new film festivals like Telluride and, eventually, Sundance, mustered to deliver quality independent films to the public. New York City in particular experienced a wave of art house theater openings. To read *The Village Voice* in the seventies was to sample the enthusiasm for auteurs that aroused Harvey and Bob and animated their dreamy hope of entering the movie business.

But first Harvey had a thriving concert business in Buffalo to attend to. He and Bob tried to lure Max Weinstein to visit more, but work hindered his travel. Max was able to come to the weekend concerts of

Sinatra, Bette Midler, and the Grateful Dead. He came alone, for Miriam, recalls Bob, "never came to any concerts." Unlike Miriam, however, Max never got to witness his name on their film company, Miramax, or the apex of his son's success in Buffalo, or Bob's early marriage to Vicki, a local hairdresser with whom he would have two daughters. On the way home from work in June 1976, Max was felled by a massive heart attack. He was fifty-two, worn out by the failure of his second attempt at his own business, this time cutting and selling synthetic diamonds in one of the world's centers for authentic stones. Harvey was twenty-four, Bob twenty-two. Miriam was widowed at just fifty. To comfort her, Bob moved back to Queens for six months to live with his mother. Harvey stayed in Buffalo.

Bob was left with vivid memories of Max. To save on the costs of a skilled worker, Max trained seventeen-year-old Bob as a diamond cutter, and the son absorbed some of his father's work ethic and attention to detail. In their memories, their father would be preserved in an amber glow, but there was a hint of the cautionary tale as well, for they would remember key events in later years when negotiating contracts and pushing for leverage. Never for a moment did they forget Max's unhappiness at being an employee, not an owner, or how his lack of capital doomed the launch of his own businesses. And left little for Miriam.

In Buffalo, by 1976 Harvey was celebrated as an impresario. Old friends found that he had become imperious. Peter Adler was living in St. Louis when Harvey invited him and other high school friends to a Grateful Dead concert. It was "really generous," Peter thought, like a high school reunion. "And it was, except that when we got there, that was the first asshole Harvey I ever saw. He was bigger than life. He didn't have the time of day for us." Adler was convinced Harvey invited his old classmates to show off.

Adler's father-in-law-to-be was Ben Heller, a noted dealer in abstract expressionist art who was close friends with preeminent artists—Jackson Pollock, Willem de Kooning, Franz Kline, Mark Rothko—whose monumental works were displayed in his luxurious Central Park West apartment. One day Peter and Harvey and some of their old high school friends walked around the tenth-floor apartment, marveling at the art and the lushness of the airy co-op with its panoramic view of Central Park. Harvey was smitten. "I'm going to be this rich someday," Adler recalled Harvey boasting.

Adler was struck by another change he saw in Harvey: he thought he had become a self-absorbed narcissist. When they were all together in the Hamptons for Adler's wedding, Harvey organized a touch football game on the beach. Adler thought his father-in-law, a gifted athlete who had been a semipro quarterback, should lead their team. Harvey insisted that he play quarterback. "He was a terrible athlete," Adler says, and his insistence on being the star turned a fun game into a tense one.

There seemed to be nobody in Harvey's life to say no to him—or if they did, he didn't pay attention. The earliest credible accounts of Harvey the sexual predator start from when he gained power and fame in Buffalo. Much later, observers would note that even back then Harvey sought to dominate men and women—men through intimidation, and women through sexual trespass. Harvey himself seemed perennially unable, or unwilling, to distinguish between an avid interest in sex and the urge to impose himself sexually on others. In an unpublished essay that mingled excuses with defiance, written after being exposed as a predator in the fall of 2017 and included in court documents at his criminal trial, Harvey suggested that his sexual obsessions began with the concert business:

> I GREW UP IN THE ROCK-N-ROLL CULTURE. I STARTED PRODUC-ING CONCERTS WHEN I WAS 19 AND I WAS A PART OF THE CULTURE FROM THE GRATEFUL DEAD TO THE ROLLING STONES. I'M NOT GO-ING TO LIE TO ANYBODY AND SAY THAT THE THINGS THAT HAP-PENED ON THOSE TOURS WEREN'T ROCK-N-ROLL INDUCED AND HIGHLY SPIRITED. PEOPLE HAD A DIFFERENT WAY OF COMMUNICAT-ING AND IN AN INCREDIBLE WAY MEN AND WOMEN WERE THERE FOR THE SAME HEDONISTIC REASONS . . . AND THE CONSENSUAL NATURE OF RELATIONSHIPS.

Harvey implied he was caught up in the counterculture of the seventies, a time of more open sex, "free love," *let's abandon the straight, square establishment ways of our elders.* The same attitudes pervaded Hollywood at the time. But the statement betrays his blurring of what "consensual" might actually mean for the women. The hedonism he referred to sometimes camouflaged aggressive sexual behavior. For Harvey, one other factor propelled his emergence as a sexual beast. Not until he had power did women pay him much attention. In high school, many girls considered him a nerd. In college, fantasy women appeared in his school newspaper column but rarely in his bedroom.

After Harvey's sexual assaults were publicly exposed in 2017, reporters dug up a trove of sordid tales from the period. Wende Walsh, who was working as a waitress at Mr. Goodbar, a downtown Buffalo bar, told *The Buffalo News* that when the bar closed at 4:00 a.m. one night Harvey asked for a ride. When the car door closed, he lunged at her. "He was a guy who wouldn't take no for an answer," she said. He forced her to perform oral sex. Two nights later, he was waiting on her front steps when she came home from her shift at 4:00 a.m., and to her terror, followed her upstairs, attempted to force his way into her apartment, and he exposed himself. Fortunately her cries for help were answered by her landlord, who chased Harvey away. "Complete and utter nonsense," Harvey said of the allegation, as he has of essentially every sexual allegation ever made against him.

His dangerous reputation was spreading underground, yet nothing surfaced to intrude on Harvey's momentum. By the late seventies, Harvey and Corky were producing concerts all over America, including tours for *A Chorus Line* in thirty cities. The two partners were close enough for Corky to make Harvey the godparent to his daughter. But Harvey and Bob were ready to flee Buffalo and pursue their first love, the movies. While Harvey continued to help run the concert business, he volunteered to commute to New York City and work two or three days per week as an assistant to Julian Schlossberg, who was the vice president of East Coast production for Paramount. At Schlossberg's knee, Harvey soaked up all he could about the movie distribution business.

As part of his work for Schlossberg, Harvey said he and Bob attended a lecture series on the movie business that Schlossberg ran at Town Hall. One particular lecture lingered in Harvey's mind and would shape his gonzo approach to marketing movies. It was given by Arthur Manson, at the time Warner Brothers vice president for worldwide advertising and publicity. Manson said the missing ingredient in marketing films was often boldness. As an example, he explained how he had sold *Willard*, a 1971 horror movie about a boy with pet rats. The studio and movie theaters didn't want any rats in the trailers promoting *Willard*. Manson thought they were wrong and tested his hypothesis in two Pennsylvania cities. In Scranton, the ads were rat-free, and the eventual audiences were sparse. In Wilkes-Barre, rats abounded in the ads, and lines for the film circled around the block. Decades later, Harvey's memory of Manson's speech remained vivid. "I loved the idea that you could educate an audience for a more intelligent film. And sometimes you have to put the rat in the ad."

Back in Buffalo, Harvey would often tell musicians backstage, "I'm only doing this temporarily. I'm going to be making movies." Phil Collins, then of the band Genesis, which performed for Harvey & Corky in February 1977, was the first performer who seemed to listen. "Hey, we made a movie," he told Harvey, describing a rock concert movie Genesis had made the previous year. No one had bought the film for distribution. Harvey bluffed his way into convincing Collins he could solve his problem. "Harvey told them," Bob recalled, "'I have the perfect guy for you. My brother Bob knows everything about distribution.'"

"I knew nothing," Bob later admitted. At the time, Bob did not have access to a single theater outside of Buffalo. The bluff worked, nevertheless. *Genesis: A Band in Concert* became the first movie the brothers distributed together. They treated the movie like a concert tour. "Instead of booking theaters, God, we would rent out big music halls,"

Harvey said. "Like in Pittsburgh, the Symphony Hall there, or whatever it's called. And we would rent it for three days, and tie in with the radio station. We'd present this movie event."

Harvey and Bob's early ambitions stretched not only to distributing films, but to writing and even directing. One of Harvey's concert lieutenants was Brad Grey, a fellow Buffalo student whose rise in show business would rival Harvey's; eventually he'd run Paramount. Together they developed the story for a slasher film called *The Burning*, and Bob cowrote the screenplay.

Harvey and Bob went to New York City in 1978 to explore this first potential film deal. Harvey asked Hope d'Amore, whom Grey had recommended to Harvey as an intern just months before, if she'd like to come along. A movie buff, she was excited. And though she had heard Harvey could be verbally abusive at work, she did not fear for her physical safety. She had a boyfriend; Harvey knew that. And she thought Harvey had a girlfriend. They had a long conversation about movies and she found him "extremely engaging and charming." Harvey was a good listener, capable of conveying not just sympathy but, she thought, empathy. He asked what music she liked, what movies. "He looked me in the eye. When I talked about film and Gordon Willis, it was like I was the only one in the room." Only later did she conclude that Harvey was not listening, but calculating.

When they arrived in New York, she waited while Harvey checked into the Park Lane Hotel. He came back from the check-in counter and said, "There's only one room. There's been a mistake. We're going to have to share a room." Alarm bells did not go off for her, since college students bunked together all the time.

In a poignant interview for a 2019 BBC documentary about Weinstein, *Untouchable*, a trembling, tearful d'Amore, now in her early sixties, looked into the camera and described what happened next. She got into bed; Harvey stretched out on the couch. She woke up to find he had climbed into her bed and was pressing his naked body against hers. She tried to resist, but she was all of one hundred ten pounds. Harvey had a not very romantic riposte: "Do you really want to make me an enemy for five minutes of your time?"

She tried to push him away, but he persisted. "I just thought," she remembered, "if I just shut up it would be over in five minutes." Instead, over the next hour, she said, Harvey forcibly performed oral sex on her, then intercourse. ("Another event that never happened that way," Harvey insisted.)

For weeks after their return, Harvey offered her gifts, which she refused. He never discussed with her what happened in that hotel room. She retreated into a shell and became sullen, depressed. Without warning, she was suddenly fired by an aide.

Hope d'Amore seems to have been Harvey's first rape victim, and he was learning what he could get away with.

At the time, she did not discuss what happened that night, fearful of Harvey's power. She didn't tell the police, remembering how Harvey would crow, "I own the cops in Buffalo because they work at my concerts." She was convinced he owned the press as well—Harvey & Corky Presents was an important local advertiser. "Nobody would have believed anything I said." Ashamed, she did not tell her boyfriend, even after they married. Nor did she tell her mother or sister. She punished herself with questions. *Why didn't I object when Harvey said we had to share a room? Why did I trust a man who said he owned the cops? Why did I say nothing? Why did I continue to work for him? Was I guilty of sending signals that my body was available to him? Was I too ambitious? Was it my fault?*

Harvey and Bob got their financing for the film, a riff on the classic urban myth of a serial killer stalking kids at a summer camp, which included the debut of two talented unknowns: Holly Hunter and Jason Alexander. Eventually released in 1981, the movie was not a success—the meager box office receipts were half the $1.5 million the movie cost to make—though in years to come it would enjoy some cult devotion for its campy excess. Despite the reputations they would develop for bringing quality movies to the big screen, Harvey and Bob's early years in the film business were scarred by many juvenile dead ends that took them awhile to escape.

Harvey never escaped his sexual adolescence. During the production of *The Burning*, another college intern, Paula Wachowiak, was told to go to Harvey's hotel room to get his signature on several checks. This might be the earliest reported incident of what would become a classic Harvey move: he opened the door wearing only a small towel around his waist, invited her inside, dropped the towel as he sat her on the bed, complained of a kink in his neck, and requested a massage. She refused.

"My first response was, 'Oh my God!'" she later told *The Buffalo News*. "Then I thought, 'This is fine. I'm just going to look at his face, get the checks signed and get out of here. These are sophisticated people, they do this all the time.'" She assumed, as would many others over the years, that his behavior was normal in show business.

Harvey insists it never happened. "Another urban legend," he said when I asked about Wachowiak.

A study of ninety-two rape victims interviewed in emergency rooms, written just a few years before Harvey's earliest alleged assaults, was among the first scholarly efforts to probe the range of emotions such women experienced. "Fear of physical violence and death was the primary feeling described," concluded Dr. Ann Wolbert Burgess and Dr. Lynda Lytle Holmstrom in their paper, "Rape Trauma Syndrome." They found that half the victims moved their residence after the assault, even if it had not taken place in their home. But fear and vulnerability were not the only reactions. Some women blamed themselves. Some told no one of what happened. Some retreated into a family cocoon. The authors likened the range of emotions to the stages of grief Elizabeth Kubler-Ross famously ascribed to patients facing death.

Hope d'Amore described to me the years of trauma she endured after Harvey's alleged assault—the medications for depression, the divorce, the move to San Antonio to be near her sister. She did not speak of her experience until the *New York Times* exposé appeared in October 2017, almost four decades later. Then she called Jodi Kantor, one of the two *Times* reporters who would win a Pulitzer Prize for exposing Weinstein, prepared to tell her story now that she knew there was someone ready to listen.

3

THE BOTTOM-FEEDERS

(1979–1988)

While Harvey was maneuvering to exit the music business in Buffalo, leaving the management to Corky, in 1979 Bob permanently relocated to New York to open a small office on West Fifty-Sixth Street, with Miriam Weinstein serving as the receptionist. It was Bob's idea to name the nascent company Miramax, a mashup of Miriam and Max, and Harvey instantly embraced it. Miriam was ecstatic, once telling a reporter, "It was the ultimate compliment for a mother and dad. Sometimes I slip into a film all by myself . . . and look at the logo as the movie starts."

The office space was a two-bedroom apartment, with Harvey in one bedroom, Bob in the other, and Miriam and the remainder of the staff crowded together in the living room. Money to fund Miramax came from Harvey and Bob and Corky Burger's personal savings. Together, Harvey and Bob chipped in twenty-five thousand dollars; Corky contributed somewhat less for his ownership stake. When Harvey relocated to New York full time, they soon moved to their first real headquarters, a slightly larger office at 18 East Forty-Eighth Street, just off Madison Avenue. Miriam Weinstein often brought rugelach and cookies for the small staff and was thought of by them as a warm Jewish grandmother.

It was around this time that each brother made a fundamental change: Harvey's weight began to balloon as he ate like there was no sating his hunger. And Bob now insisted that no one call him "Bobby" any longer.

Back in Buffalo, Harvey had been the dominating older brother, but from day one of Miramax's 1979 launch, Harvey and Bob were equal partners. They were genuine partners, talking constantly, sharing ideas, sharing the same sensibility. They saw themselves as outsiders. This was not a pose, a business tactic. They were genuinely defiant, determined to assault the Hollywood establishment. This became their brand. They believed the big studios were conspiring with theater owners to block quality independent films in order to make room for lesser commercial fare. Their Friday movie nights in Buffalo—and an utter confidence in their own taste—had convinced Harvey and Bob that audiences could be taught to like superior movies. Miramax would find the films, get them onto screens, and compel viewers to flock to them.

In fact, their real competition in acquiring films would come from the handful of other independent studios. The brothers' competitive zeal, coupled with their constantly simmering anger, led them to trash just about everyone. They bad-mouthed independent competitors. Bob would sometimes verbally insult them at film festivals; Harvey would sometimes threaten physical harm—against Tom Bernard, the copresident of Sony Pictures Classics; against Bingham Ray, the president of United Artists; and against Jonathan Taplin, the sales executive for the movie *Shine*, who Harvey believed had used him to bid up the auction price. Harvey reportedly grabbed Taplin by the shirt collar and screamed, "You fuck! You fucked me!" When Deb Newmyer, the producer, attempted to calm him, Harvey called her a "bitch" and was thrown out of the restaurant.

This was similar to their approach to negotiations in the music business. It was war—a zero-sum game, with only one winner. Other independent film executives may have shared their love of movies, but they were grouped as the enemy. But their prime enemy remained the giant Hollywood studios and the movies they were manufacturing in the late 1970s. "*Spartacus* was one of my favorite movies, and I've always considered Hollywood imperial Rome," Harvey told me some years later. "The arrogance of power that's exercised out there stupefies me." He believed big studios strong-armed theaters, actors, directors, and producers to comply with their wishes, while pretending they were truly interested in artistic freedom. But all that was glimpsed from a distance, on the wrong side of the fence. Harvey had lived in only two places, New York and Buffalo. His enemies were abstractions, which allowed him to hate them more.

Whether the high-handedness of the Hollywood studios fueled the rage the brothers seemed to thrive on is uncertain. What is clear is that Harvey saw himself as different. He was not a "suit," a term employed by real or imagined artists to describe studio executives who behaved like penny-pinching accountants who didn't read scripts. He refused even to wear one, preferring dark T-shirts and colorful suspenders. His one concession to vanity over the years seemed to be a perfect row of capped white teeth, which he flashed with a luminous smile.

Bombast aside, Harvey and Bob knew the movie business was changing dramatically. They were electrified by a vision. The decade from the midsixties to the midseventies had been a golden age for quality studio movies from talented directors: Arthur Penn's *Bonnie and Clyde*, Mike Nichols's *The Graduate*, Robert Altman's *McCabe & Mrs. Miller*, Stanley Kubrick's *A Clockwork Orange*, Francis Ford Coppola's *The Godfather*, Roman Polanski's *Chinatown*, Martin Scorsese's *Mean Streets* and *Taxi Driver*, among many others. Peter Bart, who was vice president of production at Paramount and later the editor of *Variety*, said that this period was "the last great time for pictures that expanded the idea of what could be done with movies." Peter Biskind, in his illuminating book *Easy Riders, Raging Bulls: How the Sex-Drugs-and-Rock 'n' Roll Generation Saved Hollywood*, wrote: "It was perhaps the last time Hollywood produced a body of risky, high-quality work—as opposed to the errant masterpiece—work that was character-, rather than plot-driven, that defied traditional narrative conventions. . . . These were often films without heroes, without romance, without . . . anyone to 'root for.'"

For the studios, the record-breaking success of blockbusters like Steven Spielberg's *Jaws* in 1975 and George Lucas's *Star Wars* in 1977 was addictive. Studios wanted films to blanket the nation's movie theaters, to offer moviegoers an entertainment escape. "Teenagers became the biggest moviegoing audience and never gave up that throne," said Orion Pictures cofounder Mike Medavoy. Films like *Top Gun*, *The Karate Kid*, *Raiders of the Lost Ark*, and *Ghostbusters* beckoned teenagers, and the studios compulsively followed.

The preoccupation with blockbusters and movies that tickled the fancy of teenagers coincided with another change in Hollywood: corporate giants like Gulf and Western, Sony, News Corp, and the Music Corporation of America acquired studios, making them subsidiary companies. "The result of that is that instead of the movie business being the business you were in, you were merely a cog in a broader industry," said Barry Diller, who ran Paramount and Twentieth Century Fox before his current incarnation as CEO and chairman and the largest shareholder in IAC (InterActiveCorp), a digital media holding company. The corporate owners were not satisfied with 5 to 7 percent profit margins. They demanded what they called "franchises" or "tent pole" movies with endless sequels. They hired budget-conscious executives to run their studios. Box office receipts and swelling profits were the measure of success, not memorable movies.

This was the Hollywood Harvey and Bob railed at. At the same time, the brothers understood this left a void for the kind of independent movies that enthralled them as teenagers. Miramax was by no means the first independent company to distribute these movies. New Line was launched more than a decade earlier, distributing a roster of forgettable movies like *Sympathy for the Devil*, *Sister Street Fighter*, and *Magical Mystery Tour*, but also a raft of foreign films they distributed on college campuses and elsewhere, including their first Oscar winner,

Get Out Your Handkerchiefs. Janus Films was still active, a legendary movie distribution company responsible for introducing American audiences to the work of the great auteurs of world cinema in the 1950s and '60s, including Bergman, Antonioni, and Kurosawa. With his encyclopedic knowledge of movie history, Harvey knew all this. He also knew of Donald Rugoff, a man seemingly forgotten by history but vivid to a cinema buff like Harvey. In the 1960s and '70s Rugoff's New York company, Cinema 5, successfully distributed art house and foreign films. Owen Gleiberman once described Rugoff as an "ill-tempered Jewish monomaniac vulgarian who reveled in his power, berated and harangued his employees . . . scarfed deli sandwiches with gobs of mustard dribbling down his shirt, cut distribution deals with gangster panache—and, through it all, showed exquisite taste in movies, as well as a virtuoso instinct for how to get people into theaters to see them." In a real sense, he was the proto-Harvey.

The Weinstein brothers may have been true believers in art house cinema on some level, but they also got into that end of the industry because they could. "The easiest way to get into the business was in the art film business," said Sony Classics' copresident Tom Bernard, then an executive at UA Classics. "You could buy a small movie in Europe for fifty thousand dollars, and if that hit, you bought more." The Weinsteins were not trying to build a studio; they couldn't afford to produce movies. They aimed to distribute inexpensive films produced by someone else, earning a 10 percent or so slice of the revenues received from the theaters. Distributing small movies was their first baby step into the movie business.

On their first trip to the Cannes Film Festival, in 1981, the brothers finagled a room at a ground-zero hotel, the Majestic, an enormous white Art Deco pile on the beachfront. But they had to share a bed in a room they complained was the size of a closet. They patrolled the bustling lobby and ground-floor lounge, acting as if they were important regular attendees, but they felt an arctic blast from what they perceived as the Hollywood establishment. The brothers returned with not much to brag about. The initial Miramax releases included films that did not match their *400 Blows* ambitions, including *Goodbye Emmanuelle*, an erotic film they purchased for twenty-five thousand dollars and would distribute. Harvey and Bob were frustrated, and blamed the movie industry for conspiring against them.

The first quality movie Miramax successfully pursued was *The Secret Policeman's Ball*, an Amnesty International benefit film featuring members of Monty Python. By this point, the filmmakers had given up trying to find an American distributor; Martin N. Lewis, who had helped produce it, liked the Weinsteins' noisy enthusiasm and made a deal with Miramax, but was puzzled by curious delays to the release. He'd mentioned to Harvey that he was working on a sequel, which had more Python material and a better director. Lewis hoped to sell it to a bigger, more professional outfit for good money once the junior-varsity team at Miramax made a success of the first film. Harvey kept promising a release but harangued Lewis several times a day, insisting that he had to have the sequel. Harvey finally succeeded in acquiring rights—but cut the two films with their two different directors into one, releasing them as *The Secret Policeman's Other Ball* in 1982.

Lewis, who had been a successful public relations and marketing executive, was appalled when he looked closely at the amateurish marketing campaigns the Weinstein brothers fashioned, a poor attempt at Python wit. He understood the value of controversy better than Harvey at the time, and threw the equivalent of a Frank Sedita smoke bomb, creating a TV ad that stations would have to censor. Knowing that Jerry Falwell's Moral Majority was on the warpath to expunge sex and violence and lewd language from movies, he crafted a commercial featuring Graham Chapman, the most respectable looking of the Pythons, wearing a women's tutu and fishnet stockings while standing in front of the American flag and declaring that he spoke for "the Oral Majority" and objected to the "lewd, lascivious" content of the film. Miramax submitted the TV ad to several New York television stations, which summarily rejected it. Miramax accused the stations of censorship.

Saturday Night Live ran the ad on "Weekend Update" as if it were one of their sketches, and the movie took off. "It grossed like an amazing six million dollars, which for an independent movie was fantastic," Harvey crowed. The film became Miramax's first success—and, for several years, its only one. At most, Miramax distributed just four movies a year; the company was barely profitable for most of its first decade.

Harvey and Bob realized they had to acquire more movies and throw them against the wall to see what stuck. They knew that other inexpensive independent films were making money. New Line's 1984 horror movie, *A Nightmare on Elm Street*, cost less than $2 million and generated a then astonishing $57 million at the box office. By the 1980s, thanks to the proliferation of video stores desperate for movies to line their shelves, independent films were not as reliant on movie theaters. Successes that defined the new age included Merchant and Ivory's *A Room with a View*, Spike Lee's *She's Gotta Have It*, Stephen Frears's *My Beautiful Laundrette*, Neil Jordan's *Mona Lisa*, and movies by directors like John Sayles, Louis Malle, Gus Van Sant, and Joel and Ethan Coen.

Propelled by competitive ambition, Harvey compulsively sought to learn more, almost like a reporter scribbling life-lesson notes from successful people, and from the books and movies he voraciously consumed. In those early years of Miramax, Harvey absorbed knowledge from John Eastman in particular, a lawyer who represented some of the biggest music moneymakers in the world, including Paul McCartney, Billy Joel, and Andrew Lloyd Webber. Eastman counseled that Harvey needed to own the rights to the films Miramax produced, just as Eastman had negotiated to assure that McCartney owned the rights to his music. When Miramax distributed films, it did not own them. But if it financed the production of a film, ownership would mean Miramax could create a library of films, forever generating revenues by renting the film to theaters, international distributors, TV stations, cable channels, video stores, and products based on movie characters. "John Eastman explained the music publishing business and how you could own these rights forever," Bob Weinstein recalled. All Harvey and Bob could do was file that advice away, because Miramax did not have the deep pockets to produce and own its films yet. But they now had a goal.

In the coming years, Harvey chose to ignore a second piece of advice imparted by John Eastman. In any negotiation to distribute a movie, Eastman advised, the end result should be "a win-win" for both sides. In addition, in a negotiation, "if you knock someone down, pick them up." Harvey preferred: if you knock them down, stomp them. Although Harvey boasted of Eastman's acute business advice, as Eastman watched Harvey build Miramax, he was struck that Harvey had "no friends," and was unlikely to make many.

After a few years of commuting to Manhattan from Buffalo, the relationship between Harvey and Corky came to an abrupt end. Harvey and Bob wanted to be the sole co-owners of a business carrying their parents' names. Corky was effectively running their concert business, and he made a bad trade, exchanging his interest in Miramax for Harvey's half ownership of the concert business. Possibly after a decade he had had enough of partnering with Harvey. Corky remained in Buffalo, continued to promote concerts, and several years later launched Media Projects International, a company that syndicated TV game shows internationally. "Money wise, I'm fine," he told his local newspaper in one of the few interviews he's ever granted. "I'm doing great. I don't have to work another day in my life." When the reporter asked Burger about Harvey she was "met by a grimace," and Corky admitted that he had not spoken to the godparent of his daughter in a decade.

Aside from his three former college roommates, Harvey had one reliable friend: Bob Weinstein. "Bob was the more regular guy," said one longtime Miramax executive, who described flying with the brothers in the days before Harvey picked up the habit of chartering private planes. "On a plane, Bob would play poker; Harvey would work. Bob had friends from high school; Harvey had few true friends." Donald Rosenfeld, a movie executive who is proud to call himself a lifelong

Weinstein adversary, says that Bob was more reclusive, Harvey more the networker: "Bob was the kind of guy who knows all the baseball statistics, but Harvey knows all the baseball players."

Because Bob was quieter, his role was often underestimated, though the brothers were equal partners. Tom Freston, who then ran Viacom's MTV and WH1, said, "I thought he was like Mr. Wolf in *Pulp Fiction.* He cleaned up the mess."

Bob was not so quiet in the frequent, no-holds-barred verbal battles in the office. "They were always fighting with each other," said one former assistant. "Bob was much more fiscally conservative. Bob was much more careful." Bob was more the businessman. Harvey was impulsive, instinctual, unrestrained by budgets. Miramax was cash strapped, yet Harvey spent rashly. These fights would continue for decades—yet the bond between them seemed unassailable. Staffers knew they fully trusted no one but each other. "It was hard to get between the two of them," remembers William Morris agent Robert Newman, one of the original Miramax employees in 1980. "It was beyond friendship. It was elemental." To criticize Bob to Harvey or Harvey to Bob was an invitation to office Siberia. Each would often cite Max Weinstein's admonition to them as boys: *Be like the Kennedy brothers. Always protect each other.* Bob would later write, "Not a day goes by that we don't speak to each other at least five times." We are, he continued, "not only each other's partner but best friend as well—an alliance that cannot be broken."

Even the disastrous experience of working on the 1986 movie *Playing for Keeps* did not sever their relationship. When they were in Buffalo in the late '70s, the brothers cowrote a script about teenagers who inherit a large house in a small town and convert it to a rock-and-roll hotel resort, a story loosely based on what they had done with the Century Theatre in Buffalo. This movie they would produce and therefore own. Harvey and Bob induced a London company to put up $4 million to make the movie. With insufficient experience and excessive hubris, they decided to codirect and to coproduce it. A then-unknown actress named Marisa Tomei had a supporting role. A producer of the movie was Alan Brewer, Harvey's childhood friend and the first of a succession of Miramax executives who would be hyperbolically described as "the third brother." There were only two brothers.

Playing for Keeps was a gigantic distraction for Harvey and Bob, helping explain why Miramax distributed only three forgettable movies that year, two Australian films and a Danish one. Shooting the movie in rural Pennsylvania was also a costly debacle, each brother dismissing as crap a scene the other directed. Brewer said they once insisted on shooting the same scene twice, first directed by Harvey, then by Bob. (Bob Weinstein denies this.) With no prior experience to teach them that actors need reassurance and to be listened to, not yelled at, the tension on set was excruciating. On the day of the premiere, Harvey, furious because he could not find material he wanted in order to make a TV ad for the movie, lashed out at Brewer, grabbing him by the collar of his sweater and punching him. Brewer pushed him away and fled for the elevator. "Harvey began to attack me again. This spilled into the street," Brewer later told *The Hollywood Reporter.*

This was not the most disturbing experience on the set of *Playing for Keeps.* During filming, according to Brewer, a young female crew member came to his office in tears. She told him that Harvey Weinstein asked her to visit his hotel room to assist with something. As Brewer recalled her account, "He forced her on the bed and held her down and went down on her. I asked her if she wanted to call the police or confront Harvey. 'No,' she said. 'I just want to keep him away from me.'" Traumatized, she still wanted her job. At the time, it was often unclear to women that a frightening or shaming encounter they'd experienced could legitimately be considered criminal sexual assault or rape, and it would be decades before women were encouraged to report workplace harassment. Women in a male-dominated field like film knew exactly how hard they'd striven to get the precious industry job, and how difficult it might be to find another.

The movie folded after a single week in theaters, effectively ending

Harvey and Bob's directorial ambitions. It also ruptured the friend-ship between Brewer and Weinstein. Brewer never worked with Harvey again. But Brewer, like many others after him, did not act on what he'd learned, despite his disgust. Harvey's female victim had told him she wished to keep her job, not make a scene.

A twisted culture was developing in the Miramax offices. By failing to control his temper, Harvey was intimidating, and thus controlling, everyone around him. In a rage, he would throw ashtrays or phones or framed pictures at male staffers, slam the wall, sometimes punch some-one. Former Miramax executive Mark Lipsky recalled a fellow execu-tive who once ran into his office exclaiming, "Call the police, Harvey just attacked me." He said Harvey struck him outside the building. No one called the police: these remained private Miramax matters.

More commonly, Harvey verbally abused staffers. He was less ver-bally brutal to women, remembers Cynthia Swartz, who then worked in public relations. "He would completely emasculate a man in a meet-ing." (His methods of controlling women took place out of sight.) A onetime senior Miramax male executive who does not want to be named described working at Miramax: "It was like walking on eggshells every day. It was an irrational workplace."

A few years later, in 1990, Miramax released *The Krays*, a British biopic about a pair of homicidal brothers who ruled the London under-world but were dominated by their doting mother. The likeness was irresistible, and staffers began referring to the brothers as "the Kray-zies." Fear permeated the office. The constant violence, actual or im-plied, became workaday, and before long executives and assistants were coaching each other how to survive it. Some staffers absorbed the at-mosphere by aping Weinstein-like aggression. If Harvey and Bob yelled, they yelled. If Harvey and Bob's temper erupted, theirs did too. Re-quests were demands. Abnormal behavior was normalized. A Miramax culture was forged.

People working for Harvey had two jobs: their Miramax job, and their job placating or avoiding Harvey. Employees wondered: *Can I get through the day without being yelled at? What if I criticize a movie he might have liked? Do I apologize or stand my ground? What can I do to make Harvey happy? What if Harvey insists on a Saturday meeting and ruins my family's weekend? What if he fires me?*

"They did with me what they went on to do with many, many people: they offered me a position that no other employer would have done," remembered Lipsky. "I came in as the head of sales and marketing. They were very good at handing out titles that were unavailable elsewhere, and at that point they owned you. Where were you going to go?" No matter their title, everyone felt like they were Harvey's assistant. And Harvey had help. Bob played the role of supporting actor in creating a fearful workplace, for though Bob was thought by some coworkers to be a better human being, he, too, had a volatile temper and dark moods. Bob, with his bushy eyebrows and closed-mouth smile, was intimidating. In the office, though, fear of Harvey was dominant.

Harvey's sexual aggression magnified the weirdness of life at Miramax. An anonymous female employee recalled two job interviews before she was hired. Before the first, she was briefed that Harvey was a bully. She was confident: "I can handle that." Before the second at a hotel, "I did get warned about him going into the bathroom and masturbating. But that person was very gossipy and I didn't think it was realistic—it sounded so out there." Three decades later, she admits her naïveté "feels a bit ridiculous now."

If he was warm when he entered his hotel suite after dinner to work with a female assistant, Harvey would say, "I need to be comfortable," take off all his clothes, and parade naked. Aghast when he first did this, various assistants would summon the nerve to ask him to get dressed. "Oh, pull yourself together," he would say in his deep, gravelly voice, as if disrobing at work was normal. It didn't matter whether you were a senior executive or a staff assistant; if displeased he would, seemingly out of control, rage at you, call you "a moron," or sometimes heave an object at you.

Many women would come forward in the wake of the 2017 *Times* and *New Yorker* exposés with claims that Harvey sexually abused them in the 1980s, including actress Cynthia Burr, who told of Harvey aggressively kissing her in an elevator, unzipping his fly, and pushing her head down on his penis. If true, it was an unusually reckless attack for him; he would generally favor the discreet spaces of hotel suites and the safety of his own private office, whose door he would lock after assistants had shown a young woman in for a meeting. Harvey would later deny all claims that he ever forced sex on anyone. His victims never publicly complained, so it's reasonable to assume Harvey felt little danger of being exposed—and thus he grew bolder. In the '80s, rape complaints were still often dismissed as the accusations of hysterical or vindictive women. But it's possible that the sheer brazenness of Harvey's assaults provided their own cover. Who would believe such out-of-control acts?

In the second half of the 1980s, Miramax employees hoped a new Harvey would emerge with the arrival of a new assistant, Eve Chilton, with whom he was clearly infatuated. She cut a striking figure, always immaculately attired, her long blond hair flowing to her back, reserved but always with a ready smile for coworkers. Harvey was not shy about his feelings. Daily, a dozen red roses were delivered to her desk, flamboyant if not artful. He lingered by her workstation. He invited her to the Venice Film Festival and meetings in Europe. Staffers cringed at Harvey's behavior, gossiped about it, but remained hopeful Harvey was changing, softening. Eve found Harvey funny and charming; she was drawn to his power, even perhaps to his rough edges. They quickly became a couple, inseparable despite their differences. Eve was more reserved and formal; Harvey craved attention and was a mesmerizing talker. "Behaviorally, she was the diametric opposite of Harvey," longtime Miramax senior executive Mark Gill said. The journalist Peter Biskind, the film historian who wrote a compelling study of Miramax, Sundance, and the birth of modern independent film, wrote, "There may have been something of Kay Corleone in Eve; when

Harvey didn't want her to know something, he figuratively shut the door on her, and she was content to avert her eyes."

While Eve had the outward self-possession of someone whose Protestant bloodline traced back to the first attorney general of the United States, friends said she was self-conscious that her looks were marred by a prominent port-wine-stain birthmark, like Mikhail Gorbachev's, that covered much of her forehead. Acting like the producer of a movie, Harvey encouraged her to get the birthmark removed with laser treatment. He was not immune to insecurities about his own appearance, as would emerge. Perhaps Harvey felt attracted to such vulnerability and relished the power implicit in being able to transform both Eve's confidence and her appearance. This pattern of rescue and dependence would recur with wife number two.

Whatever the dynamics between them, the new couple seemed blissfully happy. The kid from the ground-floor Queens apartment now spent summers at a family compound in a gated community on Martha's Vineyard. The Chiltons were members of the upper-crust West Chop Club, and Harvey enjoyed holding court there. He was getting closer to the refined life he'd admired in the Rothko-and-Pollock–lined apartment overlooking Central Park.

Harvey's social network changed accordingly. His new Vineyard friends were financiers like Dirk Ziff and Steven Rattner, Comcast CEO Brian Roberts, retail executive Mickey Drexler, singer Carly Simon.

The setting was different, but not Harvey's attire or eating habits. These Eve was powerless to change. John Schmidt, who was the chief financial officer at Miramax from 1989 to 1992, remembers visiting Eve and Harvey on the Vineyard. "Harvey was at West Chop in a polo shirt with food on his shirt. I wondered: What do the oligarchs of the American Revolution think about this?"

Eve and Harvey married in November 1987 at a private club in Manhattan, with Bob serving as best man. Eve was thirty-two, Harvey thirty-five. They honeymooned in St. Barts, bought a duplex on Central Park West, and in 1994 purchased a sprawling 8,800-square-foot white Colonial on six acres overlooking the water in Westport, Connecticut, later adding an additional guesthouse. They would adopt three daughters—Remy (known as Lily) in 1995, Emmy in 1998, and Ruth in 2002. Despite his work schedule and travel, Harvey was an attentive father, often driving his daughters to school each morning, delighting in the time he spent not only with them but with Bob's two older daughters from his first marriage. "Harvey was a good father to his girls and a good uncle to my two kids," Bob Weinstein said.

They did not forget their mother. In 1995, Harvey and Bob purchased a nearby Westport home for Miriam for $825,000, not far from Harvey (Bob lived in a Central Park West apartment). Miriam was proud of her boys, thrilled to attend their movie screenings, happy to eventually have a total of five grandchildren, who she doted on. "Harvey was devoted to my mother," Bob said.

Marrying Eve did not curb Harvey's gluttony. Eve worried about his health, hiring a trainer whom he dutifully paid and then chased from the office. She phoned Harvey's assistants constantly to ask, "Is he sticking to his diet?" Eve knew Harvey had impulse control issues. Pass around a tray of cookies and the tray would not get past Harvey.

Nor did his new domestic bliss diminish Harvey's ravenous sexual appetite. One of his new Vineyard male friends was appalled to hear the now-married Harvey "brag about famous actresses he slept with." Sex has long been currency in Hollywood. Some of these encounters were doubtless consensual; many might have been transactional. But many—and we are still learning how many—were in another category altogether.

Lysette Anthony, a British soap-opera actress, said she was introduced to Harvey in the late eighties when she was eighteen or nineteen, and told she must have dinner with him. Late one night when she answered the door in her nightgown, she said Harvey shoved it open and raped her in the entrance of her own home. "He pushed me inside and rammed me up against the coatrack in my tiny hall and started fumbling at my gown. Finally, I just gave up. At least I was able to stop him kissing me." Harvey has denied the claim, which, like others, did not become public at the time of the alleged assault.

Harvey was famed for lack of impulse control, but that does not satisfactorily explain these alleged attacks, or the careful choreography that got actresses into rooms they had no idea were perilous; such entrapment would have required some degree of advance planning. The earliest accusations against Harvey date back to Buffalo in the mid-seventies, and if these newer claims are true, then he was by now ten years into a career as a serial sexual transgressor, honing the tactics that proved effective and efficient. No ugly accusations had stuck to him. Harvey didn't seem to worry about being exposed as a sexual predator.

He did worry about his company.

By the late eighties, he knew that scrappy Miramax might go under. The movies he was buying to distribute—*Caribe*, a replica of *Miami Vice* that one critic called "abysmal," *Crazy Moon*, a romantic comedy a reviewer described as "vapid," *Ghost Fever*, a haunted-house comedy so bad the director, Lee Madden, demanded his name be erased from the credits—were not filling even small movie theaters. Harvey and Bob shared a fear that Miramax might go bankrupt. They were buying more movies than they should have, extracting rich salaries, spending more than they were taking in. Miramax was operating, Harvey said, "hand to mouth. I mean, literally, we didn't know whether the paychecks were coming in or not." In the office, chief financial officer John Schmidt recalls, a sense of panic spread. The atmosphere in the Forty-Eighth Street office was stormy. The decibel level of the yelling rose. Faced with one $250,000 bill from a firm that provided lighting for a Miramax film, Harvey told Schmidt, "I'll give them $150,000, if they want my business next year."

Schmidt asked, "What if they refuse?"

"Tell them to go fuck themselves!"

Bob and Harvey were battling more and more, with Bob struggling, and failing, to curb his brother's unrestrained spending—to distribute too many movies, to reserve too many hotel suites, to invite a too-large contingent of staffers to make a splash at Cannes and other festivals, to show off his largesse by picking up dinner tabs for actors or directors at the next table, to fly up to the Vineyard on weekends. Bob was fatigued, ready to give up: "I was offered a job that year from United Artists to be a film booker for sixty thousand dollars a year. I said to Harvey, 'This business, it's hard to make ends meet. I have a wife and two kids. We need a hit.' We took a walk. That was a euphemism for 'Let's get a slice of pizza!' Harvey said, 'Let's give it another year.'"

Miramax's financial travails were neither unique nor solely attributed to Harvey's extravagance. The entire independent movie sector was struggling. The market crash of 1987 had dried up investment capital. By the late eighties, only a half dozen independent films had grossed as much as $5 million. To the moviegoing public, Miramax was almost invisible. "No one had ever heard of the movies I was working on," said Amanda Lundberg, the second person hired in Miramax's public relations department.

After a decade at Miramax, the Weinstein brothers were exasperated. Looking back, Bob called this decade: "Phase One. We were a boutique. A niche company." Those were aspirational terms. Miramax was a bottom-feeder. If it failed to escape Phase One, the next phase would be unemployment.

4

THE BARNUM AND BAILEY
OF THE MOVIE BUSINESS

(1989–1993)

What Bob Weinstein called Phase Two arrived in 1989, when Miramax danced away from its financial crisis. The business pattern for the company over the next four years of Phase Two would repeat itself over the brothers' career together: there would be a cash drought, followed by a few movie successes, followed by excessive spending, followed by a drought, followed again by a few hits. There would be screaming matches—over Harvey's profligate spending, over what films to buy and how to schedule them, over anything at all, for these were explosive personalities—followed by brotherly apologies. A steady drumbeat of sexual assault rumbled through this frenetic churn, perhaps giving Harvey a sense of control and dominion lacking elsewhere, with his escapes ensured by the victims' shamed silence.

Harvey and Bob were almost broke in 1989 when a British venture-capital firm, Midland Montagu, spying a relatively inexpensive way to get into the movie business, invested $3.5 million in Miramax in exchange for a small stake. The investment allowed the brothers to open a $25 million line of credit, making it possible for them to distribute

more movies and to coproduce some foreign films. The cash infusion
enabled Miramax to distribute *Scandal*, a stylish, racy film about the
British Secretary of State for War John Profumo's extramarital affair
with a nineteen-year-old model, an indiscretion that brought down the
Conservative government. It was the first movie Miramax opened wide,
to more than art house movie theaters. *Scandal* was seen on what, for
Miramax, was a record number of screens—four hundred—and grossed
a healthy $15 million against their $2.35 million investment. It was,
Harvey boasted, Miramax's first "breakout film." For the launch, Harvey devised one of his marketing smoke bombs. Fascinated by how
much publicity the film *Angel Heart* received from its X rating, he urged
the producers to include nude shots of the star, Joanne Whalley, at the
same time railing publicly against the rating system. *Scandal* received
an X rating for its brief incestuous moments and Harvey got his publicity, though he cannily cut three explicit seconds, ultimately landing
the film an R rating that allowed it to open wide.

The film demonstrated, Bob chimed, that "we could make a commercial movie. We showed theaters we could take an art house movie
and broaden it."

With the infusion of cash, Miramax that year acquired for distribution another movie about illicit desire: Steven Soderbergh's cool, laconic
Sex, Lies, and Videotape, a study of a marriage coming apart under the
pressure of secrets and betrayals. Soderbergh was just twenty-six when
he wrote the movie on a yellow legal pad in the eight days it took to
drive cross-country from New York to Los Angeles. He raised a total
of $1.2 million to direct the movie in Baton Rouge, Louisiana, which
he accomplished in a single month.

The movie centers on an impotent man, portrayed by James Spader,
who videotapes women confessing their sexual histories. A buttoned-up
Andie MacDowell volunteers to discuss her sexless marriage to a cad
(Peter Gallagher) after finding out he is having an affair with Mac-
Dowell's younger sister (Laura San Giacomo). In the end, these two
repressed people—MacDowell and Spader—find each other. Among

the movie's feats was to titillate audiences without being salacious. Laura San Giacomo tormented Peter Gallagher by telling him she masturbated for Spader's camera, but no such scene was shown. Entranced audiences may have wanted MacDowell and Spader to make love after the charged scene when she turned his handheld camera on him, but Soderberg had Spader shut the camera off when they kissed, and this discretion was one of the most striking moments of a film that demonstrated that less can be more.

In the winter of 1989, the film was screened at the Sundance Film Festival in Park City, Utah, launched by Robert Redford earlier that decade and now the foremost independent film festival in the United States. It met with rapturous approval, winning the Audience Award as their favorite dramatic movie. A bidding war ensued, which Miramax eventually won by chasing competitors with a hefty $1 million bid to distribute the film to theaters. "They didn't even own the video rights," Soderbergh said. "I was sort of wondering, Are these guys nuts?" Soderbergh was taken, as other directors and actors would be in coming years, by the Weinstein brothers' passion for his film, by their marketing savvy, and by their daring claim that they would top any rival bid by one hundred thousand dollars.

The deal for *Sex, Lies* "was Bob all the way," Harvey said of his brother, who would for the next decade be as engaged as Harvey in making art movie decisions. "He was the guy who stood up and when we saw this movie, brought it back from Sundance, screened it for our staff. Bob said, 'This movie's gonna gross seventeen million dollars.' In a room full of people who thought he should be confined to a mental institution, I said, 'It'll gross six or seven million.' But Bob said, 'No, it's gonna gross more.'"

Miramax brought the movie to the 1989 Cannes Film Festival, whose organizers balked at introducing what they understood to be a sex movie into the competition for the prestigious Best Picture award, the Palme d'Or. Harvey insisted the movie was not prurient, threatening to show it elsewhere and to publicly call out the timidity of Cannes executives. Though Harvey had yet to develop real clout, the festival relented. Up against stellar competition—Jane Campion's *Sweetie*, Emir Kusturica's *Time of the Gypsies*, Jim Jarmusch's *Mystery Train*, and Spike Lee's *Do the Right Thing*—*Sex, Lies* won the Palme d'Or.

In marketing the movie Harvey reversed course. He played up the sex angle on a movie that, despite the title, featured more talk than sex. He employed still photos of the actors emphasizing their skin and erotic embraces. Cleverly, Miramax opened the movie in New York and Los Angeles only, allowing word of mouth to build before expanding to five hundred theaters. Eventually, the film transcended the art house category, grossing a then impressive $25 million at the domestic box office. It exerted a profound influence on the style and scope of subsequent independent films. It became, Peter Biskind would write, "the big bang of the modern indie film movement," comparable to the impact *Easy Rider* had on studio movies in the 1970s. Harvey and Bob were giddy over their success, convinced they had arrived with a movie that showcased Miramax as the rare studio that offered a welcoming home for artists. As would be true later when Miramax teamed with Quentin Tarantino, *Sex, Lies* served as a talent magnet for Miramax.

The Weinsteins made two other shrewd acquisitions in 1989, winning Miramax its first Oscars: *Cinema Paradiso*, a sentimental film about the transformative power of movies that brought tears to Harvey's eyes when he first screened it, captured the Best Foreign Film award; and Jim Sheridan's *My Left Foot* starring Daniel Day-Lewis, who received the Best Actor nod. A marketing effort Harvey used to promote *My Left Foot* attracted notice. Day-Lewis played a man whose cerebral palsy was so severe that he had virtually no control of his body except for his left foot, but with it he learned to write and paint. Aware of the fondness of politicians for celebrities and the cameras they attract, Harvey arranged for the actor to testify before the Senate committee that was considering the Americans with Disabilities Act. Senators who might have skipped a less glamorous hearing materialized to shake Daniel Day-Lewis's hand. Harvey also arranged a screening of the

movie for members of Congress, who clamored to appear with the actors and actresses Harvey also invited. A shower of press notices followed. The braiding of Hollywood and politics would become a Harvey
hallmark.

From ignominious beginnings, Miramax took the lead in the independent movie sector in the early 1990s with such acclaimed movies as
James Ivory and Ismail Merchant's *Mr. and Mrs. Bridge,* starring Paul
Newman and Joanne Woodward, Stephen Frears's *The Grifters,* and the
Madonna documentary *Truth or Dare.* But after *Sex, Lies, and Videotape,*
Cinema Paradiso, and *My Left Foot,* the spotlight was on the Miramax
brand itself, not just the films they distributed. Ambitious actors and
directors want to be associated with challenging movies, movies that
enhance their reputations and are celebrated at film festivals and with
Oscar nominations. So agents began to steer their talented clients to
Miramax. And when agents and actors visited, they were no longer
greeted by fifteen or so employees in the grim warren of West Forty-
Eighth Street, but by a small army of almost forty employees at Miramax's new 6,000-square-foot office on the third floor of 375 Greenwich
Street, a co-op building half owned by Robert De Niro, now a neighbor
and new Harvey friend. Miramax's presence in this once industrial
neighborhood, dotted with factories and unmarked concrete buildings
on the windy far West Side of Manhattan, would help boost Tribeca
into one of the hippest neighborhoods in the city.

Harvey's deep knowledge of movies also held great appeal for what
Hollywood refers to as "the talent," the actors, writers, directors, and
cinematographers. "A large part of the reason filmmakers would later
feel so protected and comfortable with him is because he could go toe-
to-toe with anyone about film history," observed a former assistant who
rose to a major executive position and, as with some former employees,
does not want his name in the same sentence with Harvey's. "He was
able to not only endear himself to filmmakers who cared most about
the art that they were making, but also as somebody who was set apart
from a world of studio executives who lacked his knowledge and

passion." *Passion* was the word Soderbergh invoked to describe why he wanted to work with Harvey.

Ambitious talent began to see Harvey as a career maker. "Miramax had such cachet as a movie company," Gwyneth Paltrow said years later, in describing Harvey's allure. "When I first met him at the Toronto Film Festival, I was really young. Someone said to me, 'Harvey Weinstein would like to meet you.' It felt so hugely important. My God, this is a huge moment. This guy was making the kind of movies I wanted to be in."

Paltrow had reason to be starstruck. When she met Harvey in Toronto, she had yet to star in a movie, though she had the sweet, blond beauty of a Grace Kelly and an impressive Hollywood bloodline. Her mother was the acclaimed actress Blythe Danner, and her father was Bruce Paltrow, the executive producer and creator of the memorable TV series *St. Elsewhere*. She had performed in summer theater in Williamstown and appeared in supporting roles in several films, including Steven Spielberg's *Hook* in 1991. At the age of twenty-two she would land her first supporting role in a Miramax film, 1994's *Mrs. Parker and the Vicious Circle*, a forgettable look back at the writer Dorothy Parker's role as a charter member of the Algonquin Round Table. Still, it was the first of many acting roles Harvey would bestow on her, and he would come to see her as emblematic of Miramax's soaring success.

Whatever insecurities Harvey's bluster and need to dominate strove to conceal, he was in agreement with the young Paltrow about his talents. He believed implicitly in his ability to read and fix a screenplay, and by extension, to edit a movie. "Harvey had a safecracker's feel for films, and the charisma to go with it," said John Eastman. "When he sat down with a director, he could say, 'This is how I see you making this film.'"

Telling directors how they might make a movie is, of course, why Harvey was increasingly disparaged as "Harvey Scissorhands," a bully in an editing room. The moniker was affixed to Harvey by Elliott Stein of *The Village Voice*, who would cite many films—*Cinema Paradiso*,

Scandal, The Little Thief, The Thin Blue Line—that Harvey imposed drastic cuts upon. Often, viewers felt he had wielded the scissors well. For example, Giuseppe Tornatore's original released version of *Cinema Paradiso* was 155 minutes long. To the chagrin of the director, Harvey insisted it be shortened to 124 minutes. Years later, Tornatore released what he says was his preferred 173-minute version. It was widely disparaged by the same critics who adored Harvey's edited version. But the impatient slashing down to the quick sometimes created tension with the very filmmakers Harvey claimed to revere.

Louis Malle was the head of the Cannes jury the year *Farewell My Concubine* won and was outraged when Harvey subsequently cut ten minutes prior to its U.S. release. The esteemed director suggested that Miramax had no right to wreath its print ads with the Palme d'Or. "The film we admired so much in Cannes is not the film seen in this country. . . . It doesn't make any sense."

Miramax's sudden success helped inspire a change in the big movie studios. The studio giants did not alter their appetite for teen-oriented action movies and sequels, but in the early 1990s they decided to copy Miramax by creating their own independent movie labels. Turner Broadcasting acquired New Line, which later became a division of Warner Bros.; Sony launched Sony Pictures Classics; Twentieth Century Fox introduced Fox Searchlight Pictures. Paramount's Vantage entered the fray too, as would Universal's Focus Features.

Other revenue spigots opened for Miramax and the studios. Megaplex movie theaters proliferated in the nineties, each with a dozen or so screens that required content, which gave a boost to independent and foreign films. Of greater significance was the massive expansion of video rental stores. "The emergence of the home video market and independent film in the U.S. were symbiotic," said Henry McGee, former president of HBO's Home Entertainment. The explosive growth of home videos coincided with the success of *Sex, Lies*. And starting with *Cinema Paradiso*, suddenly the foreign films championed by Miramax—the films that spoke to Harvey's first love—were selling. Time Warner's

HBO offered Miramax still another fresh revenue source: pay-TV deals to play Miramax movies on HBO. "Harvey was able to combine his artistic and marketing acumen with the checkbook of Time Warner," McGee said. Over four years, HBO licensed several dozen titles from Miramax, with the fees often exceeding $1 million per film.

When Harvey was selling a movie, McGee recalled, "he refused to take no for an answer. . . . In the years I was involved with movies, only one executive called me at home at night: Harvey Weinstein." Harvey felt no compunction about calling late to bluster and cajole. But while Harvey was the public face of the company, the nitty-gritty of contract negotiations was Bob's province. The Weinstein brothers quickly grew reliant on the sales they generated from HBO and from the video stores renting VHS cassettes, including the rapidly expanding Blockbuster, which would ultimately have over ten thousand stores worldwide.

In the early nineties, Harvey and Bob were regular attendees at movie festivals like Sundance, where critics, movie buffs, industry chiefs, and underlings watched four or more movies in a row, side by side with the actors and makers whose names scrolled onscreen. Right along with them, making rapid strategic, aesthetic, and financial calculations, were Harvey and Bob, as well as teams from the other independent studios scouting for films to distribute. Harvey relished the festival atmosphere, the parties where he could schmooze and grandstand and be on the lookout for fresh talent. The frenzied dealmaking and air of bacchanalia suited his restlessness and his roving eye, though he never drank, disliking the taste of alcohol and, no doubt, liking to maintain a level of control by staying sober.

Miramax brought an unprecedented competitive edge to the acquisitions game. Harvey flooded the festivals with a cadre of talented youngsters, who did whatever they could to secure an early look at a film with buzz. They courted hot filmmakers almost to the point of stalking them, crashed cast and crew screenings, and were rumored to bribe projectionists and lab technicians to access prints. Negotiation tactics when trying to lock down a film were a combination of a Senate filibuster and a Stalinist interrogation, sometimes lasting ten to twelve hours in a crowded hotel room, as happened with the thriller *Run Lola Run*. Director Tom Tykwer eventually stormed out after a screaming match with Harvey, who went in pursuit. "I heard these footsteps coming down the hall behind us, boom, boom, boom. We got into the elevator, and these hands grabbed the doors at the last moment and forced them open." Tykwer went with Sony.

Understandably enough, within the independent movie sector, Miramax was widely disliked by competitors. "I had a grudging respect for their taste" and their marketing ideas, said Bob Shaye, then the CEO of New Line. But Harvey "was a bully," he said, who threatened to destroy employees who left Miramax and constantly vowed to file lawsuits or intimidated people by physically cornering them in hotel lobbies or elevators when he didn't get his way. To some, Bob Weinstein was even more fearsome. Ira Deutchman, a pioneer in the independent movie world, had been a consultant to RCA Columbia Pictures and early on shared his enthusiasm for *Sex, Lies* with the Weinsteins, becoming a consultant to Miramax, a bridge between them and Soderbergh. After the movie's success, Deutchman was recruited to become a senior executive at New Line. At a Museum of the Moving Image dinner, Harvey walked over and generously congratulated him. Not Bob, who was pugnacious. "Bob shook my hand and said, 'We're going to bury you.' At the time, I heard that Bob was more of a pit bull than Harvey."

"I did not use those words," Bob Weinstein insists. "I might have said, 'You're the competition now.' We were upset to lose him. He was one hell of a marketing guy. And he loved movies." Among executives in the movie industry, Harvey and Bob were increasingly controversial, famed for their crude and sometimes ruthless behavior. "Harvey took pride in not paying bills," recounted Miramax's former chief financial officer John Schmidt. "But when you stiff a filmmaker you are stiffing the very lifeblood of what your business is. The whole independent film business is based on championing the small guy."

A famous clash occurred over Ivory and Merchant's 1990 film, *Mr. and Mrs. Bridge*, starring Paul Newman. Miramax was to distribute the film. When they screened the movie for the Weinsteins, Ivory once told a reporter for *The Wrap*, "Bob and Harvey got up during the screening and left, and missed the last third entirely." Later, the Weinsteins at first blamed a "family emergency," then claimed they were unhappy with the convoluted ending and wanted it shortened, though Ivory said they never saw it. Harvey insisted on testing the audience reaction at a screening at New York's Paris theater. With their fame ascendant after the success of *A Room with a View*, Merchant and Ivory resisted, demanding to be treated as artists with a vision and not workers for hire. The relationship was fraught. At one marketing meeting, an argument flared between producer Ismail Merchant and Harvey. The verbal fisticuffs became so intense that Merchant and Weinstein challenged each other to a real fistfight. Out to the street they marched, but no blows were exchanged. To achieve a truce, Paul Newman intervened to successfully block a Weinstein "solution," threatening to do no publicity for the movie unless Harvey backed off. He did. The film received respectful reviews from critics but attracted a modest $12 million domestic box office.

Merchant and Ivory vowed never to do another movie with Weinstein. Reflecting Miramax's growing power, a decade later they relented, agreeing to partner on *The Golden Bowl*. Again, Harvey demanded changes. Again, Merchant Ivory resisted, and decided to buy back Miramax's part ownership of the film. Ivory told journalist David Carr, "He's both a genius and an asshole, and unfortunately those things seem to go together."

In one sense, Harvey's bullying has always been commonplace in the movie business. Some of the most legendary Hollywood moguls— Adolph Zukor, Louis B. Mayer, Jack and Harry Warner, Harry Cohn, William Fox, Samuel Goldwyn—were famously overbearing and often brutal personalities. Temper tantrums are common among studio heads, producers, agents, lawyers, showrunners, directors, and actors alike. In

2021, producer Scott Rudin was compelled to step aside after he was exposed as a frightful bully. But even in this context, Harvey Weinstein's sadistic behavior stood out. Those who witnessed his outbursts described not a lovable rogue or someone as demanding of himself as of others, but rather a man with little self-control, whose tone of voice and body language seemed dangerous; at times, Harvey appeared about to burst with fury, his fists clenched, his teeth grinding, his large head shaking as he struggled to restrain himself. Sometimes he failed and physically assaulted people.

Donna Gigliotti worked at Miramax for three and a half years as an executive vice president of production and was a key movie decision maker who went on to win Academy Awards as a producer. A welcoming personality who had officemates gravitating to her desk, Gigliotti sat on the other side of a wall from Harvey's office. "I was sitting at my desk one day and thought we were hit by an earthquake," she said. "The wall just shook. I stood up. I learned that he had flung a marble ashtray at the wall."

Sometimes when one of Harvey's assistants made a mistake, Mark Gill recalls, they were ordered to go to a large chalkboard and write "I am a moron" one hundred times, then sign it and place the chalkboard in the lobby. By the early nineties, *Fortune* magazine listed the Weinstein brothers as among the worst bosses in America. As he often did when criticism could not be dodged or easily refuted, Harvey confessed, insisting he was undergoing a process of self-reform. "I think I was a bad boss. . . . I had a bad temper," he said. "I think I yelled at people way too much." He blamed being "a perfectionist and a micro manager. I still have some tendencies of doing that now, but they're way rarer to what I was then. And, I think, Bob too."

Harvey's assistants would say these confessions were cyclical, and inevitably followed by a return to old habits. They feared Harvey's sharp mood swings; feared he would explode when he couldn't find the peanut M&M's they hid because he was a diabetic, feared not having a pack of Marlboros or Carltons or a can of Diet Coke within reach when he demanded them; feared sitting across from him in a restaurant because he shoveled food in his mouth so quickly while speaking that he sent food projectiles across the table.

Successful staffers figured out subtle ways to manage him. After graduating with an art history major from Oberlin College, Amy Israel was hired at twenty-two as the assistant to the director of acquisitions and promoted at age twenty-six to be cohead of the acquisitions department with Jason Blum. She discovered that the surest way to keep impulsive, restless Harvey in his seat during a screening of a film she wanted to buy was to bring in a plate of freshly baked cookies. "This way I could keep Harvey in his seat long enough for me to get to the end of the film. He would just sit there and eat the whole plate. I thought it was a pretty clever strategy." Israel was not aware he was diabetic, since Harvey's health issues were closely guarded by his assistants, and with the way he ate it was hard to imagine he had diabetes.

Israel toiled for nearly eight years at Miramax. Looking back, she appreciated an often overlooked Miramax cultural virtue: "By starting at Miramax so young, you grew up in a culture where you learned how to think outside the box, where every closed door presented itself as a challenge in how you could break it down—either by using your intelligence, street smarts, or sheer force of will. Harvey would task you with a seemingly insurmountable mission and you would say to him, 'No, this is impossible.' He would show fifteen ways it was possible. You learned very quickly how to adapt to pull off the most incredible feats." If a staffer mentioned to Harvey that they just finished a really engrossing book, Harvey would ask questions, pressing to know the story—and if he was sufficiently intrigued, he'd demand they get on a plane the next day to visit the author to lock the book up for a movie. Many employees came to work with their passports, not knowing if they'd be told to jump on an international flight that day.

Whatever Harvey's flaws—Israel described him as "terrifying"—she also described the rare benefits that working for Harvey offered. She believes some of the "best people in the movie business" were nurtured at Miramax because the Weinstein brothers ran Miramax as "a meritocracy." Among those who went on to prominence and success were Jason Blum, founder and CEO of Blumhouse Productions, which produced *Get Out* and *BlacKkKlansman*; Donna Gigliotti, who would win Academy Awards as producer of *Shakespeare in Love* and *Hidden Figures*; Mark Gill, until late 2021 the president and CEO of Solstice Studios, an independent movie company; and Scott Greenstein, president and chief content officer of SiriusXM Radio. "As a young person coming up," Israel remembered, "if you were passionate, smart, and had taste, if you were a hustler, and could find the films first and close the deals fast, you could do very well there. At age twenty-six I was corunning a department of twenty-eight people around the world. When I discovered a Japanese film called *Shall We Dance* that I wanted us to acquire, he agreed immediately and put me on a plane to Japan by myself to get the deal done." This gentle comedy-drama about lonely people finding themselves through ballroom dance charmed critics and earned a profit of $9.7 million at the box office.

Even the most junior underlings were given opportunities, but "No" or "I don't know" were not acceptable answers to questions posed by Harvey or Bob. A former assistant (who preferred not to be named, fearing that Harvey's scandalous sexual behavior would tarnish his reputation) recalled, "You couldn't say to them, 'I don't know. I'll go ask so-and-so in the marketing department.' They expected you to know everything." By contrast, if you worked at a Hollywood studio as "a production executive or a development executive or a marketing executive, you pretty much stayed in your box." Over more than a decade, this assistant was promoted to a succession of senior executive roles.

Miramax was truly an entrepreneurial place to work. "I admired the fact that everything was possible," said Gina Gardini, who started working there as an intern right out of Northwestern's respected film school and rose over the next fourteen years to supervise Miramax operations in Europe. "I admired their relentlessness." Harvey's refusal to take no for an answer was often a virtue, particularly with his overpowering personality. "He was the most charismatic man I ever met in my life—when he turned it on," Gardini added. Once at lunch in a Fort Worth, Texas, restaurant with prominent NO SMOKING signs, he was asked to stub out his cigarette. He rose and went table to table, asking patrons for permission. He got it, of course.

What puzzled those who worked for Harvey was that he did not switch on the charisma more often. It was as if Harvey could not control the unpredictable emotions seething within. Peter Biskind described him as "a preternaturally charming man who is nevertheless a roiling cauldron of insecurities, in which self-love and self-hatred contend like two demons, equal in strength, canniness, and resolve. To listen to him for any length of time is to be continuously entertained, but battered as well by relentless waves of hubris, and drowned by apologia, false humility, and self-pity."

Many believed the rage that bubbled just below the surface was a volcano that Harvey could not prevent from erupting, its lava blotting out what he was able to accomplish when he bent his considerable intelligence to sympathetic listening. It is also possible that he got the results he wanted with less effort when he showed his more fearsome side.

Sayed Khorshed, Harvey's driver in New York for five years, says Harvey did not lack empathy: "He's a good man with a very good heart." He would send food out to Khorshed, invite him to screenings. Khorshed knew that Harvey could be brutal to his staff. But "I know that if I needed help, he would help."

While Miramax employees respected Harvey's talents, unlike Khorshed, few liked him. "I never had a single personal conversation with Harvey. I don't think he knew if I was married or had a family," said a former senior executive who worked closely with him. Most found him cold and remote. He had few industry friends outside Miramax. Despite their scorching verbal battles and sometimes rivalry, Bob remained Harvey's best friend. And to those in the office, his only friend.

By contrast, many adored his mother. Miriam continued to bring hugs and warm smiles, bagels and cookies to the office. If she used gentle bribes as a ticket into the arena of her sons' lives, their employees did not seem to mind. On her frequent visits she wore fashionable two-piece suits and colorful scarves, her bright red hair fixed just so. She would park in the paneled conference room when Harvey and Bob were on the road, leaving her as the center of attention as the youngish staff would gather round. She wanted to know all the details about who was dating whom and any wedding plans. She was a delicious gossip and enjoyed rehashing the Miramax screenings her sons sometimes brought her to. She boasted of how Harvey and Bob each called her daily, which is what she expected these employees would do for their parents. John Schmidt, the CFO who came to detest the Weinstein brothers, said, "I kept thinking, 'How did this kindly woman produce those two guys?'" And yet Harvey and Bob made a running gag out of how domineering she was.

Harvey and Bob were notoriously impatient, Gina Gardini remembers, but not with Miriam—"Bob and Harvey were never short with her. Or bothered by her." Harvey "always talked about his mother," recalled Vicki Gordon, a senior *60 Minutes* producer who got to know Harvey while covering entertainment stories and was someone he tried to hire. "He was a momma's boy." For many years, Miriam dated Arthur, a Queens teacher whose last name was unknown to those at Miramax. Harvey and Bob were content that she was happy. Her shrieking, ill-tempered presence that Harvey's childhood acquaintances described seemed to have been softened by time, or by her sons' success—although Ivana Lowell, who worked at Miramax in the 1990s and dated Bob, remembered that "when they got an Oscar, it would be 'So, where's the next one?' It was never quite good enough, whatever they did."

Certainly Miriam was enjoying her proximity to the kind of glamour she'd pored over in the glossy magazines she loved, as well as the chance to wield some mild influence. Some employees glimpsed a less attractive side of sweet Miriam. "She might have been a very difficult mother," said Jonathan Gordon, who started as a Miramax intern in

1992 and after several years as one of Harvey's assistants rose to senior executive positions, leaving fifteen years later to become cohead of production at Universal Studios. He liked Miriam, found her kind and capable of real warmth. He also came to see traces of Harvey in her. He recalled the time Miriam requested that he hire someone "because she met the girl's grandmother at the beauty parlor" and promised that her son would hire her granddaughter. Miriam didn't even know the girl, yet she told him, "'Jon, she's going to be fantastic.' Her approach to me was, 'I'd like you to do this for me.'"

Miriam's charm, people learned, sometimes ended abruptly. Amanda Lundberg, who joined Miramax's public relations arm in 1988, left in 1995, and was rehired early in the new century as worldwide head of PR, had a warm relationship with her. When Lundberg returned, she reintroduced herself on one of her visits. "Hi, Miriam. Remember me?"

"No," Miriam responded.

Shocked, Lundberg asked, "Why?"

"You must not have made an impression on me," Miriam replied.

Lundberg was struck by her lack of empathy or awareness of the effect her words had on people. "She didn't realize how it sounded. It was not deliberate." But it was a trait Lundberg saw in Harvey as well.

Consider the temptations for a man like Harvey, surrounded by women seeking opportunity and showering him with compliments about his movies, his brilliance. It is not uncommon for famous and powerful men to confuse a compliment with a come-on. Surely, this was true of fellow moguls over the life of Hollywood. Rare were moments when members of the film community harshly judged promiscuous behavior.

However, Harvey had already violated the extremely forgiving codes of behavior for men in power. His game was not seduction, but subjugation, and he sought out the vulnerable. His boastful, trophy mentality toward actresses has been noted by many, but he also prowled among his own staff.

Laura Madden, an Irish-born assistant, was hired in 1992 to work in the London office. One day, she said, Harvey asked her to come to his Dublin suite, and took a few moments to praise her work on the production crew of a Miramax movie, dangling the possibility of a promotion. The conversation quickly veered into a familiar Harvey lament: he had a stiff neck and needed a massage. Without warning, he instructed her to undress, sexually assaulted her, and masturbated over her. Then he commanded her to join him in the shower. She began to sob so uncontrollably that, irritated, he rushed from the bathroom. She recalls hearing the sounds of him continuing to masturbate on the other side of the door as she wept. Badly wanting the job, given assurances that he would not again misbehave, and somewhat reassured that he was based in faraway New York, for the next six years Madden continued as a production assistant for Miramax in London. Like many victims of sexual assault, she felt enormous guilt and shame, blaming herself for getting in the shower as instructed, and then for continuing to work for Harvey. So she kept quiet—for twenty-five years. She would be the first woman of all those who shared their experiences with Jodi Kantor and Megan Twohey to agree to go on the record.

Around this time, at the Martha's Vineyard home of the novelist William Styron, one of his heroes, Harvey met a woman who told him that her daughter, Katherine Kendall, aspired to be an actress. Harvey offered to advance her career. He asked the twenty-three-year-old to go to a screening with him and then pop by his apartment while he picked up something. He emerged from the bathroom naked, demanding a massage, and when she refused, asked for her to at least show him her breasts. She told him she was late to meet her boyfriend. Suspicious, he said he would accompany her. She jumped from their taxi and ran into a bar and begged the bartender to pretend he was her boyfriend, as Harvey watched from the taxi.

Harvey denies he assaulted her. And Kendall did not report the incident. "There were no cuts or bruises, so what recourse did I have?" she said later. "So I thought immediately: 'I better shut up. No one is going to care.'" If Harvey would assault someone so close to one of his idols, it suggests how compulsive his sexual urges were—and how certain he was that he would not be called to account.

Nor did a connection to a senior executive offer any protection. The daughter of close friends of CFO John Schmidt started working at Miramax in 1990; like many of the young women hired there, she was attractive as well as bright. Sometime later, Schmidt noticed she was no longer in the office. He asked her parents why. They gave him devastating news, telling him that Harvey had sexually assaulted their daughter, and that she had resisted and quit. Schmidt said he confronted Harvey, who, in one of the rare occasions when he acknowledged inappropriate behavior and apologized, told Schmidt that it was "a one-off." He said that he was sorry, and it wouldn't happen again. Naïvely, Schmidt laments, "I did not think it was a pattern."

Kathy DeClesis, Bob Weinstein's assistant, left the company immediately after reading a letter from the young woman's attorney announcing that he was filing a lawsuit on her behalf against Harvey. The existence of this letter raced through the office like a brushfire. This was perhaps the first time Harvey was truly fearful of being exposed. He got his lawyers to induce the young woman to sign one of Harvey's first coerced nondisclosure agreements (NDAs). He would pay to make the young woman disappear.

And so she did. In these NDAs Harvey acquired a new and powerful tool that his teams of lawyers would wield with the same frightful monotony as the assaults themselves. The Miramax workplace returned to what passed for normalcy, as it did for CFO Schmidt, who did not resign until a few years later, in 1993, burdened by guilt: "I did not leave immediately. I think about that a lot."

All these instances show Harvey cornering young women with little power. And yet successful actresses were not safe either. Harvey seemed to view the casting and production stages of his films as a kind of one-stop shopping for sexual opportunity, testing to see how far he could go in positions where he had the upper hand. As the 1992 Miramax thriller *Love Crimes* was wrapping, its star Sean Young was seated in Harvey's office when she said he pulled his penis out. "You know, Harvey, I really wouldn't be pulling that thing out because it's really not pretty," she remembered saying. "I got up and I left." Young said that Harvey punished her by spreading tales that she was difficult, hobbling her career. As she put it, "The minute you actually stand up for yourself in Hollywood, you're the crazy one."

Also in 1992, another actress, Rosanna Arquette, would make similar claims. Harvey invited Arquette to meet by dangling a potential role opposite Gary Oldman, an actor she admired. Harvey invited her to pick up the script for *True Romance* and join him for dinner in the Polo Lounge of the Beverly Hills Hotel. When Arquette arrived, she was told Harvey would see her upstairs. He opened the door wearing a white bathrobe, she said, and greeted her with: "Rosanna, I can't move my neck." He asked for a massage. She refused. She says he grabbed her hand and pushed it onto his exposed penis. She yanked her hand away. He boasted, as he often would when initially rejected by a woman, of the prominent actresses and models who'd cooperated and whose careers benefited. Disgusted, Arquette stormed out. Two years later, she did appear in another Miramax movie, *Pulp Fiction*, and did not speak out about the incident—but remains convinced that, despite giving her this small role in one of the company's signature hits, Harvey tried to harm her career by spreading rumors that she was difficult to work with.

When Arquette's account of his behavior was recently relayed to Harvey, he flatly denied it to me and said he'd be willing to take a lie detector test and to pay for one by Arquette.

The man who would become Miramax's most consequential director was a middle school dropout who got his cinematic education from reading books, watching TV, and working in a Los Angeles video store, where he spent days and nights coaxing customers to watch his favorites. It was a biography virtually designed to make Harvey love Quentin Tarantino. One of the video store customers misheard Tarantino's recommendation of Louis Malle's elegiac World War II film *Au Revoir les Enfants* (Goodbye, Children) as "Reservoir Dogs," and the title lodged in his mind. He set out to write a script about a ring of incompetent but shockingly vicious jewel thieves infiltrated by an undercover cop. He showed the script to the dancer and actor Lawrence Bender, who had an inexpensive horror movie as his single producing credit. Bender was excited, and persuaded a friend to give it to Harvey Keitel, a respected actor whose career had been somewhat overshadowed by Robert De Niro's. Keitel loved the script and knew that Tarantino was insisting on directing the movie. Keitel felt you should believe in the talent. He felt that about himself too. Remarkably, given the raffishness and inexperience of the writer and producer, he signed on as the lead, on the basis of which Bender raised $1.5 million. Shown at Sundance in the winter of 1992, *Reservoir Dogs* was both lauded and condemned for its violence. At the end of the Sundance screening, an audience member rose and asked Tarantino to justify all the blood.

"I don't know about you, but I love violent movies," Tarantino shot back. "What I find offensive is that Merchant-Ivory shit." Like Harvey, Tarantino enjoyed behaving like a rebel. His put-downs of critics and those he considered vanilla moviemakers were avidly recorded by the press.

The buzz around *Reservoir Dogs* spread, and after the film was shown in Cannes, Harvey and Bob jumped in to sign on to distribute Tarantino's movie. Its rabid intensity attracted applause from critics and members of the film cognoscenti. *The New York Times'* chief film critic, Vincent Canby, welcomed Tarantino to the ranks of "first-rate new American" directors, and Keitel was rewarded for his faith in Tarantino and his script by a flood of attention and a new mantle of *cool*. But the movie's feral violence limited the size of its audience—it netted just $2.5 million at the box office, less than half its box office in the U.K.

However, Harvey achieved something more important than a financial success: Tarantino's loyalty.

Tarantino recounted his initial decisive experience with Harvey over this, his first released movie. Harvey liked the movie but wanted a market research focus group screening to test the audience reaction. "I just hate those fucking things," Tarantino said. But he relented and attended the focus group screening. Afterward, he and Harvey met alone in the darkened theater. Harvey told him the audience hated the bloody scene where Mr. Blonde tortures a bound cop and slices off his ear. "People who could really appreciate the movie and enjoy it, that scene cuts their head off. . . . So we can have a much bigger hit if you were to cut that scene out." Harvey had shown the movie to his wife, Eve, and her sister as well, and they got up and left in the middle of the screening (although they went back in to see what happened). Despite that promising sign, Harvey was convinced women would reject the movie.

"You know what, Harvey?" Tarantino responded. "This is the movie I wanted to make; that's my favorite scene in the movie. I'll never be able to watch it if we cut that scene out. . . . No, I'm keeping the torture scene in."

Aware that he had lassoed a rare talent, almost instantly Harvey relented. "Well okay. Then we're not gonna touch the movie." Harvey "was the opposite of a bully," Tarantino said. (Harvey was also clearly wrong about the ear scene, which became iconic.)

Tarantino's movie was a sensational reputation builder, but Miramax had been teetering near bankruptcy and *Reservoir Dogs*'s box office couldn't pull it back from the brink. "I thought the company could easily go out of business," CFO John Schmidt said. "Harvey was an uncontrolled spender on films," as well as first-class flights and restaurants. His impulsive enthusiasms were a mounting concern, and a source of tension with brother Bob, who kept a close eye on spending. "The hardest part of my job," said Agnès Mentre, who as director of acquisitions invested in movies, "was to convince Harvey not [to overspend] to make a movie" or to distribute it. Mentre was married to Ken Jacobs, then a senior partner at the investment bank Lazard Frères (and now the CEO). "Harvey was scrambling, and running out of money," recalled Steven Rattner, a friend of Harvey's and then a partner at Lazard. "My recollection is that Ken came to me on a Friday afternoon and said, 'Harvey has reached out to me. He's got financial problems. Will you come downtown and see him with me?'" When they met, Rattner said, "it was clear the company was broke. Harvey started yelling at me: 'Get Felix [Rohatyn, the foremost rainmaker at Lazard]. Felix can call someone.'" There was no one for Rohatyn to call who would pour money into a sinking ship.

Miramax was saved from drowning by Neil Jordan's *The Crying Game*, which was released two months after *Reservoir Dogs* and benefited from an extraordinary marketing campaign mounted by Harvey. The movie was set in Northern Ireland, where an IRA soldier played by Stephen Rea befriends a black British prisoner the IRA has kidnapped (Forest Whitaker). Whitaker senses the kindness in the IRA soldier who is guarding him and asks that, after he is shot (for his execution is a certainty), his captor deliver a message to his girlfriend, played by Jaye Davidson. Rea falls in love with this alluring, haunted woman with delicate features. The movie's startling zenith arrives when Rea, shedding Jaye Davidson's robe, freezes at the sight of a penis. At the time, transgender life was almost invisible to the mainstream, and this plot twist had real power to shock. But when *The Crying Game* opened in England, it flopped with critics and the public. The revelation had been exposed in the critics' reviews, draining its power. "I regret not buying *The Crying Game* when I worked at New Line," said Ira Deutchman. "I had a hard time figuring out how to market it if you knew the ending. Harvey was brilliant."

As the film's distributor, Harvey's great insight was to create buzz by asking the public to become coconspirators in keeping the movie's big secret. For a whopping hundred thousand dollars, Harvey commissioned a Gallup poll asking the public whether they wanted to know the ending before they saw the movie. An overwhelming number said they did not. Harvey used this evidence to try to convince critics not to divulge the secret in their reviews. When the Associated Press planned to go ahead with the spoiler, Harvey called the editor. "I'm begging. You're not hurting me financially. You're ruining the movie for audiences." AP scrapped the review. Harvey flew Davidson to Egypt and ordered him to lay low during the promotion period, lest anyone suspect that the actor—who'd been scouted at a Derek Jarman wrap party and had never acted before—was male. Harvey's marketing ploy elevated the buzz around the movie to Hitchcockian proportions. Former Miramax marketing chief Mark Gill admired Harvey's gift for orchestrating attention-getting conflict, but this was a case of artful concealment rather than agitprop. "Harvey was clearly the Barnum and Bailey of the movie business in the late twentieth century," Gill said. "He was just so much better than everybody else."

Unlike *Reservoir Dogs*, *The Crying Game* became a true crossover success, grossing almost $63 million, smashing through the $25 million threshold that was seen at the time to be the proverbial glass ceiling for independent films. Neil Jordan won an Oscar for Best Screenplay. Davidson received a nomination for Best Actor. Miramax movies received twelve Oscar nominations that year, half of them for *The Crying Game*. One third of the 1993 nominations for Best Picture, Best Actress, and Best Actor would go to independently financed films, and Miramax was leading the charge.

The success of the movie saved Miramax, and Harvey instantly started spending again—on movies and on the public display he felt would lure moviemakers. Miramax enjoyed some other surprise successes around this time: *Like Water for Chocolate*, which had languished unbought, but became the highest-grossing foreign film ever released in America after it got the Scissorhands treatment; the low-key charmer *Enchanted April*; *Passion Fish* (a favorite of Miriam's when it was screened—Harvey was attentive to his mother's tastes); and *Strictly Ballroom*, Baz Luhrmann's directorial debut.

After the triumphant showing at the 1993 Oscars, all of Harvey's shouting and conniving, his shrewd strategizing and bold Hail Mary passes, appeared to be paying off at last. The Walt Disney Company outbid Ted Turner to acquire Miramax. The outsiders were coming inside.

Disney recognized that Miramax had what Disney lacked: "Disney was in a different kind of business," then CEO Michael Eisner said years later, looking back on what would prove to be an exceptionally stormy relationship. "We were in the event movie business, the expensive movie business. We had a very tiny library, no real live-action library. I thought their volume, their quality, their international appeal, would be good for Disney." Miramax stood for something. "The Miramax name may be the only brand in the movie business other than the Disney brand." One of the facts of the film business is that the studios producing hit films get no real branding credit for the movie. The film that edged out *The Crying Game* for Best Picture was Clint Eastwood's *Unforgiven*, and it's safe to say that the general public that flocked to theaters came to see a Clint Eastwood movie, not a Warner Brothers movie. But Eisner believed the public was aware that *The Crying Game*, or *Sex, Lies, and Videotape*, or *Reservoir Dogs*, was a Miramax movie, just as they were aware *Snow White* was a Disney movie. And more to the point, the creative community knew it.

Negotiations were tense. The brothers worried that they were signing over their autonomy. As the Disney executives waited for him to sign, Bob pored once more over the 50-plus-page agreement, agonizing over its ramifications, assuming that Disney was out to screw them—possibly, said a former Disney executive, because that's how the brothers did business themselves. Since Miramax *was* the Weinsteins, Disney had insisted on taking out life insurance policies on them but struggled to find anyone to underwrite the risk. However apprehensive they were, Harvey and Bob saw the Disney acquisition as their breakout moment, to be seized avidly while they were on one of their business upswings. They now could slip those hands into Disney's deep pockets. They wanted to do more than buy and distribute other people's movies; they wanted to produce more films of their own—but until now they had lacked the resources. In 1992, for instance, Miramax released twenty movies, but produced only three of them; the rest they signed on to as distributors.

The distribution fee for circulating a movie in theaters gave Miramax a negotiated 10 to 20 percent of the movie's grosses. To produce a movie is to own it, as John Eastman had explained to Harvey years before. By owning its movies, Miramax would own what is known as the back end, or access to the box office grosses, plus the TV and video and sequel and other potentially lucrative rights.

To say nothing of the thrill of crafting the work from the ground up. The brothers had both nursed ambitions to be moviemakers and not just merchants. The producer's power to decide very much appealed to Harvey, with his worship for filmmaking and belief in his own talent to craft a successful film.

Fundamentally, Harvey and Bob were haunted and shaped by what happened to their father. Max Weinstein briefly fulfilled his dream by opening his own stall to cut jewels, with a window on Forty-Seventh Street to display his work. In his essay about his father, Bob explained the perils that defeated Max and had threatened Miramax: "The heady days of the first sales passed, and competition from some of the bigger boys on the Street increased. . . . Gradually, as with so many small businesses, the economic pressure took its toll on Max's window. It gets difficult to ride out the tough times when you need to make changes but lack the capital to implement them."

Harvey and Bob were convinced they could avoid Max's fate because they had something he didn't: When Max started his business, Bob said, "he lacked the capital, but he also lacked a partner. . . . He didn't have the dynamic of Bob and Harvey."

Miramax in 1993 was still a relatively small company, with revenues of $100 million and after-tax profits of $8 million. They did not have the cash to sew up the directors who'd delivered their hits. Universal offered Jim Sheridan of *My Left Foot* a $3 million deal that Miramax couldn't match. "It broke my heart," Harvey said. After the disappointment of his follow-up to *Sex, Lies*—the surreal biopic *Kafka*, which grossed only a tenth of its budget—Soderbergh jumped ship to Gramercy, the art house division of Universal. Harvey knew he needed more resources to compete.

Harvey came to understand that the movie business is unusual because long-term relationships are rare. Most businesses thrive on a stable workplace, but in Hollywood the agents and lawyers who represent talent don't seek stability; they seek to create insecurity at the studios they negotiate with. The talent that comes together to work on a movie disperses at the end. Unlike in the studio system of old, where actors and directors were under the long-term control of the studio, most everyone in the movie business is a freelancer.

Harvey was enthusiastic about the sale, and hopeful that Disney's money would grant him more control. The workforce would expand exponentially, but the Miramax culture did not change: it remained a fearful, if exciting, place to work. Harvey was still consumed by his demons. He was convinced the Hollywood Deep State conspired against him, maybe including his new corporate owners, and his battles were just beginning. Attacked, and attacker—this was Harvey Weinstein as he perceived himself, and Harvey as others saw him.

Just a few months into the Weinstein-Disney relationship, sometime in the winter of 1993–94, the actress Annabella Sciorra was invited to a dinner in New York with Harvey and others, including Uma Thurman, who had just finished filming *Pulp Fiction*. Sciorra had attracted attention for her coolly scorching turn opposite Wesley Snipes in Spike Lee's *Jungle Fever* in 1991, and in the hit thriller *The Hand That Rocks the Cradle* in 1992. She'd recently wrapped a Miramax movie, *The Night*

We Never Met. She enjoyed being part of the Miramax community, regularly attending their screenings and parties. When she got up to leave the dinner, Harvey offered to drop her off at her Gramercy Park apartment. She said good night to him in the car and was getting ready for bed when there was a knock on her apartment door.

She opened the front door slightly, and, to her shock, Harvey barged past her. She ordered him to leave. Harvey grabbed at her nightgown, shoved her on the bed, and raped her.

She said nothing publicly. She described her trauma: "I wanted to pretend it never happened. . . . I spent a lot of time alone. I didn't want to see any people." Psychologists who work with rape victims say Sciorra's response—denying to herself that the rape occurred, withdrawing from friends, escaping into drugs and alcohol—is not uncommon. Her promising career faltered. "I just kept getting this pushback of 'We heard you were difficult. . . .' I think that was the Harvey machine." Nor was her time in his sights over. He would stalk her for years, on several occasions showing up late at night at her hotel room at Cannes or during a London shoot to bang on the door and demand entry. It was as if, once he asserted his will over a woman, he believed she should be available to him in perpetuity.

It's impossible to know whether Sciorra's claims of what occurred that winter night in Gramercy Park came back to Harvey in later years— if he felt regret or tried to explain it away to himself; if he grasped the gravity of what he'd done, or if he returned to the memory to savor his sense of mastery; if he went home to his wife afterward and told her it had been a pleasant enough evening, just another work dinner. But it marked a passage for Sciorra from before to after, and now her life was on a different course. She would tell her story on the witness stand in courtroom 1530 almost three decades later.

THE CULTURE
OF SILENCE

(1993–1997)

Disney studio chief Jeffrey Katzenberg midwifed the marriage between Disney and Miramax. Unlike most members of the Hollywood establishment, Katzenberg enjoyed a relaxed, trusting relationship with the Weinsteins. A short, lean, tightly coiled but popular Hollywood notable, Katzenberg drank as many Diet Cokes daily as Harvey and was famous for scheduling at least two consecutive breakfasts and lunches most days, between juggling hundreds of phone calls. He was one of a handful of people Harvey hailed as "a mentor," though Katzenberg was just two years his senior. Katzenberg reciprocated, calling Harvey "a force of nature. An extraordinarily articulate storyteller and filmmaker. I decided I wanted to buy his company." Katzenberg and his boss, Michael Eisner, weren't always on cordial terms, but here they were on the same page.

Colleagues at Disney agreed but were wary. "The question we had was discipline and staying within budget," said Peter Murphy, Disney's chief strategic officer at the time, who had so much influence under Michael Eisner that he was known as "the enforcer." They negotiated what they thought was a reasonable but generous contract. In addition to the $61 million, plus incentives, bringing the purchase price to about $80 million, almost every penny of it pocketed by Harvey and Bob, the contract named them cochairmen, provided an annual salary to each of $1 million, and offered a bonus pegged to Miramax's profits. There was considerable unhappiness about the deal among the one hundred or so Miramax employees, who were not invited to share in the jackpot. When the brothers announced the deal in the Miramax screening room, they promised bonuses, but these would never arrive. "Harvey and Bob said, 'We're going to get rich.' They meant only they would get rich," recalled Miramax public relations executive Amanda Lundberg.

With Disney's money, Harvey now had the power to own the movie—to commission scripts, recruit directors, cast actors, control the entire production—and not simply share in a relatively small slice of its revenues. After the theaters took roughly half of the grosses, as the producer—often with a studio producing or distribution partner to defray costs—Miramax and Disney, like other studios, would pocket most of the rest. Harvey could now compete for expensive movies with the major Hollywood studios. And with more dollars, he also aimed to branch out beyond the movie business, becoming a media as well as a movie mogul. Miramax would still attend the film festivals and compete to buy independent films to distribute to theaters around the world. But the profits on a successfully produced film dwarfed the margins on a film the studio distributed.

Miramax's contract with Disney stipulated an annual budget for Miramax of $700 million to cover movies, marketing, and overhead, or seven times the revenues Miramax generated in its last year as an independent company. Only many years later did Disney admit that it discovered the Weinsteins put their thumb on the scale and slipped in a major contract loophole: their annual bonuses were based solely on the movies they released that year, meaning that if Miramax did not release dozens of duds, their bonuses would not shrink, though the money devoted to make the movies would never be recovered. Harvey may have been careless in how he spent money, but with Bob's help he was shrewd at pocketing it.

Under their contract, the Weinsteins were free to make creative decisions without interference, as long as they lived within what Disney called financial and creative "boundaries"—Miramax was not to spend more than $30 million on any movie; they were not, the contract read, to "release any picture which contains excessive or gratuitous violence, or excessive or gratuitous sexual content"; nor were they to "release NC-17 or X-rated pictures without Disney's" prior approval. Harvey and Bob were each to be rewarded a performance-based monthly bonus of $241,660 over the next sixty months, which Disney saw as an installment payout to boost the purchase price and was separate from their annual bonus. To fire either Weinstein required the scaling of a very unusual high wall: only a felony conviction, not the more common executive contract language that stipulated an arrest or indictment, could permit a termination. Apart from these "boundaries," Murphy said, "Harvey wanted to believe he didn't report to anyone."

Harvey made that clear immediately. "The first Sunday after the deal closes Harvey sends me the script for *Pulp Fiction*," Katzenberg remembered. It would be Quentin Tarantino's second movie for Miramax. "He said, 'It's great.' After reading it, I called him and said, 'Harvey, on what planet is this not an NC-17 movie?' He made a great pitch. He said it was a comeback movie for John Travolta and Bruce Willis. He said, 'Tarantino is a genius. This will be a cultural phenomenon.' He was right."

With Disney's deeper pockets, Miramax could afford to produce *Pulp Fiction* for $8.5 million, which was basically Miramax's entire after-tax profit the year before its acquisition. It was the first movie Miramax fully financed under Disney. After the artistic success of *Reservoir Dogs*, Tarantino had been offered numerous directing opportunities, including *Men in Black*. Then just thirty years old, exhausted after doing the global festival circuit for *Reservoir Dogs*, he decided to move to the red-light district of Amsterdam, where he spent three months in a one-room apartment feverishly writing the screenplay for *Pulp Fiction*, a blackly comic ensemble thriller about a couple of chatty hitmen, a boxer preparing to throw a fight, some hapless stick-up artists, and the seductive girlfriend of a powerful drug lord, all set in the grittier corners of Los Angeles. Tarantino was joined by his screenwriter buddy Roger Avary, a fellow clerk from their video store days—the two had wanted to be the next Joel and Ethan Coen—and they mashed together stories they'd worked on for years. These became seven sequences that leap back and forward in time, spiced with multiple murders and viciously clever twists. At the time, Tarantino was under contract to TriStar Pictures, which had invested nine hundred thousand dollars in him to write the script, money that Miramax had lacked. His producer on *Reservoir Dogs*, Lawrence Bender, had given the 159-page script to the studio in May 1993, with "LAST DRAFT" written on the cover in bold letters, Tarantino's way of signaling that he would allow no changes.

Baffled by the convoluted narrative and the raw violence, particularly a scene where pieces of a victim's brain are splattered all over the back seat of a car, TriStar rejected the movie, which allowed Harvey to swoop in, as he would years later when Fox abandoned *The English Patient* or Universal stepped away from *Shakespeare in Love*. As described by Mark Seal in *Vanity Fair*, Harvey's assistant, Richard Gladstein, handed him the script as Harvey was racing from the office to fly to Martha's Vineyard on vacation.

"He called me two hours later," Gladstein recalled, "and said, 'The first scene is *fucking brilliant*. Does it stay this good?'" Gladstein said it did.

Harvey called an hour later after reading the scene in which the assassin, Vincent Vega, is shot and killed as he steps out of the bathroom in the apartment he's staking out, having been reading on the toilet. "Are you guys crazy?" Harvey blurted, as if he were talking to Tarantino, not his assistant. "You just killed off the main character in the middle of the movie!"

"Just keep reading," Gladstein advised.

Harvey shot back, "Start negotiating! We're making this movie."

The movie starred John Travolta as Vega and Bruce Willis as Butch

Coolidge, an aging boxer fleeing a gang boss (the story line Avary contributed); each actor saw the film as a daring comeback opportunity after some fallow years. Travolta and Willis and the other prominent actors—Samuel L. Jackson, Uma Thurman, Harvey Keitel, Rosanna Arquette, and Christopher Walken, among others—worked for practically nothing. Harvey transported most of the cast to strut the carpet at the 1994 Cannes Film Festival, where *Pulp Fiction* won the Palme d'Or for Best Picture. It was Miramax's first blockbuster, grossing $108 million domestically—fifty times the gross of Tarantino's first film, and almost double the box office of *The Crying Game*—and $214 million worldwide. No other independent film had ever been shown in more than one thousand theaters or topped the $100 million box office threshold.

Because Harvey started with the conviction that *Pulp Fiction* was not "an art house movie" but rather "a smash hit" fit to be shown in thousands of theaters, he made an unusual decision, deciding to take the movie to multiple film festivals around the world between winning the Palme d'Or in May and the movie's opening in October 1994. Tarantino was dazzled by the way Harvey marketed his movie. The blanket festival treatment meant critics watched the movie two or three times, writing "about it along the way, and then just constantly getting the word out about the movie coming." Tarantino believed that had he signed with any other studio, "it wouldn't have been *Pulp Fiction*. It would've been *L.A. Confidential*," a critically acclaimed neo-noir crime movie that, despite its impressive $126 million box office, did not attract the larger audiences it deserved because the studio "was too scared to go all the way with it." What Miramax proved with *Pulp Fiction* was that the right independent film could escape the art house ghetto and galvanize a huge audience.

Tarantino and Harvey became tight. Both men could be socially awkward. Both men took pride in their ability to verbally dominate an argument and to seduce someone on the other side of the negotiating table. But Tarantino, brash and logorrheic as he could be, had an artlessness and generosity to him early on that many noted. He began to send some of his favorite Chinese movies to Harvey, who called him one of his Jedi Masters: "I didn't know any of these guys—Jet Li, Jackie Chan—and I learned them early. Because Quentin was so far ahead of the curve, I love Chinese cinema."

Tarantino's public praise of Harvey came from a place of genuine affection and respect. Like him, Harvey was a cinephile unafraid to act on his instincts. Tarantino compared Harvey and, to a lesser degree, Bob, to Jack Warner, David O. Selznick, and Adolph Zukor, the Hollywood moguls of old, which was exactly how the Weinsteins wished to be perceived. "They run the place. Nobody else in town, even with the Palme d'Or, would have had the confidence to say, 'This is going to be a smash hit. We're going to open in the biggest number of theaters we can.' Warner Bros. and the other studios would have been scared of it." Other studio heads, Tarantino said, had "power, but they're ultimately employees." With a few notable exceptions—the team of Robert Daly and Terry Semel at Warner Brothers, or Katzenberg and Eisner at Disney—the lifetime of studio heads usually ended quickly. Insecurity was a constant curse. Studio heads worried about losing the support of their distant corporate bosses. They worried about shareholders, about betting too much on a movie that flops, about spending too much to market a film, about being blamed when a prominent actor or director fled to another studio.

If Harvey was good for Quentin, Quentin was also good for Harvey. Actors and directors and producers flocked to Miramax. Harvey started calling his company "the house that Quentin built." He told Peter Biskind, "I never had to tell any filmmaker around the world anything other than one thing: 'We were the company that made *Pulp Fiction.*'"

Harvey and Bob were as comfortable working under Katzenberg as Tarantino was under the Weinsteins. The brothers trusted few people beyond each other, worried that people aimed to trick them. Harvey's instinctive default posture was always to be mistrustful of others, to look for their angle, their hidden agenda, their plan to *screw* him. "He trusted no one," says Jonathan Gordon, who started as Harvey's assistant in the early 1990s and rose to become a senior Miramax executive. "I think he thought it was foolish to take people at their word."

The brothers appreciated that Katzenberg did not mince words or hide what he thought. He would stab you in the chest, not the back, which is how the Weinsteins saw themselves. However, in August 1994, Katzenberg and Eisner suddenly parted ways. The two men always had an uneasy relationship. Eisner was never comfortable with the often brusque Katzenberg. And Katzenberg felt Eisner disparaged him as his "Golden Retriever," withholding the respect he deserved after building the film and studio profits from several million to $800 million in a decade. Eisner's president and trusted chief operating officer for two decades was the beloved, low-ego Frank Wells, and after his sudden death in a helicopter crash while on a skiing trip, the ever-impatient Katzenberg pressed Eisner to move him into Wells's office and his role overseeing the entire company. Eisner had trusted Wells. From day one, Wells had assured Eisner he did not want his job and was content serving as his number two. Eisner did not feel comfortable with the aggressive Katzenberg, who insisted that Eisner had promised him that role if Wells decided to leave. To Eisner, Katzenberg's raw ambition was unseemly so soon after a beloved colleague's death. To Katzenberg, Eisner was a liar. Although no studio matched the profits of Disney over the previous decade, and Katzenberg was a gifted executive, his departure was a reminder that personal factors, not just business factors like financial performance, often sway decisions.

Katzenberg marched off to found DreamWorks with Steven Spielberg and David Geffen. He was not sorry to be out from under Eisner, but he was sorry to abandon Harvey. "I had an amazing rapport with Harvey," Katzenberg said. "I saw the good Harvey," someone he admired for his taste in movies, and for being direct. Years later, when Harvey was exposed as a sexual predator, Katzenberg was one of the first Hollywood executives to denounce him. Katzenberg says he was shocked to learn of Harvey's sordid behavior with women over many years.

Joe Roth, who succeeded Katzenberg as studio chief, wished he saw the good Harvey more often. Soon after accepting the job, Roth flew east for lunch with the brothers at the Tribeca Grill, the restaurant below their offices co-owned by Robert De Niro, of which the Weinsteins owned a tiny slice. "I walked into the restaurant thinking I was going to help them," Roth said. "They were paranoid about me." They stonily eyed Roth like detectives sizing up a suspect. Roth exclaimed, "Hey, wait a minute. I'm here as the head of the studio and I'm here to help you."

"What do you mean, *help*?" Bob Weinstein asked.

Roth thought: *What did I get into?* He quickly saw that though the Weinstein brothers no longer owned the company, they still very much acted as if they did.

This would be Disney's perennial headache. In the words of chief strategy officer Peter Murphy, "We realized Harvey was undisciplined financially and we had to try to constrain Harvey and Bob in terms of the number of films they made and the capital they spent. That was the financial box we tried to build. But they kept trying to pierce the box and it became years of whack-a-mole." Regularly, he said, Harvey phoned and screamed at him. "I would put it on speakerphone so I could do work while he ranted for five or thirty minutes."

The tensions were manageable—or had to be managed—because Miramax was thriving. When the Oscar nominations for 1994 were announced, Miramax received twenty-two, with *Pulp Fiction* capturing seven, including Best Picture. (It lost to *Forrest Gump*.) Tarantino was honored along with cowriter Roger Avary with an Oscar for Best Original Screenplay.

With Disney dollars to mount marketing campaigns and purchase movies, Miramax could bring to theaters upwards of forty movies annually, many of them now produced in-house. Suddenly, their independent studio competitors were outgunned when bidding to acquire movies for distribution. "They had more money than we did," New Line CEO Bob Shaye said. New Line would soon be acquired by Warner Bros. "Miramax became more of a juggernaut. Harvey became more of the crown prince." They threw their weight around with the theaters, trying to load them up with Miramax films and squeeze out the competition, precisely what the Weinsteins once accused the studios of doing. Jack Foley, then vice president of distribution for Miramax, said, "It was always bullying and taunting and jiving and goading and pressing and molesting. . . . If [the other independents] didn't get their openings, they wouldn't gross, and they'd be in trouble."

Harvey hadn't forgotten a lesson he'd learned from Arthur Manson's Town Hall lectures when he was a concert promoter hoping to make it in the movies: the importance of pressing theater owners to be patient, allowing word of mouth to build. When *Sling Blade*, the 1996 Billy Bob Thornton movie about a man with an intellectual disability and his friendship with a vulnerable boy, was playing to empty houses at the indie stalwart Lincoln Plaza Cinemas in New York, Harvey called the theater owner directly. "I don't care if I have to carry this movie on my back, I'm not giving it up. You cannot get rid of this movie. You'll see that audiences will come." He revamped the marketing campaign, shooting a charismatic Thornton talking about the film rather than showing him in character, and aired the spots on cable in Los Angeles in the runup to the Oscars. The audiences showed up as he'd sworn they would, and the film grossed $25 million; and then Thornton was nominated for, and won, the Oscar for Best Adapted Screenplay.

Harvey was at the time celebrated for his talent more than excoriated for his crude behavior. Those who worked with him marveled at his eye for a good script. Abby Ex, who was the vice president of production for three years and is today a Hollywood producer, believed this was the essential Weinstein talent, along with his "unique" ability to seize on a story "that will resonate with an audience. . . . He had a remarkable ability to think laterally about how to solve problems of narrative, or how to just think about storytelling in ways that are very difficult."

Meryl Poster, his longtime movie production chief who oversaw the development and making of Miramax movies, said, "He knew *The Piano* was a great movie from the script." It is the story of a woman who has not spoken since she was six, sold by her father to marry a frontiersman in nineteenth-century New Zealand. She sails across the world with her young daughter and her beloved piano, which her new husband forces her to leave behind on the beach. Another man hauls the instrument over the mountains and sells it back to her, key by key, for the right to watch her play, and a complicated game of seduction ensues that shades slowly into love. After reading it, the year before the release of *Pulp Fiction*, Harvey signed on to distribute the movie in America.

Jane Campion wrote the screenplay and directed. Harvey may have been a sexual brute, but he was an early champion of women directors. With Harvey cheering, Campion became the first female director to win the Palme d'Or, and until 2021, when director Julia Ducournau won for directing *Titane*, the only woman to have done so. The mute pianist was portrayed by Holly Hunter, her coarse and uncomprehending husband by Sam Neill, her daughter by Anna Paquin, and her lover by Harvey Keitel, who was on a roll for Miramax. Critics rhapsodized. Roger Ebert described the movie as being "as peculiar and haunting as any film I've seen." Hunter won the Best Actress Oscar, the eleven-year-old Paquin Best Supporting Actress, and Campion Best Original Screenplay. For a movie that cost only $7 million to make, its $40 million domestic box office was a resounding financial success for Miramax.

His ability to spot the promise of *The Piano* could be traced back to those days in Queens when young Harvey, forced to stay home with an eye injury, ingested books with the same lust he had for food. "To me, it's about words. It's about the book," he told me, explaining what makes a good movie, in 2002 when I was profiling him for *The New Yorker*—an exceptionally rare comment for a studio exec, who might focus instead on the actors or director. He passed on buying a Roman Polanski–directed movie, *Death and the Maiden*, which turned out to be

a box office dud. Harvey knew why: "I don't think it was because Polanski directed it poorly. . . . They don't make good movies unless they
have a good script."

When he wasn't working with a Campion or Tarantino is when
Harvey Scissorhands often surfaced. Once in his office, I watched him
edit a film by Scott Spiegel, *My Name Is Modesty*, based on the exploits
of the comic-book character Modesty Blaise (incidentally, the book *Pulp
Fiction*'s Vincent Vega is reading in the bathroom just before he is shot
is Peter O'Donnell's *Modesty Blaise*). As Harvey intently watched a tape
while chain-smoking Marlboros and gulping Diet Cokes, a Miramax
production executive dutifully took notes. After a few minutes, exasperated, Harvey declared, "There's another way to begin the movie, which
is here in the casino." *Cut, cut, cut*, he told her. "Less is more. This whole
scene can be played faster. You're dying here. Cut the guards out here."
After speeding through the two-hour tape in forty minutes, Weinstein
told the production executive, "You get the idea." Harvey had a satisfied
look, knowing his editing ideas made sense. Still, the director was not
present to see what Harvey was doing to his creation. When I asked
about the absent Spiegel, Harvey defensively responded, "Of course,
these changes are subject to the director's approval."

Absurdly, he insisted in one of our conversations that "the idea of
me bossing around a director is unheard of." The late, esteemed director Bernardo Bertolucci would dismiss this claim as preposterous. Harvey insisted his 1993 Miramax film *Little Buddha* be cut from 140 to
123 minutes, threatening not to release it to theaters and letting it go
straight to video. Bertolucci relented. But he got in the last word, saying, "He's like a little Saddam Hussein of cinema."

This kind of criticism of Harvey was not yet commonplace. In the
midnineties, Harvey Weinstein was still mostly regarded as a colorful,
shrewd character who delivered superb films. His temper tantrums were
seen as mere tactics. His excesses, including threatening violence against
competitors to acquire movies at film festivals, were either not widely
known or rationalized away by those who admired his films and kept

score by whether Harvey's movies wowed critics and made money. Furthermore, rumors of Harvey's infidelities were not shocking in a film community where pressuring women for sex was not unusual. And if members of the community heard that Harvey sexually harassed or chased women—though almost uniformly they would later deny that they had—was silence so very out of the ordinary in Hollywood? Rape was out of the ordinary.

Harvey saw himself as a Medici of the film business, a discerning patron and collector of a stable of talent. Many staffers saw him this way as well. Cohead of Acquisitions Amy Israel recalls how Harvey dominated: "He micromanaged everything from making the film to marketing the film, to publicizing the film, in such a way, with such care and tenacity, that things got done that you could never imagine." She screened *Il Postino* for him at the Toronto Film Festival in September 1994. It is a sentimental story of a friendship between the exiled Nobel Prize–winning poet Pablo Neruda and an Italian postman who recites from his verses to woo the woman he loves. Harvey sat in the back of the theater with his mother, whom he brought to the festival. By the end of the movie, Israel said, "he was crying, and within minutes he came up with the entire marketing campaign for the movie," which featured no stars from the film. Instead he recruited celebrities like Julia Roberts, Sting, Glenn Close, Madonna, Samuel L. Jackson, and Andy Garcia to read poems by Neruda (whose book sales jumped) and released them as part of the movie's soundtrack.

Harvey savored his growing power, yet at the same time saw himself and Miramax as outsiders, as David with a slingshot. But Miramax, standing on the shoulders of the second-largest media company in the world, had become a Goliath.

Disney dollars also liberated Bob Weinstein, allowing him to produce well-made commercial movies, and to slip out of Harvey's shadow. Two years before the acquisition, he had started a division to produce a modest number of forgettable films. But with Disney's money, in 1994 he scaled up Dimension Films to produce horror films, suspense thrillers, comedies, teen fare—films Harvey was not likely to take an interest in, and that Bob genuinely loved. An early success was *The Crow*, starring Bruce Lee's son Brandon, who had tragically died eight days before the end of filming in an accident with a stunt revolver the crew had equipped with live rounds instead of dummy ones. Where studios saw a cursed production, Bob saw opportunity. He bought the unfinished film, using a stunt double and digital effects to complete Lee's remaining scenes. The film opened at number one and grossed an astonishing $51 million; *Rolling Stone* called it a "dazzling fever dream" and Roger Ebert wrote that it was the best version of a comic-book universe he'd seen, and a greater film than any of Bruce Lee's. Dimension would eventually generate more profits than Miramax, with movies like the *Scary Movie* franchise, Wes Craven's *Scream*, plus a total of eleven Robert Rodriguez films.

Bob had talent and wanted the world to know it. "It gave me my own thing," Bob said. "Harvey was running Rolls-Royce, and I ended up running General Motors. Harvey was doing these pristine cars, and finicking with them. I'm going, 'I wonder what the masses want?' Harvey was so gracious. He would say, 'My brother's making all this money, and it just gives me more money to make movies.'" While Bob was still cochairman and involved in Miramax's movies and management, having his own division to run lessened tensions between the brothers. They still screamed at each other in the office, but Harvey was delighted Bob had his own sandbox. It also meant that Harvey had more freedom. Disney kept its hands off, just as it did with Miramax movies.

Wes Craven's *Scream* was Bob's huge breakthrough success. The screenplay, by Kevin Williamson, was submitted in the fall of 1995 to Dimension and to Cary Woods, a producer who worked closely with Miramax. He excitedly shared the script with Drew Barrymore, who agreed to join the cast. As with Harvey Keitel and *Reservoir Dogs*, once Barrymore signed on, the movie was green-lighted by Bob. The screenplay was sent to director Wes Craven, who practically invented the teenage slasher film with movies like *The Last House on the Left* and *A Nightmare on Elm Street*, the first feature film starring Johnny Depp.

Scream, meant to be both a legitimate horror movie and a wicked send-up for fans of the form, follows the classic trope of a high school student—played by Drew Barrymore—pursued by a mysterious killer. A flirty call with a stranger turns into the revelation that he is holding her boyfriend hostage and will kill him if she gets any horror trivia wrong. Both teens are gruesomely killed by the white-masked murderer, with buckets more blood to follow as the film revisits slasher-movie clichés with a gloss of postmodern irony.

The proposed title of the film, *Scary Movie*, worried Bob. He wanted humor in the movie, but he wanted it truly to *be* scary. "Is it a funny movie with scares?" he asked the writer. "Or is it a scary movie with humor?"

He was pleased when the writer said, "It's a scary movie with humor." To help make the point, the title of the movie was changed to *Scream*.

In addition to Barrymore, the young and sweet-faced cast included relative newcomers like Neve Campbell, Courteney Cox, David Arquette, Liev Schreiber, and Rose McGowan, who caught Harvey's eye. His interest in her would haunt them both.

When the movie was being shot in Santa Rosa, California, Bob became an annoyance to Craven. He screened the daily rushes and complained they were not scary. He didn't like the wig Barrymore wore. He called Craven in the middle of one shoot to berate him. "What kind of studio head calls a filmmaker in the middle of shooting and kicks him in the balls and expects him to work the rest of the day and do good work?" Craven told Peter Biskind.

Next Bob complained about the "goofy" white mask the slasher was wearing. He said he wanted scenes filmed with the actor wearing four different masks. Craven refused to comply. A compromise was proposed: He would show the finished first scene to Bob. If Bob liked it, he would leave them alone. If he didn't, Craven would walk away from the film. Whether or not he liked it, Bob signed off on the now-iconic white mask.

Weeks later, when the rough first cut of the movie was delivered to Bob, he watched it with Harvey. Bob was ecstatic, as was Harvey. "You guys were right," Bob declared. "I was wrong—I was so wrong it's fucking amazing. Anything you guys want, anything!" Woods's coproducer, Cathy Konrad, told Biskind, "That was it. We never heard from him again. I have to say it was one of the greatest calls I've ever received from a studio chairman in my life."

Marketing wisdom held that horror movies should never open around the jolly Christmas season. Bob defied convention and opened the movie just before Christmas 1996: it was an enormous success. The movie would gross $173 million worldwide. The success of this movie, Bob would say, looking back, "opened the eyes of the Hollywood community that low-cost good horror and thriller movies could have massive returns. More than 20 years later, the studios are now making horror films as a staple of their film slates."

Marcy Granata, who joined Miramax in 1994 as publicity chief, met Harvey before she met Bob. And her recruitment reveals how the brothers operated. A former theater publicist with straight black hair, she had worked alongside Mike Nichols and Michael Bennett, and then for Columbia Pictures, credentials that impressed Harvey. She knew little about Miramax when she first met Harvey at a Museum of Modern Art screening she was doing for Steve Martin's *L.A. Story*. She didn't see his name on the VIP list and was told by her boss, "That's Harvey Weinstein. He crashes everything to get to know people."

The next time Granata encountered Harvey was at the Toronto Film Festival, where she was promoting Martin Scorsese's *The Age of Innocence* and Robert Redford's *A River Runs Through It*. Harvey was promoting *The Piano*, and she was amazed that he took out full-page

New York Times ads for a small-budget film. "Hollywood was not used to seeing this. We had no ads for our movies." She thought, "My God, this guy believes in his movies."

A Hollywood executive who was offered a senior communications job by Harvey declined it and recommended Granata, who was recently married and wanted to move to New York to be with her husband. Harvey, determined to expand now that he had Disney to pay for it, interviewed her in New York. When she walked into the busy hotel suite, Harvey was on the phone discussing casting a certain actor for a role. When he got off the phone he announced that he planned to hire the actor for the role and asked her opinion. She asserted that he was wrong for the role, explaining why.

"He loved that," she said, adding that she would come to respect that Harvey welcomed disagreement "as long as you could back it up." Without clearing it with Bob, Harvey offered her a major position. Granata would rise over the next seven years to executive vice president of marketing and public relations, standing out as a strong woman who barked back at Harvey.

But before she could join Miramax, Granata had to get past Bob. When stories in the trade papers announced Harvey had recruited her, she says Bob Weinstein phoned her and in a loud voice harrumphed, "We don't self-promote at Miramax!"

"I called my lawyer," Granata remembered, "and said, 'Maybe we shouldn't do this.'"

Her doubts were eased somewhat when four dozen roses were delivered to her office with a conciliatory note from Harvey and Bob: "We look forward to working with you." This was a familiar pattern at Miramax: screams followed by gifts.

Granata was surprised to learn that Bob Weinstein had real talent. "When Bob came in a room and looked at an ad or a commercial," she said, "he could laser it and tell what was wrong or missing in it." She recalled a conversation she once had with Miriam Weinstein: "Miriam once told me, in her words, 'Bob had been trained by Max. He had the patience and focus of Max, who had the patience and focus to cut stones. Bob saw what needed to be fixed.'"

Looking back, David Boies, who would become Miramax's prime attorney and was close to each brother, noted that the more successful Bob was in his own realm, the better the brothers got along. "Harvey thought Bob was good at commercial movies and Harvey was good at art."

"Bob was more prudent," remembers Mark Gill, who played a vital role at the company, first working as president of marketing in New York and then as president of Miramax Los Angeles, leaving in 2002 to head Warner Brothers' independent film division. And while Harvey was celebrated for his eye for a story, some Miramax executives believed Bob was more adept as a script editor. "His ability to fix a script was better than Harvey's," said Meryl Poster, who joined Miramax in 1989 and would serve for many years as Harvey's chief movie production deputy. Bob's skill, associates believed, stemmed from his ability to focus on the forest, not the trees, which led him to concentrate on whether the narrative worked. Because Harvey was more of a micro-manager, too often he spent time hacking down trees and battling the screenwriter or director before he addressed the storytelling.

The Weinstein brothers were alike in this respect: in the office, each could be scarier than a Wes Craven slasher. They shared hair-trigger tempers and were indiscriminate yellers. Bob had gone through a messy divorce in 1991 with his first wife, and subsequently began to drink heavily. For the next ten years he says he was a functioning alco-holic, with sometimes erratic bursts of rage. B. J. Rack, a producer who worked with him on *Scream*, said, "He has peaks and valleys that are really extreme. . . . One second he'll say to you, 'Yeah, that's a good idea,' and then, like that, without breaking eye contact, 'I hate it,' like a switch." Harvey did not drink or take drugs, but his moods also shifted abruptly, and he had never seen any upside to hiding his contempt or irritation if an employee wasn't quick enough for him. One morning not long after Mark Gill joined Miramax, he arrived for work at 8:00 a.m. with Harvey right behind him. Harvey asked a question, and Gill's answer did not satisfy him. Harvey started yelling at him: "Strap your brain on when you show up in the morning, you fucking idiot!"

Rather than take it personally, Gill quickly became accustomed to Harvey and treated his outbursts as Harvey's way of saying "Good morning." Like many fellow Miramax employees, he had begun to normalize the aberrant behavior. Besides, he said, "I also realized it probably had nothing to do with me, it probably had everything to do with the fight he just had ten minutes before." Gill was not so understanding when Harvey, in a not uncommon fit of rage in the mid-1990s, angrily heaved a ten-pound urn at him. "I had to duck," Gill admitted. He could not recall why Harvey heaved the urn, which suggests such fits of rage were fairly normal. Eric Robinson, who started working at Miramax in 2000 as Harvey's assistant and rose to a senior executive position over the next decade, still trembles recalling the time Harvey "threw me up against the wall at the Savoy Hotel in London at two a.m. because he blamed me for a minor screw-up." When Harvey lost his temper, staffers knew he had lost control. "You were expected to do what he wanted—or else. You never knew when he would explode," said Abby Ex. It was almost as if Harvey became another person, staffers frequently said.

The unstable atmosphere in the office infected staffers' perceptions. One day Gill considered him a monster; the next, he called him a genius. Harvey, said the executive who worked beside him for eight years, "had four things going for him that, on a scale of one to ten, were all ten." The four were: creative skill, analytical skill, the ability to persuade, and showmanship. "And you just never see all of those things together in one person. In fact, usually you're lucky if you get one of them." But Gill, an executive whom Harvey relied on, also saw that these talents were "inseparable from his dark side. . . . For some reason you couldn't get all that genius without the ego, certainly without the anger, which is arguably one of the biggest parts of it, and without the sort of degradation of employees and other people."

In other words, Harvey's success in the movie business was sometimes helped along by his vices. His lack of impulse control, his obsessive behavior, his unwillingness to accept no for an answer, his volatility and stubbornness and bullying sometimes served him well in a negotiation, in getting movies made, in marketing them, in bulldozing actors and directors to succumb to his wishes.

Although Bob was quieter, more introverted, and considered a more decent human being, he could sometimes be just as fearsome as his brother, as Marcy Granata experienced—and this contributed to a divide that further fractured the workplace and created a sense of tribalism and threat. "All of the people working for Harvey were terrified of Bob," said Agnès Mentre. "And all of the people working for Bob were terrified of Harvey."

Bob Weinstein responds, "She's fifty percent right. You can guess which fifty percent I think was right."

While Bob and Harvey fiercely defended each other against what they perceived as outsider assaults, tensions between them would build and ebb. Initially, the brothers had offices next to each other at 375 Greenwich Street, separated by a thin wall. Like ringside spectators at a boxing match, staffers could not miss their loud arguments. Nor could they avoid the circuitous way Bob and Harvey often dealt with each other. "Harvey would say, 'Go tell my brother,' instead of talking to him," said Jason Blum, who was cohead of acquisitions with Amy Israel and who today is the founder and CEO of Blumhouse Productions. "Constantly they both told people, 'Talk to my brother.'" It wasn't as if the brothers were estranged—yet—but each knew that a cooler voice that wasn't steeped in decades of sibling strife might persuade the other to yield to an argument.

Not for a minute did Blum and other Miramax employees fail to understand that they worked for a family company—not for Disney.

"There was no hierarchy other than Harvey and Bob," Blum said. Separated by three thousand miles from their parent company and dominated by two assertive bosses, Blum said, "We worked for Harvey. He would bad-mouth Disney. He would say, 'Disney doesn't know what they're doing.'" Though Disney was signing his checks, Harvey resented Disney and Michael Eisner, and had no problem showing it. The brothers appeared at one company retreat wearing matching T-shirts that said CORPORATELY IRRESPONSIBLE. Harvey found it almost intolerable to be in a position where someone might have the right and the responsibility to rein him in.

In the midnineties, a scandal enveloped Hollywood when Heidi Fleiss was arrested for operating a lucrative prostitution business, popular among actors and executives. The press was alive with tales of the "Hollywood Madam." The industry trembled with terrified questions. Would she give up names in a plea bargain? Which of the mighty would fall when she did? And yet throughout Fleiss's state and federal trials in 1994 and 1996, which led to a seven-year prison sentence, few names of her customers seeped out. The Hollywood omertà was as sturdy as a police department's blue wall of silence.

Maybe that's why Harvey had no fear that his own sexual predations at Miramax would be exposed. Certainly his sexual transgressions showed no signs of diminishing.

One of his assistants was always assigned to travel with Harvey, whether in a car or an airplane. Jonathan Gordon, who performed this role during this time, recalled the first time he checked into the Peninsula Hotel in Los Angeles with Harvey: "Mr. Weinstein, here's your room key," the man at the desk told him. "Mr. Gordon, you're on the same floor."

"Whoa, whoa. He doesn't stay on the same floor as me," Harvey interjected. "He's an assistant. He's lucky he's staying in this hotel. You put him somewhere else."

Gordon had two thoughts: One, Harvey was appalled at the thought
that his just-out-of-college assistant deserved the same accommodations
as the head of the company. And two: "He probably doesn't want me
to see what he's up to." On subsequent trips he said Harvey would tell
him, 'Call so-and-so and tell her I'm coming to town and see if she
wants to have a drink tonight.'"

One morning when he came to Harvey's suite, Gordon saw a cham-
pagne bucket and two glasses, one of which was untouched; he knew
Harvey did not drink. "It was clear that he was having extramarital
stuff going on." Clearly, people who worked at Miramax knew of his
troubling behavior and felt uneasy. Male executives privately advised
female employees not to go alone when summoned to a meeting at one
of the hotel suites where Harvey liked to work. Mark Gill, who became
president of Miramax's West Coast office, recalled, "I'd say, 'Okay, well,
somebody's going with you. Or I'll go with you. Or you're not going.'"
Despite the clear indications that he knew what danger being alone
with Harvey posed for women, Gill claimed he had no idea there was
a risk of "sexual assault." What he feared, he said, was what he called
"sexual harassment," which he defined as "him reaching for consensual
sex . . . chasing people around the couch." Most everyone who worked
at Miramax, he continued, "knew that he was not faithful to his wife
and was cheating on her with some consensual relationships." In Gill's
distinction between the two, one shared by many who worked for Harvey, "sexual assault" was equivalent to a serious felony, while pressing
women for sex, normally described as "sexual harassment," was wrong,
but a misdemeanor. Splitting hairs in this way meant that employees
could acknowledge to themselves that lines were being crossed but could
still justify staying in the meaningful jobs they had worked so long and
so hard to achieve. Many allowed themselves to see not an assault but
an exchange taking place, in which a powerful man and an attractive
woman each offered something the other wanted. This is likely how
Harvey himself saw his predations.

Missing from this armchair analysis was an appreciation of the terror Harvey's victims experienced, and an understanding of the long half-life of the trauma. Not simply nightmare memories of the assault—which could range from groping to violent penetration—but also self-blame (Had you signaled you were available? Did you fail to struggle enough? Did you say *NO* forcefully enough?); guilt (Did you too eagerly seek assistance for your career?); and shame over the burden of a squalid secret. You were left with the knowledge that silence—even in self-preservation—meant Harvey, unchallenged and unrestrained, could do the same thing to someone else.

Hillary Silver's narrow escape suggests that Harvey's behavior was not a secret for many Miramax employees, despite later protests of ignorance. In late 1997, Silver was twenty-seven years old and a rising Hollywood agent, but she longed to enter the film production business. Hollywood friends wrote to Harvey and a January 1998 interview was arranged with Miramax's human resources department. She entered the elevator at 375 Greenwich Street, and it happened that Harvey was in the same elevator. "He looked at me from head to toe" and said hello, she recalls. He asked where she was going and she said she had an appointment with HR.

"I'll show you where the office is," he said, marching her to HR. "This is Hillary Silver," he said. "When she's done, send her to my office."

"I thought, this is really a friendly, hands-on place," Silver remembered wryly. She was stunned when the HR executive delivered her to Harvey's office and Harvey announced, without consulting HR, "You're hired."

Ecstatic, she left for a scheduled month of travel abroad. When she returned and checked in with HR about her start date, the executive told her some coworkers wanted to take her out for a welcoming drink.

"Listen, I'm going to cut to the chase," the HR executive told her at the Red Stripe lounge in Soho. "You do not want this job."

"What do you mean?" she said, puzzled.

"You're going to be scratching his back. You'll be giving him massages. You seem like a very nice person. This is not something you would want."

With tears in her eyes, one of the two women at the table—who worked on Harvey's team of four assistants—chimed in that she had just quit. "I hate him. This job is awful," she blurted.

Silver decided not to show up for work the next day, instead writing a letter declining the job. "When I first heard the news nineteen years later that Harvey Weinstein was a sexual predator and a friend said I dodged a bullet, my first reaction was, 'How did this happen?'" she said. "People who worked there knew about this. Three sweet people warned me. What about the other people who worked for him? They knew about this. He wasn't an isolated criminal. Why is only he held accountable? Why not the other people who enabled his behavior?"

Amy Israel, a bright, forceful woman who, like a handful of female Miramax staffers—Marcy Granata, Zelda Perkins—was not intimidated by Harvey, was one of a larger number of executives who came to feel Harvey was untrustworthy with women, and she sought to protect employees. Of the many who claimed, "'I never knew anything,' I find that hard to believe," she said. "Many people, including myself, didn't know the criminal extent of his behavior, but a year after I started at the company, I heard that the woman I replaced as an assistant had gotten a payout. From that moment on, I made sure that anyone who worked in my department was never alone with Harvey. This was particularly important because my department was the one that flew around the world with him to film festivals."

Harvey had tried the infamous massage line on Israel herself while she was working the important Toronto Film Festival as a junior staffer. A male assistant had walked her into Harvey's suite and disappeared, and Harvey had moved in on her. Quick-witted, she said she had to call her mother, which defused the threat. A year or so later, during a dull screening, he idly suggested, "Why don't you take off your shirt and do some cartwheels?"

"Go fuck yourself, you fat fuck," the pugnacious Israel shot back. At this, he apparently lost interest. Harvey could retreat when someone pushed back, though many women describe freezing with fright at his tactics, or hastily calculating the cost to themselves of his anger and affront if rejected. It also suggests that harassment was a constant, low-rumbling threat for women employees. Oppressed by what she suspected Harvey might have done to others, Israel would open up years later to Jodi Kantor and Megan Twohey, the *New York Times* reporters who first publicly exposed Harvey.

Others admit they knew Harvey sexually abused women and kept quiet. Paul Webster, who worked at Miramax in the 1990s as a senior executive, confessed to being a Harvey enabler in a 2018 PBS *Frontline* documentary, *Weinstein*. He acknowledged prohibiting his female assistant from bringing requested material to Harvey's hotel suite at night. Why? "It didn't take too much brainpower to put it together that a man who was so abusive and bullying in every aspect of his life, would bring that abuse into the sexual arena. . . . I think looking back that I did know and I chose to suppress it. I chose to hide from that fact. I think we were all enablers. . . . I knew he was a dangerous character. Yet I knew he was at the epicenter of where I wanted to be."

Those like Webster who knew, or those who should have known, or those who didn't want to know, were partners in a culture of silence.

Miramax employees had hoped Harvey's seemingly happy marriage to Eve would tame him, and yet the number of assaults seemed to rise in this decade, coinciding with Harvey's increased power. Treating one woman lovingly is no guarantee that someone will treat all women kindly. In the end, the marriage does not illustrate Harvey's tender, satisfied side so much as it does a divided life and a growing willingness to deceive.

The episodes took on a numbing sameness in 1997. Actress Rose McGowan had caught Harvey's eye in Dimension's first hit, *Scream*, and was working on another Miramax film, *Phantoms*, when she got word during the 1997 Sundance Film Festival that Harvey, who she considered the big boss, wanted to meet her in the restaurant of the Stein Ericksen, a timber-framed lodge that was the ground-zero hotel at the festival. When McGowan arrived, she was told the meeting would be in Harvey's suite, which she described as being an entire floor of the hotel, with a long corridor connecting several rooms. Their meeting was very pleasant, filled with praise for her acting, before he escorted her to the door. "Walking behind me, his huge size seemed even more overwhelming," she recalled in her memoir. She claims he abruptly pushed her into a small side room with a Jacuzzi, peeled off her clothes while she was still frozen with shock, and forcibly performed oral sex on her. "I disassociated and left my body. . . . Anybody who's a sexual assault victim will tell you: the trauma does strange things to your sense of time, your memory. There are details you remember with uncanny accuracy . . . and then there are gaps in the timeline where there is nothing, nothing. . . . I'm trying to put my clothes on and make sense of what has just happened. It's like a race you can't keep up with."

Afterward, as he would do with increasing frequency when one of these incidents turned toxic and threatened his peace, Harvey got McGowan to sign an NDA in exchange for one hundred thousand dollars. She agreed, she told Ronan Farrow, because her attorney advised that no one would believe her if she pressed charges. But her muzzling chafed at her, and in later years she struggled against it, dropping public hints of the assault and then retreating. Her paranoia seems justified: Harvey would in 2017 hire a spy agency to surveil her to measure the threat she posed to him.

The same year as the alleged McGowan assault, Italian actress Asia Argento said Harvey forcefully performed oral sex on her after she was invited to a party at the Hotel du Cap-Eden-Roc, the storied haunt of Lost Generation literary expats, perched on the rocks a good half hour from Cannes, during the annual film festival; there was no party, only Harvey, and he appeared in a bathrobe and asked for a massage.

"A big, fat man wanting to eat you. It's a scary fairy tale," she told Ronan Farrow. Subsequently, exhausted by his continued pursuit, and by the damage that had been done to her sense of autonomy, she entered a consensual sexual relationship with him. "After the rape, he won." (Weinstein denied Argento's accusation and, delightedly, later accused her of hypocrisy when it came to light that she had settled sexual abuse claims made against her by a young man.)

This was a not-infrequent pattern among his victims. Succumbing created a vortex of confusion and guilt, further undermining their ability to resist or speak out. When assault was followed by seduction, how credible could the accuser be? It is a cycle familiar to those who study abused women. Dr. Barbara Ziv, a forensic psychologist and Temple University professor who has long studied why sexual assault victims keep in touch with their abusers, notes that only 20 to 40 percent of rape victims resist, and the vast majority don't report the crime.

Actress Ashley Judd remembers that in late 1996 or early 1997 she was invited to meet Harvey at the Peninsula Hotel in Los Angeles for breakfast to discuss a role in a Miramax movie. He invoked his standard opening line, complaining of a kink in his neck and asking for a massage. She demurred, but he kept coming up with new requests, asking her to pick out his clothes for him, to watch him take a shower, escalating to grabbing her arms. "I said no, a lot of ways, a lot of times, and he always came back at me with some slimy ask," she told reporters Kantor and Twohey. She described his attempt to display his power over her as "twirling the lasso." Judd said the thought that rushed into her mind was: "How do I get out of the room as fast as possible without alienating Harvey Weinstein?"

Cracking a bitter joke gave her a way out: "When I win an Academy Award in a Miramax movie, I'll give you a blow job." Two years later, Judd encountered Harvey at a dinner party for a movie premiere and leaned across the crowded table toward him, about to speak, but he interrupted to say, "I think I'll let you out of that deal we made." Judd remains certain that he spread rumors that she was difficult to work with after the Peninsula incident, and the director Peter Jackson confirmed that Harvey discouraged him from casting her and Mira Sorvino, another actress he pursued, for Jackson's *Lord of the Rings* trilogy. "In hindsight, I realize that this was very likely the Miramax smear campaign in full swing," he told a reporter for *The Guardian*.

Actress Kate Beckinsale chimed in, years later in an Instagram post, that she was only seventeen and still in high school when she was invited to a movie discussion in a hotel conference room. She was directed to Weinstein's suite. "He opened the door in his bathrobe. I was incredibly naïve and young and it did not cross my mind that this older, unattractive man"—Harvey was in his forties—"would ever expect me to have any sexual interest in him. After declining alcohol and announcing that I had school in the morning, I left."

What is unclear is whether Harvey considered that, even without sex, making these women uncomfortable was a success.

As ritualized in his response to accusations as he was in the abuse itself, Harvey had a few tactics to clean up any messy aftermath. First, he would stifle protest with an NDA. If not an admission of guilt, the NDAs were at least an acknowledgment of a situation that could be harmful to his business and reputation if known, and so the terms were ferociously punitive if the woman spoke to anyone—family, colleagues, press, doctors—about what happened. If rumors did emerge despite the NDA and awkward questions were asked, he would issue a blanket denial and either claim these were consensual encounters or a lie.

Harvey would not deny that he was a trader of favors. That's how he thought power was exercised. This is illustrated by the deal he reportedly offered actress Gwyneth Paltrow a few years earlier. When she was in her early twenties, Paltrow had already performed supporting roles in several Miramax movies, and pressed Harvey for a starring role. "He knew I was desperate to do *Emma*, the Jane Austen adaptation. He said, 'I'll give you that if you agree to be in *The Pallbearer.*'" This was a lackluster dramedy with *Friends* star David Schwimmer. "It was always," Paltrow said, "'You do this for me, and I'll do that for you.'"

Harvey had another trade in mind as well. He summoned Paltrow to his Peninsula Hotel suite in 1995 to discuss *Emma*. After the door was closed, Harvey grabbed her by the arms and squeezed, she recalled, trying to coax her into the bedroom for a massage. Shocked, she refused. She told her then boyfriend, Brad Pitt, who spotted Harvey weeks later at the theater for the opening of *Hamlet* and threatened him with bodily harm. "If you ever make her feel uncomfortable again, I'll kill you," Pitt told Paltrow he shouted at Harvey. "I am so grateful to Brad," she said. "Because he leveraged his power and fame to protect me—when I was no one—and he scared Harvey."

Harvey sought to placate the prominent actor, assuring him it would not happen again. Despite his rage, Pitt would appear in two more Harvey-produced movies (*Inglourious Basterds* and *Killing Them Softly*).

Harvey did not try to placate Paltrow; instead, he phoned and yelled at her. "He said some version of, *I'm going to ruin your career*," she later claimed. She managed to mollify him and continued her climb to the Miramax mountaintop.

Why, I asked Paltrow, did she continue working with Harvey and Miramax after that?

She could have been speaking for much of Hollywood when she answered: "We all knew he was hitting on all of us. It was sort of an eye roll." Of course, it was more. But she says it was not common knowledge that he sexually assaulted women. The "bind" so many were in, she said, was that "he had so much power. He was making all these great movies. And I was about to be in those movies. How do you calibrate that? We all wanted to make excuses for a lot of his behavior over the years because of the movies he was making." Paltrow rejected the casting couch trade she was offered and said he never accosted her again.

THE MOGUL

(1997–1998)

B y 1998, once tiny Miramax was producing and distributing more movies than any major studio—thirty-six—and on average was spending two and three times more per movie than it earlier spent to distribute independent films. "In other words," Peter Biskind wrote, "at the same time the indie world was being Miramaxed, Miramax itself was being Disneyized."

The deal with Disney granted Harvey substantial autonomy, but Miramax's rapid expansion alarmed his corporate overlords. Harvey began to ignore Disney's financial controls, exceeding the amount of money—$30 million—his contract stipulated he could spend on a movie. Michael Eisner lamented, "Harvey ceased to want to be a small, independent filmmaker. He wanted to be up with the studio heads. He wanted to be an entrepreneur, and to buy and sell things—without talking to anybody. He moved out of his agreed-upon contracts."

Picture Harvey in the late 1990s: Most days, he arrived at Miramax's offices on Greenwich Street just before 10:00 a.m., in the back seat of a black Mercedes. Harvey's office, with its exposed-brick walls, seemed too small for the large man who occupied it. There was no computer, because Harvey barely knew how to use one. An adjoining room contained the unused exercise equipment Eve had ordered. Harvey was in total command. Four assistants sat just outside his office, one of whom traveled with him everywhere, always kept him in cell-phone contact with the world, and was not permitted to ride the subway, where the cell-phone signal often did not work. The four assistants performed varied tasks: making and receiving phone calls; listening in on Harvey's calls and taking follow-up notes; interpreting Harvey's mood for Miramax executives who hovered by their desks; relaying Harvey's orders; printing out Harvey's emails because for several years he did not know how to access or compose them himself; handling correspondence, filing; making appointments for actresses Harvey asked to see; and waiting to be verbally abused.

Daniel Murray lasted one year as an assistant. He had studied film and literature at Brown, and his dream was to one day become a movie producer. He'd worked with Scott Rudin and Mike Nichols before landing a job with Harvey at twenty-five. Murray described "a culture of fear" that permeated Miramax. He was always stumped by the source of Harvey's outbursts: "His rage was over nonconsequential things. He threw a cell phone at me. He screamed, 'Jump out the window and kill yourself!' He dropped me off on I-95 on the way to Westport and screamed, 'Get the fuck out of the car!'" After quitting, Murray gave up the idea of becoming a producer and became a lawyer.

Yet, Murray adds, there were important compensations. "In the late nineties, he was making the best movies. You knew if you could survive Harvey, you'd rise to an executive at Miramax."

Five years of access to Disney resources had expanded Harvey's ambitions. He was now attending the annual summer mogul-fest hosted by the investment bank Allen & Co. in Sun Valley and was intoxicated by the atmosphere. The perennial party-crasher now saw himself as a peer of fellow attendees: giants of tech, finance, and media such as Rupert Murdoch, Bill Gates, and Warren Buffett; moguls like Sumner Redstone, who owned Hollywood studios; John Malone, who ruled TCI, the biggest cable company; and Harvey's putative boss, Michael

Eisner, who had no idea that Harvey had already started to branch out to launch subsidiary businesses of his own.

Harvey felt one of his great strengths in filmmaking was his omnivorous reading habit. Now he decided to start his own publishing company. In 1998 Harvey persuaded Tina Brown, then the renowned editor of *The New Yorker*, to exit and become the founding editor of a new magazine, *Talk*, and chairwoman of Miramax's Talk Media, supervising both the magazine and a new book division, Talk Books. He chose Liberty Island as the site of a lavish, star-studded party to launch *Talk* and celebrate Brown. "I always thought it would be cool to have a magazine," Harvey said. It was a point of pride for him that he was different from the crass moguls of old Hollywood, such as Harry Cohn: "I'm a magazine and book junkie. I don't know that Harry Cohn read magazines! I thought Tina was the best editor in America."

He proclaimed that Miramax was becoming a media empire, invoking that favorite word of media moguls: *synergy*. He envisioned that Talk Books, in partnership with *Talk* magazine, would generate movie ideas and promote his movies and their stars and directors. He lavished big bucks and executive perks on Brown and publisher Ron Galotti and their team. He dangled extravagant salaries to lure people to *Talk*, including senior CBS *60 Minutes* producer Vicki Gordon, who says he offered her $750,000 to join as a senior editor, which she declined.

Eisner remembers how he learned of *Talk* magazine: "Tina Brown called me in Aspen over Christmas and thanked me."

"For what?" he said.

"For the magazine we're doing together."

"What magazine?" he asked.

"The magazine I'm doing with Harvey."

Stunned, Eisner phoned Harvey. "We had a very unpleasant conversation. I reminded Harvey that he had no right to do this. . . . I didn't believe in the magazine business at that time." Disney had recently sold the newspapers and magazine it inherited soon after it acquired Capital Cities/ABC in 1995. "It was not what we bought Miramax for, to get into the magazine business." Eisner was enraged at Harvey for over-spending and for ignoring the financial curbs in his contract, but most of all for not behaving like a partner.

That night, Eisner and his wife had dinner with Evelyn and Leonard Lauder, CEO of the Estee Lauder Companies, and Eisner recalled, "Leonard told me, 'Harvey Weinstein is the darling of the New York press. Harvey Weinstein is winning Academy Awards. He's making movies New Yorkers love. You will not win this.'"

Eisner backed off. The tensions boiling between Disney and Miramax were reduced for the moment to a simmer.

Harvey recruited British editor Jonathan Burnham as editor in chief of Talk Books; they aimed, said Burnham, to publish about twenty-five books each year. "Harvey signed off on every acquisition we made," Burnham recalled. Harvey, on his own and unrestrained, offered extravagant book contracts to prominent people who enhanced his influence even if their books didn't sell. He signed former mayor Rudy Giuliani, before he was made famous after 9/11, to author a memoir (for an eye-popping $3 million contract); he signed superlawyer David Boies ($1 million), former secretary of state Madeleine Albright (just under $1 million), and Vice President Al Gore's daughters, Kristin and Karenna. Harvey sprinkled book contracts on journalists—NBC's *Meet the Press* host Tim Russert, Arianna Huffington, Page Six's Paula Froelich, *Daily News* gossip columnist Mitchell Fink, MSNBC's Joe Scarborough and Mika Brzezinski, *Variety* editor Peter Bart, and film critics Todd McCarthy and Marshall Fine. Burnham says he was regularly harangued by calls from people who said, "Harvey said he would publish my book," and Burnham had to let them down.

Without Bob looking over the shoulder of Talk Books—"Bob thought we were sucking Harvey's time," Burnham said—Harvey merrily spent away. Typically, he did not focus on whether the projected sales of a book justified the dollars Talk Books offered. But he paid keen attention to the content. "Harvey was an incredibly voracious reader," Burnham says. "He would ask me to send him a book and the next day he would send me notes on the book. . . . It was the only time in publishing that my boss urged me to spend more." What his editor saw in Harvey was a "galvanizing talent for creating a vision for a movie or a book."

The same furious explosions familiar to his film staff took place at Talk Books. "Harvey's toxic energy became an abusive force in the company," said Burnham. Harvey had "irrational bouts of anger"— demeaning people in meetings by declaring, "You're pathetic," or "You'll always be the weakest link in this company." Burnham described it as "the flip side of Harvey's orgiastic enthusiasm." He was, recalled Susan Mercandetti, who worked for Talk Books as a senior editor from Washington, D.C., "someone who was well read, enthusiastic, a great storyteller, funny. But a little scary." Over its five years, said Burnham, Talk published about eighty books, 10 percent (eight) of which claimed to be national bestsellers.

But Eisner was right—it wasn't the right moment to invest in the magazine business. After the anxiety-driven decline in advertising dollars following the 9/11 attacks, *Talk* would be abruptly shuttered in January 2002, just four years after its splashy launch. Talk Books carried on, was renamed Miramax Books, and Burnham and most executives exited in 2005.

When David Boies was first contacted about writing a book, Harvey called his office and announced to the woman who picked up the phone, "I'm Harvey Weinstein," expecting to be patched through immediately. His secretary had no idea who Harvey Weinstein was, Boies recalled, and Harvey tried to explain the prominent movies he had brought to theaters.

She took a message and Boies called him back. Boies says he had only cursory knowledge of who Harvey was, but agreed to have lunch. At lunch Harvey pitched Boies on writing a Louis Nizer–like *My Life in Court*, covering his career and the cases he'd tried. "I had no idea about books," Boies recalled. "But a one-million-dollar advance seemed like a lot of money."

Boies accepted the offer and ultimately wrote *Courting Justice*. Sales were disappointing, but Harvey received a return on his investment before the book was even published when Boies became his go-to lawyer, a trusted adviser who often served as diplomat for an impulsive man who needed someone to dig him out of holes he had dug himself.

Although *Talk* magazine would lose an astounding amount of money, the year before it was launched in 1998 had been a good one for Miramax and Disney, which probably fueled Harvey's optimism. Miramax produced from scratch and acquired for distribution thirty-four films, generating record-breaking revenues of $420 million, nearly half of which came from Bob Weinstein's Dimension, with movies like *Scream*. The artistic success that thrilled Harvey most was *The English Patient*, a Saul Zaentz–produced film that Miramax distributed and that brought the company its first Best Picture Oscar in 1997.

Based on a Michael Ondaatje novel, it tells the story of four people stranded in an Italian villa in the final months of World War II. A badly burned Hungarian count eager to keep his identity concealed (Ralph Fiennes) holds his nurse (Juliette Binoche) spellbound with the tale of his affair with a married Englishwoman (Kristin Scott Thomas) in Cairo on the eve of war. Scripted and directed by Anthony Minghella, the film weaves a tortuous path through secrecy, betrayal, desire, and loss; lavishly produced, it delivered both resoundingly good reviews and great box office. In all, it amassed an astounding nine Oscars. By contrast, Michael Eisner and Disney were generally applauded for making money, not for making outstanding movies, with the exception of their Oscar wins for animated features.

Good Will Hunting was Harvey's other huge success later the same year. How Harvey seduced two childhood friends and aspiring screenwriters and actors, Ben Affleck and Matt Damon, reveals much about why talent gravitated to him. Castle Rock, a subsidiary of Warner Bros., originally bought their script, but Affleck and Damon knew the studio did not want them to star and were convinced studio execs had done only a cursory read of the script. They needed to recruit another studio willing to pay $1 million to buy it back. Harvey has told the story of meeting with Affleck and Damon in many settings, each retelling portraying Harvey on the side of artistic talent.

"What do you think of the script?" Affleck and Damon asked.

"I think the script is great," Harvey answered, "but on page sixty" the psychiatrist and the professor "give each other a blow job. I don't understand that blow-job scene."

Damon and Affleck beamed, for they had inserted that non sequitur in the script as a test. Harvey recalled what they told him: "We wrote that for studio executives. You were the only one who ever pointed it out. We had meetings with Warner, MGM, Paramount. We just wanted to see who the fuck read this goddamn thing."

The movie centers on Will Hunting (Matt Damon), a twenty-year-old MIT janitor with a genius IQ who is discovered by a math professor (Stellan Skarsgård). When Will takes part in a gang fight along with his best friend, Chuckie (Ben Affleck), and is arrested after attacking a cop, his math professor mentor negotiates a leniency deal, but only if Will studies advanced mathematics and agrees to see therapist Sean McGuire (Robin Williams). Over time Will accepts then rejects help, jobs, friends, and love, leaving audiences gyrating between exasperation and joy. Slowly, Williams breaks through Damon's defenses and teaches him about putting his rare gifts to use and loving someone more than you love yourself.

The movie achieved impressive praise. According to the scoreboard kept by Rotten Tomatoes, an astonishing 98 percent of critics were enthusiastic, and 94 percent of the audience. Equally impressive were worldwide box office sales of $226 million. The director, Gus Van Sant, unlike other directors, praised Harvey for never intruding, either during filming or in postproduction. The movie was nominated for nine Academy Awards, with Robin Williams snaring the Best Actor award and Damon and Affleck the Best Screenplay. Nervously clutching the statue tightly on stage, Affleck thanked "Harvey Weinstein, who believed in us, and made this movie." Since Miramax produced the film and did not just distribute it, Harvey was particularly proud—and reaped a generous share of its profits.

Harvey's self-image was that of an artist, or at least someone who appreciated artists. He aspired to be a throwback to the early studio moguls who nursed their stars and also made important movies. "I'll never be as great as either Thalberg or Selznick," he said. As a kid who worshipped movies and the New York Yankees, in his eyes they were equal to Mickey Mantle and Whitey Ford. When I told him that some critics had likened him to extremely brutal studio boss Harry Cohn, who physically abused actresses and verbally abused most everyone— and unlike other studio founders was widely thought to be a thug with little interest in elevating audience expectations—Harvey was offended. "That's the worst thing you can say to me," he responded, going on to express the contempt he felt for industry people, explaining why he located Miramax in New York and identified as an outsider in an industry where too few executives even knew who Francois Truffaut was.

"When push comes to shove, the talent feels he's on their side," Disney's then studio boss Joe Roth said. "It's almost an animal instinct." Gwyneth Paltrow, having run the gauntlet of his sexual interest to star in many of his films, knew she was a favorite. Harvey cast her in multiple movies starting in the nineties, and later crowned her the "First Lady of Miramax." Outwardly, he treated Paltrow with respect. At the time, she declared that Harvey was a protector: "Harvey has a more old-fashioned approach to relationships with movie stars. It's very sort of mafioso—'We're all in this together.' He looks out for me."

Yet in 2017 Paltrow would find out that he tried to coerce other women by claiming he had sex with her, using her star trajectory as an example when he told one actress in 2000 that agreeing to his advances was "the best thing you can do for your career now." Deeply upset, Paltrow told an interviewer, "He's not the first person to lie about sleeping with someone, but he used the lie as an assault weapon."

For a man not noted for empathy, Harvey had a preternatural ability to detect people's vanities and private passions. Eric Robinson, who started as one of Harvey's multiple New York assistants and rose to the title of vice president, remembers when Harvey was determined to persuade Russell Crowe to star in *Cinderella Man*, a film about a scrappy boxer who rises to be the world heavyweight champion. Crowe was not interested. "Harvey had to find a way to Russell's heart. He had a band"—called 30 Odd Foot of Grunts. "Crowe had made a documentary about his band. Harvey found out that the band was performing in Milan. He dropped everything and flew to Milan to see the band perform. And he bought Crowe's unpublished documentary." After this extended courtship, Crowe agreed to star in *Cinderella Man*. It was a demonstration of Harvey's special talents as head of a studio: He would not take no for an answer. He believed that he could persuade anyone to do what he wanted. He had a nose for people's vulnerabilities or desires. And he could wield considerable charm.

But charm required concentration. Harvey's default position was anger and paranoia. He fervently believed Hollywood was out to get him, and he believed this even before it was true. He thought the movie industry resented the success he had making movies—sometimes brilliant, innovative movies—that Hollywood wouldn't touch. Although the film industry included many successful Jews, he was convinced there was more than a whiff of anti-Semitism in the way they talked about him behind his back.

Saul Zaentz, producer of *The English Patient* and a popular figure in Hollywood, was happy to bad-mouth Harvey to his face. Zaentz was an Oscar winner for *One Flew Over the Cuckoo's Nest* and *Amadeus*; the year before the 1996 release of *The English Patient*, which would win him his third Oscar, the Academy gave him the Irving Thalberg Lifetime Achievement Award that Harvey craved. *The English Patient* cost about $30 million and grossed $78.7 million in the United States and $232 million worldwide. The movie was owned by Twentieth Century Fox, but when they pressed for more famous lead actors—*Why not Demi Moore rather than Kristin Scott Thomas as the female lead?*—and fretted about the production costs, Harvey swooped in and acquired it. Miramax would coproduce and distribute the film. Yet the director, Anthony Minghella, and the crew had deferred part of their salaries to get the film made and by 2002 had still not been paid in full, nor had Zaentz received his slice of the profits. Harvey insisted that he had already paid Zaentz more than $3 million, and that Zaentz was obligated to pay the director and crew. Besides, Harvey explained somewhat condescendingly, what looks like a hit in the movie business often isn't. Since Miramax spent an additional $42 million marketing the movie, Miramax actually lost money on it, he insisted. Zaentz and Minghella knew that Harvey was employing the fake math all too common at Hollywood studios. Among the dollars Harvey was leaving out of his calculus was the $50 million Miramax raked in from the sale of broadcast, cable, pay-TV, home video, and other ancillary theatrical revenues. To induce Miramax to distribute his movie, Zaentz had ceded these additional worldwide rights to Miramax. Zaentz denounced Harvey as "a liar" and filed a lawsuit to force Harvey to pay Minghella and the crew, which eventually was settled for $20 million. Although Minghella agreed with Zaentz that Harvey had stiffed them, this decent, nonconfrontational director believed Harvey genuinely cared deeply about making quality movies, and by 2002 Minghella was directing his third Miramax movie, *Cold Mountain*.

All in all, Harvey was getting away with a lot. "There are not that many industries where there is direct contact between older, powerful men and significantly less powerful, attractive women," observed Susan Lyne, who was once president of ABC Entertainment and the founding editor of *Premiere* magazine. "In corporate life there are layers of people between senior powerful men and most females. Hollywood is a male-dominated business. Its culture has been built up over the years. That culture exploits women and makes men who have power over women believe they have rights."

As Harvey's self-image as a true Hollywood mogul in the grand tradition swelled, his abuse of women escalated. In the spring of 1998, Zoe Brock, a successful twenty-four-year-old model, attended the Cannes Film Festival. She was seated next to Harvey at a crowded dinner at the Majestic Hotel. Brock was a beautiful woman and Harvey took note, offering her a ride to her hotel; he amended the offer by telling her there was to be a party at the Hotel du Cap-Eden-Roc and her friends were coming.

It was a lie. As recounted in the *Frontline* documentary, no one was in Weinstein's suite when they arrived. (This is the same ruse he allegedly used on the actress Asia Argento in 1997.) An industry insider would claim that Harvey would sometimes take two suites for the festival, one at the Majestic and one at the Hotel du Cap, which could cost a combined three hundred thousand dollars, but which conceivably gave him two arenas of entrapment. He stepped into the bathroom and emerged naked, asking for, then demanding, a massage. He pursued Brock but she managed to get to the bathroom, locked the door, and screamed an order: *Harvey, put on your clothes!* Like a few other strong-willed, confident women who didn't show fear, she managed to escape. "It worked," she told *Frontline*. "I came out of the bathroom and he was apologizing. He started to cry. He said something in between his tears I have never forgotten, and I never will for the rest of my days: 'You do not like me because I'm fat.'"

Brock had stumbled on a vulnerability: shame over the way he looked. His friend, rich playboy Taki Theodoracopulos, wrote in a column that Harvey told him, "I was born poor, ugly, Jewish and had to fight all my life to get somewhere. You got lots of girls. No girl looked at me until I made it big in Hollywood." (When Harvey objected to other quotes in the column saying he exchanged jobs for sex, Theodoracopulos retracted them, but not Harvey's self-description.)

Brock did not report the assault to the police. In this she was like every other victim of Harvey's to date. They didn't believe the law or their employer would take the word of a young woman over a prominent Hollywood executive. Perhaps she felt guilty for accepting his party offer. Perhaps she feared he would harm her career and expose her in the press. Silence seemed preferable.

"You can think of it as kind of a cost-benefit analysis," explained Deborah Tuerkheimer, an expert on rape law at Northwestern University's Pritzker School of Law and a former sex-crimes prosecutor in Manhattan. All these reasons for not coming forward were cited in testimony twenty-two years later at Harvey's criminal trial. After years of silence from those he assaulted, Harvey had reason to feel invincible.

And even if women did speak of their experiences, it seemed to accomplish little. Daryl Hannah was one of Harvey's targets for years, culminating at the Rome premiere of Tarantino's *Kill Bill: Volume 2*, where Harvey somehow secured a key to her hotel room and burst in on her, only to be deterred by the presence of her male makeup artist. He pretended that there was a party downstairs and she needed to appear, but when she followed him downstairs, he took her to an empty room and asked her to show him her breasts. When she refused, she said she experienced "instant repercussions": the next day the Miramax plane left Rome without her. Hannah said she told many people in the industry about Harvey's stalking. "I think it doesn't matter if you're a well-known actress, it doesn't matter if you're twenty or if you're forty, it doesn't matter if you report or if you don't, because we are not believed." Both Mia Kirshner, an aspiring actress, and Gwyneth Paltrow would one day claim that they reported Harvey's bad behavior to their CAA agents, who did nothing. CAA, arguably the most influential talent agency in Hollywood, surely seemed to be confessing complicity when in late 2017 they released this statement in the wake of a *New York Times* story on Hollywood's "complicity machine," mentioning that there were eight unnamed CAA agents who should have known, sort of: "We apologize to any person who the agency let down."

Quentin Tarantino did know. In the *Times'* October 2017 front-page exposé of Harvey Weinstein, Harvey's favorite director belatedly admitted, "I knew enough to do more than I did. There was more to it than just the normal rumors, the normal gossip. It wasn't secondhand. I knew he did a couple of these things. I wish I had taken responsibility for what I heard." Actresses Uma Thurman, who appeared in three of his movies, and Mira Sorvino, whom the director had dated, had both told Tarantino that Harvey assaulted them. Thurman described her efforts to evade him: "You're like an animal wriggling away, like a lizard. I was doing anything I could to get the train back on the track. My track. Not his track."

Yet Tarantino kept making pictures with Harvey.

Little wonder that Harvey had reason to feel safe—until the 1998 Venice Film Festival.

His movie *Shakespeare in Love* dominated Harvey's attention in the late summer of 1998. In the weeks leading up to the September Venice Film Festival, Harvey was consumed with the editing of what he hoped would be a smash hit. But he was struggling with how it should end. After an in-house screening in London, Harvey planned to leave for Venice, where he was always treated as royalty, with actors and directors and producers lining up to kiss his ring. Logistical planning for this important trip was the responsibility of a twenty-five-year-old staffer named Zelda Perkins, who had come to work at Miramax two years earlier. Harvey had no reason to suspect that Perkins, whose independent spirit he enjoyed, would soon pose the greatest menace to his career.

Perkins had graduated from Manchester University and moved to New York City to be with a boyfriend. She had landed an off-camera job on a television series but longed to return to London. Perkins worked for a friend of former Miramax executive Donna Gigliotti, now a producer on *Shakespeare in Love*. Invoking Gigliotti's name at the suggestion of her boss, Perkins scored an interview with the head of business affairs and was hired as a temp in Miramax's London office. "I had no idea who Harvey Weinstein was," she said. "I knew he made some cool movies." She quickly learned he instilled fear: "Everyone went into panic when he called."

When one of Harvey's three London assistants suddenly went AWOL, Perkins received a 7:30 a.m. call from one of his other assistants, telling her that she should be at the Savoy Hotel in twenty minutes. Once again revealing that Harvey's behavior was no secret, the assistant cautioned Perkins, "Don't wear anything too revealing. If he asks you anything, don't say you don't know." When she arrived at the Savoy she knocked on one of several doors. It was the wrong door. Harvey answered. "Who the fuck are you?" he bellowed.

"Presumably I've come here to fucking help you!" she shot back.

"Get in here," he said.

Harvey liked women who dared talk back to him, Perkins learned. "Harvey humiliated and destroyed men, but he wanted strong women around him."

Perkins soon became his number one assistant in London, with a meager annual salary of twelve thousand pounds. Assistants were given lavish tips on occasion but were generally underpaid; the gratuities they enjoyed weren't tied to their salaries, which increased their dependence on Harvey. Her immediate impression: "He was vile but at the same time an extremely exciting, brilliant, inspiring person to be around. Everyone came to him, not just in movies but politics. To be around someone so powerful was exciting."

She was unprepared for the "culture shock" she experienced when first exposed to the "unreal world" of Hollywood. Perkins was not the kind of sexy young actress or statuesque model Harvey was known to chase around his hotel suite; she had brownish-blond hair loosely brushing her shoulders, was five foot three inches, and did not have a voluptuous body. But chase her he did: "Every time I was alone with him. This was his MO with every woman he was alone with. It didn't matter what you looked like. His obsession was making every woman submit."

Another Harvey obsession, she learned, was to invite aspiring actresses on the private jets he was now leasing. It was "normal" for Harvey to please many male actors by "bringing girls to all these guys. I
was like a baby learning all new stuff. It was all unreal. When you did
well organizing a trip for Harvey, you sometimes got a grand in cash. . . .
All of it was unreal, insane. You're hanging out with people who don't
live in the real world. The way actors behave, they are infantilized.
They are manipulated by people like Harvey. They get what they want."
Drivers. Assistants. Girls. And what Harvey dangled in front of them
he also grasped for himself.

"They act like spoiled babies, and their behavior is allowed because
that is the way you control them. This was my introduction to this
'adult' world. Once we sat in a club in Paris and a prominent actor was
at Harvey's table with a large group and they're all drinking and they
formed a circle around the actor. They spotted a pretty girl and she was
allowed into our circle and the actor slapped her on the ass and smelled
her. If he liked her, she'd stay. If he didn't, she'd be sent away. Everybody there should have hated that, including the girls. Yet they went
along. I was horrified by women and the effect Harvey had on them.
It was his power. Power does strange things to people."

Perkins knew that whatever city Harvey was visiting, he liked to
work out of a hotel suite. In London, she arranged for a suite at the
Savoy. By day, his office was the living room, with desks, multiple
phones, faxes, laptops, and more than one sitting area. At night, he slept
in the adjoining bedroom and, Perkins said, "Harvey always had a girlfriend coming around." Sometimes two. Sometimes, she said, he would
ask her to run out and buy him condoms, though she never cleaned up
after him, as other assistants claim they had to do. Perkins knew that
women slipped Harvey their phone numbers or business cards, which
he interpreted as a sexual invitation. At the time, Perkins didn't believe
he assaulted women. She knew he tried, in her words, "to normalize"
his weird behavior. And it was weird. When she was first hired, her
duties included rousing a half-naked Harvey out of bed and turning on

the shower for him. She was given a private warning by one of his senior assistants about how to avoid Harvey's groping, and she copied and shared these admonitions:

> *Don't sit on the couch next to Harvey, sit in the armchair.*
> *Don't wear anything revealing.*
> *Don't give him a massage. And don't let him give you a massage.*
> *Don't agree to watch him take a shower.*
> *Don't be surprised if he spends thirty percent of the time you are together "trying to hit on you."*
> *Don't be alarmed by his violent temper outbursts; it is "normal."*
> *Don't be alarmed when he returns from dinner and claims he's hot and sheds all his clothes, dictating notes completely naked or in his boxer shorts. This, too, was "normal."*

For the Venice Film Festival in September 1998, Perkins booked a suite at the five-star Excelsior Hotel on the Lido, a fifteen-minute water shuttle from the busy streets and canals of Venice. The Excelsior has hosted the festival since it began in 1932, and is the only hotel in Venice with its own beach. If you're somebody in the movie business, you expect to be welcomed at the Excelsior. Harvey stayed in one of their fifteen suites, each with panoramic views of the Adriatic. This year, Perkins traveled to Venice with Rowena Chiu, who had been hired in late July as her eventual replacement, as Perkins was to be promoted to another job at Miramax. In many ways, they were unalike. Perkins, slight herself, was three inches taller than Chiu, more assertive, more self-confident; Chiu was quiet, her straight black hair neatly parted in the center and curved over her ears, and, unlike Perkins, she cowered when Harvey yelled at her. An English literature major and former president of the Oxford Drama Society, at twenty-four she was a year younger than Perkins, born in Britain to professionals who had immigrated from China. At the coaxing of her parents, she got a law degree, but she longed for a behind-the-camera career making movies.

Chiu met Harvey for the first time in a small Soho screening room to view rushes from *Shakespeare in Love*. "There was no normal inter-action," she recalled. "He doesn't come up to you and say, 'Hi, I'm Harvey Weinstein. I hear you're testing out with my assistants.' He totally ignores you. . . . He never speaks to you. His people manage you." She and Perkins were seated in the front row. Harvey, six feet tall and overweight, sat directly behind Chiu. "And because he's such an enormous person, his breathing is noisy," she said. Worried that she might be blocking his view of the small screen, she started to rise to move one seat over.

"Sit the fuck down!" he thundered.

"Years later," Chiu remembered, "I realized this was part of the grooming process—a test of how much I would tolerate. Harvey played games of this sort impeccably, testing how far he could go."

After the screening, in the taxi Chiu turned to Perkins, and instead of protesting Harvey's rough treatment of her, she said, "Do you think I did okay?" She would get the job, but she knew she had already shown a critical vulnerability: "He wanted someone compliant," Chiu said, which was contrary to what Perkins believed. "I think he looked for weakness. . . . I feel there's a direct connection between the type of person you can swear at the first time you meet her and tell her to sit the fuck down and she sits down." Perkins saw, starkly, that those who worked for Harvey, including her, "enabled a culture around him where he was King."

Weeks later, on the way to the Venice Film Festival, the two crafted a work plan: Perkins would start in the early morning, Chiu would arrive around noon, and they'd work together up to dinner, and after Perkins departed Chiu would be on duty until Harvey was ready to sleep. Their tasks at the festival included making appointments with those Harvey wished to see, booking lunch and dinner reservations, scheduling movies to screen, taking notes from Harvey and sending along his thoughts or orders, reading incoming scripts and sharing impressions with him. Because Harvey stayed up well past midnight,

Perkins told her, he usually slept late. If she ever awakened him in the suite, she cautioned, he liked to dictate notes and would invariably seek to pull her into bed, trying "to soften you" with flattery, with questions about your favorite Shakespeare plays, about your boyfriend's profession, treating you as if you were "the most fascinating, intellectual being on the planet." With those he sought to seduce, he would often boast of the actresses he claimed to have scored with. To Harvey, Perkins explained, "the power play was perhaps more fun than the sex." He was exploring, she said, "where the boundaries were. Playing with you, like a cat with a mouse."

Perkins sought to reassure Chiu that she was not in danger of being physically assaulted, because for Harvey this form of stalking was a game, "psychological sex." She added, "His foreplay was domination, not sex." Besides, in the more than two years she had worked for him and he had paraded around a hotel suite stark naked, occasionally trying to hit on her as she was warned he would, Zelda never saw an erection. "I thought he was impotent," she told me. Despite the indignities, the trade-off of working for Harvey was "the electricity in that room. I felt like I'm the center of power in the world. He made you feel that what you were doing was an emergency, the most important thing." Power bestowed a halo on Harvey.

A psychology major at the University of Manchester, Perkins would in the aftermath of Venice dig deep into her own psyche to understand both Harvey's motivations and her own. "I wondered what weakness in me had me work for him," she said. Her answer? "I found the chase exciting and beating him thrilling. It was very frightening working for Harvey. I used to describe it as a bungee jump. You got addicted. I would come back from the hotel and say to myself, 'I survived.'"

Despite her reassurances to Chiu, Perkins had a last piece of advice: "Wear two pairs of tights," because he might try to pull one pair off.

When Harvey and Perkins came back to the Excelsior from an event that night, Chiu did have on two pairs of tights. She was making notes while reading scripts. The first thing Harvey did was take off all his clothes and put on a robe, which he kept open. "I need to be comfortable," he declared. He opened a Diet Coke, lit a cigarette, and plopped in an armchair.

Before Perkins left for her room, she had whispered: "Keep me on the speed dial on your mobile. Or call me if you need anything." Soon after she left, Harvey and Chiu talked in detail about the ten or so scripts she had read. He interwove script talk with personal questions: *What Shakespeare plays do you prefer? Tell me about Chris, your boyfriend. What does Chris do?* Told that he was an investment banker, Harvey said, *I would really like to meet him.*

Harvey was now in full seduction mode. He told Chiu she was "super smart," and he could see her one day with a big Miramax job in New York. "Bring Chris to Nobu sometime. What bank does he work for?" Maybe, Harvey said, "I can get a job for your boyfriend." The questions got more personal: "Is he your first boyfriend? Did you have sex with him right away? Is he the only person you ever slept with?" He told Chiu that he liked Chinese girls because they were discreet and could keep a secret.

Soon, as Perkins predicted, Harvey asked for a massage, and then for other sexual favors, interspersed with compliments. Chiu's confusion in the moment is telling. He was inexorably boxing her in with his power over her as her boss, with his physical heft, and with his psychological manipulations.

Tense and on the alert, Chiu nonetheless complied, massaging his acned back, then allowing him to massage hers. His requests, she said, persisted over several hours, escalating as Chiu tried to call his attention back to their work. He asked her for oral sex. He cornered her on the bed and cajoled, "It's really hot in this hotel room. I can't even bear to have my robe on anymore. Why don't you take off your tights?"

Despite Perkins's warning, she removed the first pair.

Holding her down on the bed by clamping her thin arms above her head, Harvey yanked off the second pair, wheedling for her to remove her underwear. "One thrust and I'll pull out, I promise," he said. He tried to hold her down. That is how close he came to raping Chiu. Nevertheless, what Harvey allegedly did meets the legal definition of a sexual assault, which is a felony.

Somehow, Chiu managed to slide off the bed, with her knickers on. She was determined to keep them on. At that point, she thought: "It's still a game. He wasn't angry, because I was worried he would be angry." She knew that if he was angry, "I would literally be raped. I wanted to keep it nice, because he likes the belief that he was a Don Juan. He wanted to believe that he seduced me. That I couldn't resist his charms." She remembered how he went ballistic earlier that night when the hotel had only plain and not peanut M&M's, which he liked to shove into his mouth by the handful. She knew that if Harvey now flared up at her, he would be "out of control. I mean, it was like another person had taken over his body."

All Harvey's assistants knew, Perkins had said, that the key to surviving with Harvey was simple: "You didn't want to get him angry."

In the suite, Chiu started to cry. She thought Harvey feared she would scream. This altered their dynamic. Now, she sensed, Harvey "wanted to feel like he wasn't a rapist." She invoked Zelda's name, as if he would fear her maternal wrath. "Zelda is really worried about me," she pleaded. "She told me to check in on her at two a.m. at the latest." Harvey did not try to prevent her from racing from the suite. She immediately went to Zelda's room, which was as usual on another floor, for Harvey didn't want his assistants to spot who was entering or leaving at night, or to locate in the more expensive rooms. Chiu banged on Zelda's door. Despite her panic, Chiu was concerned that she was being "really intrusive because she was in there with a boyfriend." Perkins opened the door. Chiu's face was as white as the sheet Perkins had wrapped around herself.

"Are you okay?" Perkins asked. It was the knock she'd feared.

Chiu lied: "I'm fine." It was 2:00 a.m. and she didn't want to intrude any further, so she did not share what happened. When she went to her room, she worried Harvey would track her down, warn her to keep her mouth shut.

Together again in the suite late the next morning while Harvey was out, Chiu frantically described to Perkins what happened there the night before. Perkins thought Chiu was in a state of shock. They sat on the carpeted living room floor, both crying as Chiu recounted Harvey's attempted rape. "Even though she was only twenty-five and I was twenty-four, it's like she was my parent," Chiu said. Perkins knew Chiu made a mistake; she "let that first boundary be broken" when she massaged Harvey's shoulders and allowed him to massage hers. So Harvey assumed what he did next was "consensual." It was easy to "lose your footing" with Harvey, Perkins said, recalling the first time he entered the hotel suite in the Savoy and peeled off all his clothes except his underpants. Shocked, she objected. "Oh, pull yourself together, Zelda," he snapped, treating her as a naïve child. Harvey had succeeded in normalizing a transgression he repeated many nights in London.

But after Chiu shared what Harvey had done, Perkins refused to accept his behavior as normal. She knew Harvey was having a very important luncheon with Martin Scorsese and others on the terrace of the Excelsior, a lunch he was anxious about because he worshipped Scorsese, and the fabled director had always declined to make a movie with him. Perkins marched to the restaurant. Harvey was at the head of the table, his back to her. She tapped him on the shoulder. He turned and growled, "What?"

"Harvey, you need to come with me," she commanded. "Right now!" Like a few strong women who worked for Harvey and talked back to him, Perkins could sometimes wield authority over Harvey.

Harvey followed her to a corridor of the hotel. He towered over her, but, she says, "I felt so angry that I felt invincible." She asked, "What happened last night?"

"Nothing happened. What did Rowena say?"

"Oh, you didn't fool around with her?"

"Nothing happened. I swear on the life of my wife and my children."

"I know you're fucking lying then," she countered. As she later re-called, "That was his get-out-of-jail card that he always used when he was in big trouble."

She said Harvey looked worried, and she yelled: "Harvey, if I find out you are lying to me, I am going to fuck you."

Chiu likened Perkins to a "one-woman activist warrior . . . a one-woman Erin Brockovich story."

Perkins threatened to report Harvey to the police. And that was something none of Harvey's sex victims—an unknowable number but stretching back decades—had ever done before.

W hatever fear Harvey might have had of being exposed was al-layed by a belief, reinforced now that he was a mogul, that he was entitled to the same "casting couch" privileges enjoyed by earlier Hollywood bigwigs, the explanation he would in time openly use to excuse his behavior. He lived in his own reality distortion field, insist-ing to me in 2002, when I asked him about his behavior with women and with his staff, that he had tamed his volatility and temper. He admitted he cheated on his wife, but said his extracurricular sex was always consensual. He was a calmer man, he said, because with "the corporate luxury" Disney afforded, he had found "peace." We are "re-laxed, relaxed, relaxed. Because the economic success was overwhelm-ing. We had enough money to do whatever we wanted."

However, by 1998, five years after Disney had acquired Miramax, there were more than a few hints that Disney would not allow him to do whatever he wanted. Eisner had surrendered to Harvey on *Talk*, but admitted that "this was the beginning" of a break in trust. Tensions and conflicts intensified. "Every day there was an issue." Eisner was stunned by Harvey's seeming inability to control his impulses. Small transgres-sions spoke volumes. There were prominent NO SMOKING signs through-out Disney's offices, yet only Harvey would walk out into a hallway and light up. Eisner had heard about the time Harvey was desperate for a cigarette and yanked the smoke detector from a bathroom on a transatlantic Concorde flight. Peter Murphy, head of Disney's strategic planning department, shared the intensifying level of frustration among Disney executives: "Harvey did not think he reported to anyone." If Murphy challenged him, he remembered, "it was a little bit of Dr. Jekyll and Mr. Hyde. He could be charming. He could be polite. . . . At other times he was completely crazed, selfish, narcissistic."

As he became more and more puffed up with his own importance, those working for Miramax thought his behavior became more extreme. It was a terrifying "top-down" company, ruled "by fear and manipulation," said Eric Robinson, who worked at Miramax for over ten years. The Dr. Jekyll side of his personality, as his L.A. president Mark Gill had said, was his enormous talent. But Mr. Hyde was inseparable from that. The "genius" was linked to "the ego" and "the anger."

What Gill witnessed, as did Perkins and Chiu, was that Harvey's narcissism smothered his ability to empathize with others—to comprehend, for example, the distress he caused Rowena Chiu. Most people learn empathy through the pain they have experienced. For a few, the welter of their own emotions and desires means others effectively don't exist.

Harvey had always escaped exposure, so often that he was by now inured to the danger. But he had never encountered someone as determined to expose him as Zelda Perkins.

THE ART OF THE NDA

(1998)

Z elda Perkins and Rowena Chiu did not occupy Harvey's thoughts
in the days after he returned from Venice, though they should
have. For Miramax, 1998 was a vintage year, the summit of
Harvey's mogul years. His soon-to-be-released film, *Shakespeare in Love*,
was generating enormous buzz. There was once again widespread talk
about Harvey's golden gut. In the nineteen years since its founding,
Miramax had dazzled audiences with many celebrated movies, and by
1998, it was America's dominant independent movie studio, accounting
for an estimated 80 percent market share of all independent movies
released in the United States. Harvey gloried in his power. His influence in Hollywood grew year on year. With the studios increasingly
chasing big-budget action movies, Miramax became the preeminent
gatekeeper for the sort of prominent roles that could define an actor's
career, as with Gwyneth Paltrow, or revive it, as with John Travolta.

And then came the pinnacle of his success.

Shakespeare in Love was not a predictable slam-dunk hit. Screenwriter Marc Norman had written the first version of the script and
presented it to director Edward Zwick a decade earlier. Unhappy with
Norman's screenplay, Zwick hired playwright Tom Stoppard, who'd

already won three Tony Awards, to rewrite it. Zwick enticed Julia Roberts to portray Viola, but she insisted that Daniel Day-Lewis play the role of Shakespeare, and when he turned it down, Roberts pulled out six weeks before the film was to be shot. Now unable to lure a studio to bankroll the film, Zwick turned to Harvey Weinstein. Harvey not only agreed to fund the movie, he volunteered to serve as a producer, an unusual move by a studio head. And an unusual role for Harvey. Harvey also decided that Zwick—the man who brought him the film— was the wrong director, and he plucked from genteel obscurity the Cambridge-educated John Madden, whose résumé included four episodes of the TV series *Prime Suspect*, several modest plays, and some radio series. But Madden was literate, a student of Shakespeare, and Harvey was convinced he would not invite ridicule from students of the Bard. The role of Viola, Harvey offered to Kate Winslet, flush off her *Titanic* success, but she passed. Harvey then offered the role to Gwyneth Paltrow, who had beguiled audiences with her sparkling turn as the blithely interfering title character in *Emma*, a movie that cost only $7 million to make and generated a respectable box office of $22.2 million, along with critical acclaim.

The cast was filled out with Joseph Fiennes as a limpid-eyed Shakespeare, supported by classic British stalwarts such as Judi Dench as Queen Elizabeth I, Colin Firth, and Simon Callow, and in a bit of playful casting, Ben Affleck as Ned Alleyn, the founder of an acting troupe and a bit of a buffoon. (Affleck and Paltrow became a couple on the set and dated for three years.)

After filming wrapped in June 1998, postproduction was a struggle. Harvey was dissatisfied. The original Tom Stoppard ending had Viola lying dead, with a modern New York City skyline as a backdrop. Harvey hated it, thought it was a downer, Mark Gill said. The focus group research showed the audience agreed. But since the lovers were parting, how to shoot a happy ending? The second version was too saccharine. "Overnight, Harvey came up with the idea" of an ingenious new ending, remembered Gill, which drew the characters of the film back into the Bard's own work. Director John Madden shot this bittersweet new ending, in which Viola is compelled by the queen (Judi Dench) to follow through with her arranged marriage to Lord Wessex (Colin Firth) and sail with him to Virginia. "Write me, Will," are her parting words. He then immortalizes her in *Twelfth Night*, a romantic comedy featuring an incandescent Viola.

The film was finally ready to be released in December 1998. It was an immediate box office hit, ultimately generating $289 million worldwide. To justify his producer credit, Harvey claimed he took a leave of absence from his executive duties at Miramax to work on this movie, which Mark Gill dismissed as "complete bullshit."

Harvey cranked up another masterful marketing campaign. He launched the campaign by persuading First Lady Hillary Clinton, who would be likely to respond to the bold female roles acted by Gwyneth Paltrow and Judi Dench, to host its world premiere in New York on December 3, 1998. It was a brilliant choice; her presence assured massive press coverage. And there were boffo reviews. Lael Loewenstein of *Variety* wrote, "Exquisitely acted, tightly directed and impressively assembled, this lively period piece is the kind of arty gem with potentially broad appeal that Miramax certainly knows how to sell." When the Academy Award nominations were announced early in 1999, *Shakespeare* received a stunning thirteen Oscar nominations. Nevertheless, Steven Spielberg's *Saving Private Ryan* was favored to win Best Picture.

Determined to score an upset, Harvey mounted an unusual campaign, accompanied by extensive advertising and a team of semiretired publicists serving as canvassers, whose task was to contact fellow voting Academy members who represented the desired demographic audience. Harvey knew that the actors' branch of Academy voters was by far the largest. "He bet," said Mark Gill, "that *Shakespeare in Love* had an advantage there because the characters were playing actors. It was a story about the stage." The appeal to actors' love of their craft was irresistible. Paltrow and the film's other marquee actors and its director were all dispatched to court Academy voters. Phone banks were provided for

staffers to call them. A screening was held in a retirement home heavily populated by Academy members. For only twelve thousand dollars,
Meryl Poster sent DVDs of the movie to Academy voters, an idea she
credits to Bob Weinstein.

Although this was a notably extensive campaign, Oscar campaigning did not begin with Miramax. The technique of sending screeners
to many, not all, Academy voters was first pioneered three years earlier
by director John Boorman for his mediocre movie *The Emerald Forest.*
Nevertheless, Oscar campaigns fundamentally changed because of Miramax. Producer Irwin Winkler's 1976 movie *Rocky* won Best Picture
without paying for a single ad. In Miramax's wake, Oscar campaigns
intensified. Twenty years on, Netflix would spend more money on its
winning campaign for *Roma* than the $15 million the movie cost.
Screeners are now routinely sent to all Academy members.

Harvey's vigorous campaign didn't just promote his own movie; it
contained a negative component. Terry Press, who oversaw press relations
for DreamWorks, Spielberg's studio, warned Spielberg, "Harvey is saying all this shit about your movie." She'd heard that Harvey and Miramax were mounting a whispering campaign, planting the seed that
after a sensational beginning, *Saving Private Ryan* flattened into a pe-
destrian war movie. Reporters constantly called Terry Press, telling her
that Miramax executives, including Harvey, were telling them, "The
only thing amazing about *Ryan* is the first twenty minutes, and then
after that it's just a regular genre movie." This was the first time, Press
told *The Hollywood Reporter,* "I was exposed to the idea of a 'whisper
campaign' against another movie."

At first, Spielberg didn't want to believe it. But the negatives would
have an impact on Spielberg's movie, and further corrode Harvey's reputation. Although Harvey denied the stories, few believed him. Mark
Gill concedes, "Harvey would say, 'It's the greatest opening twenty-four
minutes. After that, you fall asleep.'"

When, on the night of the Oscars, the winner of the Best Actress
award was announced, a broad smile creased Harvey's face as Gwyneth

Paltrow, drenched in tears, thanked "Harvey Weinstein and everybody at Miramax Films for their undying support of me." She had come a long way from the interview in the Peninsula Hotel room where he'd tried to exact an ugly trade. Steven Spielberg applauded as lustily as Harvey did, for Paltrow was his goddaughter. But Harvey and the Miramax team were particularly thrilled because they now thought they had a shot at winning Best Picture.

Bob was sitting in the audience with his mother, Miriam, and Annie, his second wife. "I remember Harrison Ford opening the envelope and I feel he paused for a second because he saw that *Saving Private Ryan* was not the winner," Bob said. "I knew we won."

The five producers of *Shakespeare in Love* had not expected to capture the Best Picture award, but they'd agreed in advance that if they did, they would come up onstage together and David Parfitt would say a few words, followed by Donna Gigliotti, who would speak for the rest. Just before she left her hotel for the ceremony, Gigliotti recalled, Harvey and Bob phoned and insisted that if they won, Harvey must speak. "The threat was implicit," she said. "You must do this."

From a nearby seat, Harvey first embraced Eve, then raced onstage. He stood behind the movie's four other producers, intensely shuffling and scanning a sheaf of folded papers on which he had jotted notes. It was unusual for a studio head to accept an award, but Harvey insisted he be credited as one of the five producers. At the Oscars, winners are allotted two minutes. Gigliotti and Parfitt quickly thanked a few people, and as producer Edward Zwick—who'd been fired as the first director—moved toward the microphone, Gigliotti, who stood before the microphone, stopped him by publicly thanking Harvey and beckoning him to speak. With the bunch of papers protruding from his front pants pocket, Harvey stepped forward while Zwick stepped back.

Harvey thanked Disney and his parent company CEO Michael Eisner for giving "me great latitude and support"; his studio producing partners at Universal; executives at Miramax; his brother, Bob, "who is my partner and best friend every day"; his "loving" wife; his two "rotten" daughters (their third daughter had not yet been adopted); his nieces; and "my mother, Miriam, the Miriam of Miramax, who makes Jewish mothers look good." In all, Harvey spoke for two minutes and fifteen seconds, or two thirds of the time they were on stage, before he was silenced by music. Zwick, who fathered the idea for the movie, and fellow producer Marc Norman, who had written the first draft, never had a turn at the microphone.

At the Governor's Ball and the after-parties that night, Harvey lingered until 4:30 a.m., clutching his Oscar, one of seven that *Shakespeare in Love* won. For him, it was an unusually joyous night. There were no brusque orders to staffers, no temper tantrums. For Mark Gill, who was one of those Harvey thanked from the stage, the "vivid" memory that stayed with him is that this was "one of the only nights or days I ever spent with Harvey where there was a whole evening where he didn't yell at me. And I was one of the ones he liked."

The most vivid memory for Steven Spielberg's team was of being cheated. Well-connected movie promoter Peggy Siegal remembered attending the Governor's Ball with her friend, *New York Post* gossip columnist Claudia Cohen. They stopped at Spielberg's table, and Cohen's ruby earring fell beneath the table. Cohen crawled under the tablecloth to search for it and heard the alarmed voices of aides warning that Harvey Weinstein was barreling across the room to embrace Spielberg. The director hurriedly walked away. Cohen located her earring and had her scooplet.

Early the next morning, Harvey, convinced Spielberg's team would savage him for his alleged campaign to sabotage *Saving Private Ryan*, summoned his staff to meet. "Harvey came in like a drill sergeant," recalls Marcy Granata, his marketing and public relations chief. "He gave orders to manage the press," to persuade them that Miramax was innocent. They weren't, as Mark Gill conceded.

Harvey was certain that his triumph with *Shakespeare in Love* was the moment when the industry decisively turned on him, plotting to drag down Miramax, the crude, underhanded louts who stole the Oscar from Spielberg. Years after the award, he still bridled, exclaiming, "It's easier to say that we manipulated the process than to give credit to the movie. So it's part of that whole 'blame Miramax.'"

As usual, Harvey was at ease portraying himself as a victim. But Harvey was now a target of fierce Hollywood criticism. Both his friend Jeffrey Katzenberg and David Geffen, who founded DreamWorks with Spielberg, told *The New York Times* they were enraged at him. Bill Mechanic, chairman of Fox Filmed Entertainment, blamed Harvey for turning "the Oscar process" into "an expensive political campaign. . . . It's no longer about the material or the merit. It's about how much media money you spend. It's not what the academy founders set out to do."

The euphoria on the awards stage and at the Governor's Ball did much to blot from Harvey's memory the peril he had faced six months earlier, after the Venice Film Festival. At first, he gave little thought to what happened in the hotel suite with Rowena Chiu or in his confrontation with Zelda Perkins. Like his many previous sexual escapades, he had reason to assume this one would also leave no wake, that silence would again reign.

Zelda Perkins, who had labored to support *Shakespeare in Love*, took no special joy in its Oscar wins. She and Rowena Chiu were left with bitter memories of their unprecedented effort to call Harvey to account. When they returned to London in September 1998, they debated whether to report the attempted rape to the police. Perkins wanted to blow the whistle on Harvey; although she was the victim, Chiu wanted to keep her job—quitting would be hard to explain to a subsequent employer, and she would have experienced hell with nothing to show for it. And she didn't want her family to learn the shameful details.

Perkins decided to confide in Donna Gigliotti, who had a storied career, beginning as an assistant to Martin Scorsese on *Raging Bull*. She served as an executive vice president at Miramax from 1993 to 1996, producing several films. Now a lead producer on Miramax's *Shakespeare in Love*, she had worked closely with Perkins, scheduling meetings with Harvey and those working on the movie, getting him to make phone calls. While Gigliotti was not a Miramax employee, during the editing of the movie in the fall she often parked in their London office. And to Perkins, the ever-calm Gigliotti was, at forty-three, a grown-up. Perkins decided to confide what had happened in Venice. She was surprised by Gigliotti's reaction: "I thought when I told Donna that Donna's reaction would be more stratospheric than my reaction—I thought I was telling the parents and now shit would hit the fan and she'd know what to do."

"I remember Zelda being really confident that telling Donna would lift the lid," recalled Chiu.

"Donna didn't even bat an eyelid," Perkins said, which "told me that he had done it before, that she was not a person of any moral standing." In Perkins's view, Gigliotti was therefore an enabler.

"You better get yourself a lawyer," Perkins recalled Gigliotti telling her, which she interpreted not as advice from a friend and female mentor, but as a brush-off.

Donna Gigliotti said this interpretation was absurd, for it was the first time she ever heard that Harvey sexually abused women. She said she initiated the conversation with Perkins after noticing that she "looked gray to me. I said to her, 'What's wrong?'" After Perkins opened up, Gigliotti did phone her New York lawyer for advice, was advised they needed an employment lawyer, and then arranged and participated in a conference call with Perkins and the New York employment lawyer, Anne Vladeck. Chiu, torn about her course of action because she didn't want her parents or boyfriend to know, never spoke with Donna Gigliotti, whose advice was tendered to Perkins. Gigliotti would also advise Zelda on the terms of their NDA, which would be the third NDA I'm aware of after the secretive one he signed the previous year with Rose McGowan and the earlier one with the young woman who was a family friend of John Schmidt. Later, when Perkins told her Harvey's lawyers were offering to pay them a measly one year's salary, Gigliotti said she told her, "You go back and ask for at least 200,000 pounds," which Perkins confirms. As a thank-you, Gigliotti said she received "a beautiful Montblanc pen" from Zelda.

So she did help? I asked.

"Absolutely, she helped me," Perkins said.

Chiu had a different view: Yes, but. "She first and foremost protected her own career and made sure she could continue working with Harvey. She was about forty, with a future and career that she had to protect." In addition to adding an Oscar to her mantel for *Shakespeare*, eight years later Gigliotti would go on to produce three additional Miramax movies, and also rejoined the Weinstein Company in 2010 for one year as president of production, later serving as a producer on Weinstein's *Silver Linings Playbook*. Ultimately Chiu finds it difficult to look past what she interprets as Gigliotti's passivity: "She knew what Harvey did, yet she continued working for Harvey."

The truth is not black or white. "The notion that I was protecting my career is false," Gigliotti said. "The truth is, I jeopardized my career by advising them." Gigliotti is a charming person, who looks you in the eye when speaking and, unlike many puffed-up denizens of Hollywood, asks questions and listens to the answers. Factually, she insists, she did not regularly work for Harvey. After *Shakespeare in Love*, she became president of production for Barry Diller's USA Films and claims she did not see or speak to Harvey Weinstein for almost a decade. In 2008, when her friends Anthony Minghella and Sydney Pollack were both terminally ill with cancer, she says Harvey approached her in Cannes and asked if she'd step in as producer on their film *The Reader*, which was nominated for an Oscar in 2008. In 2010, when the head of production at the Weinstein Company stepped down, Harvey offered the job to Gigliotti. Needing health insurance to "cover an urgent preexisting medical condition that required surgery," and knowing that employer plans covered preexisting conditions, she said she accepted a one-year executive job at the company that by design expired in mid-2011. She was contractually obligated in 2012, she said, to complete work as one of three producers for *Silver Linings Playbook*.

Clearly, Gigliotti did not make a clean break from Harvey. But she was not an acolyte. He did not appear to dangle work in front of her, despite her involvement in the huge success of *Shakespeare in Love*—or if he did, she did not accept it. Because the NDA that Perkins and Chiu eventually signed required them to share the names of everyone they told about what happened in Venice, Gigliotti assumed Harvey knew she had advised them, she told me. And she did later try to help me expose Harvey's assault in Venice.

But did Donna Gigliotti challenge Harvey? She said she confronted him and asked point-blank if he'd assaulted Chiu. "He told me that he and Rowena were having an affair and he broke it off." That Gigliotti would think that Harvey had an extended affair with his cowed assistant is risible, and both Perkins and Chiu derisively laughed when they heard this is what Gigliotti reported. If it really is what Harvey told her, it suggests he had an arrogant belief in his powers of persuasion. Or that he thought Gigliotti was asking him a question she didn't really want answered.

N ow, though, Harvey was aware of his peril. Employment attorney Anne Vladeck advised Perkins and Chiu to hire lawyers in London, since any criminal charges would be brought there. They retained the London firm of Simons Muirhead Burton, which advised that because the incident took place several weeks before, it was too late to go to the police because there was no forensic evidence, no witnesses, they had failed to report Harvey to the police at the time, and the incident took place in another country. The best course of action still available to them, the lawyers advised, was to resign by invoking "constructive dismissal," which means they were resigning due to a hostile work environment, and then seek a settlement.

Perkins and Chiu notified Harvey by fax that they were quitting Miramax, they had retained lawyers, and they might file charges against him. That evening, Harvey left various voice messages on Perkins's phone, alternately wooing her with praise, then raging into the phone, then begging her to please call him. Perkins saved the messages. "I'm coming to London tonight," he said on one. "I want to meet you and Rowena in a bar. I want to make you guys happy. Whatever you want."

Miramax employees were aware something unsettling had happened overseas. Many called Perkins's cell phone—she puts the number of calls at twenty. She didn't return a single one, though she listened to messages pleading with her to call, not to quit Miramax. Chiu, two decades later, harshly dismissed these callers. "How can I not think of them as enablers?" she asked. "The entire industry is enabling. It's dominated by white, male producers who have a lot of money, who are frequently using and abusing women who are young." And those young women were "desperate to work in film."

Rowena Chiu came to believe that Harvey deliberately created a culture to normalize the abnormal. She grouped Harvey enablers into three categories. The first were those who "knew Harvey had a bad reputation, but they had never experienced any of his shenanigans." A second group knew "he was seducing actresses and being unfaithful to his wife but did not know that he was an assaulter or a rapist." The third group, she believes, were the hard-core enablers "who knew what Harvey was doing and turned a blind eye." Harvey, she continued, "could not have done this for decades—for three decades—without a huge system of enablement set up around him. And that's not just men at a senior level. It's women as well." Think, she said, of the female assistants "training other female assistants, 'Oh, this is how you avoid roving hands.'" Perkins had said these things, too—even experienced them—though she now acted decisively when she saw proof of serious trespass. But it was not always easy for staffers, when caught inside the labyrinth Harvey had built to normalize aberrant behavior, to shake off his distortions and call the depravity by its name.

The day after Harvey was warned that Perkins and Chiu might file charges against him, Katrina Wolfe, who at that time worked for Miramax business affairs executive Steve Hutensky, watched Harvey hurry out of his office and enter Hutensky's, slamming the door. Soon Hutensky came out and asked her to pull the employee files of Zelda Perkins and Rowena Chiu. She was instructed to book Hutensky on the next day's Concorde flight to London.

Perkins and Chiu met with Hutensky soon after he landed in London. They referred to him as "Harvey's attack dog." He served as a resource for the heavyweight London law firm Allen & Overy, which had represented several Miramax movies, and would negotiate an NDA with Perkins and Chiu. The NDA sessions lasted up to twelve hours, and Perkins recalled a morning session that resumed at 5:00 p.m. and ended at 5:00 a.m. the next day. They were forbidden pen and paper and escorted to the bathroom. "You lost track of time and space. We were two young women shut in a room full of lawyers talking in legal riddles, and we were not able to tell anyone what we were doing."

With Hutensky's support, the London law firm bullied Chiu and Perkins to accept Harvey's terms: They must not tell anyone what occurred in Venice, including their families, and if they wanted to speak to a psychiatrist, they must first get them to sign an NDA with Harvey's London law firm—effectively barring the women from seeking help. If they broke silence, the penalty would be to forfeit their individual payments of 125,000 pounds, or just over $210,000 each. Harvey's initial offer had been for one year's salary; this revised offer, prompted by Gigliotti, represented ten times that amount, though less than Gigliotti suggested. It seemed a large sum to the women. In addition, they were required to provide a list not only of everyone they had told of what happened in Venice, but contact information for their parents, siblings, boyfriends, and closest friends. This was purely an intimidation tactic, with no real legal consequences, though that was not apparent from the language. They would abide by it to the letter for years. Perkins and Chiu also had to agree not to testify in any civil or criminal case against Harvey Weinstein. And neither side could ever publicly disparage the other.

Perkins and Chiu fought hard but knew they could not successfully prosecute Harvey. Their primary aim became to curtail his predaceous behavior. They issued their own demands, which were eventually accepted. It was agreed: 1) Harvey would seek therapy to address his aberrant behavior. 2) Harvey would be terminated by Miramax if he sexually misbehaved again and tried to cover it up. 3) The parent company, Disney, would be informed if Harvey, to avoid sexual harassment claims, entered into any further NDAs. 4) Harvey would overhaul the HR policies and practices at Miramax, ensuring staff safeguards, and would appoint three "corporate complaint handlers" to investigate sexual harassment or assault at work. 5) Harvey would provide Perkins and Chiu with a letter of recommendation for prospective employers who might wonder why they left Miramax. In return, they would turn over all documents and material relating to their work at Miramax.

"All of these demands were to be met in exchange for our silence," Perkins would later write. "Our silence was the only bargaining tool we had. It had been made clear to us by our lawyers that our route to justice through the courts was almost impossible to navigate." The only reason we have such a detailed picture of the anatomy of a Harvey NDA is because both Chiu and Perkins would eventually break it. Many other women would sit at similar tables and sign NDAs with terms harsh enough that the signers could not bring themselves to flout them, even after the extent of Harvey's criminality had been revealed.

Asked multiple times to comment on the women's claims, Hutensky refused. He did, however, tell people that Harvey's London law firm negotiated the NDAs and as Harvey's business affairs executive he did not act as a lawyer in the negotiations, which is nominally true. And although he has told others that he was only peripherally involved in the negotiations and that the final document contained no admission of guilt by Harvey, in fact Perkins said, "Steve was present through the negotiations . . . he was very much the aggressive lead according to my solicitor. He was definitely present the day of Harvey's apology and signing of the agreement and initialed every page of the agreement himself with Harvey." The multipage NDA document mentions Hutensky twice, once as the go-to person at Miramax for Perkins and Chiu should they seek help to get a job in the movie business, and second in saying that they should "direct all requests for employment references solely to Steven Hutensky."

Hutensky has told people that Harvey said his relationship with Chiu was "consensual." Since Hutensky sat in the room that finalized the NDA, he knows that what happened with Rowena was not consensual. And he knows the NDA's "I'm guilty" terms Chiu and Perkins insisted Harvey agree to before they would pledge to be silent. Although Hutensky should have known Harvey was a sexual predator in 1998, he continued to work for him until 2004.

On the fall day the parties were to sign, Harvey appeared in the offices of his law firm with Hutensky. It was the first time Perkins and Chiu had seen Harvey in months. With all the lawyers present, Perkins later wrote, "we hoped this would give us protection from the screaming, shouting or humiliation from him that we had come to expect. . . . I had fixed a grim and (I hoped) impenetrable expression on my face—ready for a barrage of abuse. However, what we were to hear was extraordinary and completely unexpected." Suddenly, "Harvey launched into what became an apology, an admission, a groveling plea asking us to stay in his employ."

Their lawyer raced to take down what Harvey said:

> I truly apologize for the pain I've caused you. It is not window dressing in the contract. I was leading a stupid life, wrong for wife and marriage, seeing a psychiatrist, thought very highly of you, considered you friends, want to move forward if that's possible, thought both incredibly bright, anything I can do. . . . I would hire you both back in a second. Want to express how sorry I am. Acted incorrectly. I'm a hypocrite. Love my wife and children. Strange as it seems, I

like both of you. . . . Sometimes I don't know when it's consensual. Trying to learn. Maybe I don't recognize my power in these situations. I'm an adulterer and I'm not proud of it. I acted incorrectly. But I'm a good man. . . . I hope one day—and it sounds astounding given the way you are both looking at me—but I hope one day we can be friends. I'm truly moved by what you said.

Chiu was stunned: "He dropped, what seems to me now, an atomic bomb: 'I sometimes don't know when it's consensual.'"

Harvey's legal team understood the significance of that sentence. It was a contradiction of Harvey's frequent assertion that he "never engaged in nonconsensual sexual activity with any of my accusers."

"Our lawyer was busy taking notes during the meeting and once it finished and we held fast in our wish to continue with signing the agreement," Perkins wrote, "Weinstein's lawyer turned to ours and asked for the notepad. The lawyer was told the deal would be off if the notepad wasn't handed over."

Perkins had a clever idea. "I asked Weinstein and his team to leave the room so we could confer with our lawyer. We were given five minutes. I hurriedly whispered to our solicitor—fearing that a recording apparatus was hidden in the room—to call a secretary and dictate the note over the phone. Our lawyer was concerned with the ethics of this, but I argued it was only a problem if they asked us if we had made a copy and we did not disclose it. If they asked, we would admit it. But if they didn't, were we doing anything wrong?" There was no listening device in the room. Their lawyer dictated his notes, and when Weinstein and his lawyers returned, he handed over his notebook. Perkins, Chiu, and Harvey signed the NDA.

Their case is a rare glimpse into the anatomy of an NDA—rare because of their courage in flouting a punitively restrictive contract. Two decades later, Perkins would write that a parliamentary investigation into whether NDAs should be legal had recovered the dictated memo of Harvey's startling speech. But she was told that the way the note was created meant it could not be used in court, and thus, she lamented, it "will never be able to be used in any of the cases against Weinstein." Indeed, Perkins would not testify at his trial, and to date it does not appear that the note, nor Harvey's statement, has been introduced in any of the cases against him.

But in 1998, Perkins and Chiu left the offices of Allen & Overy exhausted and grimly victorious, certain the provisions in the NDA they just signed would deter him from committing additional sexual assaults. For a time, they stopped fearing Harvey Weinstein.

It's impossible to say whether Harvey believed at any point that he was capable of the change he vowed to make with such apparent conviction. What he did know was that he had managed to slip out of another tight jam. He employed intimidation, money, and lies to extricate himself from these jams, as he would the following year when John Connolly of *Premiere* magazine had gotten a tip that Harvey allegedly raped a former assistant during the Venice Film Festival and induced this woman and another to sign NDAs. Connolly, a former cop, hired a private investigator in London, who discovered their names. Connolly said he called each of them and they refused to talk. Hearing that Connolly was sleuthing, Harvey had a friend reach out to him to arrange a meeting at the Tribeca Grill. "We were excited," recalls *Premiere*'s then editor in chief, Susan Lyne, who had heard the rumors about Harvey and now thought they could convert rumor to fact. Connolly recalled that Bob Weinstein joined his brother for the meeting.

"Listen, kid," Harvey began. "I know where you're going, but I'm a married man and this was consensual. I know you're an ex-cop. I'll take a lie detector test for you."

"I believe you," Connolly eventually responded, too easily convinced.

At what point did Harvey seduce him with a $500,000 Talk Books contract for a book on Bill Clinton's conspiracy-minded critics? It's not clear, but Connolly did sign such a book contract. It is also unclear how much information Connolly truly had on what happened in Venice.

Much later, he would tell me that he contacted Chiu but because she did not want to be exposed in 1999 as a sexual victim, "I have kept this woman's secret for more than 20 years."

Rowena Chiu insists she never spoke to Connolly in 1999, or after.

For Harvey and Miramax, 1998 turned out to be a glorious year. He had reason to feel invincible. He once again slipped out of a potential sex scandal. His Oscar mantel was getting crowded. Miramax was cruising on all cylinders, its bulging revenues making it difficult for Disney to clamp down on its excesses. Despite the criticism in Hollywood of his Oscar campaign, Harvey was lionized in the press as a movie industry giant, a bigger-than-life character, a figure worthy of magazine profiles. Actors, agents, directors, producers wanted to be in business with him. No one in the film community needed to cite his last name. If you said *Harvey*, people knew who you meant.

By 1999, Harvey's perceived power, and his desire to put it to use, was such that even his parent company feared him. A senior Disney executive reluctantly conceded that this was true: "Disney was intimidated by Harvey's ability to create a bad reputation for Disney by getting into a public fight that would not be good for the Disney brand." Already, stories appeared with some regularity in the press from unnamed sources asserting that Disney was this play-it-too-safe corporate bureaucracy unwilling to take chances. The advantage Harvey had, the executive said, is that the press "idolized him" and subscribed to his narrative that "Disney was preventing him from being an artist," trying to "muzzle him" and violate his promised autonomy. "Anything we said against him would put us in a negative light with Hollywood talent, and agents, and the press. Disney needed talent, and agents, and the press. It's a perception game." To read accounts in the Hollywood trade press or *The New York Times* in these years is to appreciate how successful Harvey was at spinning his side of the story—and to get a whiff of what he'd done to threaten others.

"I'M THE FUCKING SHERIFF OF THIS FUCKING LAWLESS PIECE-OF-SHIT TOWN"

(1999–2002)

The brothers landed a new long-term contract in 1999. They would each receive a salary of $1.75 million the first year, rising each year to $3 million by 2006, $2 million more than their $1 million annual salary at the start of their Disney relationship in 1993. In addition, each received six hundred thousand Disney stock options pegged to the price of the stock—as the stock price rose, so did the value of their options—and an improved formula to boost their annual bonus. According to internal Disney documents, between 1993 and 2003 the Weinstein brothers received between them, including the initial purchase price, total compensation of $297 million.

This was a rich contract, if entered into somewhat joylessly by Disney, and with telling new protections. The amended contract permitted Disney to terminate the relationship six years after signing, for what Disney internal documents described as "willful misappropriation" of money, "gross negligence," or "conviction of a felony." The final provision was carried over from the original contract, but the first two were new. The contract kept in place the $30 million ceiling Miramax could spend on a movie, plus restrictions on what types of movies Miramax could make—no "gratuitous" violence, "deviant sexual" behavior, NC-17 or X-rated movies.

By one measure—revenues—internal Disney documents revealed that Miramax revenues climbed from $36 million in 1993 to a robust $1.259 billion in 2003. But a vast financial reporting chasm yawned between Miramax and Disney, never surfacing as a public issue though it remained a private source of conflict between them. They could not agree on some basic financial facts. The Weinsteins, for instance, asserted that they delivered to Disney operating income of $143 million in 2001, a poor performance year; internal Disney documents disputed this, saying that Miramax actually lost $108 million after bonuses were paid.

The chasm was even wider than they realized. Disney's contract with the Weinsteins unwisely continued to predicate their bonus on profitability. "And the Weinsteins manipulated the system based on the movies released," conceded one Miramax lawyer. By refusing to release movies expected to bomb at the box office, Miramax saved marketing costs, and the movie's losses were not subtracted from that year's profits, and thus their bonus. They also spared themselves the embarrassment of flops. "There were hundreds of millions of dollars of unreleased movies," the Miramax lawyer conceded. Not true, countered Disney: the claim that Miramax saved hundreds of millions of dollars was preposterous because even if the movie was not released that year, the costs to make the film were charged to Miramax's budget. But, as noted, what Disney's response overlooked is that unreleased movies did not incur marketing expenses or box office losses. Disney chose not to make this a public issue. With their acute consciousness of the value of the Miramax brand, it's possible that Disney also understood the value of not diluting it by releasing duds. It was not an insane strategy, if one could afford it.

But could they? Another source of friction, Michael Eisner conceded, was that Harvey began to spend big-studio-like $100 million–plus money on pictures—*Cold Mountain, Gangs of New York*—that far exceeded Miramax's $30 million spending ceiling. Eisner fumed, but outwardly he remained a permissive parent.

Eisner's indulgence was based, in part, on his ambivalence. He knew how to read a spreadsheet, and as angry as he often got at the Weinsteins, he was generally pleased by the numbers, especially the ones Bob Weinstein's Dimension division was producing. *Scary Movie*, a slasher send-up directed by Keenen Ivory Wayans that spoofed Bob's own spoof, *Scream*, grossed $157 million at the box office in 2000. *Scream 3* was also a hit. Dimension's profits helped offset the losses related to Harvey's extravagant spending, and would over the next five years account for an estimated three quarters of Miramax's profits. But it was Harvey who brought the cachet. Another reason for Eisner to avoid a bloody war that might harm Disney more than Miramax was simply the power of Harvey's renown. "We would go to festivals and every filmmaker wanted to sell their movie to Harvey," said Agnès Mentre, who was a senior executive at Miramax for fifteen years. "They knew more people would see their movie if Harvey was behind it."

When asked to describe Harvey's power, Michael Eisner put on his sociologist hat and identified four components, all related to the fear Harvey instilled in Hollywood: He could deny you a role in a movie. Or he could decide not to make your movie. Or he could embarrass you with a press leak. Or he could attack you publicly. Eisner assured me that he was not afraid of Harvey. It's worth noting that Eisner is at least three inches taller than Harvey and a commanding presence. And yet Eisner, too, trod cautiously when it came to battling Harvey in the court of industry opinion. Anthony Minghella likened Harvey to a bull, "exhilarating" if he's charging alongside you. "If he's charging toward you, that's a big force to negotiate."

Harvey reveled in showing off his influence in small ways as well as large. Once, late in the evening at the Peninsula Hotel in Los Angeles, Harvey was in the restaurant with his teenage daughters and a young actress he wanted to impress. He asked, "Would you like to meet Meryl Streep?"

Harvey grabbed a phone and called up to Streep's room. "My family is here. All my girls. Would you come down and say hi?"

Streep was exhausted. "I was there promoting a film of his," she recalled, recovering from the press junket's grueling relay of back-to-back interviews—but she got dressed and came down.

Harvey was a pro at projecting power. He had the hubris to call studio executives and frame a request as a command. Former CEO of the Fox Network Group, Tony Vinciquerra, said he didn't even know Harvey years earlier when he phoned his office and demanded, "I need to talk to him at two p.m. today."

What happened to actress Ashley Judd is instructive. It's a testimonial to his power that even after Harvey repeatedly pressured Judd for sex in the mid-1990s, she subsequently agreed to perform in two additional Miramax movies, including *Frida* in 2002, a shoot that would be plagued by his intimidating outbursts. Aspiring actresses needed to gain fame before their hair turned gray, and Harvey knew it.

The press was a key component of that power. Harvey claimed as social friends Rupert Murdoch, *Vogue* editor Anna Wintour, *Vanity Fair* editor Graydon Carter, *New York Daily News* publisher Mort Zuckerman, CBS CEO Les Moonves, NBC CEO Jeff Zucker, and *Saturday Night Live* producer Lorne Michaels. "There was a sense that he controlled the press, that he knew powerful people," said Joseph Ravitch, a well-connected Goldman Sachs investment banker who would work closely with the Weinsteins, both before and after cofounding the Raine Group in 2009, a media investment advisory firm with worldwide offices.

Harvey did not hesitate to go over the heads of reporters who wrote about him. When David Carr was profiling him for *New York* magazine, Harvey repeatedly contacted executives at Primedia, the magazine's then owner, and Caroline Miller, the editor, blustering and cajoling them to try to tone the piece down, treating this and other profiles as a Miramax campaign he was critiquing rather than a journalistic profile he was subject to. Simultaneously, he sought to intimidate potential sources, to say nothing of the women he silenced. Some in the industry were frustrated by his self-engineered Teflon. "There is one story that needs to be told about this guy, and you are not going to tell it," one New York film executive challenged Carr.

Harvey also aggressively courted gossip columnists, sometimes seeking to buy their favor. He recruited Richard Johnson, then editor of the *New York Post*'s Page Six, to write a script for a movie, *Jet Set*. The project stalled, and Johnson said, "I didn't get a penny," but the deal still elicited his agreement to become a movie business partner of Harvey's. Roger Friedman, a prolific gossip writer for Fox News and others, insisted, "I never took money from Harvey" to write a book or a script. Yet, when pressed, Friedman acknowledged that Harvey financed a Miramax music documentary he narrated.

If you were a gossip columnist, Harvey was a compelling figure. The *Post*'s Cindy Adams said with affection, "He's always available for a quote, whether you want one or not." When Mitchell Fink first moved to New York as a gossip columnist for the *Los Angeles Herald Examiner*, and then for the *New York Daily News*, the number one thing he said he had to do was "get to know Harvey Weinstein. . . . He was the Hollywood guy in New York. There was no one remotely close to Harvey when it came to Hollywood stuff. I needed access, and Harvey gave me access. I was invited to all his parties. I saw celebrities on couches with drugs." In return for access, such celebrity tales were off-limits.

Peter Biskind first started investigating the Weinstein brothers for *Premiere* magazine way back in 1991. "Before I had made a single phone call, Miramax had agitated the publisher by threatening to withdraw its advertising from the magazine, and the next thing I knew, Harvey was writing columns for *Premiere* and I was his editor." The exposé was abandoned.

Lloyd Grove, who covered the entertainment world for *The Washington Post* before penning a gossip column for the *Daily News* and *New York* magazine, tried to break Harvey's allure for reporters down this way: "He was always available. Not like Trump, who would call back in five minutes. Harvey was very tactical. Trump wanted his name in print. Harvey had a point to what he was doing." Harvey also wanted reporters to think he was their friend. "You know I'll always help you," he told Grove. And when he helped, Harvey was not just smart and knowledgeable; he was funny and enjoyed swapping and leaking gossip. When Harvey wanted to kill a story, he offered Grove a trade: drop the story, and "I can give you so many better items."

When that didn't work, Harvey escalated to coercion: "He told me he was a friend of Mort Zuckerman," Grove's publisher.

When that didn't work, Harvey moved to a work threat: "I'm not going to let you in any Miramax screenings."

If that didn't succeed, Harvey finally escalated to what sounded to Grove like a threat of violence: "I'm the scariest motherfucker you'll ever have as an enemy in this town." Grove treated this as an empty threat, which on this occasion it was.

Harvey set himself up as a benefactor. He would hire Sharon Waxman of *The Wrap*'s daughter as one of his many summer interns, as he would Anna Wintour's daughter, Bee Shaffer, and President Obama's daughter Malia.

Which begs an obvious question: What role did a lax press play in enabling Harvey's behavior? A press corps quick to jump on any hint of scandal rarely followed up on the many hints in the next decade that Harvey abused women. Punk singer-songwriter Courtney Love in a 1995 interview offered this advice to young actresses, which seemed to be a hint of something untoward: "If Harvey Weinstein invites you to a private party in the Four Seasons, don't go." In her memoir, Ivana Lowell wrote of Harvey: "Tales of his trying to seduce every young actress in town were infamous." A *30 Rock* episode on NBC had Jane

Krakowski's character exclaim, "I'm not afraid of anyone in show business. I turned down intercourse with Harvey Weinstein on no less than three occasions, out of five!" These asides did not provoke media investigations.

D uring Harvey's annual Christmas vacation in St. Barts with Eve and their daughters at the end of 1999, when he was forty-seven, he came down with what was described as a life-threatening bacterial infection. Years later, Phoebe Eaton, a reporter for Graydon Carter's weekly online publication, *Air Mail*, claimed that the rare ailment was Fournier's gangrene, whose effects are often decomposed testicles, plus a hovering, foul smell. Obesity and diabetes are risk factors for this fast-moving infection that often targets the genitalia, sometimes through a superficial wound or tear in the skin. Harvey was afflicted by both diabetes and obesity, but he flatly denies he suffered from Fournier's gangrene.

In any case, he was emergency airlifted off the island and hospitalized for more than a month, under another name, at a New York hospital with no one but family members and a few old Buffalo friends allowed to visit. Miriam Weinstein, always beautifully attired, her red hair done up, began to appear in the office more regularly during Harvey's illness. Sometimes, Miriam was nearly as assertive there as she had been in the Weinstein home. She commanded aides to be sure the press was kept unaware that he was in the hospital.

Bob ran the company in Harvey's absence and visited his brother daily. He felt moved by the suffering he saw in the hospital, which tapped into a sentimental streak Bob did not hide. Bob was more of a bleeding heart than his brother and had a predilection for somewhat sentimental personal essays about his family. He was frustrated by Harvey's inability to be more empathetic. In what he called a "Love Letter to Brother Harvey," published in *The Hollywood Reporter*, he once gently rebuked his brother:

"Harvey, we've been through so much, been so blessed, but when you think about it, what's it all for? I mean, in the end, it's going to end badly. How do you live with that knowledge?" Now, I'm truly the more sensitive of the brothers, prone to thoughts and questions like this, but I was astonished to hear a deep silence on the other end of the phone. . . . 20 seconds, 30 seconds, finally he responded: "Did you get the grosses on *Cider House Rules*?" I burst out laughing. It wasn't that Harvey was cold of heart. . . . He realized there is no real answer other than understanding the meaning you give each moment. And at that moment we had *Cider House Rules* in wide release. So I gave him the answer: "Harvey, the grosses are really good."

In time Bob would come to think that he had given his brother too much credit. Perhaps there had been no reflection on life's meaning; perhaps Harvey was not capable of it.

When Harvey was released from the hospital, he was forty pounds lighter, had quit smoking, and had a long scar on his neck from a tracheotomy to permit a breathing tube to slide down his throat, and another scar from an operation on his stomach. For a time, Harvey said he was chastened, determined to change.

But the weight would pile back on, the chain-smoking reignite, and the brawling escalate. At the start of the new century, Harvey's wars with talent agents also escalated. He enraged them by calling their clients directly. Studios were irate when he sought to share their profits but not their risks. Universal was furious when Harvey resorted to extortion by refusing to release John Madden, the director of *Shakespeare in Love*, from a two-picture contract to direct a movie for Universal and Working Title—unless Miramax was made a partner and also received domestic distribution rights to *Bridget Jones's Diary*. Harvey had similar battles with Sony Pictures over *All the Pretty Horses* and with DreamWorks when

he refused to release Lasse Hallström to direct *Catch Me If You Can.*
Harvey insisted that everyone in Hollywood did the same: "Every time
Steve Spielberg has gone up to the plate and said, 'I want to direct a
movie,' the same people who criticize me go and get half the movie."

Few would argue that Hollywood is a serene place populated by
priestly, disinterested men and women. Clearly, such extortionate demands had a long history in Hollywood, which called it dealmaking.
But Harvey stood out. He was unusually "mistrustful," as longtime
Miramax executive Jonathan Gordon has said. Harvey was "capable of
screwing people to such an enormous degree because he assumed everybody was going to take advantage of him that same way." And to Harvey, starting in Buffalo, a negotiation was a zero-sum game; there could
be only one winner.

The assiduous consolidation of power was a form of self-protection
as much as it was ego gratification. He was doing his best to bank favors
and showcase connections. By now, Harvey's political clout was widely
known. He screened movies for the Clintons at the White House, once
bringing the Hollywood couple of the moment, Brad Pitt and Gwyneth
Paltrow. He spent a weekend at Camp David. He was a pal of Bill
Clinton's when the president vacationed on the Vineyard in the summer, and thought of himself as a confidant of Clinton's. "He would brag
about counseling the president who, as Harvey told it, was in the 'dog-
house,' something Harvey assured the president he knew a lot about,"
recalled Marcy Granata. "And so he would describe himself as a good
shoulder for the president in Martha's Vineyard over the summer of the
Lewinsky scandal. We believed him, but who knows if any of that is
actually true." Granata's reaction to Harvey the fabulist was similar to
those who wondered whether his many boasts of the famous actresses
he had slept with were true. One member of Harvey's "Martha's Vineyard Mafia," as Harvey called them, remembers being shocked at how
Harvey, in a crowded room, once regaled guests with tales of the prominent actresses he had conquered.

What was clearly true is that Harvey and Bill Clinton became close enough for Clinton to share personal insights about his friend. Asked about Harvey's sometimes compulsive behavior, Clinton told me, "Something happens to you when you're a child and makes you feel that if you really want to have an impact in life you have to be in a hurry. And you can't be a milquetoast. And I don't know much about his life before he got involved with politics, but there's something there that planted a deep yearning in him that would let him define the work of his life, at least in part, by how much he got done how quick. And I think that guys like him—and me—if you're not careful you miss a lot of the other things in life."

Harvey's fundraising feats were undeniable. He orchestrated major giver parties in 2000 for Al Gore's presidential candidacy and Hillary Clinton's run for the U.S. Senate, cochairing a Radio City Music Hall fundraiser for Gore and a Roseland birthday party and fundraiser for Hillary Clinton. He sprinkled his money on Republicans as well as Democrats, raising two hundred thousand dollars for the reelection of New York Republican governor George Pataki in 1998, and lobbying Democrats to support Republican mayoral candidate Michael Bloomberg in 2001. In all, between 1998 and 2002, Weinstein said he and his wife gave candidates a total of $750,000 and raised $14 million more.

While a generous donor and fundraiser, he remained the bellicose micromanager. The Roseland party he helped choreograph for Hillary Clinton in 2000 became an obsession. Nathan Lane was the master of ceremonies, and Harvey insisted on doing a run-through of Lane's jokes. "Harvey was concerned about the propriety of some of Lane's material, and they got into an argument about it," recalled actor James Naughton, who directed the entertainment. Suddenly, Lane remembered, "Harvey became Tony Soprano," and ordered him to cut this joke and that joke.

Lane refused. Towering over the five-foot-five Lane, Harvey bellied him into a corner. "I'll ruin your career."

"You can't hurt me. I don't have a film career," the Broadway actor shot back.

Hillary Clinton tried to assuage Lane, apologizing for Harvey's eruption, but asked if he'd please cut some jokes.

On stage minutes later, Lane waited to introduce Cher, because she was caught in traffic. Stalling for time, he announced to the audience, "In the meantime, I'm going to do all the jokes Harvey Weinstein wanted me to cut."

Appearing on Seth Meyers's *Late Night* show years later, Lane got in the last word by recounting this scene.

Harvey's behavior, said producer Jane Rosenthal, who cochaired the Roseland event, "was insane." Harvey said he did not threaten Lane but simply told him, "Don't do this material." He feared it was too risqué, and Republicans would pummel Hillary for it.

Over the years, when Hillary Clinton's aides were reportedly warned of Harvey's abusive ways, particularly with women, these warnings had no obvious impact on the Clintons' fealty to Harvey. Disney executives insist they were never warned of Harvey's abuse of women. But when Michael Eisner was alerted to Harvey's political activities, he took action. He increasingly worried that Harvey was muddying Disney's family-friendly brand. "He was forcing executives to make political contributions, which he shouldn't be doing," said Eisner. "And we put a stop to it immediately." Disney had always played it politically safe, proud to split its political donations equally between Democrats and Republicans. Eisner was mortified to read news reports that 80 percent of Disney's combined contributions flowed to the Democrats; this, he complained, was "because of the Miramax money, which Harvey didn't report to Disney."

Power altered Harvey's self-perception. He became what Marcy Granata, who by now had developed a jaundiced view of her boss, called "Citizen Harvey," a nod to *Citizen Kane*, the classic Orson Welles film about a media mogul who makes a failed run at a political career. "When Harvey Weinstein jumped into national politics . . . he overextended himself doing this and he also got very full of himself." His ambitions grew. He joined the board of the Robin Hood Foundation, a nonprofit organization dedicated to fighting poverty in New York City, and got chummy with rich new friends like Robin Hood founder and hedge fund billionaire Paul Tudor Jones. He helped recruit others to the board, including Gwyneth Paltrow. "He got terser and terser. . . . The political piece not only inflated his ego but it also amplified his anger. He felt superior to everyone because he was someone who had the president 'on his phone' as well as a few Oscars in his pocket. The main film business suffered because Harvey Weinstein was taking his eye off of the ball a lot," recalled Granata. The more his ego was stoked, the hotter the furnace roared.

His brother Bob concurred: "I used to say to him, 'Harvey, you're becoming a one-name person. You're becoming Harvey.'" Once Bob erupted at Harvey because his brother kept doing TV interviews about their movies and subbing for Piers Morgan, who had replaced Larry King on CNN. "You've lost your rocker. You're out of control."

"No, the pictures need promoting," Harvey responded.

"Harvey, you're promoting yourself!"

Early on Election Night 2000, Harvey hosted a book party for a friend at the Tribeca Grand Hotel. He lost it and erupted when *New York Observer* reporter Rebecca Traister, whose calls he had ignored all week, asked about a stalled Miramax film project. Irate that she would interrupt to ask a question unrelated to the book he was celebrating, Harvey began stabbing his finger into her shoulder and shouting that she was "a cunt" and "a bitch," and people should be happy he was installing order as the "fucking sheriff of this fucking lawless piece-of-shit town." Traister's colleague at the *Observer*, Andrew Goldman, was there to cover the book party; he had angered Harvey that summer by writing that "Harvey's Angels are flying the coop," identifying a handful of his PR executives who quit because the "backstabbing" in the office and "the micromanaging Harvey Weinstein" exhausted them. When Goldman heard Harvey yelling at his colleague, he intervened to try to calm Weinstein. Harvey erupted at him as well, trying to snatch Goldman's tape recorder and grabbing him in a headlock and dragging him outside. Goldman's tape recorder remained on, capturing everything. So, too, did the many flashing press cameras.

Yet the next day not a single picture appeared in the press. The first sentence in the pictureless *New York Post* story placed the blame on "a couple of pushy reporters for the *New York Observer* [who] pushed Miramax chief Harvey Weinstein to the breaking point." A senior Miramax executive, when granted anonymity, candidly explained why there were no incriminating pictures: "Harvey ran a favor system. He would try and build up goodwill with reporters even if he had no idea how or whether he would ever tap into it. But when something like this came up, he would say, 'Look, I gave you all this access. I did you this favor. So you guys should be able to make the decision not to run it.' In the gossip and paparazzi space, things were even more transactional."

A Miramax press representative apologized, sort of: "Nobody acted like Albert Einstein, including Harvey. It was regrettable behavior on both of their parts."

More than regrettable, thought Marcy Granata. She dared confront Harvey, who was traveling to Florida to promote Al Gore. She got him on the phone and asked whether he used the "C-word" with Traister. Harvey was impatient and dismissive. "I wanted him to apologize, but he went on a rant to justify himself," she said. "He claimed he was a victim of 'gotcha' journalism, of two reporters who lied to get access to his book celebration."

She pressed about the "C-word," saying she would rather quit than deny it to reporters if it were true. Harvey now had reason to fear Granata would resign; she was especially important to Harvey because he relied on her marketing talent and her fearless candor.

Usually when confronted about something embarrassing that he did, Harvey would deny it by saying, "It's not true. I swear on my kids' life!" With Granata he went further. "Dripping with sincerity, he asked, 'Have you ever heard me use that word?'" She had not. "He then invoked his oldest daughter, Lily, whose smiling face was pictured on his watch, to fervently deny he would ever use such a word. 'I swear on Lily's life that I didn't say it. I swear on Lily's life.' Harvey used the only person I thought he ever really loved as a shield. He didn't say Eve or Miriam. He said Lily. I believed him because he swore on Lily's life. It turned out to be a big dark lie, the worst lie he ever told me." But this lie, like others, allowed Harvey to wiggle out of a potential staff crisis.

Harvey kept getting into fights. At a Los Angeles event around this time, he spotted *Vanity Fair* editor Graydon Carter, the cofounder and former coeditor of *Spy*—a magazine that in the past had ridiculed the Weinstein brothers and crafted what cofounder Kurt Anderson called a "rough kind of vivisection of Miramax." Harvey bellowed at Carter, "I hear you're doing a story on me?"

"No, we're not," Carter responded.

"Well, I hear you are," Harvey said.

"We're not—I would know," Carter said.

"I could do a story on *Spy* and all the drugs used there," Harvey said.

Carter, with a laugh, replied that *Spy* didn't pay its writers enough money to buy drugs.

"I have my own magazine now!" Harvey said, somewhat childishly, and they glared at each other before Harvey interjected, "Let's take this outside."

Carter thought they would have a fistfight. Instead, he said, "the second we hit the outside air, he put his arm around me and said, 'Graydon, you're a great editor. I just wanted you to know that. I hope my magazine will be half as good.'" Carter was unpersuaded. "It was all for show. To look good. To intimidate me." Harvey insisted the exchange with Carter was civil, adding, "We went outside to take a walk." Six years after this encounter, Harvey's Talk Books outbid others to offer a $1 million advance to Carter and Anderson for a book on *Spy* magazine. Sometimes Harvey greased palms before he knew exactly what he wanted, as seemed to be his intention in offering a book contract to famed litigator David Boies; sometimes he reached for his checkbook to please stars, as he did by flying actors on private jets. Of course, the money was plentiful because it was Disney's money.

Back at the dingy Miramax office in Tribeca with its low ceilings, empty coffee cups and boxes strewn about, the belligerence Graydon Carter or Rebecca Traister experienced was increasingly on display daily. Entering the office was "like going into a lion's cage, and you didn't know whether the lion was tame or crazy," said Charles Layton, who long served as Harvey's right hand for business. "Every day at Miramax was a continuation of the infighting and drama of their childhood."

"Two or three times a week Harvey seemed out of control," Jason Blum recalled. "The culture was brutal and familial. . . . Harvey's assistants were as powerful as senior executives. If an assistant called and said, 'Harvey wants this,' you did it. . . . There were two groups of people: Fifty percent left in the first year. The other percent complained, and also loved him. Harvey was a disciplinarian and a provider." Unlike those on the staff who found Harvey cold, impersonal, Blum sometimes saw another side. "When my grandmother died, the biggest bouquet of flowers was from Harvey." When Jonathan Gordon's younger brother suddenly died of a cardiac arrhythmia in Los Angeles, his parents were away on vacation. Without being asked, Harvey chartered a plane to fetch his parents and fly them to Los Angeles.

Such magnanimous gestures could go a long way to inspire loyalty. "There was a feeling of us versus them," said Katrina Wolfe, who joined the company as a lowly assistant in 1998 before rising over the next decade to senior vice president of production and casting. "We didn't feel we were part of Hollywood. We were in New York. We were a tribe." The fierce, defiant, and proud culture Harvey and Bob spurred helps explain Miramax's success.

Employees banded together, in part, because they had to. United in fear of Harvey (and to a lesser extent, Bob), many members of the tribe were pulled one way by his magnetism, and the other by his bullying.

His needs were a furnace that required constant stoking. A former Miramaxer recalled, "It felt like everyone was his assistant. The philosophy was that the company runs best when Harvey is happy, so you have to make sure things run smoothly. . . . It was like tending to a giant, belligerent, disgusting baby. His moods dictated so much that you constantly thought about whether he was tired, hungry, thirsty, cold." The employee, who chose to speak anonymously, described chaotic, febrile days where anything that pleased Harvey and preserved the peace was a net good.

Inevitably, Harvey induced people to view his most outrageous acts as small trespasses, and these were shrugged off, laughed at, or endured. Someone who could put a reporter in a headlock after screaming he is the "sheriff of this fucking town" is someone taking a sledgehammer to reality. Fear distorts reality. To stay in Harvey's orbit, one had to accept that words and actions beyond the pale were normal.

C itizen Harvey was the orchestra conductor for the post-9/11 fundraising concert at Madison Square Garden, helping assemble an amazing array of performing talent—including Paul McCartney, Bruce Springsteen, Billy Joel, the Rolling Stones, Elton John, Jay-Z, Destiny's Child, and Eric Clapton. They raised $35 million to honor the families of police and fire first responders who had sacrificed their lives. In talking to the press, Harvey usually played up his role, and not that of his other cochairs, James Dolan, who owns the Garden; John Sykes, the president of Infinity Broadcasting; and Robert Pittman, the president of AOL. "He was beginning to make this about him," says someone who played a big role in organizing the concert. "Unlike most of the talent who volunteered and gave because they wanted to, Harvey wanted people to know," observed a senior Miramax executive.

In the spring of 2002, a series of confrontations that approached violence would lead to what Harvey claimed was a come-to-Jesus moment. In January 2002, on the night of the Golden Globe Awards in Los

Angeles, Harvey had an ugly encounter with Stacey Snider, the studio chief of Universal. Miramax received three Golden Globes that night, but its Best Picture candidate, *In the Bedroom*, lost to Universal's *A Beautiful Mind* (a coproduction with DreamWorks). The Golden Globes had become a weathervane often indicating which way the Oscars might go, and because it was deemed important, campaigning beforehand could be fierce. A false rumor was making the rounds that John Nash, the mathematician plagued by schizophrenia on whom *A Beautiful Mind* is based, was an anti-Semite, and Harvey was convinced a story would soon appear in the press pinning the whispering campaign on him. He blamed Snider for insinuating to reporters that he was behind it.

When Harvey spotted Snider at a CAA after-party that night in a restaurant, he cornered her in an alcove across from the bar. To the petite Snider, he was a fearsome sight—his eyes dark and glowering, his fleshy face unshaved. Towering over her, he jabbed a finger at her face and screamed, "You're going to go down for this!"

Snider assured him that she had not accused him of spreading the rumor, and that they were friends. Of course, she did believe Harvey had spread the rumor. She reported the altercation to her boss, Barry Diller, chief executive of Vivendi Universal Entertainment, who would soon be quoted in the press labeling Harvey a "bully."

Harvey was still seething about Diller's quote when he spotted him on the terrace of the Hotel du Cap-Eden-Roc at *Vanity Fair*'s annual dinner during the 2002 Cannes Film Festival. Loud enough to galvanize an audience, he yelled at Diller, "Why'd you call me a bully?"

"You are a bully," Diller replied as the two men stood toe-to-toe before a hushed audience of actors, directors, models, and fellow executives. Diller's back was to the railing, high above the rocks and water below. "Harvey started to move toward me," Diller said. "I see this gorilla person coming toward me. I'm physically afraid, but don't want to admit it. I'm backed up to the railing and worried I will flip over onto the rocks. I shout something at him—the way you shout at a bear! He paused, and I turned and ran down the steps."

Weeks later, when reporting a *New Yorker* profile of Harvey, I asked him, "Did you threaten Snider and nearly attack Diller in Cannes?"

"I yelled, perhaps too loudly," he said contritely.

Harvey volunteered that he telephoned Snider and Diller to apologize.

"It's time to be a statesman," Snider told Weinstein when he called; she appealed to his vanity, telling him that if he ever wanted to win the award he most coveted, the Academy's Irving G. Thalberg Memorial Award, he would have to change. Weinstein said he was chastened. "This year, I decided to take Stacey's advice," he told me. "I'm going to go out of my way. It's like Ariel Sharon—you can't be a lion in the desert and then not govern properly. At a certain point, it's time for the firebombing to be over. You've got to know when the revolution has succeeded. Why do I have to keep fighting?"

"The thing I hate most about myself is my temper," he confided, before pledging: "Every year that I have a public argument, I'm gonna leave a hundred thousand dollars to Paul Newman's Hole in the Wall Gang camp. And it's really motivating me."

Although Harvey was a longtime generous supporter of Newman's camp, he did not carry out his pledge to donate a hundred thousand dollars every time he exploded in public. He might have gone broke had he honored the pledge.

Now that he had turned fifty, Harvey insisted that he was a changed man, that winning laurels and brawls mattered much less to him now. "No, I've really gone in a different direction. . . . You say to yourself, 'I'm fifty, wait a second. Hang on.' I've done a lot and there's not much more to do. And there's not that much more time, if you really think about it. You know what? More Martha's Vineyards, more family, more this, more that, more human things at the end of the day."

In any event, his tantrums did not cease, nor did his longing for "family" reduce his sexual appetite. Mixed in with the coerced encounters were more ambiguous entanglements. Katrina Wolfe worked for Harvey and Bob for a decade, becoming a senior casting executive; early on, as Steve Hutensky's assistant, she'd witnessed the flurry around the Perkins/Chiu settlement. Today she is president of production for AG Studios. She recounts how Harvey would call her with requests to arrange meetings for him with certain actresses. After he met them, she said, "Many times I would get a call out of the blue from Harvey asking me to help an actress—'Maybe there's a part in an American movie. Maybe she can meet with a casting director.'"

Did Wolfe think he was having sex with them?

"We always whispered, but most of the time I could not tell whether he slept with them. We had no illusions about him being faithful." Despite the solicitousness of Miramax employees toward these women, she described many as haughty. "They treated us as if they were Harvey's wife." In the computers of Harvey's assistants, these women were listed as "F.O.H." (Friends of Harvey), women whose names and contact information and what city or country they lived in were kept on digital file. Possibly the flagrant adultery served as a smokescreen for the assaults, allowing staffers who were not in the hotel suite to see only the cheating.

It is doubtful Miriam knew about his sexual behavior. Once, Marcy Granata recalled, there was a Page Six item in the *New York Post* suggesting that David Carr, who was profiling Harvey for *New York* magazine, might be looking into whether Harvey abused women. Miriam was upset. "Harvey didn't call, but to my surprise, Miriam did," Granata said. "I was in the process of breaking my contract to leave the company, but I took the call from home because it was rare to get a call from Miriam. I had never had a conversation with Miriam about Miramax business. . . . She got on the phone and was a different person. Very terse and strict: 'How could you do your job and let something like this happen? Why are people saying these things about my son?'" Miriam seemed shocked, as if it couldn't be true. The press had to be making up tales that her son abused women.

Granata told her that she had to ask her son that question. "I told Miriam that Harvey's personal life was not my job, nor was it something I discussed with him. Miriam was mean and aggressive that day. I felt like I was on the phone with Harvey."

Meryl Poster was close to Harvey and Bob and was seen as a loyalist, someone who quickly and publicly came to their defense, and years later would alert Harvey that the media aimed to expose him. Poster had a closer relationship with Miriam than most Miramax employees, yet after Harvey was dethroned, she said of Miriam: "She created these monsters. I never knew how she did."

Harvey was proud of his record of supporting women directors and actresses and would speak of it often—pulling it over himself defensively like a too-small coat once the 2017 *New York Times* and *New Yorker* exposés exploded. But the fraught production of the 2002 film *Frida*, about the Mexican artist Frida Kahlo, who was famed for her surreal and vivid self-portraits, suggests a different story line. Years afterward, Salma Hayek, who produced and starred in the film, wrote an op-ed for the *Times* in which she described Harvey as "my monster." He hounded her throughout the production, pressuring her for sex. She tabulated her many refusals:

> *No to me taking a shower with him.*
> *No to letting him watch me take a shower.*
> *No to letting him give me a massage.*
> *No to letting a naked friend give me a massage.*
> *No to letting him give me oral sex.*
> *. . . And with every refusal came Harvey's Machiavellian rage.*

By her account, Harvey, frustrated and furious that she was not acquiescing to his demands, set impossible tasks for her as producer, and complained bitterly that her portrayal was not sexy enough. He threatened to shut the movie down unless she agreed to film an explicit lesbian love scene with her costar Ashley Judd. Hayek agreed to do it, but wrote of the shoot:

My body began to shake uncontrollably, my breath was short and I began to cry and cry, unable to stop, as if I were throwing up tears. . . . Since those around me had no knowledge of my history of Harvey, they were very surprised by my struggle that morning. It was not because I would be naked with another woman. It was because I would be naked with her for Harvey Weinstein. . . . My mind understood that I had to do it, but my body wouldn't stop crying and convulsing.

Hayek's description of her extreme physical reaction has an echo in Annabella Sciorra's account of her rape by Harvey, with its mental dissociation and physical distress, as well as the testimony of others at his criminal trial.

Ashley Judd, of course, had been the recipient of Harvey's unwanted hotel-suite attentions five years earlier, but had slipped away without igniting his dangerous rage. Nevertheless, he seemed determined to extract some form of sexual submission from her, as from Salma Hayek.

The troubles of *Frida* were not over. Harvey disliked the final cut, which he found too long, and at a test screening where the movie rated highly with viewers but not high enough for Harvey, he had an altercation with director Julie Taymor. In a fury, he ripped up the audience questionnaires and threw them at her feet, threatening to sell the film straight to HBO rather than give it a theatrical release. According to several witnesses, he moved intimidatingly close to Taymor's beau, Elliot Goldenthal, who had composed the score, and said, "Why don't you defend her so I can beat the shit out of you?" This outburst came a few months after Harvey told me he was a changed man.

In the end, the film won six Oscar nominations, including a Best Actress nod for Hayek.

Despite Harvey's frantic concerns that he would be exposed after the 1998 Venice Film Festival, four years later he seemed unconcerned that Salma Hayek or any other victim of his would publicly accuse him. Harvey had ignored the stipulations he agreed to in the NDA he signed with Rowena Chiu and Zelda Perkins. Miramax had not instituted new policies and structures to prevent sexual harassment. Perkins had negotiated the right to select a therapist for him and attend the sessions, but after struggling unsuccessfully to schedule them, she stopped trying.

In 2002, Zelda Perkins received a call from Donna Gigliotti. "She rang me," Perkins recounts, "and she said, 'I know you want to get Harvey. I know you want to see justice done. So I have this journalist, he's going to bust Harvey. He's doing a story on him, and you need to talk to him.'"

Perkins was not interested. "Zelda became angry," Gigliotti recalled, and told her, "This is my story to tell. I will tell it in my own time." If Perkins spoke, she would break her NDA, forfeiting her settlement and facing the threat of an expensive lawsuit. "I suggested she tell the truth about Harvey Weinstein as she knew so much more and would be a more powerful voice," Perkins explained. "But she intimated her position and career made that impossible." The call infuriated Perkins, who already felt that she had sacrificed a great deal of her life after confronting Harvey in 1998. She hung up on Gigliotti.

I was the journalist Gigliotti wanted to introduce to Perkins. In the last half of 2002 I spent months reporting a Harvey Weinstein profile for *The New Yorker*, and I had been told many on-the-record stories of Harvey mugging people, throwing things at them, threatening physical violence, terrorizing them, and asserting his domination, all of which would be reported in the profile. In the course of my reporting, some whispered that Harvey sexually abused women. It was usually very vague.

After I quizzed her about these whispers, it was Donna Gigliotti who first told me of the assault on Rowena Chiu and the NDA that Chiu and Perkins had signed. I believed that Harvey's sexual assaults were just an extension of his bullying and need to dominate that I had reported, and I was determined to unearth facts. But *The New Yorker* does not traffic in rumors. I needed women to go on the record. And I couldn't locate anyone who would speak out. Gigliotti said she couldn't because "Zelda had clearly told me it was not my story to tell."

I thought maybe court records would reveal what happened, so I scoured court records in London and the U.S. for NDAs but came up empty. I later realized that by intervening early and paying for an NDA before charges were lodged in a courtroom, Harvey had sealed them from public view. The reason I could not find NDAs was because they never reached a court. They were private, not public, documents, locked in the safes of Harvey's lawyers. Unbelievably, no copies were given to his accusers. Neither Perkins nor Chiu possessed one. Had I published what I then thought I knew, I would have written that Chiu was raped by Harvey, instead of Harvey attempting rape and Chiu narrowly escaping.

Despite the NDA's terms that stated Harvey would write positive recommendations for the women, Zelda Perkins had not been able to get a job because she could not satisfactorily explain in job interviews why she left Miramax. In two job interviews, she told me years later, male executives asked if she had given Weinstein a blow job. Harvey's shadow was so dominant she had to leave the industry to escape it.

With help from Donna Gigliotti, I tracked her to Guatemala, where she was training horses. I saw Gigliotti as a vital ally. She assured me that if Perkins would speak on the record, she would probably confirm her account. Once more, Perkins refused to violate her NDA and told me she would not answer my questions.

I heard that Chiu was working in Asia, but I had no luck locating her; when I succeeded in interviewing her years later, Chiu said she would not have spoken if I had. She filled out the details of her life after Venice: On job interviews she encountered the same obstacle Perkins had—her inability to say why she exited Miramax left her interviewers suspicious. Finally, Harvey rehired Chiu. It was as if he'd studied Thomas Hardy's novel *Tess of the D'Urbervilles*, or, just as likely, Roman Polanski's adaptation *Tess*, whose title character fled the man who violated her, but in the end returned, feeling she had no other option. It was an insurance policy of sorts: if any rumor slipped out, he could say that if he had really done something bad, Chiu wouldn't still be working for Miramax. She received a three-year contract to move to Hong Kong to help oversee Miramax's Asian films, but in fact had little to do. Clinically depressed, she said she visited a total of eight psychiatrists, none of whom could help because "I was not allowed to talk about Harvey," her assaulter and currently her boss. Had she not been consumed by fear, which was the NDA's primary function, perhaps she would have told one of her psychiatrists; surely they would have kept what their patient said in confidence.

At the time, she was living with Chris, her investment banker boyfriend of seven years, but never told him about the assault, nor did she tell her parents and sister. Twice, she said, she rented a hotel room and "tried to commit suicide," swallowing pills. Without telling Chris, she fled Hong Kong, abandoning a job meant to silence her and a relationship strangled by a secret. She returned to London, where she got a graduate business degree before moving to the U.S. and a job at the World Bank. She would marry a tech entrepreneur, move to San Francisco, have four children, and keep what happened in Venice to herself—until Harvey's past was prized open in 2017.

I confronted Harvey about Rowena Chiu and Zelda Perkins in my final 2002 interview, one of about a dozen hours of one-on-one interviews we conducted. We were alone in Miramax's small uptown office on Broadway. I had never mentioned their names before.

Harvey, at the Venice Film Festival in 1998, did you rape Rowena Chiu? Did you pay her and Zelda Perkins each 125,000 pounds to sign NDAs?

He rose from one end of the tiny conference table and moved to face me. He was standing, I was seated. His fists clenched, his shoulders raised, his lower lip trembling, he glowered. I thought he might throw a punch and I was seated, an easy target. So I stood up.

As soon as I rose, he started to sob uncontrollably. *If you write that, it will end my marriage to Eve and humiliate and make the lives of our three*

young daughters miserable. This was a consensual relationship. I was not a
good husband. But I'm not a sexual predator. The only reason I paid money
and had them sign NDAs was to protect my family.

Not for a second did I believe Harvey. I had been reporting this profile for months, delving into his behavior, his vows, and to me it sounded
like the lie Harvey told Marcy Granata when he swore on his daughter
Lily's life that he was telling the truth. But with no victim willing to go
on the record, I was dealing with hearsay, assertions I could not prove.
As my editors and I wrestled with what to publish about Harvey's aberrant sexual behavior, I realized a back door might exist that would expose
what Harvey had done. I had to find out whether the NDAs were paid
for by funds from Miramax or Disney, the corporate parent. If a corporation paid, perhaps a crime had been committed. At a minimum, shareholders would be irate at how their investment dollars were spent. Even
without a single woman coming forward to lend their name to expose
Harvey, under-the-table corporate expenditures would allow *The New*
Yorker to publicize why, and for what, the money was spent.

Fearful that the profile would reveal his assault on Rowena Chiu,
and perhaps others, days prior to publication Harvey requested an off-
the-record meeting with me and David Remnick, the editor of *The New*
Yorker. We met in an upstairs conference room of *The New Yorker*'s
parent company, Condé Nast, joined by deputy editor Pam McCarthy
and *New Yorker* counsel Ed Klaris. Harvey was accompanied by his
attorney, David Boies. I had known Boies and became a social friend
after I covered the 1999 Microsoft antitrust trial for the magazine and
for a subsequent book. After his successful prosecution of Microsoft,
Boies was hailed as a public servant for taking a leave from a lucrative
private practice to work for the government.

After being seated, it did not take long for Harvey to issue a threat—
If The New Yorker *seeks to publish this salacious story, I will seek an injunction to block publication.*

You can't do that, Boies gently interrupted, tapping his client's arm.
The First Amendment prevents such prior restraint or censorship.

Harvey was suddenly quiet. I interjected: *It's Tuesday, Harvey. The magazine closes late Thursday and is published Monday. We need you to come back tomorrow with the cancelled checks showing how you paid for Rowena Chiu's and Zelda Perkins's NDAs.*

The next day Harvey and David Boies returned, this time accompanied by Bob Weinstein. We were in a conference room dominated by a long table. David Remnick and I and Ed Klaris sat side by side facing the windows. Across the six-foot-wide table sat Bob and Harvey and David Boies. Harvey and Bob had grim expressions, the kind you could imagine Israeli and Palestinian officials wore in a negotiation. There was no chitchat. With a publishing deadline the next day, I asked to see proof of who paid for Zelda Perkins's and Rowena Chiu's silence. David Boies slid two cancelled checks across the table, each from Bob Weinstein's personal account. He agreed to make the payments, Bob Weinstein said, because his brother told him Chiu was blackmailing him. The payments, Harvey again said, were to protect his family.

My back door slammed shut. Our scheme to ensnare Harvey by showing he illegally siphoned corporate dollars from Miramax or Disney to silence his sexual victims was dead.

Bob Weinstein saved Harvey. This brought to mind a comment Michael Eisner had made to me about the brothers: "They are extremely loyal to each other. They may fight, but if someone comes in between they close ranks."

The meeting ended with Harvey uncertain whether the profile would contain accounts of his sexual abuse. Remnick and I were also uncertain. We had on-the-record accounts of Harvey's verbal bullying of studio executives Stacey Snider and Barry Diller, of director Julie Taymor, of his threat to punch *Vanity Fair* editor Graydon Carter, of heaving objects and vile words at staffers, of apologizing for his temper and promising, as he had for years, to reform. All of which were included in the published profile. But there were huge gaps in our reporting. We didn't have a single woman willing to go public with an account of how Harvey sexually abused them. We only had whispers. We didn't then know what was in the NDAs. We didn't have a detailed description of what really happened in the Venice hotel suite.

The decision of what to publish belonged to the editor of *The New Yorker*. Thursday morning, deadline day, we conferred at length. Remnick explained his decision by referring to a 1992 exposé by the newspaper where he once worked: *When* The Washington Post *reported on its front page that Senator Bob Packwood sexually assaulted women, it quoted ten women by name describing what he had done to them. We have no one on the record. We can't publish anonymous accusations.*

I agreed. To escape a "fake news" claim, journalism must establish facts and offer proof, not conjecture or opinion. I believed Harvey was guilty of beastly sexual behavior. But I lacked proof. The profile ran in December 2002. Although Harvey was relieved that his sexual compulsions were not revealed, he was mightily displeased with his portrait. And yet, once again, the "sheriff" of this lawless town had managed to escape being exposed.

TWO DIVORCES

(2002-2005)

By the end of 2002, Harvey's foremost concern was not whether he would be exposed; it was Miramax's rocky relationship with Disney. They had ordered an audit, concerned that his financial books weren't transparent and that the Weinstein brothers had engaged in "creative accounting." At the time, Eisner publicly downplayed the audit, saying in dry bureaucrat fashion, "Whatever audit was going on is a normal audit about how you account for a personal-services contract that related to Bob and Harvey." The brothers saw it differently, thinking it was an attack on their independence. They hired attorneys David Boies and Bert Fields to challenge the audit.

In fact, Michael Eisner was agitated. After a four-year run, *Talk* magazine was shuttered in 2002, vindicating his conviction that the magazine business was a mistake. Disney lost an estimated $55 million on *Talk*, half of it charged to the company's magazine partner, Hearst Communications, which was just as eager to stem the losses. Confirming his concern about Harvey's sway over the press, Eisner said he was also upset that Miramax was leaking "its earnings to the press, and they weren't true." Internal documents sent to Eisner showing Miramax's revenues, expenses, and earnings on each movie revealed that while Miramax claimed total profits of $1.156 billion between 1993 and 2004, Disney recorded pretax Miramax profits of barely $125 million, just 10 percent of what had been declared. An internal memo sent to Eisner by his strategic planning department under the heading "Summary of significant Miramax issues over the last year" focused on what the department concluded was excessive spending, including steep salaries for *Talk* magazine executives, losses on Rudy Giuliani's $3 million book contract, private airplanes, and "significant overages" on spending for Martin Scorsese's film *Gangs of New York*. Harvey would spend four times his $30 million contractual limit on the film.

Eisner's unhappiness was matched by Harvey's. He was enraged by what he saw as Disney's intrusive management. It galled him that Disney refused to finance *The Lord of the Rings*. He had proposed to Eisner that Disney help finance Peter Jackson's trilogy at a then estimated cost of $180 million. Too expensive, Eisner replied. Besides, Harvey told Howard Stern many years later on the radio, Eisner told him no one cared about "these hobbits and elves and dwarfs."

Harvey told Stern he had read *The Lord of the Rings* in college and was convinced it would have a worldwide audience. "It was action, heroic. . . . The subtext was World War II, and how we deal with evil." Forgoing ownership, Miramax became one of its producers with a relatively small investment in exchange for 5 percent of the movies' grosses. Bob Shaye of New Line decided to finance the three movies with Time Warner's money. Instead of the $120 million Miramax and Disney split from their 5 percent of the gross, New Line's profit totaled $2.5 billion. It was, Harvey said in 2002, "a colossal mistake" by Disney, and not just because of the lost box office. The movie characters, he said, could have been featured in Disney theme parks and merchandise, creating a gigantic self-generating revenue stream.

Somewhat defensively, Eisner challenged Harvey's assertion: "They came to us with the request for a $180 million budget, as a first step, without even a script. These were guys who were supposed to be making movies for $15 million, tops [the contractual figure was $30 million],

and we were already losing money with them as they continually violated their arrangement with us. It was an easy pass at the time. In
hindsight, we probably lost a lot of money on it, but with the information we had about them at the time, it wasn't worth the risk. Speaking
of hindsight, I always believe that what you do make is more important
than what you don't make."

By 2002, Miramax needed some good business news. Staring at
losses, for the first time Miramax was compelled to institute significant
layoffs—about seventy-five employees, or roughly 20 percent of the
staff. Between 2000 and 2002 there was also a voluntary exodus of
longtime senior executives, most of whom felt exhausted by Harvey, and
some of whom had enticing new opportunities. Those who departed
included West Coast president Mark Gill, the two coheads of acquisitions, Jason Blum and Amy Israel, CFO Bahman Naraghi, publicity
and marketing head Marcy Granata, and Dimension number two Cary
Granat.

More jarring, personal tension between Harvey and Bob escalated.
Once, Bob said they spoke "at least five or six times a day," so much
that Bob's wife would complain when the phone rang late at night: "It's
him. I know it. It's him—don't pick it up." The constant dialogue between Harvey and Bob had ended by the early years of the new century.
Bob was the brother who scoured the books and fretted about spending
encroaching on profits, and he was increasingly impatient not just with
Harvey's spending but with what he saw as his lack of focus. At the
same time, Bob admits he was wrestling with his own demon: alcohol,
which further eroded his relationship with Harvey. Bob could be volcanic. Although Harvey lost control when his temper flared, he was
impatient with drinkers who lost control when they drank.

The tension in the relationship between Bob and Harvey was reflected in the locations of their offices. When Miramax renovated its
third-floor offices at 375 Greenwich and expanded to 13,000 square
feet and another floor, a large office was set aside for Bob close to
Harvey's. He chose not to occupy it, preferring to establish Dimension's

headquarters on the fourth floor, before ultimately moving to 99 Hudson Street, a block away. "The less I saw him, the better I felt," Bob said of his brother. He believed his brother's attention had wandered from the artful movies they loved to *Talk* magazine and Talk Books, to politics, to a quest for expensive, blockbuster movies. "I had the view that Harvey started acting out of an arrogant belief he could do anything." Increasingly, the relationship between the brothers mirrored that of a married couple who one day professed their love, and the next day consulted their lawyers. In coming years, this tension would intensify.

The tempestuous relationship between Harvey and Bob caught me in the middle when I was reporting my 2002 *New Yorker* profile. Bob, averse to anything that smacked of self-promotion, refused to participate in the profile. Although regular pleas were made to him through his brother and through Matthew Hiltzik, the company spokesman, three months expired before Bob finally consented to an interview. When the hour arrived, Bob's demeanor suggested that he'd been imprisoned in the room with the reporter. He announced that he would only talk off the record and only about Miramax's business. Told that these were not acceptable ground rules, Bob screamed at me and threatened to leave; Harvey was summoned, and after many minutes of soothing, persuaded Bob to acquiesce. Twenty minutes into the interview, I mentioned that Harvey had spoken of their father, Max, and had urged me to ask Bob about him.

Bob again erupted, demanding that Harvey return to the room. When Harvey came in, Bob yelled at him for daring to talk about Max, insisting that Harvey knew Bob was writing his own essay about Max for *Vanity Fair*. Harvey tried over the next half hour or so to calm his brother, to no avail. Bob politely apologized to me and ended the interview. Weeks later, Bob—whose essay was eventually published in *Vanity Fair*—was still yelling at Harvey for betraying him, and Harvey was now pleading with me to placate Bob: "Please, Ken," he'd say. "Don't mention Max. Bob is really upset."

The brothers had other differences. Despite his volatility, Bob was more introspective, capable of climbing into himself to understand why he behaved a certain way and correct it. Harvey could not or would not. Bob and Harvey also differed on their perceptions of their relationship with Disney. Bob said he did not share Harvey's annoyance at Disney's micromanagement of Miramax. "Harvey was the one who was frustrated with Disney." Bob actually concurred with Disney's alarm at Harvey's spending: "He looked at it as if he had the Federal Reserve on his side, free money."

While it sounds as if Harvey and Bob were at war, it was actually a cold peace. Meanwhile, the battles with Disney were mushrooming. And Harvey was spending less time at home, his sour disposition and unusually frequent travels to Europe chilling his relationship with Eve.

Yet whatever pressure Harvey was feeling, he remained confident he could hurl smoke bombs to deflect attention. Defend by attacking was his default strategy. If he worried about a divorce from Disney, or from Bob, he masked it. When I proposed to profile him for *The New Yorker*, Harvey at first refused to cooperate. Failing to persuade him, I said I would report the profile without his cooperation. Sometimes this is an empty journalistic threat, because a profile without the voice of the subject of the profile risks both superficiality and reading like a prosecution brief. I had not yet decided whether this was a bluff. But Harvey, perhaps fearing journalistic digging into his marriage with Disney and Miramax's finances, perhaps confident he could seduce me, decided to cooperate. For the next several months his office and employees were open to me. We each thought we could manipulate the other.

One day in his New York office in the summer of 2002 was a fairly typical day. A dozen or so of his executives gathered to discuss which movie Miramax should enter in each of the big festivals—Sundance in January, Cannes in May, Venice in early September, and New York and Toronto in the fall. These festivals generated favorable publicity for

Miramax movies, aroused critics, served as early-warning signals for films in trouble, and were shopping centers for Miramax to acquire movies. A major prize in an important festival might start the dominoes falling toward the Oscars.

The staff and Harvey gathered in a modestly furnished, cramped conference room down the hall from his office. On this hot day, Harvey wore gray suit pants, a dark-gray wool three-quarter-sleeve shirt, and red suspenders. He was informed that the New York Film Festival had turned down *The Hours*, the film based on Michael Cunningham's Pulitzer Prize–winning novel about Virginia Woolf that Miramax was distributing. Harvey lit a cigarette and reacted stoically to the news. "This is a worry," he said. "That movie needs help"—from critics and film festivals. He was much less stoic when told that the New York festival had also said no to *City of God*, Miramax's evocative film about life in the Brazilian ghetto. "You're kidding," Harvey exclaimed. "This is one of the best films we ever made. It's in Portuguese. They're morons!"

Perched precariously on an Aeron chair at the end of the conference table, Harvey pounded the carpeted floor with his right heel and chain-smoked. Cynthia Swartz, who worked in publicity and supervised Miramax's Oscar campaigns, turned the conversation to the Toronto festival. DreamWorks, she said, was considering a "huge retrospective for Spielberg," and she wanted to know whether she should counter with an effort to celebrate Martin Scorsese, the director of their big movie of the year, *Gangs of New York*.

"Leave it," Harvey said. "I thought *Minority Report*"—a Spielberg film—"was the best movie I saw this summer." He switched the subject to the Venice festival. "Should we play *The Hours* in Venice or wait for the Berlin festival?" One problem, he said, was that he hadn't yet seen *The Hours*, because its producer, Scott Rudin, a man whose appetite for conflict matched Harvey's, wouldn't screen it for him, and Harvey wouldn't commit himself to showing it until he had. "Why don't we put our foot down on this," he said, referring to the standoff with Rudin.

"Tell him, 'Harvey doesn't want to go to Venice.' It's good to scare them. Find out when he has to deliver the print to us." Harvey relished the idea of making a man he detested squirm. And Rudin, who felt equal disdain for Harvey, asserted to me that Harvey was not telling the truth, insisting that he "had already seen the film once in London and had professed to like it a great deal."

Weeks later, Harvey got around to viewing the movie, walking downstairs from his office to a small screening room. He sat in the center of the room; the seat to his left was occupied by Scott Martin, head of postproduction for Miramax, who had spiked hair and three small silver hoops in his left ear. Martin had joined the company eleven years earlier and always sat next to Harvey at screenings because, Harvey said, their tastes were similar.

The Hours oozed talent. It was directed by Stephen Daldry, with a screenplay by David Hare, and it starred Nicole Kidman, Meryl Streep, and Julianne Moore. It opens with Kidman, as Virginia Woolf, putting stones in her coat pockets and drowning herself in a river. Weinstein and Martin, whispering together, instantly agreed that the Philip Glass score—in particular, the loud, thumping opening music—was too melodramatic, and that the film's pacing was too slow. The screening over, Harvey said he liked the movie a lot, but didn't think it was ready to be shown at the Venice festival later that month. "This movie is only ninety percent. Great director . . . but it's over the top. Great acting."

Harvey held that some things in a movie couldn't be fixed—a bad performance, a mediocre screenplay—but that it was possible to do a lot with editing and music. Yet he seemed troubled by having to decide whether or not to show the film at Venice, although it was hard to dismiss the thought that he enjoyed tormenting Scott Rudin. "Do I be the good Harvey or the bad Harvey?" he asked. "Do I argue to fix the movie? Do I argue that the scene where Virginia Woolf is kissing her sister is too long?" He knew Rudin would make the final call, but, since

Miramax had international distribution rights, Harvey got to decide about Venice. And his decision would be to nix Venice.

Rudin, like Weinstein, had produced many outstanding movies; and, like Harvey, he had a reputation as a bully.* He once sent a memorandum to Allison Jackson, the executive in charge of special projects at Paramount, which read, "Be aware that the only thing separating my hands from your neck is the fact that there are three thousand miles between us." He sent copies of this note to all of Jackson's superiors.

When Rudin was told of Weinstein's decision on the Venice festival, he was, predictably, furious—but he insisted *The Hours* would open as planned on December 27, 2002.

As the film distributor, Harvey lacked the authority to edit the movie. But he could subvert Rudin. After *The Hours* was screened in Los Angeles in August, Weinstein wrote directly to Sherry Lansing, the head of Paramount, which jointly financed the film with Miramax. "I received the scores for last night's screening of 'The Hours' and I was very disappointed, as I am sure you were. I definitely think that not going to Venice was the best decision. . . . We can have a great movie, but the music hurts. The music is so overused, repetitive, intrusive, schmaltzy and too telegraphic. Additionally, I share your concern with finding the right cuts and the right text to make the ending more satisfying." Ultimately, Rudin made some of the music and tempo changes that Weinstein sought. Nevertheless, Todd Haynes's *Far from Heaven* filled the slot at Venice *The Hours* would have occupied. Later, Rudin, still angry, said of Weinstein, "He had never been willing to discuss anything with me related to the finishing of this movie." Untrue, countered Harvey.

---

* In 2021, Rudin was publicly exposed as a sometimes-vicious bully and felt compelled to suspend serving as a producer and volunteered to seek therapeutic help.

Rudin was so offended by Harvey's behavior that he sent a gift-wrapped box to him containing twenty-seven cartons of Marlboro Lights and a note: "Thanks for all the help on *The Hours*. Best, Scott."

Harvey claimed he laughed at the gesture: "I much prefer Scott Rudin sending me cigarettes and wishing me a premature burial than the guys in Hollywood who spend five hours on the telephone behind your back putting a knife into you." He described Rudin as "this fantastic producer, who has great taste." But he took care to add that his belligerence "makes me look like Mary Poppins." Perhaps not surprisingly, when I visited Rudin to discuss Harvey, he described Harvey's brutal treatment of the Miramax staff as appallingly unacceptable. Yet when a staff assistant entered his office and didn't have an immediate answer to a question, Rudin became another person, raining loud, vile insults on the hapless aide. As with Harvey, I wondered whether Rudin was aware of the monstrous behavior that terrified his staff. Neither Harvey nor Rudin saw themselves as a despot, but that's how they were perceived by many of their employees.

Sometimes Harvey angered the very filmmakers he championed, as happened with Martin Scorsese in 2001 and 2002 when he was directing *Gangs of New York*. Scorsese had been noodling the idea for the movie for two decades, since he read a 1927 book by Herbert Asbury, *Gangs of New York: An Informal History of the Underworld*, about the violent gang wars between Catholics and Protestants in nineteenth-century New York that helped shape the future of the city. Scorsese worked with his best friend, Jay Cocks, on the screenplay. Scorsese needed a great deal of money to realize the vision, and though he'd resisted Harvey's blandishments in the past, the Disney dollars lured him in, as did Harvey's most captivating quality: his embrace of quality films. Harvey agreed to produce the movie in 1999, but he told Scorsese the script "was good but not great" and that he needed to fire Jay Cocks.

This was their first disagreement, and Harvey won. Scorsese reluctantly told his friend that he had to bring in a new screenwriter at

Weinstein's insistence. The director recruited Steven Zaillian and Kenneth Lonergan to rework the script. He cast Daniel Day-Lewis to portray the Nativist Protestant gang leader, "Bill the Butcher," Leonardo DiCaprio to portray Catholic gang leader Amsterdam Vallon, and Cameron Diaz to portray pickpocket Jenny Everdeane, DiCaprio's love interest and the protégée of Bill the Butcher. To re-create nineteenth-century New York, Scorsese built a complex set of buildings in the 400,000-square-foot Cinecitta Studios in Rome, including the infamous Five Points slum in lower Manhattan. There were furious disagreements between a strong-willed director and his producer, with Harvey complaining that costs exceeded budgets by 25 percent, that the movie was too long, clocking in at over three hours, and that it had to be more commercial. A film that began shooting in late 2000 would not be released until December 2002.

Harvey spent a remarkable sixteen weeks on the set in Rome. He and Scorsese tried to muffle stories that they were feuding, and at one point they issued a statement about "their terrific working relationship" and how much "fun" they'd had, but for the most part the relationship was neither terrific nor fun. Although Scorsese, like Spielberg and a handful of other directors, had absolute "final cut" approval, meaning he alone controlled what appeared on the screen, Harvey hovered, pressuring for edits. With his prodding, *Gangs* was postponed while it was shortened from more than three hours to two and a half. Scorsese's friends said he was miserable working with Weinstein. The one friend who would say this for the record, Jay Cocks, described it as an "awful" experience—except that, in his rather magnanimous view (given that he was fired from the project), "the movie turned out so well."

Seated in the small screening room of his Park Avenue office, Scorsese praised Harvey for being "ruthlessly honest," for his "enthusiasm," and for his ability to get things done. Still, Scorsese conceded that the description of the movie set as *fun* was "a euphemism" to "psych myself" and the actors and crew; of Weinstein he said, "I found

Harvey really imposing on me." Actually, the director had mirrors installed on the video monitors so he could see Harvey coming up behind him.

Scorsese admitted he was not the easiest person to work with. "I have to be told stuff—only I don't like to be told anything. I took two of his nine ideas. I kept telling him he should direct. He's all over the product, the grammar."

Scorsese did, however, appreciate Harvey's genuine love and knowledge of good movies, and his hunger to keep learning. As he did with Tarantino, Harvey had turned for instruction to Scorsese, also naming him a Jedi Master. "Marty would give me a movie every Saturday night to watch with info about the making of the movie. So over three years, I saw eighty films that Scorsese gave me from his personal library." He rattled off some of them, including David Lean's *Oliver Twist*, Pietro Germi's *Divorce Italian Style*, Tay Garnett's *The Postman Always Rings Twice*, and Michael Curtiz's *Mildred Pierce*.

The battles between Weinstein and Scorsese over *Gangs* bled into a larger battle with Disney. Harvey announced that the movie cost just under $100 million, while outside analysts who track the movie industry estimated the true cost at $120 million. A May 4, 2001, internal memo from strategic planning addressed to Eisner described the movie as exceeding budgets.

Compared with its costs, its box office results were tepid; it grossed just $77 million domestically and a total of $194 million worldwide. *Gangs* was nominated for ten Academy Awards, winning none. Few could muster up passionate feelings for it, as they could for such memorable Scorsese films as *Raging Bull* or *Taxi Driver*. Miramax losses were offset that year by the success of *Chicago*, the musical, whose domestic box office zoomed to $170 million and which captured a Best Picture Oscar. Although Harvey said Miramax lost no money on *Gangs*, another internal Disney memo reported that the true bottom line for *Gangs* is that it lost $6 million. The good news for Miramax was that

Chicago made \$125 million. Harvey could not understand why Disney did not show more appreciation for these profits. Disney could not understand how he overspent so cavalierly.

To read internal Disney memos from this period is to sense a rapidly approaching crisis. Although Miramax had been profitable, Disney was increasingly distressed by what it saw as Miramax's profligate financial decisions and its mismanagement. Trust between the marriage partners was leaking away like air from a punctured balloon. Harvey did not behave like a partner, Disney asserted. In 2003 there were more than a few unreleased Miramax movies thought to be duds. And, Disney claimed, the Weinsteins were exaggerating their profits in another way. In 2002, for example, Miramax claimed profits of \$48 million. But Disney said this was a false number because it did not include Miramax's overhead costs of \$50 million, meaning that Miramax actually lost \$2 million that year. By inflating profits, Eisner said, between 1999 and 2003, the Weinsteins claimed bonuses totaling \$162 million. (Disney's contentions deserve some skepticism, for in a later memo to Eisner and chief operating officer Bob Iger, Disney's planning department reported that although Miramax claimed profits in 2002 of \$142 million, the true profits were only \$43 million. This is not the loss of \$2 million that another Disney memo trumpeted.)

One of Harvey's qualities that enraged Disney but aroused the devotion of its recipients was his sometimes impulsive generosity. Director Anthony Minghella remembered how during the 2003 filming of *Cold Mountain* in South Carolina, Jude Law's wife, Sadie Frost, went into labor and the actor asked to fly home to England to be with her, since she'd had episodes of postnatal depression in the past. Minghella was startled when Weinstein announced that he would send a plane to take Law to England and agreed to pay the cast and crew for four days while they waited for Law to return. "He demands loyalty, and he gives loyalty," Minghella said. Harvey said the decision to stop shooting cost

Miramax $1.1 million. He could not resist adding, "Ask Jeffrey Katzenberg or [Universal chair] Stacey Snider if they'd make the same decision!" Or: ask Disney.

Disney's displeasure with Miramax's management targeted Harvey, not Bob. Dimension's movies, including *Spy Kids* and *Scary Movie*, beefed up the revenues of Miramax, and Bob kept Dimension's overhead low. It drove Disney batty that Harvey charged over four hundred thousand dollars to Miramax's budget for Fabrizio Lombardo, who was listed as head of Miramax Italy, even though he was also employed by another company. A charmer, Lombardo traveled every year to Cannes with Harvey; among Miramax's employees he was known as "Harvey's procurer," which he denied. Of this, Disney claimed ignorance. They insisted Lombardo be terminated because they said his salary was unjustified.

Disney had come to the conclusion that Harvey was making too many movies, spending too wildly. Constantly, he reassured Disney executives that by spending more he was about to strike gold and enhance Miramax's brand. "Harvey was a selfish businessman," Disney's Peter Murphy said. This was reflected in how he dealt with Disney and those he did business with. "A good businessman would adopt a win-win philosophy in dealing with partners or with those you negotiate with. It is not sustainable to say, as Harvey did, 'I win, and you lose.' To burn bridges, as he did, is not good." The perceived lack of financial discipline was confirmed to Disney when Harvey, in 2003, a year after *Talk* had closed, joined with a handful of investors, including Mort Zuckerman and Jeffrey Epstein (yes, that Jeffrey Epstein), to make an unsuccessful bid to acquire *New York* magazine, despite knowing how displeased Eisner was when he launched *Talk* magazine (which had shut down with losses of $55 million). More worrisome, an internal memo addressed to Eisner reported that "Miramax overspent its approved 2003 production budget by $179 million."

Disney was also unsettled by the strange dynamics between the Weinstein brothers. "They would come to meetings together," remembers Murphy. "Sometimes they would be on the same page. Sometimes they would sit on the same side of the table and argue with each other like a cartoon."

However, the brothers were aligned against Disney in support of Michael Moore's film *Fahrenheit 9/11*. Moore's political documentary eviscerated the administration of George W. Bush, his war in Iraq, and what Moore said were its cheerleaders in the press and corporate America. Harvey and Bob Weinstein and Miramax were involved in helping fund Moore, without telling Disney. Michael Eisner said he was blindsided: "I was watching the 2003 Academy Awards and Michael Moore won for *Bowling for Columbine*. His speech was viciously anti-Bush. The next day at a Monday staff lunch, I hear that Moore is making a movie about Bush to be distributed before the 2004 presidential election." Days later Eisner had lunch with Ari Emanuel, head of the William Morris agency, who happened to be Harvey's agent, representing him with potential studio partners and negotiating on his behalf with Disney. At this lunch Eisner learned that Harvey was helping fund Moore's documentary. "I told Emanuel I would not allow that film to be distributed by an arm of Disney before the election." Disney was apolitical. Miramax's contract with Disney placed restrictions on certain types of movies, and *Fahrenheit 9/11* was one. Emanuel said he understood, Eisner said, "and immediately took it to Harvey." Eisner put his thoughts in writing, and said Harvey concurred. Miramax would not distribute the movie.

A year later, Peter Murphy asked Eisner, "Have you seen *Fahrenheit 9/11*?"

"No."

"You ought to see it," Murphy said.

"Why?" Eisner asked.

"We own it!" Murphy said.

Indeed. Harvey and Bob had helped fund and produce Moore's movie, personally advancing Moore $6 million. Eisner again felt betrayed. But so did Harvey. He and Bob shared Moore's anti-Bush stance, and felt Eisner was trying to squeeze the rebellious spirit out of them. Hadn't Disney promised Harvey and Bob creative freedom? Harvey insisted—with good reason—that it was a powerful movie, though he preposterously claimed it wasn't controversial. Disney insisted that Harvey's involvement violated their employment agreement.

To Harvey's mind, Michael Eisner's opposition to Moore's movie proved he had lost his nerve. Harvey sniffed weakness. He knew that after two decades as CEO, Eisner's star had dimmed. A shareholder revolt the previous year had forced Eisner to step down as chairman, ceding the position to former Senate majority leader George Mitchell. For the first time in years, Disney's animation unit was floundering, as was its movie studio. Disney parks had not yet recovered from 9/11's impact on tourism. Eisner was in a messy business dispute with Steve Jobs of Apple, and it had turned nasty. And Eisner felt pressure from his board and shareholders to relent and finally choose a number two, thus naming a likely successor. When Robert Iger was selected, Eisner was further diminished by speculation that he was on the way out.

Harvey chose to try to go around Eisner, which proved a miscalculation. Disney chairman George Mitchell, a Democrat, was living in New York with his second wife, and Harvey made it a practice to invite them to Miramax premieres and parties. Thinking Mitchell might be his ally against a weakened Eisner, Harvey secretly visited Mitchell and persuaded him to watch the Moore movie, insisting it wasn't controversial and would make a lot of money. He pleaded with Mitchell to lead the board in overruling Eisner. Mitchell, a skilled diplomat who negotiated a peace pact between warring factions in Northern Ireland, did ask Eisner at a board meeting if there wasn't some middle ground for compromise.

To Eisner, a compromise with Harvey on this issue was akin to negotiating with terrorists. He put his foot down on Michael Moore's film, and Mitchell and the board backed him. "I told Harvey to sell it," Eisner said, "but told him that Disney gets half the profits for the Disney Foundation." In fact, Moore's movie was a brilliant investment. It not only won Cannes's Palme d'Or, but by selling $119 million worth of admission tickets at American theaters and a total of $222 million worldwide, it became the highest-grossing documentary of all time. Nevertheless, Eisner and his executive team and board were exasperated dealing with untamable Harvey. Miramax was a small company that consumed an inordinate amount of Disney's executive time.

While Disney was fatigued with Harvey, their anger blinded them to why his relentlessness sometimes boosted business. Harvey was frequently mocked in Hollywood for zealously promoting charming but slight movies as if they were *Citizen Kane*, as he did a few years before in an unsuccessful campaign to capture an Oscar for the movie *Chocolat*, a romantic comedy starring Juliette Binoche as a single mother who settles in a hidebound French village and opens a small chocolaterie, whose delicious treats soon win over hostile villagers. The too-sweet story takes improbable twists and turns, including an on and off and on again love affair between Binoche and self-described "river rat" Johnny Depp.

When the movie came out, Andy Seiler, a Hollywood watcher for *USA Today*, lacerated the Oscar campaign Miramax mounted for *Chocolat*, which sold it as a spiritual movie that promoted tolerance, inducing people like Jesse Jackson to proclaim its healing powers. Seiler found it a slight movie, and thought Harvey was playing tricks on the public.

Harvey reached out to Seiler and said, "I love this movie. . . . I'll tell you what. Let's pick an audience anywhere in the world. Anywhere. You tell me and I'll fly there." And at the end of the movie "let's ask these people what they think of this movie."

Seiler chose Washington, D.C. Harvey urged him to bring his wife. At the end of the movie, Harvey went up on stage and asked, "How many of you liked this movie?" Most hands shot up. He asked why, and audience members volunteered that it was "transformational," it preached "tolerance," and though it seemed to be about chocolate it had a much deeper meaning. Before they left the theater, Harvey turned to Seiler's wife. "What did you think?"

"I liked it," she said. Eyeing her husband she added, "I don't know what his bug is." The resistance of critics to the charms of *Chocolat*—it received a mediocre critics score of 62 percent on Rotten Tomatoes—triggered Harvey's paranoid conviction that the movie establishment was arrayed against Miramax.

That anger and raging persistence extended to his own corporate team, and his behavior toward them ranged from tactless to harassing. Skip Brittenham, the prominent Hollywood attorney who had represented Miramax, recalled how exhausting Harvey could be. Harvey once "called and started yelling at me. I hung up and didn't return his calls. He then had his secretary call my office every fifteen minutes for an entire week. He sent me flowers and chocolates." Brittenham and his secretary were tired of the barrage. "I said I would talk if he stopped calling. I told him, the next time he yelled I would quit. And I did."

Harvey's relentlessness drove him to dig himself into a deeper hole with Disney, which ordered new audits of Miramax. Convinced that Disney was withholding funds from Miramax, Harvey asked pit-bull Los Angeles attorney Bert Fields to audit Disney's financials, deeply offending the company that owned his company.

To outward appearances, Harvey and Eve had a happy home life. They doted on three daughters and spent many summer weekends on the Vineyard. Eve accompanied Harvey to Miramax movie premieres and awards shows. Harvey and Eve had been married for sixteen years when he met British-born clothing designer Georgina Chapman, twenty-seven, a beautiful former model and aspiring actress, at a London cocktail party in 2003. Harvey was not discreet about his new infatuation. By 2004, Harvey was spending half his time in Europe. He openly wooed Georgina. She'd struggled with disabilities: born with femoral anteversion, which caused her toes to point inward, making walking clumsy, and diagnosed with dyslexia at age eight. She found Harvey a rock to lean on, as Eve had. He seemed to relish boosting her confidence and creating opportunities for her—often dragooning other people into the process. He promoted Georgina for small acting roles at Miramax, sometimes showing up on the movie set to watch her perform. He would urge actresses to wear the outfits designed by her new upscale couture label, Marchesa. He booked Georgina into New York hotels under the name Postel, Miriam's maiden name and the surname Harvey used for his hotel liaisons. He had always been a flagrant philanderer, observed Eric Robinson, who began working as Harvey's assistant early in the new century. "It boggled our minds how Eve didn't know."

Maybe she did know. By this time, frost had settled over the relationship between Eve and Harvey. Harvey was home less often, and when he was, he often arrived late and seemed distracted. Eve was the engaged mother of three young girls, and she apparently felt very alone. She was pleased when Harvey arranged a weekend visit to Capri. Perhaps the magic of their relationship would return. She did not know they would be joined by a business associate.

Jonathan Burnham was in Europe on a scouting trip for Talk Books when he received a message from Harvey to join him and Eve in Capri for the weekend. Burnham declined, only to receive another message that Harvey had already cancelled Burnham's flight home and booked him on a plane that would get him to Capri. It was a tense weekend of long, bored silences between Eve and Harvey, whose mind was plainly elsewhere.

Not long after they returned from Capri, in May 2004, Eve reached a separation agreement with Harvey. For Harvey, it was costly. According to the 48-page document first revealed by Chris Francescani of ABC News, Harvey agreed to: gift Eve half of his six hundred thousand Disney stock options (at an average share price of $26.30, the options were worth roughly $15 million); give her either $11.5 million or half the value of his just-over-$20 million of liquid assets; give her half of his 401K plan at Disney; and keep her as the beneficiary of half of his $6 million life insurance policy, with their daughters receiving the other half. In addition, he would make annual payments of $500,000 to Eve; cede ownership of the Central Park West duplex to her; provide $250,000 annually for child support until their three girls were in their early twenties; subsidize their private school, camp, college tuition, and expenses; pay for a nanny, driver, and vacations; and fund a $1 million trust for each daughter to access on graduating from college. Both Eve and Harvey signed his favorite tool of conflict, an NDA, preventing them from speaking of their marriage.

That same year, according to an internal Disney memo, Michael Eisner drew up divorce papers as well, a year before Harvey and Bob's contract was to be renewed. Initially, without consulting the Weinsteins, he presented to the Disney board these terms: Disney would retain Bob Weinstein and Dimension and sever ties to Harvey, though Harvey's new company would distribute his brother's films. Eisner might have found Bob difficult, but he knew few studios gushed profits like Dimension. "The typical Hollywood studio achieved a modest seven percent debt-free return on their cash investment in their movies," said Joseph Ravitch, who was Harvey and Bob's investment adviser. "The guy who blew everyone away was Bob Weinstein. Dimension generated a twenty-two percent debt-free return on their movies."

When this plan was proposed to Bob, he rejected it. Bob had successfully enrolled in an upstate New York New Directions treatment center for alcoholism, felt more settled, and said he did not wish to be separated from Harvey. Besides, the brothers were united in fury that Disney insisted on keeping the many hundreds of movies in the Miramax library, and on retaining the Miramax brand name. On August 24, 2004, Eisner dispatched a letter to the Weinsteins "to terminate their services effective September 30, 2005"—in thirteen months. In return, the Weinstein brothers would receive an estimated $140 million severance payment.

"It killed Harvey that Eisner would not let him keep the Miramax name. 'It's my parents' name!'" he shouted at Eisner, remembers Joe Ravitch.

It killed Miriam Weinstein as well. "She called me," remembers

Eisner. "She said, 'You have to give the Miramax name to my boys. It's named after me and my husband.'" Eisner was not persuaded. "Disney put billions into Miramax," he says.

By the time of the actual divorce in September 2005, Bob Iger had replaced Eisner as CEO. Iger had no emotional investment in the Weinsteins. To Iger, divorcing them was strictly a business decision. There were more important Disney business issues he was determined to tackle, like repairing Disney's fractured relationship with Steve Jobs and Apple. To Eisner, it was more personal. He disliked and distrusted Harvey. He was convinced Harvey had betrayed his contract. Besides, Harvey was a pain in the ass.

Harvey and Bob felt entitled to be upset with Disney. They had delivered the quality movies they promised when they partnered with Disney twelve years before. Miramax released more than three hundred movies under Disney, generated ticket sales of $4.5 billion, and collected 220 Academy Award nominations and 53 Oscars, including three Best Picture wins, for *Shakespeare in Love*, *The English Patient*, and *Chicago*. The Weinstein brothers believed Eisner and Disney reneged on their vow not to micromanage Miramax. To them, Disney was stealing the Miramax name. It infuriated Harvey that Disney executives like Peter Murphy disparaged him as a poor businessman. "Peter Murphy," Harvey countered, "was such a good executive that he helped Michael Eisner to turn down *The Lord of the Rings*, which would have made millions of dollars for the company. . . . I always made money."

To maintain an illusion of power, Harvey threw another smoke bomb, announcing that Miramax had fired Disney. In an interview with Sharon Waxman for *The Wrap*, Harvey falsely claimed what he had been telling others: "Disney offered Bob and me $9 million each to stay in 2005, and we said no. We were never let go." He claimed Miramax produced one third of Disney's studio profits, which was untrue. He said Miramax was profitable in its final years at Disney, which his own people say was untrue for Harvey's movies, though not for Bob's. Harvey treated this divorce as another marketing campaign.

As genuinely upset as the brothers were with Disney, Bob Weinstein insisted they were not upset with each other. They were still secretly negotiating terms of their divorce with Disney when on the eve of the March 2005 Academy Awards, Miramax hosted a party at the Pacific Design Center. Before an audience that included Leonardo DiCaprio, Cate Blanchett, and Martin Scorsese, Bob Weinstein, still privately smoldering with anger toward Disney, rose and declared, "No event or person will ever break up the brothers Weinstein."

This, too, would prove to be untrue.

10

"WE CAN TALK ANYBODY INTO ANYTHING"

(2005-2010)

Ever the shrewd marketers, Harvey and Bob saw the March 2005 Academy Awards and the annual gathering of Hollywood's elite as an opportunity to capture attention for the launch of their new business enterprise. Even though they were still officially Disney employees until September of that year, the brothers would give a Queens middle-finger salute to Disney. Their employees reported to the same Miramax offices in Tribeca, but they received new business cards with a new company name: The Weinstein Company. Aside from Harvey and Bob, most Miramax employees didn't ever think they worked for Disney. Nor, if you listened to Disney, did Harvey and Bob.

As was true under Disney, Harvey and Bob planned to produce as well as distribute movies. They claimed the new company would be liberated from Disney's overcautious micromanagement and fumbling bureaucracy. They would thrive in television as well as movies. They treated the Disney divorce as a jailbreak, though for the first five or so years the new company was imprisoned by its own mistakes.

They started strong. Aided by Joe Ravitch, then of Goldman Sachs, the new company would initially be financed by $1 billion, half from shareholders in the new company and half from debt the company would assume. The Weinstein brothers were designated cochairmen. Among the three classes of stock—A, B, and W—they owned W shares, which awarded them voting control. Goldman Sachs was one of the eighteen outside investors, including film producer Tarak Ben Ammar's Quinta Communications, the SoftBank Group, investment giant Fidelity, ubiquitous media financier Vivi Nevo, and hedge funds Perry Capital and Wellington Management. Peter Murphy of Disney was impressed that the Weinsteins succeeded in attracting "a fairly illustrious group of high-caliber, sophisticated investors." But he was skeptical and said so. "A Goldman partner called me before they were investing. I was really candid and told them they should not invest because the Weinsteins were bad partners."

Harvey and Bob received what can only be described as a sweetheart contract. As long as they were united, their W stock granted them total decision-making control. No investors, no board of directors, could overrule them. And for the board to terminate either Harvey or Bob "for cause" was a stupendously high bar. In what can be taken as Harvey's certitude that his sexual deviance was unassailable, the contract required that either brother first be convicted of a felony for "moral turpitude," and only "after the exhaustion of all possible appeals" could they be dismissed. If either were accused of sexual harassment, for instance, even if there was documentary evidence, the board was not to investigate. Instead, the board had to wait to see if either was convicted in a court of law. A second definition of "moral turpitude" in the contract involved the misuse of corporate funds. Here, too, the contract provided an unusual escape hatch: the guilty party would be granted "a cure" period, allowing them time to fix the financial fraud as if it were a mere mistake, and to demonstrate they were "cured" of whatever impulse drove them to cheat. Their annual pay was not extravagant by Hollywood standards—just over $2 million plus bonus participation—but with this added sweetener: in all subsequent contracts, Harvey and Bob were promised "equal or better terms."

Most Miramax employees made the move to the new company. Miriam Weinstein still visited to dispense rugelach and keep an eye on her boys. And given the sheer volume of sexual assault accusations that would later be lodged against Harvey during his years at the Weinstein Company between 2005 and 2015, his sense that he was unassailably safe continued.

Miriam Haleyi was twenty-seven when she briefly met Harvey in 2004 at a film premiere in London. She had been working in London for producer Michael White, a mentor who suffered a series of strokes. Seeking work, she attended the Cannes Film Festival in 2006, where Harvey invited her to his suite at the Majestic. She asked if there might be a job for her in New York; he asked for a massage. She refused. Yet she was hired as a production assistant on his TV fashion show, *Project Runway*. Because her tourist visa did not allow her to work in the United States, she was paid in cash. When the show wrapped for the season, she wrote to thank Harvey, who invited her for drinks and told her she could return to work the next season as well. She thought his obvious first flare of sexual interest in her had vanished now that she was an employee. She was invited to his SoHo apartment for a drink. Without warning, he began to grope her and slather her with kisses, chasing her into the bedroom where, despite trying to make him stop, he sexually assaulted her.

Many years later, Haleyi would give a full account of this assault as a principal witness at Harvey's criminal trial.

After the mugging that day, Haleyi told a roommate what occurred, but refused to call the police. She feared she would lose her job, and thus her visa. A month later, she received an invitation from Harvey to meet for drinks at the Tribeca Grand Hotel. Although his office was next door and he now lived in a SoHo apartment with Georgina, who he professed to love and would marry, Harvey often had the company rent a suite near his office at the Greenwich Hotel, for between $750 and $1,400 per night. According to Glenn Cunningham, vice president of security at the Tribeca Film Center and also director of security at the hotel, the suites were rented starting at 6:00 p.m. under the name Max Postel, a combination of his father's first name and his mother's maiden name. A Weinstein assistant met Haleyi at the bar, escorted her to Harvey's suite, and left.

Once in the suite, Haleyi said, Harvey ordered her to undress. She lay there motionless, not fighting back, surrendering to his assault. To Harvey's way of thinking, since she came to his suite, it was consensual. To Haleyi, this was rape. Like other Harvey victims, she dared not share what happened with the police. She worried that an accusation would be read as seeking attention and money. And she was burdened by guilt, wondering whether by agreeing to meet him again so soon after he had assaulted her that she had signaled to him that her body was available. She kept her job, but not her sense of self.

It can be dizzying to track all the charges of rape and assault that have emerged against Harvey, and the detailed composite picture they paint is of a man who was constantly, compulsively hunting women. Embarrassed, fearing retribution, perhaps needing to deny what occurred, the women who claimed to be his victims did not notify the police, ever. Years later, when reporters asked about his alleged victims, Harvey would not deny he had sex with his accusers. Rather, he simply declared that the sex was consensual.

Meanwhile, Harvey somehow balanced his sexual lust with his new love. He seemed focused on enhancing Georgina Chapman's career. Chapman had launched her upscale Marchesa label in New York in 2004, and prodded by Harvey, prominent actresses—Scarlett Johansson, Jennifer Lopez, Cate Blanchett, Anne Hathaway, Penélope Cruz— walked the red carpet wearing Marchesa. When Harvey wanted a celebrity to show off Marchesa's dresses, he exerted pressure. Jennifer Aniston was starring in a Weinstein Company movie, *Derailed*, in London. She would tell *Variety* that Harvey visited her on the set and tried to "bully" her, handing her a catalogue of Marchesa gowns and saying, "I'd like you to wear one of these to the premiere." The choice of dress for an actress was not a frivolous one—a successful look secured extra red-carpet coverage—and it was usually made in consultation with a stylist and the actress's management team. Aniston said the intensely romantic dresses were not her style. Harvey commanded, "You have to wear the dress." She refused.

After dating for four years, Harvey and Georgina wed in December 2007 at Harvey's Westport, Connecticut, home, a prim and dignified Colonial on Long Island Sound with private steps to the beach. It was a quarter century since the launch of Miramax; Harvey was fifty-five, his bride thirty-one. He had asked her to marry him just one month before. The ceremony was conducted under a tent lit by chandeliers and brimming with roses despite the 28-degree chill. The guest list featured many of Harvey's powerful friends—Rupert and Wendi Murdoch, Blackstone Group CEO Stephen Schwarzman, Madison Square Garden owner James Dolan, who served as an usher, Quentin Tarantino, Anna Wintour, Robert De Niro, Graydon Carter, *Daily News* publisher Mortimer Zuckerman, CBS CEO Les Moonves, NBC CEO Jeff Zucker, actresses Jennifer Lopez, Renée Zellweger, Cameron Diaz, and Naomi Watts, and those Harvey referred to as his "Martha's Vineyard Mafia"—his best man, investor Dirk Ziff, Comcast CEO Brian Roberts, J.Crew CEO Mickey Drexler, and financier Steven Rattner, who also served as an usher. Rupert and Wendi Murdoch's two young daughters were flower girls. The night sky was lit up by fireworks launched from a barge on Long Island Sound. Guests sat for a wedding video that was akin to a this-is-your-life tribute to Harvey, with toasts from Bill Clinton, Matt Damon, and others who could not attend. Aside from stroking his ego, the ceremony—just two years into the launch of the Weinstein Company— was a marketing campaign reminder that though Harvey's company did not carry the Miramax name, he was back, as powerful as ever.

Left out of the official wedding party was brother Bob, who had been best man at Harvey's wedding to Eve. "I was demoted," Bob told me with a laugh years later. "You can't ask for a better description of the fact that we were estranged." It is emblematic of their roller-coaster relationship that Bob went from declaring brotherly solidarity with

Harvey in March 2005 to saying of his brother's wedding two years later that it was a "corporate wedding. He's handing out ushers and best man on his understanding of value—to him." And the video, he remembered, "went on and on. . . . I could feel others felt embarrassed, embarrassed because of the ego. It spoke of total insecurity: 'I need everyone to know that all these famous people are my friends, and they like me.'" Bob was invited to speak after the video. He was fond of Georgina, who he describes as "very warm and effervescent, with a great sense of humor." But because his relationship with Harvey was by now more remote, he was not as close to her as he had been to Eve. He said he began with a tongue-in-cheek remark: "If I had known I could have shot a video and not been here tonight, I would have gladly taken that offer." Harvey feigned a laugh.

"It was a strange night," confirms one prominent guest. "Weddings are traditionally celebrations about the bride—or at the very least, the couple. This was all, I mean *all*, about the groom. There were speeches and videos after the ceremony and all made reference only to Harvey." If Georgina was offended, she betrayed no clue.

Georgina knew Harvey was her champion. He had jumped, feet first, into the fashion business. Besides actively promoting Marchesa and befriending *Vogue* editor Anna Wintour, with whom he would often sit in the front row at fashion shows and who became a good friend to Georgina, he produced TV shows featuring models, including the TV show he hired Miriam Haleyi for, *Project Runway*. The fashion business was also a cover for Harvey's insatiable sexual appetite. Years later, eleven models came forward to accuse Harvey of sexual misconduct, ranging from unwanted kisses to groping to rape.

Determined to jump out of the gate quickly with the new company, and without Michael Eisner and Peter Murphy hovering, Harvey made a series of deals. The company aligned with Metro-Goldwyn-Mayer to distribute its movies domestically, a not uncommon move among studios looking to share costs. The Weinstein Company launched TV shows—*Marco Polo, Models of the Runway, Mob Wives*. Its biggest hit, *Project Runway*, made stars of designer Michael Kors, model Heidi Klum, and editor Nina Garcia. In fashion, the company acquired Halston's clothing brand, and licensed the option to revive the Charles James brand. Celebrities were asked to wear his wife's Marchesa label if they were in a Weinstein movie. His production companies were frequently involved in fashion-themed movies, including Madonna's *W.E.*, Robert Altman's *Prêt-à-Porter*, and Tom Ford's *A Single Man*. Stars of Weinstein's films—Charlize Theron, Renée Zellweger, and Winona Ryder—all appeared on *Vogue* covers in 2007. Harvey made additional investments that took him perilously far out of his area of expertise. He pushed to invest in cable networks, acquiring 25 percent ownership of Starz and part ownership of art-focused Ovation TV. In advertising, Harvey promised to place products in their movies, inducing WPP, the world's largest advertising and marketing holding company, to invest $25 million for 5 percent ownership of the Weinstein Company.

Like other media executives, Harvey believed media companies needed to diversify by investing in other businesses. The problem was that the Weinstein Company failed to make the right investments. And the movie business was not a fast-growth business. Harvey longed to be a mogul, a man with a wide wingspan, with multiple businesses gushing revenues. He knew he was smarter than most. He was fascinated when he learned that businessman Sidney Frank built his Grey Goose vodka brand by relying on marketing, including placing Grey Goose in movie scenes and TV shows. It drove Harvey wild to see actors he worked with promoting Grey Goose in their movies. He was convinced he could do it better in his movies. *Who the fuck was Sidney Frank?* Harvey famously did not drink, but one day Joe Ravitch entered his office and was startled to see six bottles of vodka arrayed on Harvey's desk. "They all taste the same," Harvey, puzzled, told Ravitch. Harvey understood that what mattered was building a brand. Who better to do that than Harvey Weinstein? "I can do that with Halston. I need to invest in brands."

The Halston investment was a flop. A monumental business mistake was not acquiring Marvel Entertainment, the company that created familiar comic-book characters like Spider-Man, Iron Man, Captain America, the Avengers, and Black Panther. Marvel approached Joe Ravitch, who was advising Weinstein. "Marvel was then trading for nothing. They probably would have taken stock in the Weinstein Company," Ravitch said. "Harvey turned it down. He said, 'Marvel's a flash in the pan.'" The man whose company thrived on horror movies reacted like a snob. "Harvey didn't like the superhero stuff." And where was Bob Weinstein, whose more commercial tastes generated lofty profits for the company, and whose first Dimension smash was *The Crow*, based on a comic-book character? "Bob wasn't involved at all," Ravitch said. "Harvey was pretty dismissive, so it never got to Bob."

When asked about Marvel, Harvey emailed back in 2021 that the idea wasn't "locked up," and to finance it we "would have had to raise $500 million more, with no access to capital. In retrospect, Disney did a better job." To pay for it, "I would have been trying to figure out [how] to make 5 English Patients."

Disney was not about to miss out on another franchise opportunity like *The Lord of the Rings*. For $4 billion the company acquired Marvel in 2009, and over the next ten years transformed comic-book characters into sixteen movies that generated an astonishing $18.2 billion in global box office.

Strategic mistakes were common in the rapidly changing media landscape. Rupert Murdoch's News Corp spent $580 million in 2005 to purchase a social media site, Myspace, that was meant to outrace Facebook but quickly floundered; Murdoch sold it six years later for $35 million. To be in the media business in the first two decades of the new century was to live in dread. Advertising dollars were being siphoned by Google and Facebook. The cable bundle was coming apart, as consumers were choosing to reduce their monthly costs by shopping for à la carte services like Netflix. Google's YouTube was enticing young viewers, and these consumers increasingly spent their free time on social networks like Facebook rather than going to the movies. By the new century, megaplex movie theaters were overbuilt and rents were going unpaid, leading owners to either declare bankruptcy or say those screens that remained must be used to display action and sequel movies for multiple viewing times, crowding out independent movies. This, coupled with the drop-off of DVD sales and shuttered video stores, impacted the Weinstein Company. Not until streaming emerged as a dominant platform in the latter half of the second decade of the 2000s would independent and foreign films receive a boost. With so many choices, the audience for network television plunged. Media companies, like News Corp, that owned newspapers saw circulation and ad dollars nose-dive.

Before their eyes, the Weinstein Company and its studio brethren witnessed a classic collapse of a business they had relied on. Once, Blockbuster's nearly ten thousand video stores ruled the video rental business. They produced a steady stream of high-margin profits for the studios. But Blockbuster, like many other legacy businesses, strove to shield its existing franchise, and paid too little attention to looming digital disruptors.

Blockbuster became an instructive example of a media company frozen in time. Its lush profits were partly dependent on charging late fees to tardy customers, charges that at one point generated an extra $200 million annually but alienated customers. Hoping to compete, Reed Hastings and Marc Randolph launched Netflix in 1998, mailing movies from their website. When the internet bubble seemed to burst in 2000, decimating many digital upstarts and creating red ink for Netflix, Hastings and Randolph visited Blockbuster's offices in Dallas with a plea for Blockbuster to purchase Netflix.

"How much would Blockbuster need to pay for Netflix?" CEO John Antioco asked.

"Fifty million," they responded.

End of meeting. And, eventually, the end of Blockbuster, whose expensive stores and limited shelf space could not compete with a company with no store rents and with unlimited shelf space, since Netflix was mailing DVDs and eventually streaming movies over the internet. Blockbuster was forced to declare bankruptcy in 2010. Netflix now produces its own original programming, and in November 2021 its stock was valued at more than a quarter of a trillion dollars, making it more valued than Disney.

If Harvey's frantic diversification efforts were not fatal to him, his deal with WPP would, in time, threaten his rule in unexpected ways. The deal initially granted a board observer seat to Lance Maerov, a WPP executive vice president who headed corporate development and supervised WPP's venture investments. Maerov, who was thirty-nine when he met Harvey Weinstein in 2005 and was the chief dealmaker for WPP in North America, reported directly to CEO Martin Sorrell. A sociable man with a dimpled smile, Maerov was an experienced hand, serving on the boards of many companies WPP invested in—but he was instantly shocked by what he witnessed at the Weinstein Company. At his first board meeting, Harvey and Bob had different opinions about a film, and started yelling at each other. They argued over how much Harvey was spending to market a movie, about whether to acquire a certain movie, about Harvey spreading himself too thin and gambling on the company's fate with risky investments. Harvey had immense faith in his own "golden gut," his business instincts. He truly believed that without him the Weinstein Company would wither. He was hardly alone in that view.

Brawling between Harvey and Bob occurred at most Weinstein Company board meetings, Maerov discovered. "It got very personal," he said. And over the years it got worse. Bob Weinstein acknowledged the vituperative exchanges with Harvey at board meetings: "Ninety percent of them were financial. Harvey would agree to a budget and a day later he would ignore it by buying a movie outside of the budget. I would say, "Why are we at this board meeting if you do not comply?" Added Maerov, "It may have started over financial issues, but they quickly deteriorated into personal attacks initiated by Harvey against Bob." Harvey, as witnessed by Glenn Cunningham, head of security for the Greenwich Hotel, would bark at Bob, "You're a fucking idiot! Mom was right!"

None of the verbal eye-scratching at board meetings was described in the sanitized board minutes.

In its first five or so years, the Weinstein Company was perched on the edge of the proverbial cliff. Eager to make a statement that the Weinsteins were back, between 2005 and mid-2008 the company produced or distributed sixty-five movies—including *Elite Squad*, *Shut Up & Sing*, *Sicko*, *Zack and Miri Make a Porno*—none memorable and few moneymakers. Without the Disney vault behind them, and with questions surfacing as to whether the Weinsteins had lost their touch, the company was draining its investors' money. On top of this, the recession of 2008 struck with hurricane-like force. There were layoffs. "We never knew if we were getting paid the next pay period," Abby Ex, vice president of production and development, recalled. "We never knew if we would show up one day and the doors would be locked. I was constantly having to pitch rich equity up-front investors on our slate to see if they would invest. Harvey would bring in these rich guys who wanted to just jump into Hollywood."

Bob Weinstein was alarmed that Harvey's attention had wandered from the movie business in general and from the quality movies he excelled at. "He was like an athlete who stopped training and going to practice and thought they should get by on their natural talent and experience. Harvey lost his focus." He and the board knew this, Bob said, but the board "had no power," and without Harvey's weighted vote, neither did Bob—unless he joined with the board against his brother, which he was unwilling to do.

Harvey was desperate to bring in those "rich guys" because he was losing the support of Goldman Sachs. Seeking to curry favor, he sometimes invited Goldman partners to attend the Academy Awards and movie premieres. Nevertheless, the investment bank started to lean on Harvey, and he eventually did what an early mentor, attorney John Eastman, warned him never to do: sell all or part of his library. A senior Goldman executive said the Weinstein Company "was out of dough" just several years after the company was born. In exchange for the retirement of an astounding $335 million in debt, Goldman and its insurance company would acquire from the Weinstein Company a total of two hundred of its movies, with the Weinstein Company retaining more than one hundred titles and permitted to manage the entire library. Representing the Weinstein Company in this debt restructuring deal was H. Rodgin Cohen of Sullivan & Cromwell. Once enough sales from the library were made to retire the Goldman debt, the Weinstein Company could reclaim ownership. After Goldman acquired the library, with any money that came in, the executive said, the company was required to first repay the Goldman loans. Yet the Weinstein Company continued to churn out movies. The Goldman executive explained how: "Harvey violated the covenant [the original contract with Goldman] by investing in movies, not repaying loans."

Harvey had recruited an important creditor in 2008: the best man at his wedding, Dirk Ziff, a billionaire investor who with his two brothers was heir to the Ziff Davis publishing fortune, and who Harvey convinced to lend the company $75 million. Later, Ziff converted this loan to equity in the company and joined the board; and subsequently, to help extract Harvey from Goldman, his close friend James Dolan had his AMC Networks purchase the 150 films remaining in the Weinstein Company library, stipulating that Harvey would control the library.

What saved the company from bankruptcy, the senior Goldman executive said, was Quentin Tarantino's 2009 World War II movie, *Inglourious Basterds*, a scabrous, often hilarious alternate history story of two plots to assassinate Nazi Germany's leadership. The movie grossed an astonishing $321 million worldwide, more than *Pulp Fiction*. Harvey displayed his usual verve in marketing Tarantino's movie. For example, he phoned Larry Hackett, the editor of *People* magazine: "Larry, I want the cover."

"Harvey, this is *People* magazine," Hackett answered. "We do Julia Roberts movies."

Harvey countered by offering Brad Pitt, one of the movie's stars. Five days before the film debuted, the headline on the cover of *People* read: BRAD OPENS UP TO *PEOPLE*.

Of Weinstein, Hackett told *The Washington Post*, "He had this way of bending people to his will. Michael Eisner didn't call you. Alan Horn didn't call you, but Harvey did. Harvey was the Trump of the movie industry. He knew what was a good story. He knew how it worked. He knew what a deadline was. He knew about the care and feeding of gossip columns."

Harvey was grateful to Tarantino for helping the Weinstein Company defy corporate death. And Tarantino was grateful for Harvey's relentlessness and was willing to stump for the faltering company that was throwing itself behind his film.

Asked once how two strong-willed guys could happily make so many movies together, Tarantino said, "He's a tough cookie . . . but I look forward to him being a tough cookie." He told of the many arguments he had witnessed between Harvey and other filmmakers, and said, "I'm usually on Harvey's side."

Tarantino then added an observation that helps explain why Harvey was convinced he could wiggle out of any jam through cajolery or bullying, or both: "One of the reasons me and Harvey get along really well," he said, "is we kind of both work under the assumption we can talk anybody into anything."

11

BLOOD, BROTHERS

(2011–2015)

High from another Tarantino hit, Harvey was once again bullish, convinced the Weinstein Company had escaped its doldrums. He felt liberated to spend, although the Weinstein Company's overall losses exceeded the money *Inglourious Basterds* earned. When informed that Disney planned to cash in and sell Miramax and its library, Harvey jumped in feet first, teaming with investor Ron Burkle to make a bid. "But after reaching a verbal agreement with Disney," his investment adviser, Joseph Ravitch, said, "Harvey pressed to renegotiate to get better terms." Disney rejected their bid, and in 2010 sold the library for $660 million to an investor group.

Harvey has offered two different versions of why the library deal collapsed. In one email to me he blamed Ron Burkle, who thought Disney's math was off and reduced the offer price by $30 million, insisting that he, Harvey, "told Burkle that Disney would not go for it. He didn't listen. They lost it. They lost the prestige of it and the library itself. It was the single biggest disappointment of my career." He went out of his way not to blame Ravitch, who he called "a visionary who aided the company and is an asset to any company he deals with."

In a later email, Harvey blamed Disney, claiming their rejection was spiteful. If he were a failed businessman as they'd claimed, he countered, how could they have "made hundreds of millions of dollars" on a company they paid only $80 million for? "Disney sold Miramax for $660 million. That said it all," he said.

Harvey continued to spend prodigiously. Between 2010 and 2017, the Weinstein Company spent a total of two hundred thousand dollars on Greenwich Hotel suites. The company also paid extravagantly for suites at three other Harvey favorites: the Peninsula and the Montage in Los Angeles, with the daily rate at the Peninsula starting at $1,500 and suites at the Montage costing up to $7,500; and the Savoy in London, where a modest suite is listed at $3,555 per night.

These suites were often used by Harvey to meet young women eager for career help. Usually, Harvey relied on a conveyor system to funnel women to his suite: One of Harvey's assistants would schedule a meeting. Next a specific Miramax executive—casting, or television, or movie production—would be invited for the start of the meeting, then be excused to leave Harvey alone with his quarry. Lucia Evans, who would appear in Harvey's original indictment charging him with forcing her to perform oral sex on him, described a disturbing smoothness to the way the staff handled the choreography of a meeting. "It feels like a very streamlined process. . . . Female casting director, Harvey wants to meet. Everything was designed to make me feel comfortable before it happened. And then the shame in what happened was also designed to keep me quiet."

In 2011, an assistant in Harvey's office invited Jessica Mann, a twenty-five-year-old aspiring actress he had met at a party, and her friend, Talita Maia, for late-night drinks at the Montage Hotel bar. Harvey came alone, and told them, Mann recalled, "You guys are perfect for this film I'm producing. It's a vampire film." The bar was closing, and he said, "Let's go upstairs and I'll give you the script." Jessica was wary, Maia excited.

In his suite, they sat on a couch. Harvey went into the bedroom (many women have reported that he would give himself an injection to get an erection before sex), returning after a moment to stand in the doorway and bellow, "Jessica, come here."

She rose and Harvey grabbed her arm and slammed the bedroom door closed. "He was pushing me back and trying to kiss me like crazy. The more I fought, the angrier he got."

She said she tried to calm him with mollifying compliments. His next words, she recalled, were, "'I'm not letting you leave until I do something for you.' He went down on me. I started to fake an orgasm to get out of it."

There were no scripts for the vampire movie in the suite. Although Maia witnessed Mann pulled into the bedroom by Harvey, and presumably could hear sounds from the other side of the door and saw a distressed friend emerge from the bedroom, Mann said that Maia, equally ambitious to break into acting, urged her to stay in touch with Harvey.

Many staffers insisted they did not know he abused young women like Jessica Mann. At first, senior executive Abby Ex said, "I didn't think he was a predator. I just thought he was a man who had impulse control problems. It spanned across all areas—in his rage, in food, in power, in awards, in money, and in women. And so it was sort of like the casting couch on acid." But experience taught her that Harvey was a sex fiend, and she would be one of the few women who dared grant an on-camera interview denouncing Harvey to Ronan Farrow, which NBC did not air. Two of Harvey's assistants, Sandeep Rehal and Michelle Franklin, would eventually file a civil suit alleging: "Harvey Weinstein's sexual abuse and conduct, and his use of the office, TWC [The Weinstein Co] and staff to enable it, was common knowledge in the office." Rehal claimed she "was required to manage the stock of Caverject shots for his erectile dysfunction. . . . Every time Harvey Weinstein went to meet a woman at a hotel, in the office, or elsewhere, which occurred on average at least three times a week when he was in New York, Ms. Rehal was required as part of her job to provide Harvey

Weinstein with a shot, which she placed in his jacket pocket or in a brown paper bag."

After dozens of women came forward as victims in 2017, as we've seen, Quentin Tarantino admitted that for at least a decade he carried the knowledge that Harvey had assaulted actresses Mira Sorvino and Uma Thurman. "I wish I had taken responsibility for what I heard," Tarantino told *New York Times* reporter Jodi Kantor. "If I had done the work I should have done then, I would have had to not work with him."

But work with Harvey he did: on subsequent films like *Jackie Brown*, *Sin City*, *Kill Bill: Volume 1* and *Volume 2*, *Inglourious Basterds*, and *Django Unchained*.

Producer, actor, and creator of the hit TV series *Family Guy*, Seth McFarlane had been told by his friend, actress Jessica Barth, that Harvey asked for a naked massage during a 2011 business meeting at his Peninsula Hotel suite. She fled. It was with Barth in mind that MacFarlane, when hosting the 2013 Academy Awards and announcing the Best Supporting Actress nominees, pointedly joked, "Congratulations, you five ladies no longer have to pretend to be attracted to Harvey Weinstein."

Some inside the Weinstein Company were concerned that Harvey's behavior imperiled the company. Irwin Reiter, the company's executive vice president for accounting and financial reporting, would share with Jodi Kantor and Megan Twohey the email he wrote Harvey in 2014. After naming female victims of Harvey's sexual abuse, Reiter wrote, "Stop doing bad shit." Harvey confronted him and denied it. Reiter kept silent. A year later, Sandeep Rehal had begun to tell Reiter and a few other executives some of the humiliating requirements of her work managing Harvey's assignations. She later said she was too scared to reveal the not-so-veiled threats he had leveled: telling her he could have her younger sister kicked out of college, and alluding to Rehal's unpaid student loans. Rehal said he told her, "You are at Harvey Weinstein University, and I decide if you graduate."

Harvey blandly denied the existence of a casting couch in a 2014 radio interview with Howard Stern:

Stern: I gotta figure every starlet in Hollywood wanted to at least blow you . . . ?

Harvey: [chuckles]

Stern: Did you ever get to experience the . . . I'm gonna say the mogul aspect? Do a little coke, hang out with you, you know, I don't know, Julia Roberts. Give you a hand job. Something. You never got any of that?

Harvey: Howard . . . it doesn't work that way.

Stern: It doesn't really?

Harvey: No. I'll tell you who it works that way for. It works that way for the actors . . .

Stern: No, come on. Every girl knows that if she's a competent actress and she could get on your good side, you could make her a star over-fucking-night. Don't fucking tell me it doesn't work that way.

Harvey: Howard, I wish. The movies are too expensive. The risks are too great. It doesn't happen that way.

Five years later, Stern commented on Harvey's hypocrisy: "In other words, he knew everything you should do and say. This is not a guy who didn't know better."

In the roughly one hundred physical abuse claims that have been lodged against Harvey by women, there is only one video that actually shows Harvey as predator with prey, and it occurred on September 29, 2011, when Melissa Thompson, twenty-eight, thought she had a meeting with the Weinstein Company's marketing department to pitch her company, Intercast, and its digital marketing platform. Harvey had seen the recent Columbia MBA graduate with friends in a restaurant and noticed that she was attractive. He introduced himself and she mentioned her company, said she was their director of business development, and touted Intercast's new technology platform. He invited her to make a business pitch to his marketing team.

When Thompson arrived at 375 Greenwich Street, she was not sent to the marketing department but instead ushered into Harvey's office. She sat at a conference table and turned on her laptop and its camera to record this business meeting. She wore a bare sleeved top and skirt, her large black glasses perched on her head. When Harvey entered wearing a white T-shirt, his large belly protruding, his facial hairs untrimmed, he called out to his assistants, "Do not interrupt. Do not interrupt," and he clicked the lock on his door. Thompson rose and extended her hand. Harvey ignored her hand and instead pulled her to him in a hug, rubbing her back in a circular motion for a few seconds, before releasing her.

Harvey positioned a chair on the corner of the table maybe a foot and a half away from Thompson and facing her. "Am I allowed to flirt with you?" he asked, a perfect row of white teeth lighting his face.

"A little bit," she answered, smiling back at him.

He told her he had a movie that would soon appear about Marilyn Monroe, and asked how her digital marketing tool might work to promote the movie.

Leaning toward him with a big smile, she explained how it would work, displaying video examples of her company's work on her laptop.

Seemingly enthused, Harvey said, "You just tell me what I can do and it's going to happen." He turned to her and added, "It's fun when we do this."

She moved her face maybe a foot from his and smiled.

"But I'm actually seriously having a conversation with you," he said, reciprocating with a smile.

"Good, we can do both," she said, flirting back.

She discussed the different ways her digital company could make movie trailers and could use Facebook Likes to promote his movies.

"OK," he said. "I'm going to use your service on *Marilyn Monroe*."

As he said that, Harvey placed his right hand under the table and caressed her bare thigh.

She looked straight ahead, seemingly trying not to frown or appear upset, but also not welcoming.

He lifted his arm and started to rub her bare shoulder as she displayed data showing her company's marketing success.

"The data is so hot," she declared, leaning toward him and poking his arm.

"It is hot. You're hot," he said.

She laughed.

He put his right hand all the way up her skirt. "Let me have a little part of you. Can you give it to me?" he asked.

"Uh-uh, that's a little too high," she said, before changing the subject to other marketing campaigns they could do for his company.

After a few more minutes, Harvey told her, "I've got to go edit a movie, but I'll meet you somewhere." He suggested a drink at 5:30 that evening at the Tribeca Grand Hotel.

That evening she waited in the lobby bar sipping a Diet Coke. When he arrived, he did not sit down but instead abruptly placed cash on the table to pay her bill and told her to follow him. She said she thought they were going to a conference room. They went to his suite, where she claimed he dispensed with seduction and forcibly and brutally raped her.

Sky News reporter Hannah Thomas-Peter, who Thompson shared the video with in 2018, asked her on air, "Do you think you might have encouraged him?"

"I don't think I purposely encouraged him," she answered, going on to explain that she was confused and scared. She wanted to make a sale and not offend him. She kept thinking, "What do I do?" Terror came over her, which she said she struggled not to show, when "at some point his whole affect changed and he looked like a predator. His eyes became dark."

The next morning she emailed a friend, "I fucked something disgusting and I did not want to. It happened." Weinstein and his lawyers believe this email confirms that their sex was consensual. Thompson's lawyer, who filed a civil lawsuit against Harvey, says it demonstrates her revulsion.

But Harvey controlled a piece of business she wanted for her company, so she returned to the Weinstein Company office. This time Thompson carefully made sure she was accompanied by a male executive. They eventually made a deal to assist on marketing a 2012 movie, the Margaret Thatcher biopic *The Iron Lady*.

Despite the dangers posed to his company by his sexual compulsions, plus his extravagant spending, his volatility, and the unseemly verbal brawls between the brothers at board meetings, Harvey was blind to any potential threat to his power from within. Whatever the problems, he continued to believe that without his unique eye and talent, the Weinstein Company would collapse.

But he failed to prevent Goldman Sachs from fleeing. Eager to escape serving on the dysfunctional Weinstein Company board, in 2013 Goldman Sachs partner Gaurav Bhandari, who often disagreed with Harvey, with the support of Goldman, requested that board observer Lance Maerov of WPP replace him as the lead outside director.

This became a consequential decision, for Maerov instantly became a serious irritant to Harvey and his docile board. Although Maerov had long attended board meetings as an observer, he remained shocked at the rancor at the meetings. Worse, as he now had access to the books, he was shocked by the business of the Weinstein Company. He became convinced that Harvey was distracted by the pursuit of power and personal wealth. He saw that Bob's Dimension movies made money; Harvey's often didn't. "Bob's movies cost nothing. They may have been garbage. But he didn't have to send fifty people to Cannes. Harvey's overhead was probably ten times what Bob's was, which is one thing that created the rift between them."

Maerov was persuaded that as a businessman, Harvey, unlike Bob, was "incredibly unsophisticated. If he was negotiating a deal on a picture, he was very sophisticated. In terms of thinking of the company from a financial or operational or organizational standpoint, he had no competence. He was not a manager. He did not understand the basic principles of profit and loss." If Harvey understood the principles of accounting, Bob conceded, "he ignored them. If a picture grossed thirty-eight million dollars, Harvey wanted it to hit forty million. He would spend more money on marketing than was budgeted for appearance's sake."

Still, because of his drive and talent, once again the Weinstein Company would bounce back from a spate of movie whiffs.

If quizzed by Lance Maerov, Harvey could instantly cite *The King's Speech* to demonstrate that he could still hit home runs. Although the company only distributed and did not produce this movie, it was nominated for twelve Academy Awards and captured the Best Picture Oscar in 2011, grossing a remarkable $414 million worldwide. *The King's Speech* centers on the future King George VI and his struggle to overcome a debilitating stammer with the help of an irreverent speech therapist, who becomes his close friend. After his brother abdicates the throne for the twice-divorced Wallis Simpson, he becomes a wartime king, giving speeches that bolster the nation through the ordeal of the Blitz.

Harvey's marketing campaign for the movie captured the hearts of moviegoers and Academy voters alike. "Harvey would find the message to communicate to Academy members with one sentence," marveled publicist Peggy Siegal, who over a long career represented many studios, including Harvey's. "He would put that sentence in an ad, a TV spot, a T-shirt. And that message would give you a thrill. For *The King's Speech* it was 'Find Your Voice.'"

The next year another picture he chose to distribute, *The Artist*, was

a box office home run despite the skepticism of his executives, reinforc-
ing his belief that the company's success was dependent on him. On his
way back from China, Harvey had stopped in France and screened the
movie, shot in black and white, which delves into the relationship between an older silent film star and a young actress as his career is
jeopardized by the shift to talking pictures. Convinced that a mostly
silent black-and-white movie starring unfamiliar French actors would
flop, American distributors had shunned it.

Smitten by the film—he was often susceptible to movies that were
love letters to the movies—Harvey brought it back to New York and
asked his vice president of production, Abby Ex, to screen it. "I watched
it," she said, "and I thought, 'What the fuck was he thinking?'"

When Harvey was focused, Bob Weinstein always had confidence in
his brother's movie taste. Soon after they acquired *The Artist*, Bob ad-
miringly said of his brother, "I remember asking Harvey what he thought
about when he screened a movie he didn't make. He said he never thinks
about the price they wanted but only whether he liked it or not. There
was a clarity in that thought. He felt if he liked it, hopefully the audience would like it. If it was black and white and silent, it didn't dissuade
him. He felt it was his obligation to market the movie and not let negatives stand in the way." The movie would go on to receive ten Academy
Award nominations, winning five in 2012, including Best Picture, Best
Director for Michel Hazanavicius, and Best Actor for Jean Dujardin.

But movie success could not overcome for Abby Ex the abusive
corporate environment Harvey created. After just three years at the
company, she was eager to flee what she called a "toxic environment. . . .
He constantly verbally abused me, he constantly was psychologically
torturing me," she recalls. He would curse her, call her names, threaten
to fire her. "It wasn't until much later that I started to experience the
effects of it—flashbacks, panic attacks," she said. Like a soldier returning from a war zone, she suffered from post-traumatic stress disorder.
Although she was never assaulted by Harvey, she understood how his
sexual abuse was related to his verbal abuse.

What convinced her she had to get out was riding in the back seat of a car with Harvey in Los Angeles when he asked a female colleague from New York sitting in the front passenger seat to play a movie on one of his four car screens. She couldn't get it to work. Harvey went into a rage and started punching the back of her seat. Bruised and furious, the woman brought a lawsuit against Harvey, which he settled, keeping her complaint silent.

Despite these awful memories, and her decision to expose Harvey in a recorded interview with Ronan Farrow, Abby Ex nevertheless extolls his talent: "He's a genius. . . . He knew what would resonate emotionally with people, and that's what he would use in the marketing materials. He just had a knack. . . . I learned more working for Harvey in those three years than I did in any of my other experiences combined." She believes what she learned from Harvey's tutelage has helped make her a successful producer.

With movies he distributed, Harvey Scissorhands might try but had fewer opportunities to edit. But with movies he produced, Harvey asserted himself, perhaps more so after the success of *The Artist* and *The King's Speech*. Meryl Streep recalled her experience in 2012 while making *The Iron Lady*, directed by Phyllida Lloyd. Harvey never appeared on the set, she said. "He would come in at the end and drive everybody insane. . . . He would come in at the last minute and decide that he knows how it should be edited."

Were his editing suggestions bad?

"In his mind it was to make it more commercially viable. Sometimes that's not why you make a movie about an aging prime minister." The director, she added, "did not accede to his demands."

Harvey saw another way to leave his fingerprints on a movie when he and Bob made a personally satisfying deal in 2013 to ally with the new co-owners of the Miramax library. The owner of the library, Colony Capital, agreed to rely on the Weinsteins to create sequels and TV series and stage productions from the hundreds of films that were now in the Miramax library. Without Harvey's relationships and creativity,

Colony Capital's Tom Barrack, Jr., said of the film library he owned, "we didn't have the art form. If I called Quentin Tarantino and said, 'I have a great idea how to do a *Pulp Fiction* TV series,' chances are it would be a very short conversation."

Yet as happened before, a companion of success was Harvey's inflated sense of his own power and the sometimes brutal way he exercised it. He was skilled at using muscle to achieve his ends. When Canadian documentary filmmaker Barry Avrich set out to make a documentary about Weinstein, Harvey tried to persuade him to drop the project. Avrich persisted. Harvey tried charm. Avrich persisted. Harvey reverted to threats to block his future work. Avrich persisted. In the end, Harvey got his way. By 2011, Harvey had induced his close friend James Dolan, CEO of the Madison Square Garden Company and owner of the New York Knicks and New York Rangers as well as IFC Entertainment, to buy *Unauthorized*, Avrich's Harvey documentary. The film was buried—released only in Canada and, Avrich wrote, "on IFC's obscure download service, SundanceNow.com, with zero publicity. You had to be a tracker dog with a keen nose to find it."

Although Avrich was disappointed his movie had been buried, he was oddly grateful that Harvey "answers my emails almost immediately."

When Avrich asked him for a copy of *The Imitation Game* to show for the Floating Film Festival in January 2015, he said Harvey responded, "Yes, but I'm going to need a favor in return."

"OK, what's the favor?"

"I don't know yet," said Harvey, sounding like Don Corleone telling the trembling funeral director who asked for a favor: "*Someday, and that day may never come, I would like to call upon you to do me a service in return.*"

· Gina Gardini, who supervised Miramax's operations in Europe, believed power had gone to Harvey's head and he "felt entitled. He expected to get a last-minute reservation at the best restaurants in Europe, to get prime ministers to return his phone calls. Harvey acted like a head of state." She recalled the time Harvey flew to Rome for the church wedding of Fabrizio Lombardo (a man she respected but who was disparaged inside the company) and the temperature in Rome climbed above 100 degrees. In Harvey's eyes it was like attending a wedding in a steam room. Gardini was flabbergasted when Harvey told her, "I want to talk to the pope to get permission to install air-conditioning."

Joel Klein, who was Mayor Bloomberg's reform-minded schools chancellor, had met Harvey only a few times in social settings when Harvey phoned and announced, "I want to talk to you about my driver's son." Harvey had supported Bloomberg and assumed the schools chancellor would be eager to accommodate a request. According to Klein, Harvey said, *My driver's son attended a public high school in the Bronx and he wasn't eligible to graduate because low grades kept him below the necessary credits. I want him to graduate with his class. I assure you that the boy will attend summer school classes to boost his credits.*

That won't work, Klein responded. *Our citywide policy is that students can no longer promise to attend summer school and automatically graduate; they had to first complete summer school classes to earn the extra credits.*

He wants to graduate in June with his class, Harvey insisted.

Not possible. It would violate citywide policy, Klein said.

Harvey lost his temper, Klein said, and he remembered Harvey's exact words: "I'm telling you this has to be done! You're fucking me. You'll pay a price for this."

Harvey did not get his way.

Harvey's version: "Nonsense. I had no driver who had a son in the Bronx, none of my drivers work in the Bronx, and I never said that to Joel Klein. I don't think Joel Klein said any of that." (Klein stands by his account of the phone call, which was recorded.)

Harvey got his way at his company because he got little pushback from his board of directors. The nine-member board was dominated by friends: his former best man Dirk Ziff, a billionaire; James

Dolan, who frequently bailed Harvey out of tight spots; Marc Lasry, the billionaire CEO of hedge fund Avenue Capital Group (who only joined in 2016); Paul Tudor Jones, the billionaire CEO of the Tudor Investment Corporation and founder of the Robin Hood Foundation, whose board members included Harvey and Lasry; and Tim Sarnoff, grandson of the founder of NBC and RCA, whose company, Technicolor, did business with the Weinstein Company. These five men were joined by another Harvey loyalist, Richard Koenigsberg, a partner in a firm that served as Harvey's accountants. A seventh reliable voting ally was obviously Bob Weinstein.

Isolated were the remaining two members, Tarak Ben Ammar, a Franco-Tunisian financier and media executive based in France who personally invested in the Weinstein Company, and Lance Maerov. Ben Ammar and Maerov were increasingly critical of Harvey, and since he was based in New York, Maerov played the heavy. Only later, on a few critical votes, would Harvey loyalists like James Dolan, Tim Sarnoff, and Richard Koenigsberg ally with Maerov and Ben Ammar.

As long as Bob Weinstein was allied with Harvey, the two brothers had voting control. However, Bob was increasingly estranged from his brother. David Boies, Harvey's attorney, who was also trusted by Bob and often doubled as the company attorney at board meetings, said that Bob Weinstein was deeply troubled by his brother's undisciplined spending and, perhaps more deeply, by the way Harvey condescended to him. "Harvey didn't treat Bob with the kind of respect you might think he would have with a brother who was his cochairman. That rankled Bob, who was always the younger brother, the perceived-to-be-less-successful brother." Told that a Miramax executive praised Harvey's ability to be charming, Bob responded, "Well he wasn't very charming with me."

Bob, like Harvey, could be a sometimes frightening man to work for. But after he stopped drinking in 2004 and endured a bitter divorce in 2012 after a twelve-year marriage to his second wife, Anne Clayton, a former book editor, Bob was a calmer person. Meryl Poster, a key production executive at both the Weinstein Company and Miramax, and a confidante of both brothers, had left Miramax in 2005 and rejoined Harvey and Bob at the Weinstein Company in 2011 to run their burgeoning television business. She noticed that Bob had changed. "Bob did a lot of work on himself," she said. "He improved his behavior. He stopped drinking. He was a good father to two girls." Although Poster would continue to try to protect Harvey when the press was circling him in 2017, she describes him after she returned in 2011 as Napoleonic. "He changed for the worse. He lost his sense of humor. He became a bigger megalomaniac. I was standing by the elevator with him one day and he said, 'No one should be on the elevator with me.' I said, 'What are you, out of your fucking mind?'" Poster noticed something else: "The brothers were not talking when I came. When I told Harvey he should make up with Bob he said, 'He doesn't want to. I tried.'"

So concerned was Bob about his deteriorating relationship with his brother that he asked David Boies to arrange a lunch for the three of them, knowing that Harvey treasured his counsel as much as Bob did. Boies chose the Grill Room of the Four Seasons Restaurant, a favorite of his and of the power brokers that kept coming to their table, much to Bob's annoyance. Harvey liked to be seen and congratulated by successful people who flocked to his table; Bob would be happy eating incognito at McDonald's. But Bob was happy to put himself in David Boies's hands this day because he was deeply concerned that Harvey increasingly acted "pissed off" about everything, even after winning an Academy Award. Before lunch he told Boies, "David, you're successful. You have a beautiful attitude toward life. Can you help Harvey?"

At lunch Boies set out to awaken Harvey to a sense of gratitude, an appreciation of how far from Queens he had come, pride that Miriam had now lived long enough to bask in the success of her boys. Boies spoke of his own childhood: "I grew up in a midwestern town in Indiana, and I learned the value of things, of family. And if somebody had asked me when I was a little boy, 'Can you imagine the greatest life you could possibly have led?' I never could have come up with the life I actually led. And I'm appreciative of that every day."

Bob sat ignoring his food, tears filling his eyes. Harvey kept eating, and then said, "I don't get it. What are you trying to say?"

Bob and Boies glanced at each other and laughed, helpless to do more. Harvey was too emotionally closed off to comprehend the message Boies had tried to convey.

The breach worsened. Its nadir came after a nasty incident that occurred in Harvey's small conference room just before Meryl Poster returned to the company. Bob and Harvey had offices in separate locations and each ran their own business. But they shared control of the parent company, and its costs and profits were pooled in the same balance sheet. It was over this balance sheet that they fought, with Bob incessantly complaining about Harvey's excessive spending. The brothers were meeting with a few other senior executives around the small table in the mini conference room adjoining Harvey's office.

Harvey, you're exceeding board-approved spending limits, Bob exclaimed.

We have a slate of powerful movies coming up, and we will have hits and a burst of new revenues, Harvey assured everyone in the room.

"I've heard enough. I'm outta here," Bob declared. As he rose from his chair, "Harvey leapt up and punched me in my face. I went backwards. Blood was pouring out of my nose. My glasses were broken. I was dazed." So were the few witnesses, frozen in their chairs.

Bob staggered upright without the help of any of the shocked onlookers and said, "I'm calling the police," and as he reached for the phone Harvey slammed his beefy hand over Bob's to stop him.

Bleeding profusely, Bob tried again to lift the phone. Harvey held it down. Aghast, the other executives in the room now rushed to collect tissues to staunch the bleeding.

Harvey reverted to the habit of thinking himself the victim. "I thought you were going to hit me. It was self-defense!"

"You're a liar," Bob shrieked back at him.

When I asked about this incident years later, Harvey insisted, "He started it. After Bob pushed me, I punched him. I regret punching him. It's not the first fight we had, and he was definitely the aggressor." That is not what the executives witnessed.

Word quickly spread through the office. One of Harvey's assistants phoned Abby Ex—this was a few months before she left the company—at an off-site meeting "to tell me not to come back to the office because Harvey punched Bob and there was blood on the floor."

The punch "was a real breaking point for me," Bob said. "It led me to thinking I eventually wanted to split the company in two and no longer be partnered with my brother." In fact, one change happened immediately: "David Glasser, as COO, became my buffer, so I didn't have to deal with Harvey." This was a seminal moment. Bob didn't believe his relationship with Harvey was quite as broken as the one between former Warner Brothers founders Harry and Jack Warner, who loathed each other and stopped speaking completely; neither would eat in the commissary if the other brother was dining there. But Bob felt deeply estranged from his brother. The question was whether he would, as he always had, follow Max Weinstein's admonition. Max had begged his boys to emulate the Kennedys, to be allies and support each other. Traditionally, the Weinsteins bickered and sniped at each other nonstop, but still managed to present a united front. "Nobody will separate the Weinstein brothers," Bob had vowed.

Now, Bob thought the sucker punch severed that alliance. Looking back, he said, "Over time my relationship with my brother deteriorated more and more, including his physical assault on me as well as our disagreements about financial matters and being responsible to our board about our budgets." Harvey challenges this, insisting in an email that what came between them was not his spending but Bob's jealousy of his prominence and success. "My constant winning was a source of tension with Bob."

Yet as cochairmen, Harvey and Bob had to communicate. It was decided that the brothers would ask two lawyers they trusted and who were friends, David Boies and Bert Fields, to serve as a bridge between them, as peacemakers, as their confidants in an effort to keep the cold war between the brothers from becoming hot. "We got so tired of arguing with each other," Bob said. "It wasn't like they were lawyers. They were mediators."

On occasion, Bob brought up the possibility of dividing the company in two. Harvey would respond, "Sure . . . I'll get everything, and you'll get nothing." Dimension may have been more profitable than Harvey's films, but Bob was wary of losing what he'd built.

Lance Maerov knew the tensions between Bob and Harvey were serious. He was getting signals that Bob was increasingly pulling away from Harvey. As a consistent Harvey adversary at board meetings, Maerov hoped to ally with Bob in order to harness Harvey. "At some point in early 2014 or late 2013," he recalled, "Bob would come to me on more than one occasion and say, 'You're making a lot of good points.'" If he could align with Bob Weinstein on a board vote, Maerov knew, they could liberate the company from Harvey's control, and there was a chance the company could be saved.

But brotherly ties were sturdier than they appeared.

"I'M THE CHAIRMAN OF THIS COMPANY!"

(2015)

Harvey spotted Ambra Battilana Gutierrez, twenty-two, a Miss Italy finalist, at a Radio City Music Hall reception for a show he was producing in the spring of 2015. He brushed past people to ask who she was. She told him she was a model. He offered to assist her career, took her cell phone number, and invited her to visit his Tribeca office, telling her to bring along her modeling portfolio.

Harvey's vanity was concentrated around his power, not his looks. He was still overweight, his stomach bulging beneath the T-shirts or suspenders he wore. In recent years, he seemed even less particular about his grooming, sporting a patchy gray-and-white stubble that sometimes trapped pieces of food from his last meal. This is the Harvey Ambra Battilana Gutierrez stared at when she arrived in his office and was offered a seat on the couch. Opening a portfolio of her modeling pictures, she started to discuss her work as a lingerie model. Harvey abruptly changed the subject to ask: *Are your breasts real?*

Before she could say anything, he lunged to fondle them. Frantically, she pushed his hands away. Harvey was undeterred. Later she would say he was like a dog in heat. He ran his hands under and up her skirt and tried to kiss her. Shaken, she raced from his office.

And then something unprecedented happened: Ambra Battilana Gutierrez notified the police.

Not a single one of Harvey's previous victims, in assaults ranging over decades, had ever taken this step. While Gutierrez reviewed with detectives what had happened, Harvey, unaware, called her cell phone and requested that they meet for a drink. The detectives whispered for her to agree to meet him the next night at the Tribeca Grand Hotel bar at 2 Sixth Avenue. They planned to hide a recording device on her.

As Harvey sat down in the dimly lit Church Lounge with its array of leather couches, undercover detectives spaced themselves around the room. Harvey told Ambra how beautiful she was. He told her he would help her career, as he had helped the many actresses he name-dropped, if she would also agree to be his friend. But he said he was desperate to take a shower and asked if she'd mind waiting for him in his penthouse suite. She accompanied him upstairs but lingered outside in the hallway and would not enter the suite.

"I'm telling you right now, get in here," he ordered, the recording revealed.

"What do we have to do here?" she asked.

"Nothing," he said impatiently, clearly irritated. He had a busy schedule, and she was disrupting it. "I'm going to take a shower. You sit there and have a drink."

"I don't drink," she said.

"Then have a glass of water."

"Can I stay here [meaning downstairs] at the bar?"

"No. You must come here now," he demanded.

"I don't want to. I want to go downstairs," she insisted. Looking directly at him, she asked why he had groped her breasts.

"Oh, please, I'm sorry, just come in," he demanded. "I'm used to that. Come on, please."

"You're used to that?" she said, sounding incredulous.

"Yes," he answered, before seeking to cajole her with this reassurance: "I won't do it again."

The police had their confession. Undercover cops swarmed around Harvey, who was startled. More so when an officer said, "Mr. Weinstein, we think you should come with us."

In the back of the police cruiser on the way to the station house, Harvey, as those with power often do, started dropping names. "I know Bill Bratton"—the police commissioner. "I'll call him up." These words, said former chief of detectives Robert Boyce, were included in the detailed report he received from his detectives. Though he tried not to show it, Harvey had reason to be scared. Over the many years he had assaulted women, never before had he been physically confronted by police officers.

Nor had he ever had to refute to his former or his current wife the accusations of women who publicly claimed he sexually abused them, because none did. When he was politely released by the police that night after a brief discussion of the potential charges he might face, Harvey knew he had to say something to Georgina. He told her a complaint would appear in the press and it was a lie meant to extract money from him and attract publicity for the model. Georgina believed her husband.

This was also the first time an alleged sexual assault by Harvey received press exposure. The next day, headlines blared: HARVEY ADMITS TO GRABBING A MODEL'S BREASTS. A POLICE STING NABS HARVEY WEINSTEIN. DISTRICT ATTORNEY INVESTIGATES HARVEY WEINSTEIN. Harvey may have built a favor bank with entertainment and gossip scribes over the years, but he could not suppress a juicy news story like this.

Reliable police sources described the evidence against Harvey as unassailable. At the time, one police official told me, "We believe her. She hadn't hired a lawyer when she came to the police station. Nor had she tried to extort money. She just seemed intent on punishing Weinstein and preventing him from doing this to another woman." The police announced that they were investigating, but when I pressed they would not release the incriminating Harvey tape. Nor would the lawyer she later hired agree to share its contents.

Harvey was not thrilled to take my call, but he did, desperate to manage this potentially damaging news story. He politely said the district attorney's office had warned him not to speak to the press. "I'm on a gag order. I'm not allowed to speak." He asked if I would meet with his defense team.

The meeting took place the next day in David Boies's conference room, and was attended by Boies; Harvey's criminal defense attorney Elkan Abramowitz, a former law partner of District Attorney Cyrus Vance; and expert security sleuth Jules Kroll, whose firm had long worked for Harvey. The glassed conference room was dominated by a long table piled with documents, including her past paramours and transcripts from the trial of Silvio Berlusconi, in which Gutierrez testified as a prosecution witness but the prosecutor dismissed her testimony as not credible. This type of information was gathered not just by Kroll but by Harvey's former $3 million author, Rudy Giuliani, whose security firm had been hurriedly given a contract by Harvey to dig up dirt on her. Former mayor Giuliani did not attend this meeting. Irrespective of questions about Gutierrez's past, the present question was whether Vance would bring charges against Harvey. I left that conference room wondering how Ambra Battilana Gutierrez's credibility would hold up when questioned by the D.A.

Within days, Harvey's team mounted a campaign to sabotage his accuser's reputation. He hired high-powered public relations executive Ken Sunshine of Sunshine Sachs, who placed incriminating stories about Gutierrez's "secret life" in the press, particularly in the gossip columns. Enraged, City University and State University students, faculty, alumni, and staff denounced him for "slut shaming" and signed a petition demanding that the governor remove Sunshine as a CUNY board member. Harvey also sought help from author Linda Fairstein, who founded and led the Manhattan district attorney's sex crimes unit from 1976 to 2002; Harvey had optioned one of her novels and promised

to make it into a movie. He directed his team to send all the negative information they had on Gutierrez to Fairstein. And in a decision
that astonished those who celebrated the work of the sex crimes unit
she pioneered, Fairstein arranged a meeting between her sex crimes
unit successor, Martha Bashford, and Harvey's criminal attorney, Elkan
Abramowitz.

Harvey thought he had successfully turned around the early wave
of negative press, but the one newspaper that kept pounding him was
the *New York Daily News*. He emailed his buddy James Dolan, a member of his company's board and a friend of *Daily News* publisher Mort
Zuckerman. The publisher, like Dolan, had attended Harvey's wedding
to Georgina. Harvey pleaded:

> *Dear Jim,*
> *   . . . the Daily News is killing me and I have got to talk to you*
> *tomorrow. Everybody else is being great—everybody, including*
> *networks. People are refusing to even run the story across the board.*
> *But only the Daily News—and Mort doesn't return my phone calls*
> *anymore.*

Despite his claims to Dolan, clearly Harvey was in real trouble. The
police had a tape, the D.A. was investigating, and pictures of the attractive model magnetized a press frenzy. His employees could see that Harvey was worried, unnerved, as he had been in 1998 when Zelda Perkins
threatened a lawsuit. While employees feared for the company, Harvey's
throng of female victims had reason to hope he would finally be held
accountable. And those in the movie industry, victimized for years by his
verbal abuse, were gleeful, privately rejoicing at the humiliation to come.

But once again, Harvey seemed to escape when District Attorney
Vance decided not to file charges against him, despite the confession
they'd obtained via the wire the police persuaded Gutierrez to wear.
Bruised by his office's failure to successfully prosecute a sex-crimes
case against Dominique Strauss-Kahn, then head of the International

Monetary Fund, after the credibility of his accuser, a hotel maid, was successfully assaulted by his criminal defense lawyer, Benjamin Brafman, Vance was understandably concerned that Gutierrez's credibility would not withstand a savage cross-examination by Harvey's lawyers. Critics of Vance claimed he caved both to Harvey's power and to campaign contributions he received from his former law partner, Abramowitz, and from Boies. Unnamed police officials complained to reporters that Vance should have prosecuted.

I set out to report a story for *The New Yorker* about Harvey's sexual assaults, as I had tried to do in 2002. I sought the police tape. I identified three additional women who might come forward to expose Harvey. The first was Ashley Judd. In a recent *Variety* interview, the actress described an unnamed major producer asking for a massage in his hotel suite, which sounded like Harvey's familiar opening gambit. I contacted Judd's public relations adviser to ask if it was Harvey, and after several calls, a couple of days later I was told Judd had nothing to say. Another call was to Angelina Jolie's agent to ask about rumors that earlier in her acting career Harvey tried to accost her. The agent called back the next day to say she had nothing to say. The third call was prompted by a column in *The New York Observer* by aspiring actress Jasmine Loeb. She described a prominent producer who goaded her into a massage and assaulted her in a hotel room at the Cannes Film Festival. I phoned Loeb several times to ask if the anonymous producer was Harvey. She spoke with me but declined to say.

Jennifer Senior, then a staff writer at *New York* magazine, was optimistic that Harvey was finally trapped. She tweeted after Harvey's arrest, "At some pt, all the women who've been afraid to speak out about Harvey Weinstein are gonna have to hold hands and jump." But Harvey's abuse had endured for so long without becoming a major news event that the very length of the silence was further inducement to silence; the task of challenging him seemed too daunting for one person to face alone. Years later, after Harvey was outed, all three women would confirm that it was Harvey who had sexually accosted them.

I was compelled to abandon the story when Ambra Battilana Gutierrez, reeling from the media attention, slipped away and signed an NDA with Harvey. Without the investigative arm of the district attorney behind her, Gutierrez was left with few resources to combat powerful Harvey. In exchange for $1 million, she signed an affidavit that did not mention Harvey grabbing her breasts or running his hand under her skirt, or the secretly taped encounter in the hotel. Instead, her signed affidavit declared:

> Mr. Weinstein's stated belief that he behaved appropriately is reasonable, and the meeting [in his office] was cordial and ended amicably.
>
> I reported my interactions with Mr. Weinstein to the police due to poor advice I received from friends and representatives. I regret how the events transpired and were portrayed in the media.

Seeing Gutierrez publicly withdraw, and imagining how brutal the insinuations and the legal claims against her would have been, one can imagine why Ashley Judd and others would stay silent. However, Gutierrez had a surprise. While her public affidavit was untrue and did not share what really happened to her in Harvey's office, she cleverly retained her copy of the police tape. This would in the future plague Harvey, for the tape with Harvey's raspy voice was more authoritative than any witness.

Meanwhile, there was fallout for the company from this highly publicized incident. "The first time I was told there were sex issues with Harvey was the Italian model case," Lance Maerov said. "It was the first time the board discussed this issue." Harvey denied the accusations and acted insulted. *How dare Maerov insinuate I might be lying? I carried this company on my back, didn't I?* The board overwhelmingly agreed that he had.

When the story first made headlines, Bob Weinstein worried that his brother was a sex addict. But he was reassured when the district attorney chose not to prosecute and the Italian model signed an affidavit asserting that Harvey behaved "amicably." With the single exception of Paris-based board member and investor Ben Ammar, Maerov was alone in not believing Harvey.

Maerov insisted on reviewing Harvey's personnel file. He wanted to know if there were other sexual abuse claims lodged against Harvey. He knew the company imposed a blanket NDA for all employees, requiring that they affix their signatures to a document pledging not to criticize the company or its top executives if it might impugn the "business" or the "personal reputation" of the Weinstein Company and its executives. Maerov did not know if Harvey sexually abused any company employees and compelled them to sign NDAs. He did not know who paid the $1 million settlement to Gutierrez. He didn't believe it was the company. But could he be sure? He wondered: Did Disney ever pay for a Harvey NDA? Maerov was deeply suspicious of Chief Operating Officer David Glasser, a forty-four-year-old former actor and producer who joined the company in 2008 to run international sales but who rose quickly to become known as "the third brother," a description applied to others over the years, none of whom lasted. Since the human resources department reported to Glasser, Maerov was convinced any harassment complaints against Harvey were buried by him. Maerov and Ben Ammar, and not a few company executives, deeply distrusted Glasser, believing he was duplicitous.

To Harvey, Glasser was a competent executive who Bob and he relied on to keep the trains running on time. Glasser was closer to Bob, but Harvey thought him fundamentally loyal to both brothers. The untrustworthy person was Lance Maerov, who Harvey came to see as the unbendable Inspector Javert in Victor Hugo's *Les Misérables*, zealously intent on persecuting Harvey.

Maerov knew the company was in financial peril. By 2015, he said, "the company had never turned a profit in ten years." He was incensed that the publicity generated by Harvey's behavior cost the company a major business opportunity. Unlike the fashion and brand-ing businesses, the TV division was successful, and the company had been on the cusp of negotiating the sale of its television division to England's ITV network for just under $1 billion. Although the TV business generated a profit, its profits did not mask the company's over-all losses. However, after the blistering headlines, ITV pulled out of the deal. (Officially, ITV denied it pulled out of the sale due to the Italian model controversy.)

Further turmoil lay ahead. The Weinstein brothers' contracts were due to expire that year, and it fell to Maerov, the new chair of the board's compensation committee, to negotiate the terms. His email ex-changes with Harvey that spring were contentious. Harvey insisted that to open his personnel file was an act of distrust. The close call with Gutierrez might have been only weeks before, but Harvey, ignoring the million dollars he paid to silence her, acted as if her statement wholly exonerated him. Although Bob Weinstein did not press Harvey as hard as Maerov did in asking his brother to release his personnel file, as an act of good faith, he released his own personnel file to Maerov's com-pensation committee. "It was clear to me," David Boies said, "that what Bob was doing was to pressure Harvey to turn over his personnel file." Harvey refused. And in the end, Bob and the board, save for Maerov and Ben Ammar, declined to demand that Harvey release his personnel file. On July 31, 2015, Bob's attorney, Bert Fields, dispatched a letter to Maerov "on behalf of Bob Weinstein" that accused him of engaging "in a relentless and unauthorized campaign to force Harvey Weinstein from the company" and asserting that "your conduct will cause the loss of Bob Weinstein as well and effectively end the company."

Harvey emerged from this challenge intent on projecting strength. He told Maerov, "Bob and I both could be a hot commodity on the open market, and I do not want to go."

Maerov heard something different, and like in a tennis match, a volley of five emails went back and forth. In the first, Maerov wrote: "You said you had no intention of signing a new contract in light of other opportunities in the market that you have or could have." But, Maerov added, because Harvey was blocking the release of his personnel file, the compensation committee—he and fellow board members Tarak Ben Ammar and new recruit Jeff Sackman—was prepared to offer contracts to Bob Weinstein and to COO David Glasser, potentially leaving Harvey in the cold. He pressed Harvey to come up with a business plan that might finally offer a return to investors who had received nothing over ten years despite a start-up investment of $1 billion. How come, he asked, there were no dividends?

Furious, Harvey wanted to bring the issue to a head and requested a conference call to discuss his contract with Maerov, Ben Ammar, who had invested a total of $30 million in the company, and Sackman, a film producer whom Harvey and Bob had wanted on the board. These were the three members charged with negotiating new management contracts. Harvey was agitated about not having a new contract. Harvey the salesman said he wanted "to discuss big stuff" on the conference call. He appreciated that there was a desperate need to shore up the company's finances by selling the TV division. What he didn't say beforehand was that among the "big stuff" he wanted to discuss was the removal of his brother Bob as a coequal.

Although Bob groused about Harvey's spending and narcissism and had broached the suggestion that the company be divided, he had never voted against Harvey on the board or even suggested he should be removed. Like a spouse in an abusive marriage, some days Bob was irritated with Harvey, some days he offered praise, other days he was stuck between rage and devotion. Two months before the Gutierrez incident, Bob—whose family feelings sometimes expressed itself in sentimental personal essays—wrote a piece for *The Hollywood Reporter* headlined, BOB WEINSTEIN'S LOVE LETTER TO BROTHER HARVEY. In this public celebration of their long partnership, he regretted the fact that they spoke less than they used to. He might have been using the platform as a megaphone to reach his brother. If so, it did not succeed.

A June 2, 2015, conference call was scheduled with Harvey and the three board members on the compensation committee. Though Bob's contract was also up for renewal, he was not invited to the call. Who was invited to join the call, to the surprise of the board members, was David Glasser, whom Harvey chose to include. They were puzzled because they knew Bob Weinstein relied on Glasser, and that in recent weeks Harvey suddenly and openly disdained Glasser for being beholden to Bob. But as Quentin Tarantino had said of Harvey and himself, Harvey believed he could convince anyone to do what he wanted if he put his mind to it. So he set out to woo Glasser, which turned out to be not very difficult. Glasser quickly switched sides, jumping to Harvey's team.

On the taped call, Harvey sounds brusque, annoyed, his voice loud and his impatience leaping through the phone, as if to say: *I'm a busy man. Let's get this over with quickly. Be quiet and listen to me.* He declared that he was frustrated with the board—by which he meant Maerov. He accused them of being "bullied by Bob and making decisions that offend me, and I'm the guy who can get you the money back." He insisted, falsely, that there were three offers on the table for their TV business, including ITV's offer (Maerov had been assured by an executive there that the offer was dead). He tried to spin these board members as he often spun the press: "We got a third offer. We can't tell you who it is. We're sworn to privacy. . . . It's a big, super company." Yet you—again he meant Maerov—"almost ignore me. And I'm making you all the money."

What money? Maerov and the others thought.

In his lengthy opening monologue, Harvey announced that David Glasser was seated beside him. "David Glasser and I have decided to act in tandem. If I don't renew, he doesn't renew, and we both leave together. So you can have Bob in charge of the company, or do what you need to do in that situation." This was a threat, which Harvey tried to soften with his next sentence: "The good news is that we want to renew. We just want to be able to talk to a board [that supports us]."

Harvey now dropped all pretense and for the first time spoke directly to the target of his rage: "Lance, it's just gotten antagonistic for

us. What I would like you to do—and I'm not saying this antagonisti-
cally, I swear to you I'm not," though he was nearly bellowing. He
lowered his voice: "I think that Dirk [Ziff] or Gaurav"—Goldman Sachs
managing director Gaurav Bhandari, who had chosen Maerov to replace him on the board when he was desperate to bolt the bruising
board meetings—"should come back and take your place for a few
months to smooth sides and get a deal done for the best interests of the
company." Once again he raised his voice, directly attacking Maerov's
efforts to get his personnel file after the humiliating Ambra Battilana
Gutierrez incident. "You've dragged me through the mud," he declared,
somehow blaming the request for the personnel file for the embarrassing public fallout from his arrest.

Gutierrez's name was never mentioned. Nor was Harvey's brief
detention by the police, or the scorching headlines. It also went un-
spoken that if Harvey were charged and convicted of a felony, his contract allowed the board to dismiss him. Harvey was accustomed to not
only eluding legal culpability for his alleged assaults, but to being in
command, as he was on this call. He now summarized what he expected in a new contract. Seeking to sound magnanimous, he began:
"David and I are not looking for raises. We're just looking for a bigger
share of the profits." He did not specify what share of the profits.

The three other board members on the call remained silent, though
they could have responded, *The company has not made a profit in its entire
ten years of life. It lost $60 million in just the past year.*

The two remaining issues, Harvey went on, were selling the company's TV business, and harnessing Bob, who he blamed for a weak
slate of Dimension movies and for the company's losses, and for becoming strange—surly, unresponsive, tempestuous, generally unhinged.
The challenge, Harvey said, was to "figure out a way to make Bob
happy without jeopardizing the profits of the company, because I can't
ask David"—or other executives signing up for profit participation—"to
be affected if Bob doesn't do the right thing. We have to do this until
Bob gets better. Bob had a very bad conversation with David. David

thought he was off the charts, just emotionally up and down, screaming and yelling." Harvey, the volume of his voice rising, blamed the board for not controlling Bob's behavior or curbing his Dimension movie flops, including *Vampire Academy*, *A Dame to Kill For*, and *One Chance*. In fact, Harvey's more costly movies were a bigger drain on the budget. Harvey continued his assault on Bob, asserting that he was unhinged without citing any examples. He shocked the three board members on the call when he abruptly yelled, "I'm the chairman of this company! Just stop!" The board members had said nothing.

In a quiet voice, Maerov now said, "We are six months into 2015. . . . We have no managers under contract for 2016." This was unusually late.

Suddenly, calm, polite Harvey reappeared: "David and I will renew through 2016."

"Under what terms?" Maerov asked.

"With no salary increase," Harvey said, treating this as a benevolent act.

Maerov started to inquire about what else Harvey wanted in a new contract, but the volatile Harvey returned to cut him off: "If this is a battle, Lance, you will lose!"

"This is not a battle," Lance responded.

"It is a battle," Harvey declared, "because you are going to make it a battle because you have to have me to get this deal done. So take a beat and stop being adversarial. We will renew. We will renew through 2016. We will take twenty-five percent of the profits, and maybe we'll ask for five more. And we'll give you very generous other terms and David and I will split up how we want the profits shared, and have the same share for Bob. . . . Then you will have the security of knowing what you have for 2016. So why don't you accept?"

"Harvey, Lance has not been in management," Tarak Ben Ammar, who was allied with Maerov but whose style was to finesse confrontations, politely interrupted. Board members share a fiduciary responsibility to act in the interest of shareholders. They choose the CEO, and fire them if they fail to perform. They raise questions about the

direction of a company. But they don't make daily management decisions.

"Lance has been compromised by Bob," Harvey countered, convinced that his brother and Maerov had conspired against him.

"We don't need an outsider" to replace Lance, Ben Ammar said.

"Let Lance take a vacation," Harvey insisted.

"Who is stopping you from doing a TV deal?" Maerov sharply
asked.

"All this sturm and drang with my brother," Harvey snapped.

It seemed clear to Maerov and his colleagues that Harvey was rattled by his near-death experience with Gutierrez. Harvey was also rattled by Bob, who, as a passionate advocate of the treatment he received
to overcome alcoholism, recently told Harvey to seek help for his sex
addiction, which made Harvey suspect Bob's loyalty. It was as if Harvey
had forgotten Bob's fealty, including the time when he made out personal checks for more than four hundred thousand dollars to Rowena
Chiu and Zelda Perkins in 1998 as part of their NDA settlement.

If David Glasser were in Bob's seat, Harvey now believed, he would
feel more protected. After all, as the New York State attorney general
would report several years later, the HR department at the Weinstein
Company reported to Glasser, yet not once did he allow sexual harassment complaints at the company to surface. Maerov believed the one
person in the company who certainly knew of Harvey's transgressions
was Glasser.

Seeking to be a peacemaker, Ben Ammar said he and the board were
in agreement: they wanted Harvey to sign a new contract. "There is no
issue about that. We would like a three-year contract. It's better for
management."

"It's not better for David and me," Harvey responded. He preferred
one year, which obviously would give him more future leverage. What
he didn't say, but these board members suspected, is that Harvey hoped
to extricate himself from the adversity of Maerov and Ben Ammar by
selling the company to a friend, who they guessed was Russian-born

billionaire Leonard Blavatnik, a media investor and a financial backer of some of Harvey's movies.

Since this was not a board meeting and there was no agenda, the discussion careened from topic to topic. "This is an insane conversation," Maerov interjected, in a surprisingly conversational voice. "Harvey, the governance says you and your brother have to agree on all expenditures. So let's forget pointing fingers at the board. The board doesn't manage the company."

Jeff Sackman now spoke for the first time, trying to refocus the conversation. He noted that Harvey asked for this meeting "to talk big stuff."

The "big stuff" now came out: Harvey wanted to demote Bob. He explained: "The situation is as follows: It is very difficult to work with Bob now. This would be a lot easier if he wasn't so paranoid. Stop treating him—after he lost the original five hundred million dollars invested in the company—as a coequal, OK?" Maerov was stupefied by this claim; he believed that most of the original money lost by the company—$500 million from investors and $500 million in debt—was squandered by Harvey with his impulsive investments and extravagant expenses. To Maerov, Harvey, not Bob, was the paranoid brother.

"We can't ignore what the brother of Bob is saying," Ben Ammar said, seeking common ground. "We have come to the conclusion that you and your brother can't continue. We need to separate the two companies. We know the shitty movies he's made. We don't have the authority to deal with it." He turned to David Glasser, who he privately thought played both sides, and said, "David, you have a delicate situation. But you can play an important role because they both want you. What did I hear from Bob: 'I won't renew unless . . .'"

Before Ben Ammar could finish his sentence, Harvey loudly interrupted, "But he's not getting David! Guys, let me run my company. It's my company. You better see it that way. If you don't, you're crazy. I will accommodate Bob. David is the lieutenant and right-hand president of the company. Bob should make two movies a year and two TV series and be happy." The meager number of movies and TV series would marginalize Bob. But Harvey didn't want to pass the news of this demotion on to his brother. He wanted the board to, telling them, "You must find the balls to do that, gentlemen."

How, Ben Ammar asked, did Harvey suppose his solution would be acceptable to Bob?

Fuck acceptable! Harvey had no patience for niceties. He wanted to bulldoze his brother: "We solve it by putting him in a nice place. Say, 'Here's two movies, two series. Thank you. Be an independent producer. Cochairman. Walk around all day like you own the place. Fantastic. Be on the board. Be your combative, miserable fucking self!'" But Harvey, who relished confrontations, shied away from confronting Bob.

Bob's pugilistic attorney, Bert Fields, would fight this, Ben Ammar warned.

"You do it," Harvey bellowed. He wanted the board to establish "guidelines" for Bob to follow. Harvey's agenda was crystal clear to Maerov and his colleagues. This was a coup. Not just against Bob Weinstein, but against any member of the board who questioned Harvey.

Jeff Sackman stepped in to try to sum up, putting a more generous gloss on this diatribe: "What Harvey is saying is, 'The board has to act against Bob and don't continue to be irresponsible. But I, Harvey Weinstein, don't want Bob to be banned but to save face.'"

"Exactly," Harvey said. "Thirty percent of my and David's time is spent putting out [Bob's] fires. I am asking the board to find a solution that keeps Bob's dignity." Harvey surprised the three board members by announcing that he was pleased with the call. He signed off with this salutation: "We'll get it done."

In reality, the conference call got little done. There was no agreement on contracts, on sharing the nonexistent profits, on whether to replace Lance Maerov as the contract negotiator, on reducing Bob's role or giving him guidelines. The level of duplicity was astounding. Harvey wanted his brother murdered, but he didn't want blood on his hands.

Contractually, Bob Weinstein had equal power with Harvey, yet his fate was being discussed at a meeting he was not invited to. David Glasser, who served as the company's chief operating officer and who had told Ben Ammar days before that he was aligned with Bob, was now aligned with Harvey. Harvey excoriated Bob for the company's losses that Maerov and Ben Ammar quietly blamed on Harvey. Maerov and Ben Ammar trusted each other but knew Harvey's loyalists on the board distrusted them because Harvey did. Board member Jeffrey Sackman trusted them, but he was so alarmed by the June 2 conference call that he resigned from the board later that summer. Nor was Ben Ammar telling the truth when he told Harvey on the phone that he hoped he'd sign a new three-year contract. He and Maerov were flattering Harvey to conceal their real agenda: they hoped to either sell the company that year or force it to declare bankruptcy.

Asked years later about the call, Harvey denied what he clearly said on the taped call. When I asked why he wanted Bob demoted, he dispatched this email: "Not true. HW wanted to separate his end of the company from Bob's, that is all. HW thought BW would do better without HW opinions."

Looking back on the call, Lance Maerov believed that Harvey's loud roars and accusations were a deliberate dance around the issue he didn't want to address: releasing his personnel file. Maerov suspected the file would reveal other instances of Harvey's abuse of women, other NDAs. It was highly unusual for the head of a company's compensation committee to be denied access to an executive's personnel file. David Boies and Bert Fields had even sent him threatening letters to dissuade him from pursuing the matter.

At a screening of a company movie at the AMC Loews theater on the Upper West Side around this time, Maerov left his date in her seat before the movie started and walked to the back of the theater, where Harvey was standing. Maerov offered a courteous hello. "Harvey winds up with his right hand and starts to throw a punch," Maerov said. Harvey did not follow through, but he put his larger body near Maerov's and menacingly threatened, "I'm gonna kill you!" Shaken, the next day Maerov dispatched an email to Harvey announcing that he would not be bullied by him.

After the June 2 conference call, Maerov persisted in asking to open up Harvey's personnel file. Boies, who was Harvey's adept protector, was ready. A brilliant litigator, Boies had one flaw that colleagues reluctantly acknowledged: he was too fiercely loyal to clients and was fervently determined to win. With a near photographic memory, he loved winning at the blackjack tables in Vegas because he could remember the cards dealt to all the players. Whether his client was the government claiming Microsoft was a monopoly, or Elizabeth Holmes perpetrating the scam of Theranos, or Harvey Weinstein seeking to evade the cost of his transgressions, Boies was ferociously competitive. In the case of Holmes or Harvey, it would be said that he was too loyal, too ferocious.

At first, Boies suggested in an email to Maerov, "I will agree to review Harvey's personnel file and, if I am able to provide a written opinion that there is nothing in there that disqualifies Harvey from continuing to serve as co-CEO, there will be no further requests for personnel materials." As Harvey's attorney, Boies did not qualify as an independent auditor, and his proposal was rejected. Boies then countered by offering to turn the file over to H. Rodgin Cohen, seventy-six, the respected senior chair of Sullivan & Cromwell. Realizing this was the best they could do, Maerov relented.

Cohen was not exactly a neutral party, since he had represented the company in negotiating the sale of its library to Goldman Sachs. That fact was not noted. Boies said Cohen was willing to review Harvey's file, and if there were red flags in the file, to share them with the board. H. Rodgin Cohen was treated as if he would be the voice of God.

In a September 4, 2015, letter to the company's law firm, H. Rodgin Cohen reported that after reviewing Harvey's personnel file, "there are no unresolved claims" and "no pending or threatened litigation." This does not, of course, account for any NDAs that had been negotiated and signed—which could reasonably be interpreted as red flags themselves, especially if there were a large number. (Cohen did not respond to calls or emails from me.)

What Cohen did not report was that his son was an executive at the Weinstein Company. Cohen tried to cover his tracks by sending a personal voicemail to Philip Richter, a partner of the company's law firm, Fried, Frank, Harris, Shriver & Jacobson, reporting that "my son works for Harvey." Anxious, he followed up that afternoon with a handwritten note:

> *Phil—*
>
> *Want to make sure that you received my voicemail message this morning . . .*

NO MORE
"BOBBY" WEINSTEIN

(2015–2016)

L ate that summer, and without fanfare, Harvey's plan to sabotage Bob vanished, like smoke. The brothers, with an assist from David Boies, made a peace pact that at the time Lance Maerov didn't comprehend. He believes Bob forged a truce because "deep down he didn't believe there was a company without Harvey. And that Boies, who was a consigliere to both brothers, helped convince him." It was true: both the brothers and Boies believed that without Harvey the company would collapse.

The truce did not come without struggle. That summer Bob delivered to Boies a long and searching letter to be passed along to his brother, sometimes accusatory, sometimes grieving, that also seemed to betray a clear awareness of the gravity of Harvey's sexual misbehavior:

There have been instances of behavior that I and David Boies have had to assist u with in getting out of trouble. I am referring to a situation in England. In that case and every and I mean every time you have always minimized your behavior, or misbehavior, and always denigrated the other parties involved in some way as to deflect the fact of your own

misdeeds. . . . I am not waiting for your recovery to guide my decisions
any more. . . . Slowly I have watched you get worse over the years to the
point where from my point of view there is no more person or brother
Harvey, that I can recognize, but merely an empty soul acting out in any
way he can to fill up that space and hurt that will not go away.

Bob asked Harvey to give him and Boies his word that he would
seek counseling for what Bob considered his sex addiction. "There are
other behaviors that I will not describe that u are aware of that need to
be addressed," he wrote.

At the close, Bob made a curious comment: "As regard to other
misbehaviors that do not affect our company I have no intention or care
to police u or call u out in any way. That's not my job." He signed it,
"Love Brother, Bob."

Asked what he meant by "misbehaviors," Bob said he was referring
to Harvey's "numerous affairs."

Maerov was stunned by the renewed display of comity between the
brothers. Equally stunning, David Glasser in late July announced that
he was resigning, claiming that he was paid considerably less than com-
parable executives at other firms, and that he believed the Weinstein
brothers were hampered by directors like Maerov and others who were
subverting their ability "to move the ball forward." Yet one month later,
Harvey and Bob rehired Glasser at a much bigger salary. Still months
later, the brothers came together and agreed that David Glasser was a
slimy double agent and blamed him for helping sabotage their relationship. This was odd because Bob was unaware of the June 2 conference
call—he insists he did not learn of the conference call until I asked him
about it six years later—and therefore of Glasser's role alongside Harvey. Nor was Bob aware of the harsh things his brother said about him.
Although neither says they remember why, both brothers simply say
they came to believe Glasser was duplicitous.

It is likely that Miriam, who was then eighty-seven, also played a
role in mediating a truce between Harvey and Bob. Once when they

were yelling at each other in the back of Harvey's car, remembers Sayed Khorshed, Harvey's longtime and devoted driver, "Harvey was not listening to Bob." Sayed, who often drove Miriam Weinstein and thought she was "a wonderful lady," was concerned that Bob and Harvey might get into a fistfight and shared this concern with one of Harvey's longtime assistants. The assistant advised, "Call Miriam. She'll take care of it."

Harvey and Bob received their new contracts, but they were amended. Maerov had pushed for and the board agreed to add a Code of Conduct for its executives, which most companies have. But the code lacked real bite. If Harvey abused women, he faced only a fine: escalating from $250,000 to $1 million that he must pay if his "misconduct" required the company to make payments "to a person damaged by such misconduct."

Wily Bob Weinstein knew enough not to take his brother's word for granted. He got another alteration in the Weinstein contracts that did not seem momentous at the time but would turn out to be.

At Bob's urging, and with the support of Maerov, Tarak Ben Ammar, and David Boies representing Harvey, it was agreed that Harvey or Bob could be instantly terminated for violation of the Code of Conduct. This altered the previous contract, which stipulated that they could be dismissed only if convicted of a felony involving moral turpitude and after all appeals were exhausted. The new contract established that Harvey or Bob could be dismissed if either company cochairman (Bob or Harvey) joined a board majority in voting against the other.

"Harvey agreed," said Boies. "Why? Because he thought the company would never fire him. He was the franchise. He wanted to make peace."

Maerov, who had hoped Bob would turn on Harvey, was disappointed. "Bob seemed to make a deal," Maerov said, "that he would support Harvey if Harvey got help for his sex addiction." In fact, Bob turned on Maerov. In an email to his brother, Bob expressed pleasure that Harvey had spoken to the ITV people and possibly restored the

TV deal. Harvey clearly had not, but Bob was anxious to be on Harvey's team and to reinforce a more pro-Harvey board of directors. He wrote:

> *Harvey, this is utterly fantastic. It isolates Lance as an unreliable actor in everything. If we put the right board deck together, the right contract, and we get letters like this of support from [others] . . . we will win the board vote.*

Lance Maerov thought he understood why Bob Weinstein fell in and out of Harvey's magnetic field: "Harvey's narcissism took its toll on Bob's self-confidence. Bob has been conditioned to believe he's inferior to Harvey."

Did Bob think Harvey beat him down psychologically, I asked years later?

"Of course," Bob answered. "He beat everyone down like that. Rather than 'beat' I'd use the word 'wore' everybody down. He's a toxic person, and reason and logic was not usable against illogical behavior. So the only solution to that was detachment. That's why people get divorced."

With Bob back in his corner, Harvey had less reason to worry about dissidents on the board. In October, Harvey and Bob signed their new three-year contracts. There was no profit-sharing provision.

But Harvey took no victory laps. He was anxious about something else. Jules Kroll, whose firm had sleuthed for Harvey over many years, observed, "He was obsessed with being found out" as a sexual aggressor. Despite Harvey's contention that his sex was always consensual, after the Gutierrez near miss, Kroll said, "he was constantly in a panic. Yet he couldn't stop." And by stop, he meant stop chasing and potentially abusing women.

For only the third time—the first being Rowena Chiu and Zelda Perkins, the second being Ambra Battilana Gutierrez—Harvey had reason to panic. He learned in the latter part of 2015 that Ben Wallace of *New York* magazine was investigating his abusive sexual behavior.

Wallace had phoned Gina Gardini, who supervised Europe for the company, and she immediately asked Harvey if he wanted her to speak with Wallace. Harvey told her it was "a hatchet job," she said, but urged her to have an off-the-record conversation to "learn what the piece was about. He said, 'I'll have someone help you out. You have to talk to my friend.'"

His "friend" was from Black Cube, the private Israeli security firm populated by many former Mossad agents. Harvey had learned about the firm from former Israeli prime minister Ehud Barak, and he now hired them to do more aggressive sleuthing than Kroll's firm performed. The Black Cube operative flew to Rome to brief Gardini on how to extract information from the journalist. Gardini refused to allow her to sit in on her phone call with Wallace, who honestly told her he was investigating allegations of Harvey's abusive sexual behavior. Gardini dutifully reported to Harvey. "I told him what the piece was about and I had no information when the piece was coming out." Unable to get any victims to go on the record after many weeks of reporting, Wallace's efforts ended in frustration, as had others'. Harvey relaxed.

And then Lauren O'Connor, a promising young literary scout at the Weinstein Company, wrote a memo on November 3, 2015, circulating it to senior executives.

There is a toxic environment for women at this company. I have wanted more than anything to work hard and succeed here. My reward for my dedication and hard work has been to experience repeated harassment and abuse from the head of this company. I have also been witness to and heard about other verbal and physical assaults Harvey has inflicted on other employees. I am a 28 year old woman trying to make a living and a career. Harvey Weinstein is a 64 year old, world famous man and this is his company. The balance of power is me: 0, Harvey Weinstein: 10.

O'Connor's job at the company was to scout for books that could be turned into films, yet Harvey would order her to meet with aspiring actresses who had personal appointments with him and escort them to his suite. He instructed her to wait to greet them when they came back down to the lobby, and "facilitate introductions" to agents and managers and the casting department at the Weinstein Company. Instead of scouting books, she was, she wrote, "managing Harvey's past and present sexual conquests." O'Connor knew enough to believe if she complained to HR it would be buried. Therefore she spoke out in a companywide memo. For the first time in his four-decade career, an employee who still worked for him had openly accused Harvey. He could not suppress the information, which included damaging revelations about how some employees were tasked with keeping Harvey sexually satisfied. There could be no ignoring the memo.

O'Connor's complaint was shared just a few months after Harvey's deal with his brother. Bob Weinstein felt betrayed. Harvey had pledged to arrest his bad behavior and to seek counseling for his sexual compulsions. Enraged, Bob circulated O'Connor's pained words to company directors. The O'Connor memo "was a big deal," remembers David Boies, "because Bob got his hands on that memo and sent it to the board." In fact, Bob thought it too inflammatory to forward, and so he dictated a memo asking them to come to the office to read it. He waited a half hour before informing Harvey. When Harvey learned what his brother had done, Boies continued, he "went ballistic." Bob had also shared the memo with the board rather than the company's in-house counsel, Charlie Prince, because he feared Prince was intimidated by Harvey and would bury it.

When the board met to discuss O'Connor's claims and Lance Maerov called for an investigation, he was shocked when Harvey's close friend James Dolan backed Maerov. "I almost fell out of my chair. Bob agreed. And Richard Koenigsberg went along." For the first time, he had a majority of the then nine-member board. Boies was told the board wanted an investigation. To head it off, he assuaged them by saying former sex crimes prosecutor Linda Fairstein (who, unbeknownst to them, Harvey had recruited to counter Ambra Gutierrez just months before) would conduct an inquiry.

Before Fairstein could complete her assignment, Harvey's team—Boies insists he did not negotiate this or any other NDA—induced O'Connor to sign an NDA, as Harvey had done with so many others before. The sum of money to O'Connor in exchange for signing the NDA remains secret. But it served as her paid severance from the company. Boies informed the board, Maerov remembered, "that O'Connor had withdrawn her complaint. But what Boies did not say is that she did not withdraw her claim" of abuse. O'Connor, who bravely blew the whistle on Harvey, left her job, lost her privacy, and has endured years of expensive therapy. Today she has a good job at a media company but declined to speak of her travails, and in a brief email exchange requested that the company where she works not be named.

The issue, like O'Connor, went away—for the time being. But so, finally, did James Dolan. He'd had enough. He resigned from the board in 2016. A close business associate of Dolan's said he came to feel his friendship with Harvey was one-sided. Dolan had dutifully served Harvey's interests. Harvey had asked him to invest in TWC, and he did. He complied with Harvey's request to manage the Weinstein Company's film library that Dolan had acquired, also at Harvey's request. He agreed to buy, and bury, the Barry Avrich documentary Harvey wanted suppressed. And he invited Harvey to cohost concerts at Madison Square Garden. What had he gotten in return? In 2016, said a close Dolan friend, "Jim wrote a handwritten letter and had it delivered to Harvey. The letter said he felt used." Dolan expected that Harvey would want to talk it out. Harvey didn't, the friend continued. Days later, Harvey called and said simply, "I got your letter." He didn't discuss the letter. "Before Harvey hung up, he asked Jim for another favor. That was the last time they spoke."

Dolan was disgusted with Harvey's narcissism. Perhaps he also was concerned Harvey would damage his reputation. He certainly appeared to be burdened by guilt. Despite his wealth, Dolan seems as passionate about his amateur band, JD & The Straight Shot, as he is about his sports teams. A *Men's Journal* reviewer called him "a cosplaying bluesman . . . it's possible he can't play the guitar," and *The New York Times* mentioned his "karaoke grade" singing, but with his clout as the executive chairman of Madison Square Garden Company, he was able to persuade acts like the Eagles and the Allman Brothers to let his band open for them, and some of his songs were featured in Harvey's films. After Harvey was exposed in 2017, Dolan chose to speak out about his old friend and his own guilt via an angry, lachrymose song—"I Should Have Known"—he composed and performed in modest venues:

We were friends
Talked for hours without end
About his latest story
How to deal with fame and glory
All the girls who adored him
Catered to his every whim
Nothing he could lose
All he need to do was choose

I should've known
I should've known
I should've thrown
Myself across his tracks
Stopped him from these vile attacks
I should've known
We believed and didn't see
Through the lies he told us all
They led him to his endless fall
I should've known

Most of the Weinstein Company's board of directors could join James Dolan in his refrain. Certainly by 2015, the board was aware that Harvey had signed NDAs with two women—Ambra Battilana Gutierrez and Lauren O'Connor (though they were not aware of preexisting ones, like the agreement with Rowena Chiu and Zelda Perkins). And as 2015 neared its end, the board was aware that celebrities were no longer getting away with sexual abuse. After many months of reports that he abused women, Bill Cosby was indicted in December 2015, and later convicted, after a total of fifty women came forward to claim he not only sexually abused them but often drugged them before he raped them. After Gutierrez and O'Connor, if the board was paying attention they should have known Harvey was a ripe target.

Yet that same year the board had entered into a new contract with Harvey. As noted, Harvey could be terminated only if a majority of the board, which must include Bob Weinstein, agreed his behavior "caused serious harm to the Company." Thus the one person with the power to bring Harvey down was his brother. Although Bob knew that Harvey aggressively slept around and may have been a sex addict, Bob insists he had no idea at this time that Harvey was a rapist. He signed the personal checks in 1998 to Zelda Perkins and Rowena Chiu, he said, because Harvey convinced him he had a consensual relationship with Chiu and when he broke it off she threatened to tell Harvey's wife. Nevertheless, Bob would be accused of serving as an enabler in civil lawsuits by those who assert that he was co-CEO of both Miramax and the Weinstein Company when Harvey was incessantly chasing and abusing women. Bob has forcefully challenged the claim.

At the time, Harvey remained confident he could manage his risk. He was certain the NDAs would not be broken because signees would understand that he might pursue them as aggressively as the harsh terms allowed. And he wielded weapons beyond relying on his lawyers. Harvey knew his accusers would fear his power. In Hollywood, it was real power. He could make or break a career. When Miramax entered the fray in 1979, about one hundred movies opened in theaters annually; by 2016, the number enjoying wide release in multiple theaters was roughly the same. "Suppose there are five meaningful acting jobs per movie: that means there are only about 500 meaningful acting jobs a year," Ben Thompson, who composes a brilliant daily business blog (stratechery.com), mostly focused on digital and media companies, wrote soon after news of Harvey's sexual abuse was exposed. "Weinstein was a gatekeeper, presented with virtually unlimited supply while controlling limited distribution." If you were an actor, director, or screenwriter with Oscar dreams, Harvey was an especially important gatekeeper.

His secrets also stayed secret because in the movie business, abnormal male sexual aggression was thought to be common, fit for private whispers but not public shame. This was Hollywood's culture of silence.

I n November 2016, Harvey and Bob lost Miriam Weinstein. She was ninety. The words she chose for her tombstone were not surprising for a brassy lady: "I don't like the atmosphere or the crowd."

Miriam loomed over her sons until the very end, as Bob's essay in *The Hollywood Reporter* about her made clear. "I didn't want to hurt my mother's feelings," he wrote about his relationship with his brother. "My mother was always upset that Harvey and I were fighting."

With Miriam gone, the brothers grew still further apart. Bob arranged a private funeral for their mother at Frank Campbell's funeral home on upper Madison Avenue. Harvey wanted to invite celebrities; Bob put his foot down. Harvey organized a separate memorial service upstairs at the Tribeca Grill, inviting some celebrities who knew her, including Quentin Tarantino and Anna Wintour, and celebrities who didn't. He arranged for a tribute from Gwyneth Paltrow, who did know and care for Miriam, to be read. He padded attendance by inviting members of the staff.

Bob and his children thought Harvey was desecrating Miriam's memory and didn't attend. "It was super weird," remembered Meryl

Poster, who had long been Harvey's movie production deputy and was asked to speak. Agnès Mentre, who liked Miriam, thought the event was "quite fake, a Harvey contrivance that was more about him than Miriam." Harvey's behavior brought to mind an observation Alice Roosevelt Longworth once made about her father, Teddy Roosevelt: "He wanted to be the bride at every wedding, and the corpse at every funeral."

Bob was disgusted by what he saw as the vulgarity of using the occasion to broadcast Harvey's connections and draw sympathy, and Miriam was no longer there to soften his fury. "No question," David Boies said, "that Miriam while she was alive was a brake on the brothers falling apart. She was a very powerful person, and they both wanted her approval. They didn't want to disappoint her. Remember in *The Godfather* how Michael would not kill his brother Fredo until his mother dies." Harvey agreed: the death of Miriam collapsed a bridge between the brothers. "My mother was a strong person who helped keep the family together," he told me.

Harvey was not above using his mother's death in the service of his sexual appetite. One of his alleged rape victims, aspiring actress Jessica Mann, would testify that Harvey was crying on the phone when he pleaded with her to visit. "He needed to be consoled for his grief, and he wanted to talk to me because I understood grief," she said to a jury under oath, noting that he knew that her father had died the previous year. Upon arriving at his hotel she was shocked. "When I got there he was naked on the bed. All he wants to do is something sexual."

Harvey and Bob were on the brink of war, and not just over Miriam. Their verbal battles could be startlingly ugly. More than once Bob had heard Harvey yell at him, "You're a fucking idiot! Mom was right." While Bob was furious at Harvey for the way he paraded Miriam's death, the major source of tension between the brothers in 2016 remained economics. One Weinstein Company employee recalls, "The company didn't have the money to operate the way they wanted to. The company was virtually bankrupt." Bob castigated Harvey for not being focused on the business and for being out of the office so frequently. It would later be revealed that between June 19, 2013, and September 8, 2017, Harvey traveled outside the United States a total of 243 days.

Maerov, a pesky mosquito, regularly buzzed in Bob's ear about how Harvey wantonly spent corporate funds. Maerov cited the seventy-five thousand dollars Harvey charged the company to purchase dresses from his wife's company as a gift for a Qatari prince. "He was running his lifestyle through the company," Maerov exclaimed, his round face glowing bright red with indignation. The gift of dresses for the Qatari prince "was a bribe to get him to invest in what Harvey called 'The Animation Fund.'" Maerov shared with Bob news that Harvey paid a gratuity of thirty thousand dollars to the crew of a ship on which he vacationed and charged it to the company. "We made him reimburse the company," Maerov said.

Harvey's lawyer, Philip Richter, denied Harvey used corporate funds for his personal expenses. Yet he sent a letter to the board acknowledging that Harvey had reimbursed the company for personal expenses.

Maerov learned of what appeared to be another ethical transgression. Harvey had long served on the board of amfAR, an organization devoted to curing AIDS, and he had been chairman of the organization's annual charitable fundraiser during the 2015 Cannes Film Festival. At this fundraiser, Harvey arranged for items to be auctioned. But in return, Harvey stipulated that six hundred thousand dollars of the money raised would be given to the nonprofit American Repertory Theater in Cambridge, which had done a trial run of a musical Harvey was producing based on Miramax's modest 2004 hit, *Finding Neverland*. What Harvey didn't share, as Megan Twohey would report in *The New York Times*, was that the theater agreed that if third parties donated a total of six hundred thousand dollars toward the show, Harvey and the show's investors would be compensated this amount. If they failed to raise the six hundred thousand dollars, Harvey and the investors would get zero back.

But Harvey wanted more. Reflecting the financial pressures he was under at the Weinstein Company, he wanted amfAR to split the money raised at the Cannes auction on a fifty-fifty basis. Put another way: Harvey was using a charitable AIDS organization event to reimburse himself, building cultural goodwill as a philanthropist while skimming off the top. In the end, William D. Cohan would write in *Vanity Fair*, "Weinstein recouped all but around $100,000 of the $2.05 million he had given to" the American Repertory Theater.

His investment in Broadway plays, the extravagant time he spent on amfAR and philanthropic and political ventures, and his ethical lapses and excessive expenditures confirmed for Bob that Harvey was hopelessly distracted. Relations between the brothers became so rancorous that David Boies and Bert Fields, who had been tasked with improving communication between Harvey and Bob, started serious negotiations with the brothers to split the company in two, an idea broached on the June 2 conference call before the brothers achieved their brief armistice. After the Lauren O'Connor memo and Miriam's death, this effort to divide the company was speeded up. "There's a written document that set up a new Dimension and a new Weinstein Company," Boies said. "Bob would be chairman of a new Dimension, Harvey would be chairman of a new Weinstein Company. They divided the employees between them, and they divided the libraries and projects between them." Harvey would have zero financial interest in Dimension, and Bob would have zero stake in the Weinstein Company. But the detailed plan, prepared by the law firm Cravath, Swaine & Moore, collapsed. The company lacked the liquidity to split in two. And it was difficult to unwind deals already signed. Had they succeeded in splitting the companies, Bob Weinstein thinks Dimension would be in business today. He boasts of the "over two billion dollars in worldwide box office" his movies generated.

The company's wheels slammed into additional potholes in 2016: there were more layoffs of staffers, and the forced departure of David Glasser. Desperate for cash, the company contemplated selling the hundreds of titles in its film library. Yet Harvey still believed he could talk his way out of this, his biggest-ever business jam. With a smile, he declared to *The Hollywood Reporter*, "But, no bullshit, I think the company financially is the best it's ever been right now."

Finding Neverland did not survive, closing with a thud in July 2016. But Harvey had survived, narrowly, once again. He now knew his reckless treatment of women was a future menace. He did not know that his brother was too.

THE DAM OF SILENCE
COLLAPSES

(2016–2017)

Harvey's instinctive default posture was always to be mistrustful of others, to look for their angle, their hidden agenda, their plan to *screw* him. "He trusted no one," says Jonathan Gordon, who started as Harvey's assistant in the early 1990s and worked for him for fifteen years.

By the latter part of 2016, Harvey's distrust curdled into rampant paranoia. He doubled down on Black Cube, the intelligence company dominated by ex-Mossad agents. Harvey knew he had a bull's-eye on his back. Black Cube's mission was to be his chief spy, learning who might attack him, fishing for information about their plans by dispatching operatives to befriend suspects, and then betray them, as an agent would betray Rose McGowan.

On one level, Harvey was anxious about the business of the Weinstein Company, which by now was on life support. Even David Boies concurred with Lance Maerov's dire financial calculations that the company had lost all of the $1 billion initially invested, and "lacked the money to make new films Harvey wanted to make." Harvey's impulsive investments in Halston and other fashion, theater, and cable ventures had flopped. Not since *The Artist* in 2011 had the studio introduced a hit movie, and they had released hundreds.

But Harvey truly believed his golden gut could extract the company from its woes. He was in denial about that. But solving the company's economic crisis would not resolve his own. Whatever business anxiety he had was subsumed by a mounting terror of exposure. For four decades he had muzzled people outside the company and within it; they dared not discuss any sort of violence they'd experienced at his hands, whether it was verbal, psychological, physical, or sexual. The NDAs employees were required to sign as a matter of course assured this—and as with Lauren O'Connor, a further NDA tailored to the situation offered extra protection. Since none of his victims outside the company were allowed to keep copies of their NDAs, if they wanted to go public it would be their word against his. He was the one with the press and political connections. He could slut shame them as conniving publicity hounds who once sought to sell their bodies for a movie job. Or he'd sue them and crush them with the legal costs.

Besides, for many years Harvey had been reassured by the knowledge that males in the media business were long permitted their sexual pleasures, granted or coerced. But it was a new day. Bill Cosby would soon be behind bars. In July 2016, Fox News anchor Gretchen Carlson filed a sexual harassment suit against Fox News CEO Roger Ailes for insisting on sex in exchange for airtime, and an internal investigation showed he sexually abused others, prompting Fox to dismiss him. A month before the 2016 presidential election, *The Washington Post* unearthed the 2005 videotaped conversation of Donald Trump telling *Access Hollywood* anchor Billy Bush that as a celebrity "you can do anything. . . . Grab them by the pussy. You can do anything." Although Trump was elected, polls revealed he was a pariah to more than half the populace. In the spring of 2017, Fox's ratings leader, anchor Bill O'Reilly, was exposed in *The New York Times* as a chronic sexual harasser, compelling his advertisers to flee and Fox to terminate him.

Harvey was more paranoid than usual, determined to identify his accusers. Among them was Houston-based attorney Thomas Ajamie, who had probed his behavior toward women in an investigation for amfAR when he was asked to look into what Harvey did with the money from the Cannes auction. Harvey learned that in the course of his investigation, Ajamie had strayed into inquiring about Harvey's personal behavior. When he began his work, Ajamie said, "I did not know Harvey Weinstein. I knew his name. I interviewed people on the board. Friends in Los Angeles, in finance . . . I'd ask, 'Tell me about Harvey Weinstein.' The universal response was, 'He cheats his business partners. He threw a reporter down the stairs. He rapes women. He's a sexual predator.'"

When Harvey learned of Ajamie's probe, he did what he'd done over the years with women: he demanded, and got, members of the amfAR board to sign NDAs. Ajamie refused to sign.

Harvey was particularly agitated because he knew Ajamie did not fear him.

But Harvey's foremost concern in early 2017 was Rose McGowan, who started tweeting months before about an unnamed studio head who raped her. He worried that McGowan would break her 1997 NDA and expose him. He was convinced of this when he learned she was writing a memoir, which HarperCollins would publish. He believed if he could somehow plug the McGowan crack in the defensive dam of silence that had always protected him, he could stem a fatal flood of bad publicity. Boies described Harvey as "very desperate to find out what Rose McGowan was saying about him." Harvey fretted that McGowan was talking to reporters, including Ben Wallace of *New York* magazine, who was said to once again be probing Harvey. In a talk with Boies, whose firm administered the Black Cube contract, Harvey admitted he and McGowan had sex, but insisted it was consensual. Longtime Miramax and Weinstein Company executive Meryl Poster said Harvey, eager to undermine McGowan's claims of coercion, confided, "I have a naked picture of her," which he offered to show Poster. She declined.

In the spring, Harvey's fears spiked when a former Miramax head of production, Susan Jeanne Slonaker, emailed him a "heads-up" that "Jodi Kantor from the NY Times is working on a major profile of you . . . particularly as it relates to women." Slonaker tried to reassure him by sharing what she'd told Kantor: how Harvey displayed his respect for staff by promoting people "to positions of greater responsibility and recognition. . . . I always felt like your kid sister who you trusted enough to throw in the deep end of important projects."

Harvey, like Donald Trump, had one mode of defense: attack. He beefed up his offense. He rehired public relations specialist Ken Sunshine. To alarm newsrooms, he hired Charles J. Harder, who has aggressively sued journalists, and whose Peter Thiel–funded lawsuit had shoved the gossip website *Gawker* into bankruptcy. Harvey retained women's rights attorney Lisa Bloom, the daughter of Gloria Allred, the famed women's rights lawyer, which was as shocking to feminists as was his recruitment of Linda Fairstein. Bloom, whose new book Harvey had recently signed for a TV miniseries, was unusually aggressive. She pretended to be friends with some of Harvey's adversaries, and in calls to reporters she attacked Harvey's potential accusers McGowan and Ashley Judd as "mentally unstable." He recruited Bill Clinton's impeachment defender and crisis manager, Lanny Davis. He forwarded Slonaker's email to Lanny Davis about the good he had done for women executives, and Davis wrote back, "This is great stuff. If we can't kill this story then her comments should be included."

At the time, Harvey still believed Rose McGowan was his foremost threat, and *The New York Times*' chief source. He called David Boies in early July to alert him that the *Times* was pursuing the story. Harvey was going to call up Arthur Ochs Sulzberger, Jr., the publisher and chairman, and asked Boies to call *Times* editor Dean Baquet. It was a concerted, time-consuming campaign—of lobbying, threats, enticements—with Harvey serving as the campaign manager, which pulled him away from company business. Unlike most fully mounted campaigns, it was a private effort kept from the board and Bob and almost all company executives.

To get an early glimpse at the McGowan memoir, Harvey reached out to Jonathan Burnham, the president and publisher of the Harper Division at HarperCollins and his former editor in chief at Talk Books. HarperOne was to publish the book in January 2018. "He called to try to get hold of the book," Burnham said. "He was calling every book agent. I believe he did get—not from us—a copy of the book."

In fact, Harvey got his copy via Black Cube, whose contract specified that its mission was to: "Provide intelligence which will help the Client's efforts to completely stop the publication of a new negative article in a leading NY newspaper. . . . Any other request or requirement from the Client will be taken into consideration." Black Cube assigned "a full-time agent by the name of 'Anna' to befriend McGowan and get an early copy of her soon-to-be-published memoir," and they hired a fake journalist to phone reporters suspected of working on a Weinstein story or to phone women who might accuse Harvey of sexual abuse. Black Cube would investigate reporters, including *New York Times* reporters. For the first four months of this new contract, Black Cube was to be paid two hundred thousand dollars, plus success fees. In all, between 2016 and 2017 Harvey would pay Black Cube at least $2 million.

Secret agent "Anna" was Stella Penn Pechanac, who seduced McGowan by telling her she worked for a London asset management firm, and tendered an invitation for McGowan to speak at their annual gala. Pechanac became her confidante; McGowan at one point told her that "there was no one else in the world she could trust." Anna's cover was later blown by the *Daily Mail* in London. The pretend journalist who made calls to actresses and reporters on Harvey's target list was Seth Freedman, who also lived in England. He funneled back information from the interviews he conducted.

After reading the memoir, titled *Brave*, for some reason Harvey felt reassured, though her account of the violation was unsparing in its detail. He was relieved that the book did not name him, though it did describe him as the nameless "Monster." She wrote that she "felt so dirty. . . . I kept thinking about how he'd been sitting behind me in the theater the night before it happened," watching a scene in which she was topless. "Which made it—not my responsibility, exactly, but—like I had a hand in tempting him."

Harvey insisted he did not rape her and that they had had consensual sex in the hot tub in his suite. Although McGowan claimed she told Ben Affleck that Harvey attacked her during the 1997 Sundance Film Festival, Affleck sent Harvey an email denying this: "She never told me nor did I ever infer that she was attacked by anyone." McGowan has said she had been in Harvey's company only on the day he raped her, but she has been photographed with Harvey at industry events—once in 2005, three times in 2007, and once in 2012—including one with his arm around McGowan and one picture of them inches apart and adoringly looking into each other's eyes at the 2005 amfAR Gala in France.

Harvey believed he had evidence that could neutralize McGowan. What he didn't know was that Jodi Kantor was not solely reliant on Rose McGowan and was working with Megan Twohey of *The New York Times* on a much broader investigation.

Harvey became more frantic when he learned of still another investigation, this one by Ronan Farrow and NBC. Farrow's interest was ignited by a Rose McGowan tweet in late 2016 alleging that she had been raped by an unnamed studio head. It was not hard to learn the name of the studio head. Quietly, starting that winter, Farrow had been digging for MSNBC into allegations that Harvey abused women. Harvey learned of Farrow's sleuthing from former Republican governor George Pataki, who phoned to warn him. Harvey had carefully built a favor bank with Republicans as well as Democrats. He had thrown a book party for Pataki's daughter Allison, and raised money for the Republican governor of New York, as he had for Democrats like Senators Hillary Clinton and Kirsten Gillibrand, Governor Andrew Cuomo, and Attorney General Eric Schneiderman.

I had never met Ronan Farrow but was impressed when he phoned in the spring seeking information about Harvey. He seemed careful, not prone to leap to conclusions unhinged from facts. I was aware that he

had repeatedly denounced his father, Woody Allen, for allegedly sexually abusing Farrow's sister Dylan when she was a child, and I wondered
whether Farrow approached this story like a reporter or like a zealot.
After a long talk, I was convinced that he was a careful journalist, and
gave him access to the tapes and notebooks from my 2002 *New Yorker*
profile of Harvey, which are housed at the New York Public Library.

When Farrow visited for an in-depth interview in July, he said he
had three women on camera accusing Harvey of sexual abuse (one of
them, Rose McGowan, on the advice of her lawyer, would later pull
out), and five women with their names and faces shielded, and he also
had secured the police audiotape of Ambra Battilana Gutierrez's 2015
hotel encounter with Harvey. Farrow was clearly worried that NBC
News executives were not as enthused as were he and his equally persistent producer, Rich McHugh. Farrow had had his own daytime
MSNBC show that had been cancelled with low ratings, and not a few
NBC News executives wondered why he still hung around. Farrow said
he had a meeting scheduled for August 8 with News president Noah
Oppenheim and was hopeful he'd get a green light to air his investigative report. I was thrilled to think he had succeeded in getting Harvey's
victims to speak and would finally expose his crimes.

What neither Farrow nor I knew was that by late July, Harvey had
already stopped fretting about NBC. The NBC executives, David Boies
told me much later, had assured Harvey in July that they were not going forward with Ronan Farrow's story, and if that changed, they would
let him know.

My email to Farrow the second week in August asking how the
meeting with the News president went prompted this response: "Can I
call you from a secure phone?" I thought this was odd and even slightly
paranoid, only later learning that Black Cube was staking out his apartment and, he feared, tapping his phone.

"Oppenheim killed the story," he said over the secure phone. "He
said I'm free to take it elsewhere, but who would want it." Dejected,
Farrow was not asking a question.

Without saying why, I asked if I could call him back. I immediately phoned *New Yorker* editor David Remnick to tell him, *Ronan Farrow has finally cracked the wall of silence around Weinstein and I'm impressed by how judicious he seems.* Remnick did not hesitate. He asked that Farrow phone him. Obviously, he needed to learn more.

Harvey already knew what he needed to know from NBC. He had made multiple calls to NBC News executives in July. These executives—chairman Andrew Lack, president Noah Oppenheim, MSNBC president Phil Griffin—all say they repeatedly refused to share information with Weinstein and didn't acknowledge his frequent emails and calls. Yet soon after Harvey got off the phone with an unnamed NBC News executive a week before Ronan Farrow's August 8 meeting with the president of NBC News, he turned to his crisis consultant, Lanny Davis, and told him he felt reassured by this senior executive that the Farrow story was dead. However, Harvey could not leave it alone. Would Davis, he asked, stop by NBC on his way back to Washington and talk to the head of NBC News to confirm that the story had indeed been killed, and also pass on the message that any piece that claimed he raped Rose McGowan was false?

Davis says he demurred, not wanting to be involved in "this women's issue," but Harvey insisted.

Expecting that the News executive was awaiting his call, Davis arrived at the 30 Rockefeller Center lobby on August 2. "I called up," he said, "and asked to speak to the head of NBC News." He assumed it was Andrew Lack, who he knew, not Noah Oppenheim, whom he did not know. Oppenheim came down, to Davis's surprise. "I said, 'I understand Harvey called. My question is, Is Ronan working for NBC on a story about Harvey?'"

"No."

"Is that categorical?" Davis pressed.

"My answer is no," Oppenheim said.

Davis passed on Harvey's statement that if NBC News included Rose McGowan in a story, any claims of "rape" would be false. Davis described the encounter as "very friendly. We shook hands." Davis insisted his visit to NBC wasn't to "advocate" for the way Harvey treated women because he "wanted to distance himself" from that issue, though in a July 25 email, Davis had reassured Harvey, "You have a great record treating women well."

In an email, Oppenheim described his meeting with Davis differently:

LANNY DAVIS CALLED MY OFFICE DURING THE FIRST WEEK OF AUGUST, WITHOUT ANY APPOINTMENT OR PREARRANGEMENT, AND INFORMED MY ASSISTANT HE WAS IN THE LOBBY OF ROCKEFELLER CENTER AND WISHED TO SPEAK WITH ME. I WENT DOWN TO THE LOBBY AND, STANDING BY THE ELEVATOR BANK, POLITELY ASKED HIM TO LEAVE. MR. DAVIS SHARED HIS DESIRE TO GIVE BACKGROUND INFORMATION TO NBC NEWS ABOUT ROSE MCGOWAN, INSISTING IT WOULD UNDERMINE HER CREDIBILITY. AT THE TIME OF THIS CONVERSATION, MCGOWAN'S ATTORNEY HAD ALREADY SENT NBC NEWS A CEASE-AND-DESIST LETTER, CITING HER STATUS AS A VICTIM OF SEXUAL ASSAULT, WITH WHICH WE WERE COMPLYING. THEREFORE, I INFORMED MR. DAVIS THERE WAS NO NEED TO DISCUSS MCGOWAN AND I IMPLORED HIM TO LEAVE HER ALONE. WHEN DAVIS ASKED IF NBC NEWS WAS STILL PURSUING A STORY BUILT ON MCGOWAN'S ALLEGATIONS, I TOLD HIM THAT WE WERE NOT PURSUING ANYTHING THAT INCLUDED MCGOWAN, AND TO STOP TARGETING HER, BUT THAT IF WE DID CHOOSE TO DO A STORY ABOUT WEINSTEIN, HE WOULD BE GIVEN A CHANCE TO RESPOND TO ANY ALLEGATIONS. THE ENTIRE CONVERSATION LASTED ROUGHLY A MINUTE.

When I followed up with Davis to try to square his description of the meeting with Oppenheim's, he angrily denied Oppenheim's version. "The notion that I was targeting Rose McGowan in our conversation is a lie."

If the focus of their conversation, as Davis claimed, was on whether Ronan Farrow's story would air, then it is clear Oppenheim is not telling the truth. But if their conversation dwelled on Rose McGowan, as Oppenheim claimed, it is clear Davis is not telling the truth. Perhaps both men are not telling the full truth. Davis doesn't want to be tarnished with the suggestion that he was impugning Rose McGowan,

and Oppenheim doesn't want to be tarnished for censoring Ronan Farrow, whose reporting, following on the heels of the Kantor-Twohey
investigation, was soon to have spectacular consequences.

Whether you believe Davis or Oppenheim, or neither, NBC can't
dodge this incriminating fact: Harvey Weinstein and his team had been
assured by NBC that the Ronan Farrow story was sidelined, and Harvey knew this before Farrow was told on August 8.

NBC News offered their reasons why they decided not to air Farrow's
reporting, claiming Farrow had "not a single victim of—or witness to—
misconduct by Weinstein who was willing to be identified." Around this
time, I was asked if I'd have a not-for-attribution lunch with a senior
NBC News executive. The executive confided that he felt bad that Farrow believed NBC censored him, but said they had several people in the
News division, including two senior female producers, review what Farrow reported and all agreed he did not have the goods on Weinstein.

*What about the audiotape Farrow unearthed of Harvey admitting he
grabbed Ambra Battilana Gutierrez's breasts?* I asked him.

We're a visual medium, the executive responded, *and that was only an
audiotape.*

*That didn't stop NBC from broadcasting Richard Nixon's Oval Office
audiotapes,* I countered.

The lunch ended with the News executive insisting that NBC would
have eagerly broadcast Farrow's reporting if he had Harvey's alleged victims on camera. The testimony of victims that Farrow disclosed in *The
New Yorker,* the executive said, was only produced after he left NBC.

Farrow vehemently refuted these claims, at the time releasing this
statement: NBC executives "have now produced a memo that contains
numerous false or misleading statements. . . . Their list of sources is
incomplete and omits women who were either identified in the NBC
story or offered to be. . . . The story was twice cleared by legal and
standards [two NBC departments] only to be blocked by executives who
refused to allow us to seek comment from Harvey Weinstein."

The press too often treated these conflicting accounts as a he said, she said story, ignoring that there was a third party who could confirm or deny what Farrow and NBC claimed: *The New Yorker*, which would publish Farrow's story seven weeks after NBC said no. The person who edited Farrow's initial article in the magazine, senior editor Deirdre Foley-Mendelssohn, clearly remembers what evidence Farrow first shared with the magazine.

"He brought three women who claimed Weinstein abused them and were named, five women who said they were abused and were not named, and the police audiotape," she said. The three women named and who described what Harvey did to them, she said, were Emily Nestor (a company receptionist he had badgered for sex for a full hour despite her repeated refusals), Ambra Battilana Gutierrez, and Rose McGowan, who later withdrew her interview.

Two conclusions seem unassailable: First, NBC killed a story even though Ronan Farrow had solid evidence that Harvey Weinstein assaulted women. Second, NBC confided to Harvey Weinstein before telling Ronan Farrow his story was dead.

Why did NBC kill Farrow's Harvey Weinstein story? True, not a few NBC executives lacked confidence in Farrow's reporting chops. It is also clear that Harvey's influence mattered to decision makers at NBC. Less clear is the reason Harvey mattered. Perhaps Noah Oppenheim, who wrote Hollywood screenplays, did not want to burn bridges to Weinstein, a powerful producer. Perhaps it hinged on News chairman Andrew Lack and his wife, Betsy, who sometimes socialized with Harvey, seeing him regularly at *Vanity Fair*'s annual New Establishment confab in Silicon Valley, which she coordinated and where he would bring a hot new movie to screen. Perhaps it can be attributed to NBC CEO Steve Burke, who also oversaw Universal Studios, and was a fellow producer and sometimes studio partner with the Weinstein Company. Perhaps responsibility rested with Comcast CEO Brian Roberts, to whom NBC and Universal reported, a close friend of Harvey's and a member of Harvey's Martha's Vineyard Mafia. A fifth theory was that NBC purged the story because Harvey possessed damaging information about Matt Lauer's sexual escapades—Lauer was soon to have an explosive reckoning of his own—and Harvey traded his silence for NBC's. It is possible that any or all of these circumstances might have led to the decision to shut the story down. But to date, no hard evidence has surfaced to convincingly prove why NBC killed Ronan Farrow's story.

I n August 2017, Harvey was unaware that Farrow had found a new home for his reporting, but he was agitated about a new threat—rumblings that other women might be talking to reporters. Black Cube went to work on them. He was particularly concerned about actress Annabella Sciorra, who had angrily cut off all communication with him after he allegedly raped her in the early 1990s. He feared her because Sciorra seemed beyond his reach, unlike a number of his victims who had done the difficult calculus of what risk he posed to them, or what benefits they needed from him, or the shame they felt, a grueling calculation that eroded clarity about their victimhood and so prolonged it.

Harvey had no cell phone number for Sciorra to turn over to Black Cube. He asked his former production executive Meryl Poster, who had recently launched the production company Superb Entertainment and with whom he remained close, how to reach Sciorra. Poster contacted producer Paul Feldsher, Sciorra's friend, who texted Sciorra: "Bella. Meryl Poster asked me for your number." Poster flatly denies this, saying, "I asked Paul for Annabella's number in early 2018"—months later—"because I heard she was upset with me and I didn't understand why." But Feldsher's email to Sciorra, which was introduced as evidence at Weinstein's 2020 criminal trial, dates Poster's request to August 2017. Pretending to be a journalist and hoping to extract whether she was talking to real journalists, Black Cube operative Seth Freedman texted Sciorra on August 14, 2017:

> Hi Ms. Sciorra, it's Seth, the journalist in London. . . . Might you have time for a very quick call to help with our piece? No more

than ten minutes, and it'd be really useful for our research. . . . Thanks.

Sciorra did not cooperate, but Harvey was calmed when Feldsher assured him that Sciorra once told him her sex with Harvey was consensual. Feldsher would be his shield. He had been a consulting producer on *The Outsiders*, a 2016 Weinstein movie for which he was supposed to receive a fee of ninety thousand dollars. Harvey had stiffed him. Suddenly in April 2017, Harvey ordered that Feldsher be paid sixty thousand dollars, emailing two executives:

> *Please send $60K to Paul Feldsher asap—you can put it as a personal expense that I'll reimburse to TWC but we need to get him the money now. HW*

This suspicious transaction was revealed when Feldsher took the stand as a defense witness in Harvey's criminal trial. Neither Feldsher nor Harvey's team would explain why Harvey agreed to pay personally for a Weinstein Company contractual obligation.

Harvey remained frantic all that summer. Determined to plug another large hole, he summoned two former longtime employees who started as his assistants and rose to senior executive positions, Pamela Lubell and Denise Doyle Chambers. He didn't tell them their real mission. He explained that he needed their help on a book he was writing about the old days and asked if they'd come up with a list of actresses and women who worked for the company over the years. He added names from the roster of female "Friends of Harvey," identified on the list kept by Harvey's assistants as "F.O.H." These were identified in the first of several internal emails distributed on July 26 as the "red flags," or the women to contact whom Harvey had had some relationship with.

Harvey chose Lubell, a former assistant who over ten years at Miramax came to head the creative department in marketing and was now a Hollywood producer, to lead the effort. She wrote the email addressed to Harvey, with copies to Denise Doyle Chambers and Barbara Schnee-weiss, who had worked for Harvey for two decades on a range of projects and whose name would crop up in witnesses' testimony as being something of a fixer for him. The list contained dozens of red-flagged names and phone numbers.

When they had a full list of names, Lubell later told Ronan Farrow, Harvey "called us back into the office" and told them, "You know what, we're going to put a hold on the book." He asked Doyle Chambers and Lubell to "call some of your friends from the list and see if they got calls from the press." Weeks later, Harvey summoned Lubell and Doyle Chambers to his office and asked them to start making calls to people connected to several actresses. "It got kind of intense," Lubell recalled. "We didn't know these people, and all of a sudden this was something very different from what we signed up for." Though Lubell and Doyle Chambers were not aware of this, these names would be sent to Black Cube for follow-up.

One of the calls Lubell made was to Laura Madden, today a divorced mother of four who has battled cancer. Madden was the Irish-born woman who in 1992 took an interview with Harvey for a job in his London office, agreeing to meet in his Dublin hotel suite. He allegedly appeared in a robe, and using the shock tactics he often relied on, pulled off her clothes and sexually assaulted her. Given assurances that he would not again transgress, Madden took the job she had wanted so badly, and for the next six years worked as a production assistant for Miramax in London, reassured to some degree that he was based in far-off New York. As recounted in Jodi Kantor and Megan Twohey's book, *She Said*, Pamela Lubell, who had not spoken to Madden in two decades, phoned her. Rather than behaving in line with her assertion that this assignment was "very different from what we signed up for," Lubell did a pretty good imitation of blustery Harvey. She started by telling Madden how fortunate they had been to work for Miramax and Harvey. She asked Madden if any "cockroach journalists" had called her. She asked for assurances that Madden would not speak to them.

Madden refused to make such a pledge, so Lubell dangled a carrot: "If you ever have a project you want to make, you can bring it to me; I can bring it to Harvey." When I informed Lubell that the evidence the prosecution presented in Harvey's criminal trial suggested she had aided him in trying to squelch his sex crimes, Lubell responded, "That is absolutely not true. I had no idea, nor did anyone else he scammed." She did not explain how, after Laura Madden claimed she was scammed by Lubell, Lubell was scammed by Harvey.

At this point, there had been no press headlines about Harvey's behavior. Yet Harvey was consumed by suspicions. He wanted to know: "Who is leaking information about me to reporters?" He was convinced that "someone was behind it, and he didn't know who that was," said a senior Weinstein Company executive. Was Bob Weinstein the leak? Lance Maerov? One of Harvey's assistants? "Who is it?" Harvey kept asking. His crisis consultant, Lanny Davis, described Harvey as "emotionally volatile." His paranoia was visible to everyone in the office. Davis recalls the time he asked a mildly challenging question in a room full of people and "he shouted at me, 'Whose side are you on?'"

Despite his suspicion that Bob might be informing on him, Harvey continued to treat him as "Bobby"—condescending to him or shutting him out. He did not consult him on how to handle the danger closing in on him. He did not confide in his brother as he had when he sought his funds to sign NDAs with Zelda Perkins and Rowena Chiu. He certainly did not fear that Bob would seek to oust him from the company, which Bob now had the power to do. Harvey remained convinced that without him, the Weinstein Company would die.

Harvey ordered a security team to sweep the offices, searching for listening devices. His paranoia would not rest, but out of desperation he reached for flimsy reassurance. "Harvey hired some investigator," one adviser recalled, "to pull public stories on individuals that he didn't need a private investigator for; it could have been done in a Google search. He had them put in a binder of potential dirt on that person, and he thought, 'OK, now I've got information on them.'"

Frantically, Harvey struggled to plug holes. He had thought Kim Masters, the *Hollywood Reporter* scribe who had confronted him in the past, might again try to expose him. "He emailed me a book contract proposal," Masters said. It read:

> *Dear Kim*
> *As you may or may not know, we have a publishing arm of the company and I have an idea for a fun, Michael Korda kind of biography. Are you available to discuss today?*
> *All my best,*
> *Harvey*

"I didn't respond," she said.

The danger consumed Harvey's days. One story had been spiked, but two press organizations now menaced him. He was once again aware that Ronan Farrow was probing his life, for he received an email in September from Meryl Poster sharing an email Farrow sent to her from his *New Yorker* email address asking "to pick your brain about a story." The day after receiving Poster's warning, Harvey sent a copy of her email to his undercover operatives at Black Cube. But the bigger menace, Harvey was convinced, was that *The New York Times* had given Kantor and Twohey free rein.

Harvey thought he knew what to do, what he always did in a pinch: threaten people openly or implicitly, and call on his network of well-connected friends. One of his assistants, Alexandra Canosa, who would say she was a victim of his sexual abuse, would later file a civil lawsuit against him claiming "Harvey Weinstein verbally threatened plaintiff not to speak to anyone about his abuse." He gathered former staffers and well-placed friends in his Tribeca office, including his former chief public relations executive Matthew Hiltzik, and Linda Fairstein, former head of the Manhattan district attorney's sex crimes unit. This war room's task, according to one participant, was "trying to figure out how to deal with *The New York Times* and what was their story." Harvey's attorney Charles Harder threatened the press with lawsuits. Harvey called producer Jane Rosenthal, a cofounder of the Tribeca Film Festival with Robert De Niro, and asked her, "Did I know Jodi Kantor? Would I call Jodi and tell her how good he was on political things and with charitable contributions?" Rosenthal said Harvey phoned her twice. "I never called Jodi," Rosenthal said. He phoned his old Martha's Vineyard pal, financier Steven Rattner, a very close friend of *Times* publisher Sulzberger, and told him, Rattner recalled, "The *Times* is working on this thing. I assure you it's all bullshit. I never abused women. Can you call Arthur or somebody."

Rattner ended the call and said he never reached out to the publisher. Harvey called the publisher himself, to no avail.

Harvey now worried he had another hole in the dam to plug: he heard that the "First Lady of Miramax," Gwyneth Paltrow, might be a source for Kantor and Twohey. To take her temperature, he decided to attend a party she was hosting at her home in Amagansett, not far from his own place in the Hamptons. He attended, he insisted later, because he was asked to speak at a party for her brother, director Jake Paltrow. Harvey told me that he had a friendly private conversation with Gwyneth Paltrow at the beginning of the party.

Paltrow in an email described what occurred very differently: "It was a gathering to get investors for *Head Over Heels*, the musical. Nothing to do with Jake." Her brother was not there. "Harvey had heard about the fundraiser and invited himself." She feared that if she barred him from attending he would suspect she was a *Times* source, and she'd be exposed to his volcanic temper.

Harvey was the first guest to arrive at Paltrow's door. After Paltrow chatted with him briefly, she excused herself and hid in a bathroom to phone Jodi Kantor, asking advice on how to handle him. She said Kantor told her to "be as normal as possible" to allay his suspicions. She returned to the party, where the uninvited Harvey "decided to speak even though he had nothing to do with the show and never offered to invest (which I would have rejected). . . . Why would I invite someone

Harvey on his way into court

Bob at three and Harvey at five

Miriam and Max Weinstein

High school graduation picture

The rock promoters in Buffalo

Hope d'Amore, an intern for
Harvey and Corky's music
promotion business, who was
probably Harvey's first
alleged rape victim

Harvey and Corky with "Old Blue Eyes"

Harvey and Bob in Miramax's first office

The early days of Miramax

Miriam, who brought
pastries to the office

Harvey with Eve Chilton,
his first wife

Oscar night for *Shakespeare in Love*

With Matt Damon and Ben Affleck
on *Good Will Hunting*'s Oscar night

Quentin Tarantino
with Bob and Harvey

Harvey and his
second wife,
Georgina Chapman,
with Miriam

Harvey and
Bill Clinton

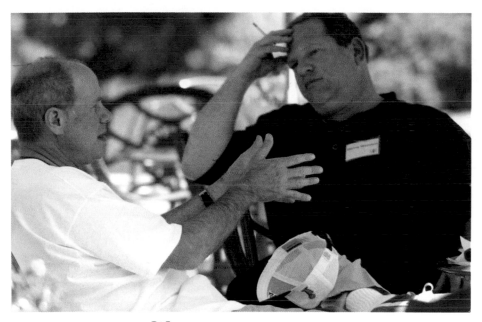

With Michael Eisner at Allen & Co.

With Jeff Bezos
at Allen & Co.'s
"mogul summer camp"

Zelda Perkins, the first employee to dare break her NDA

Actress and author
Rose McGowan, a
prominent accuser of
Harvey's

Jessica Mann entering court

Harvey survivor
Rowena Chiu speaking
at a #MeToo event

David Boies, lawyer and trusted adviser to Harvey and Bob

Barbara Schneeweiss, who was portrayed in the trial as being an enabler, with Harvey and producer Lucas Carter at a 2010 fashion show

Dirk Ziff, Harvey's best man at his second wedding and loyal board member

Harvey and Bob in better days

Robert De Niro, Jay-Z, and Harvey with Miriam

In the front row of a fashion show with Anna Wintour

Jodi Kantor, Megan Twohey,
and Ronan Farrow, journalists
who broke the story of
Harvey's crimes

Lance Maerov, more than a "pesky mosquito" to Harvey

Harvey placed
under arrest

A helping hand from best friend William Currao

Harvey's legal team of Donna Rotunno, Damon Cheronis (left),
and Arthur Aidala (right)

Prosecutor Joan Illuzzi with her boss, D.A. Cyrus Vance

The victorious team—Vance, Illuzzi, and Hast (*on the right*), Allred (*in white*), with seven of the women who testified against Harvey (*from left to right*): Taralê Wulff, Rosie Perez, Annabella Sciorra, Miriam Haley, Dawn Dunning, Jessica Mann, and Lauren Young in front

A Zoom call with a judge and lawyer from prison in June 2021

to speak at a function they invited themselves to and had nothing to do with? This guy is completely pathological."

Now officials outside Harvey's orbit at the Weinstein Company were suddenly alarmed that scandalous headlines about Harvey would soon upend their world. Lance Maerov said Megan Twohey phoned him on September 29 and told him she had a copy of the 2015 Lauren O'Connor memo as well as other evidence asserting that Harvey Weinstein was a sexual beast. She asked, *What did you and the board do about the O'Connor memo?* He told her he met with David Boies in his capacity as personal lawyer to Harvey. Boies had come back to him and said the matter had been settled and O'Connor had withdrawn her complaints.

Twohey told Maerov that Boies had lost credibility with *The New York Times*, since he was serving as an outside counsel to the *Times* at the same time his firm had hired spies from Black Cube to undermine her and Kantor's reporting, the paper believed, with his knowledge. Feeling betrayed, the *Times* terminated his services.

Boies would later acknowledge to Ronan Farrow that his firm contracted and paid Black Cube, but said the firm's involvement stopped there. He denied knowing that Black Cube sought to slur Kantor and Twohey. Yet Boies apologized: "We should not have been contracting with and paying investigators that we did not select and direct. At the time, it seemed a reasonable accommodation for a client, but it was not thought through, and that was my mistake. It was a mistake at the time." However, he added, if their investigation demonstrated that Harvey did not rape Rose McGowan or anyone else, and information "could be uncovered to convince the *Times* the charges should not be published, I did not believe, and do not believe, that that would be averse to the *Times'* interest."

Rattled by his call from Twohey, Maerov agreed to meet her that afternoon on a bench in Bryant Park. Before he did, he phoned David Glasser, who had briefly left the company but returned, oddly welcomed by Harvey and Bob. Maerov asked Glasser, *What's in Harvey's personnel file?*

Glasser, who Maerov still thought untrustworthy, instantly reported this to Harvey, and the next day Harvey phoned Maerov: "Lance, I know we had our differences, but can we just circle the wagons for me this one time?"

"Sorry, Harvey, the board has a fiduciary responsibility to explore this," Maerov said.

Harvey erupted. "I am going to destroy you because you're destroying the company! Everything [meaning any investigation] should go through David Boies."

"I don't work for you, Harvey!" Maerov shot back.

Harvey countered with another threat: Maerov had dated former model Stephanie Seymour when she was separated from her husband. Harvey had gathered the most compromising information he could on all his adversaries, and now he revealed, Kantor and Twohey would later report, "that he had obtained a letter Maerov had written to Seymour and would use it against him. The letter to Seymour," Harvey declared, "is disgusting."

Harvey was preparing for battle. He understood the battle would be a costly one. In the last six months, he started selling his real estate. He put his Amagansett home on the market, reducing the price from $12.8 to $12.4 million in July 2017, eventually selling for $11.65 million; he sold his West Village townhouse for $25.6 million, more than twice the 2006 purchase price; he sold his commercial condo in Tribeca for $6.1 million, or $5 million more than he paid for it in 1989; he sold his side-by-side Westport, Connecticut, homes—where he had married Georgina and held fundraisers for Barack Obama and Hillary Clinton—in a private sale for $16 million (the purchaser would promptly file to demolish both). In all, *The Wall Street Journal* reported, he would sell six homes for $55.9 million.

There was still another potential hole in the dam to plug, and for this Harvey would turn to his in-house counsel, Charlie Prince. With Maerov the primary target, on October 3 Prince dispatched a missive to members of the Weinstein Company board instructing them to channel any inquiries about Harvey from *The New York Times* or other publications to David Boies. The unintended effect was that now all members of the board knew something was going on—and were instantly alarmed. So, too, was Bob Weinstein, who Harvey did not share his distress with, partly because he was fuming over the possibility that Bob was talking to reporters. A board conference call was arranged for 9:00 p.m. that night.

Maerov informed the board of the *Times* investigation, and said he was told by Megan Twohey that the story would cite multiple women claiming they were sexually abused by Harvey and report that Harvey had signed many NDAs to silence them.

Dirk Ziff asked Harvey directly: "What's the truth?"

Harvey denied he had done anything wrong. Looking to deflect the scrutiny from himself, he blamed Maerov for blackening the company's good name. Abruptly, Harvey got off the phone, but Boies stayed on. Maerov was surprised when the usually compliant Ziff pressed Boies: *How many NDAs has Harvey signed over the years?*

He was aware of eight to twelve, Boies said, before adding drily, "I'm sure Harvey does not know how many over the course of his career." Boies candidly conceded, two days before the *Times* story would run, that the article would appear any day, and it would be damaging. Aside from Maerov, the board was shocked by how quickly this was unfolding. They would have been doubly shocked had Boies told them that Ronan Farrow—whose earlier NBC investigation they had not been told about—would soon resurface in *The New Yorker* with a hard-hitting report on Harvey's chronic sexual abuse. The board obviously did not know that Harvey's new attorney, Charles Harder, had already written to the magazine and described the Farrow article he had not read as "defamatory," and, blithely ignoring the First Amendment censorship concerns—concerns similar to the prior restraint argument invoked by David Boies in 2002 when he warned Harvey that he could not prohibit publication of my profile—demanded that *The New Yorker* not publish it.

Throughout the conference call, Bob Weinstein was strangely quiet.

Board members wondered: *Where does Bob Weinstein stand?* Maerov was perhaps the most puzzled. Unlike the others, he knew Bob was irate and wanted Harvey to take a long leave of absence. He didn't know if Bob would, finally, sever their bond by supporting a resolution to terminate his brother. At this point, the Harvey loyalists who dominated the board did not imagine he would be exiled. They believed, as Harvey had assiduously coached them to believe, that the success of the company was reliant on Harvey Weinstein. They granted him enormous leeway, rarely questioning the company's losses. They acted as if their primary fiduciary responsibility was to their friend.

The next day, October 4, the day before the *New York Times* article appeared, Kim Masters and Chris Gardner in *The Hollywood Reporter* disclosed that multiple sources told them the *Times* was "about to expose damaging information on Harvey Weinstein." Harvey tried to deflect the account with humor, telling the reporters: "The story sounds so good, I want to buy the movie rights." In the office, Harvey was in a foul mood. He frantically summoned Lubell, Doyle Chambers, and others to his office. "He was in a panic," Lubell told Ronan Farrow. "He starts screaming, 'Get so-and-so on the phone.'" At 1:45 p.m., his team sent an 18-page letter to the *Times* threatening to sue the paper if the story ran. At 3:00 p.m. on that same day, Harvey made an ambush visit to the *Times* offices with lawyers Lisa Bloom, Linda Fairstein, and Elkan Abramowitz in tow, demanding to speak off the record to the reporters at work on the story. Megan Twohey brought them to a tiny glass-walled conference room where her newsroom colleagues could see what was taking place. She gave him fifteen minutes. The lawyers attempted to smear the *Times*' sources as mentally unstable or morally vulnerable, dredging up past incidents the paper had already investigated and dismissed. The story would not be stalled.

Harvey decided to send an email to the board suggesting that he might take a leave of absence. But this was more a bluff than a plan. Harvey's posture was that he was victim, not villain. His mind kept racing back to the many admirable things he had done. The roughly

$500 million he claimed to have raised for important charities, including AIDS research, Robin Hood, Planned Parenthood, Paul Newman's Hole in the Wall Gang, the concerts he had staged to raise money after 9/11 and Hurricane Sandy, the female executives and directors he had hired, and the socially relevant movies he had brought to the screen.

Harvey did not have enough fingers to plug all the holes that had opened in the dam that long protected him. No one did. Harvey, and the company, were about to drown.

The October 5, 2017, front-page headline of the *New York Times* story by Jodi Kantor and Megan Twohey blared: HARVEY WEINSTEIN PAID OFF SEXUAL HARASSMENT ACCUSERS FOR DECADES. The *Times* investigation highlighted "previously undisclosed allegations against Mr. Weinstein stretching over nearly three decades." They got women on the record to share their horrific experiences with Harvey—Ashley Judd, Emily Nestor, Lauren O'Connor, Laura Madden, Zelda Perkins. They disclosed eight confidential NDAs that Harvey paid for, including those with Rose McGowan, Ambra Battilana Gutierrez, and Lauren O'Connor. "Dozens of Mr. Weinstein's former and current employees, from assistants to top executives, said they knew of inappropriate conduct while they worked for him. Only a handful said they ever confronted him." One reason was a document the *Times* dug up showing how Harvey "enforced a code of silence," with employees signing contracts prohibiting them from criticizing the company or its leaders if it would harm the business or "any employee's personal reputation."

The story quoted Harvey offering an apology, sort of: "I appreciate the way I've behaved with colleagues in the past has caused a lot of pain, and I sincerely apologize for it. Though I'm trying to do better, I know I have a long way to go."

That morning, more bad Harvey news erupted. Women who said they were Harvey's victims started to come forward, no longer feeling isolated. Leaders of the #MeToo movement celebrated the naming of a

man they considered a beast and declared the movement's commitment to exposing sexual harassment. That same morning, Harvey was
swarmed by a mob of reporters camped outside the Weinstein Company
offices on Greenwich Street. Harvey was wearing a too-tight black
T-shirt as he climbed into an SUV. He paused to say a few words before
racing off. Forgetting the occasional angry calls he had made to their
bosses insisting they be censored, or his physical threats, including once
placing a reporter in a headlock, Harvey told the reporters encircling
his SUV, "You know, I've always been good to you guys, not like those
fucking pricks who treat you like shit."

Harvey was in a fighting mood. That evening, Lisa Bloom emailed
the company board at length that the *Times* story was "largely false and
defamatory," and that Harvey would file a "defamation lawsuit" against
the paper. Harvey likely chose her from among his phalanx of lawyers
to deliver this message because she had a reputation as a staunch advocate for women's rights—and possibly because she was obliged to him
for her TV contract with the Weinstein Company. She urged the board
not to act precipitously. First Lance Maerov, then Bob Weinstein, responded in separate emails, urging her to please shut up.

That same night, the board convened for another 9:00 p.m. conference call. According to two board members, Harvey started with a sales
pitch. He announced that Michael Bloomberg, Robert Iger of Disney,
Tim Cook of Apple, and Shari Redstone of Viacom and CBS, among
others, "all pledged their support." This was untrue. He reiterated a
willingness to take a leave of absence, claiming, "Infidelity is not sexual
harassment."

Then Harvey spewed venom, trying to divert attention from the
Times report. He screamed at Bob, "You cooked the books!" meaning
he embezzled.

"You are delusional," Bob shot back.

He screamed at Maerov: "Lance, you're not that clean. I will destroy you."

"Harvey, if this were a normal company, you would have been walked out of the building," Maerov told him.

Harvey roared, "I'm coming back. There's going to be a movement to bring me back." Harvey wanted the board to issue a statement of support.

Seventy percent of the meeting was consumed by shouts, most coming from Harvey.

Speaking to the board more than to his raging brother, Bob Weinstein announced that he favored a leave of absence for his brother, and that it should be coupled with professional help. Maerov favored more drastic action. "I wanted to terminate him," he said. "But we needed an investigation." Director Tarak Ben Ammar joined Maerov in wanting Weinstein terminated; the rest of the board did not. At the end of the meeting a compromise was reached: it was resolved that the board would ask the respected law firm of Debevoise & Plimpton to conduct an independent investigation of Harvey Weinstein's behavior.

The next day, October 6, the board issued a press release stating that it took the claims in the *New York Times* story "extremely seriously," announcing "a thorough and independent investigation," and the board adopted Bob's proposal that Harvey take a leave of absence. Only four board members signed the press release. Rather than be disloyal to their friend, four other board members—Dirk Ziff, Paul Tudor Jones, Tim Sarnoff, and Marc Lasry—"ran for the hills" and resigned, Ben Ammar told *Fortune*. Hedge fund superstar Jones, the driving force behind the Robin Hood Foundation, expressed sympathy for Harvey, not his victims. "I love you," he wrote Harvey the next day, October 7, the day he resigned from the board. "Focus on the future as America loves a great comeback story. . . . The good news is, this will go away sooner than you think and it will be forgotten." Ziff, the best man at Harvey's wedding to Georgina, emailed Harvey at 7:05 p.m. on October 6—twenty-four hours after news of the *Times* story broke online—to explain, not very credibly, that he resigned from a fractious board, asserting, "I made my decisions without having seen the NYT piece."

His support rapidly eroding, Harvey had a change of mind. He now thought the best way to weather the tumult was by taking that temporary leave of absence. He greeted hostility with bravado, insisting the *Times* story was a lie since the sex had been consensual. Women, he boasted, would launch a movement on his behalf, testifying to his devotion to feminism. But behind the scenes, he was scrambling. After making up tales about their calls of support, now he wrote to prominent friends—Michael Bloomberg, Jeff Bezos, Jeffrey Katzenberg, Apple CEO Tim Cook, Goldman Sachs CEO Lloyd Blankfein, LVMH CEO Bernard Arnault and his daughter, Delphine, among others—pleading with them to write letters of support to his board. None did.

Two days after the *New York Times* story appeared, Lisa Bloom stepped down from his team of advisers; after Kantor and Twohey detailed her involvement, she publicly apologized for the part she had played for months, calling it a "colossal mistake."

Three days after the story, the remaining board members—Bob Weinstein, Lance Maerov, Tarak Ben Ammar, and Richard Koenigsberg—convened by phone to decide what to do about Harvey. He was not invited to join the discussion.

Thanks to the 2015 amendments to Harvey and Bob's contract, Harvey could be fired if he violated the revised Code of Conduct—if Bob concurred. Because the W voting shares were controlled by Bob and Harvey, the board could not fire Harvey without Bob Weinstein's assent. In a final break from his brother, Bob gave it. "I fired Harvey," Bob said. "I had the veto vote." On Sunday, October 8, the board voted to terminate Harvey Weinstein.

The real driving force behind the effort to oust him was Lance Maerov. For many years, he had been a pretty lonely voice on the board, at times clashing with David Boies or Bert Fields, always insisting that the Weinstein Company did not operate like a normal business. Despite his staunch defense of Harvey, Boies came to admire Maerov. "Harvey thought this was his company," Boies said. "He had this operating agreement that no one should ever have agreed to." The board had no control. "I think for Lance it was more trying to act like a normal director. Due diligence, keeping control, understanding the finances, controlling the finances."

Bob Weinstein, his brother and lifelong business partner, who was once hailed by Harvey as "my best friend," weeks later sent a scathing email to Harvey that his brother did not respond to:

> *Surprised that people are angry at you. What did u ever do wrong, except bully and abuse people your whole life and now say crap like everyone makes mistakes. U have hurt so many innocent women, your family, mine, me, your former employees, disgraced the name Weinstein.*

Bob said he was as shocked as the public was by the *Times* account. A year after the news broke, he said, "I knew that my brother was cheating on his wives. That's why I thought he was a sex addict and was trying to get him help for that. He was letting me believe that was his problem. Another Harvey lie. There is a perception that people assume that I knew of Harvey's criminal transgressions. I didn't know any of that." However, Bob did know of Ambra Battilana Gutierrez's complaint that prompted Harvey's arrest, though she withdrew her complaint. He knew of Lauren O'Connor's blistering indictment of the culture of the company, because he asked the board to read it, though she too seemed to withdraw her complaint. He knew of the NDA with Rowena Chiu and Zelda Perkins, because he paid the settlement.

A week after the devastating *Times* story, after ten months of reporting, the first of several Ronan Farrow bombshell pieces appeared in *The New Yorker*. Even more women—thirteen—came forward to assert that between the 1990s and 2015, Harvey assaulted or sexually harassed them. Three said he raped them. Four actresses said that after they rejected his advances, they believed, he actively sought to harm their careers. Writing of what he described as "a culture of complicity," Farrow reported:

Sixteen former and current executives and assistants at Weinstein's companies told me that they witnessed or had knowledge
of unwanted sexual advances and touch at events associated with
Weinstein's films and in the workplace. They and others described
a pattern of professional meetings that were little more than thin
pretexts for sexual advances on young actresses and models.

Thirty anonymous employees of the Weinstein Company rushed to
publish an open letter declaring, "We all knew that we were working
for a man with an infamous temper. . . . We did not know we were
working for a serial sexual predator." In an interview with *The Hollywood Reporter* a week after he'd voted to terminate Harvey, Bob Weinstein also denounced his brother as a "predator" and said that he hoped
he "gets the justice that he deserves." He said he did not believe his
brother felt "an ounce of remorse."

More than two years later, after Harvey's trial concluded, Bob would
have more clarity. He could see the distance he traveled, from arguing
with but always supporting Harvey, to being the crucial vote to terminate his brother. Looking back, he saw that his mistrustful, combative
relationship with Lance Maerov was unjustified. He now credited him
along with Jodi Kantor, Megan Twohey, and Ronan Farrow for playing
principled roles in exposing Harvey: "Lance Maerov was the most con-
scientious director who cared about the company and how it was run.
He had a great sense of ethics."

Bob, I asked, *What about your own complicity?*

"When you have been at the scene of a train wreck and think about
what you could have done to stop it," he answered, "no one that I know
of believed that Harvey was doing the things he was later charged with
and convicted of. But maybe if we had pushed harder to get him treatment for the problems we knew existed—like numerous extramarital
affairs and anger management issues—and maybe if I had gone to the
authorities after he punched me, maybe something could have changed."
It could be said that Bob's observation betrays a lack of understanding.

Because of his own experience with his alcoholism, he still preferred to attribute Harvey's sexual assaults to an addiction. In this, the brothers were aligned. But what if Harvey's problem was more serious?

Just hours after the *Times* article broke, Harvey Weinstein issued a tone-deaf statement. A fizzled smoke bomb, it failed to mollify his army of critics or distract readers still trying to metabolize the shocking report. His statement acknowledged that he had anger management issues, but now, he announced, "I am going to need a place to channel that anger so I've decided that I'm going to give the NRA my full attention. I hope Wayne LaPierre will enjoy his retirement party."

Harvey didn't grasp that for him there were no more escapes. Neither did Bob Weinstein grasp that he was now burdened with his own scarlet letter, W for Weinstein.

15

THE VICTIM

(2017)

Harvey rarely blamed himself for mistakes. A friend remembers the time they were to have lunch at the Tribeca Grill at 1:00 p.m. Harvey arrived forty-five minutes late. Instead of apologizing, he blamed his assistant, making a big scene at the table about her incompetence. "He took no responsibility," the friend said. "He called and screamed at her."

Initially, Harvey did not blame himself for the sordid accounts of his behavior described in *The New York Times* and *The New Yorker*, or for his termination from the Weinstein Company. However, he realized that if he hoped for a second act he had to be convincingly contrite, publicly admitting he needed help. At the urging of Bob, a passionate believer in the healing powers of therapy, who reached out to his brother and made peace with him, Harvey enrolled in Gentle Path, a forty-five-day treatment program for male sexual addiction at the Meadows, a rehabilitation center not far from Phoenix, Arizona. The Meadows has treated the various addictions of such celebrities as Tiger Woods, Elton John, Whitney Houston, and Rush Limbaugh. Its $58,000 price tag included such refinements as equine and expressive-arts therapy, as well as intensive counseling. The founder and senior consultant to the program, Dr.

Patrick Carnes, likens sex addiction to dependence on drugs or alcohol, portraying sex addicts as full of shame, perceiving themselves as unworthy and in constant fear they will be found out. Clinical director Erica Sarr says they "might be seeking attachment that was challenging for them in childhood." The rehabilitation program encourages patients to "drop their façades" in group and individual therapy, admonishing, "Making promises to ourselves does not work. Telling the truth does. Healing starts the moment we understand this ultimate reality."

Harvey showed little inclination to embrace that ultimate reality. He chose to stay in a hotel rather than one of the twenty-eight beds in the Meadows' adobe bungalows. He was spotted strolling around town, having meals at a diner, gabbing on his cell phone, certainly not dropping his façade with compatriots in rehab. Nor did Harvey complete the forty-five-day program. Contrition was not on conspicuous display.

Having been treated for alcoholism in 2004, Bob Weinstein knew what it took to conquer a compulsion, which he continued to think was his brother's problem. "I got off the elevator," Bob said about his own successful battle with alcohol. He remains sober to this day. Of his brother, Bob said, "In my opinion, it didn't appear that Harvey was getting or seeking the help he truly needed. I had suggested to him, based on my own experience, to commit and go to the in-patient program at the Meadows. He rejected that and decided to have doctors and therapists meet him at his hotel. I told him that was not the way to do it. You can't get proper treatment from the comfort of a hotel room while you're making business calls. I told him that was complete arrogance on his part, and the only way to get help was to totally surrender to whatever disease the doctors told him he had. I could feel that message was falling on deaf ears." Disgusted and resentful that Harvey treated his attendance at the Meadows as a publicity stunt, Bob stopped speaking to his brother.

But what if Bob Weinstein misdiagnosed Harvey's problem? What if he was not an addict, but a serial abuser, someone lusting not just for sex but for control and power over another person? Lack of guilt edges a person closer to a definition of a sociopath than a sex addict; it's one of the three defining attributes of the condition, along with narcissism and lack of empathy. Of course, there are many narcissists who lack empathy, are not guilt-ridden, and are not sociopaths. Nor do sociopaths wear identical uniforms. They can demonstrate a wide array of abusive behavior and how they describe their behavior to themselves, said Dr. Glen Gabbard, a professor of psychiatry at the Baylor College of Medicine and the author of a widely consulted book, *Boundaries and Boundary Violations in Psychoanalysis*. He's observed over three hundred sexual predator cases.

How do most sociopaths describe to themselves what they have done? They tell themselves, Dr. Gabbard says, "'I'm not a bad person.' Most say, 'That wasn't rape. Women always resist at first. That's part of the mating game.' . . . Rarely do I encounter a man who says, 'I have great regret about this.'" Often, these men have power and "a sense of entitlement that is pervasive. They feel they haven't done anything wrong. As narcissists, they believe most women would be flattered. I often hear them say, 'Women pretend they don't want to have sex, so you can't take a woman's resistance as a sign that she doesn't want you.'"

The nature of Harvey's assaults, looked at as a whole, suggests a fixation on control. More than a few of his victims said he held them down while he excitedly masturbated, dribbling semen on them. Some men are "aroused by resistance," notes Dr. Richard B. Krueger, a Columbia professor and a psychiatrist who works with sex offenders for the New York State Office of Mental Health. His wife, Dr. Meg S. Kaplan, the director of the Sexual Behavior Clinic at Columbia's department of psychiatry, said that for these men "the unknown is very exciting. Many of these individuals are saying to themselves, 'She's saying no but she's really saying yes. The sight of my erection will arouse her.' It's a complete cognitive distortion of reality."

There is little agreement on causes or cures among those who study sexual abusers. Elizabeth Jeglic, professor of psychology at John Jay College, concedes it "is a phenomenon we don't know enough about." The common ingredients to be found in such behavior, she said, include rampant narcissism and an absence of empathy. By contrast, the animating belief of the Meadows program is predicated on the "guilt and shame" of those who enroll. How to attribute guilt and shame to the Harvey Weinstein who said women were going to stage a movement to bring him back? He could not comprehend his victims' fear and panic.

Despite the ignominy, while he was at the Meadows, Harvey still harbored hopes of making a comeback. He was not prepared for the tsunami of criticism. A particularly stinging criticism came from Jeffrey Katzenberg, the man who navigated Miramax's sale to Disney and was the rare Hollywood executive Harvey admired. Desperate for help, Harvey reached out to Katzenberg immediately after *The New York Times* rocked his world on October 5, 2017. Katzenberg instantly emailed Harvey, and shared the contents of his missive with *The Hollywood Reporter*:

> There appear to be two Harvey Weinsteins . . . one that I have known well, appreciated and admired and another that I have not known at all. As someone who has been a friend of yours for 30 years, I'm available to give you advice on how to at least try to make amends, if possible address those that you've wronged, and just possibly find a path to heal and redeem yourself. Having watched your reactions, seen the actions you have taken and read your statement, I will tell you . . . you are continuing to make a horrible set of circumstances even worse.

Initially, the criticism from the Hollywood community came mostly from actresses. Unlike Katzenberg, men were mostly silent, reported *The Guardian*. The newspaper contacted twenty male actors and directors in the four days after the *Times* exposé—Quentin Tarantino, Michael Moore, Leonardo DiCaprio, Martin Scorsese, Ben Affleck, Colin Firth, Rob Marshall, among others—and initially none would comment, even though, as *The Guardian* noted, "many have been vocal about gender equality in the industry" and have forcefully criticized Donald Trump for his treatment of women. Only days later did some of these men denounce Harvey.

Rather than make amends, Harvey hired a crisis management public relations firm, Sitrick and Company. Founded by Michael S. Sitrick, its clients have included disgraced Los Angeles cardinal Roger Mahony, who was accused of doing too little to combat sexual abuse by priests, the controversial Church of Scientology, Rush Limbaugh after he was arrested for misuse of prescription drugs, and Paris Hilton, who was nabbed for cocaine possession. Sitrick would assign the Weinstein account to former reporter Sallie Hofmeister, who quickly adopted this public stance: "Any allegations of nonconsensual sex are unequivocally denied by Mr. Weinstein. Mr. Weinstein has further confirmed that there were never any acts of retaliation against any women for refusing his advances." Of course, Annabella Sciorra, Ashley Judd, Mira Sorvino, and Rosanna Arquette—who all claimed he tried to torpedo their careers—would challenge this.

Ronan Farrow made a comeback even less likely with another exposé in *The New Yorker* four weeks after the first. Under the headline HARVEY WEINSTEIN'S ARMY OF SPIES, Farrow recounted how Harvey retained Black Cube to track and spy on actresses and journalists. Farrow also disclosed how American Media Inc., publisher of the *National Enquirer*, gathered material on Harvey's accusers, alerted him to what they were saying, and then suppressed embarrassing accusations by refusing to publish them, a practice known as "catch and kill."

No crisis management firm could stem the waves of denunciation crashing on Harvey in the fall of 2017. He was expelled from the Academy of Motion Picture Arts and Sciences and the Broadway League, suspended from the British Academy of Film and Television Arts, and had his honorary doctorate from his alma mater, SUNY Buffalo, revoked, along with his French Legion of Honor.

Of more moment than the stripping of his honors, by the end of October, more than eighty women had stepped forward to claim Harvey had also sexually assaulted them, and soon this number would climb above one hundred. He had abused so many women, apparently, that his memory blurred. Actress Kate Beckinsale, who first met him at seventeen when he opened the door of his hotel suite in his bathrobe, recalled that years later "he asked me if he tried anything with me in that first meeting. I realized he couldn't remember if he had assaulted me or not." Even former allies—actresses Cate Blanchett and Julianne Moore, directors Todd Haynes and Kevin Smith—publicly condemned him.

The defection that shook him most profoundly, an associate to whom he confided recalled, was when Gwyneth Paltrow went public with the assertion that when she was a young hopeful Harvey pressured her for a massage and more. She said she always declined. Yet she has said that her relationship with Harvey "was very quid pro quo and punitive, and I always felt like I was on thin ice, and he could be truly horrible and mean and then be incredibly generous." Harvey would learn that Paltrow became a pivotal source for Jodi Kantor and Megan Twohey's October 2017 bombshell and helped them recruit at least six actresses who said they were sexually abused by him.

Unreflective and often too self-absorbed to read the feelings of others, Harvey sometimes soothed himself with the conviction that he was not a villain, merely confused about nuances of behavior. Or as he said to Zelda Perkins and Rowena Chiu, "Sometimes I don't know when it's consensual. . . . Maybe I don't recognize my power in these situations."

Closer to his fundamental attitude is what he was caught on tape saying to Ambra Battilana Gutierrez: "I'm used to that." *Droit du seigneur*, "lord's right," was said to be a medieval custom that allowed a noble to have sex with any woman under his rule on her wedding night. Historians dispute whether it ever existed as anything but myth, but the myth powerfully endured, spanning the centuries in literature and cultural memory and eventually morphing into tacit acceptance of the casting couch—and its corollaries in other arenas where men hold sway.

Harvey wasn't the first producer to dangle an acting role in exchange for sex. From the point of view of those with power in the movie business, it was a nice perk. A book Harvey often recommended was Elia Kazan's brilliant autobiography, *A Life*, in which he writes not just of the memorable movies and plays he directed but of the many young actresses he bedded, including Marilyn Monroe. Despite his immense talent, Kazan shared a primitive view of women not dissimilar to Harvey's: "All young actresses in that time and place were thought of as prey, to be overwhelmed and topped by the male." When it came to casting actresses, Kazan wrote, the dominant studio moguls—he cited Harry Cohn, Louis Mayer, Sam Goldwyn, Darryl Zanuck—"went by a simple rule and a useful one: Do I want to fuck her?" Harvey, like Kazan, perceived this to be the view of male moviegoers; and these men were in a position to act out such fantasies almost without limit. As Manohla Dargis, a chief film critic for *The New York Times*, wrote, "It is the perverse, insistent, matter-of-factness of male sexual predation and assault—of men's power over women—that haunts the revelations about Mr. Weinstein. This banality of abuse also haunts the American movie industry. Women helped build the industry, but it has long been a male-dominated enterprise that systematically treats women—as a class—as inferior to men."

It is also true that Hollywood, like the fashion or modeling business, is obsessed with sex appeal. It is a tease performed by males as well as females. A rule of thumb for most movie trailers, including Harvey's, was to highlight either the sexy female or male actor, or their steamy sex scenes. Dior, Gucci, Yves Saint Laurent, Prada, Ferragamo, or Tom Ford magazine ads usually display almost as much bare skin as clothes. The assumption animating Victoria's Secret's lingerie sales was that skimpy attire would arouse men. Ever wonder why in cop-car procedurals on television, the men wear suits and female officers often display cleavage? Feminists are not immune to promoting their sex appeal. If you watched red carpet events after Harvey Weinstein was exposed as a predator, you would have seen ardent feminists and eloquent critics of Weinstein displaying their curves and cleavage.

Harvey's perception of women seemed not to have matured beyond the reductive and often cruel attitudes of the 1950s and '60s that Kazan described. And yet Kazan did not rape his "prey." The excuse that sleeping with actresses was condoned in the industry would not have been accepted as justification for rape, even in the heyday of the Hollywood moguls. The public quickly condemned Harvey for describing rape as fitting into the somewhat less awful tradition of the casting couch.

Harvey had always wanted to dominate the culture, and now he dominated in a most unwelcome way. Because of his exposure and how it metastasized, with celebrities coming forward seemingly daily to accuse him or condemn his behavior, the #MeToo movement ignited in the fall of 2017. Over the following weeks and months, other once-mighty men would be felled by accusations of sexual assault and abuse—*Today* show host Matt Lauer (whose network, NBC, had killed the Farrow story), CBS chairman and CEO Les Moonves, actor Kevin Spacey, New York State attorney general Eric Schneiderman, hip-hop mogul Russell Simmons, comedian Louis C.K., R&B singer R. Kelly, convicted pedophile Jeffrey Epstein, *60 Minutes* executive producer Jeff Fager and anchor Charlie Rose, Senator Al Franken, Amazon studio chief Roy Price, chief creative officer of Pixar and Disney Animation John Lasseter, Metropolitan Opera conductor James Levine, editor of the *Paris Review* Lorin Stein, director Bryan Singer, photographer Mario Testino, chef Mario Batali, and in 2021, New York governor Andrew Cuomo. In addition, most of the 104 elected and appointed officials accused of sexual misconduct lost their government positions. In her book *Good and Mad*, Rebecca Traister reported that the pollster Tresa Undem's 2017 polling revealed that a "huge majority of voters—86 percent"—now understood harassment and assault were connected to "a desire for power and control over women."

Policy and other changes flowed from these revelations. Sweeping antiharassment legislation sailed through state legislatures in New York, Vermont, and Delaware. With public support, at least twelve states restricted the use of nondisclosure agreements, and some banned them either as a condition of employment or to be used in sexual misconduct settlements. Corporations imposed policies to curtail sexual harassment. In Hollywood, the screen actors union, SAG-AFTRA, imposed guidelines, urging members not to attend meetings in hotels and homes, and if they must, to bring a companion. The words of people in power changed, even if their actions didn't always match their rhetoric. Tony

Vinciquerra, the chairman and CEO of Sony Pictures, said, "The most important impact of #MeToo is it has brought full-on awareness. Everyone understands what has happened. So therefore it won't continue."

There is evidence it does continue. The Hollywood Commission, chaired by law professor Anita Hill, she of Clarence Thomas fame, in 2020 released the results of a survey of ten thousand women who work in the film capital, which came to a less sunny conclusion: two thirds of the women—67 percent—reported they had been sexually harassed in the prior twelve months, and 42 percent reported receiving unwanted sexual attention.

The aftermath of the #MeToo movement and a surge of women asserting their right to speak out introduced many salutary and overdue changes, but also some excesses. Properly irate that for too long rape victims were stereotyped or dismissed as whiners and manipulators, activists and protestors emerged with a new war cry: *Believe women*. It was publicly embraced by leaders of #MeToo and other groups that joined a nationwide protest called #BelieveSurvivors. It was championed by public figures, including presidential candidate Joe Biden, who later was placed in the awkward position of trying to tell the public not to believe a woman who belatedly claimed he sexually abused her in 1993.

Few journalists would embrace the notion that their mission is to believe, say, *all* politicians. Our job requires skepticism (not cynicism), a willingness to listen, to seek out facts, to first get the other side, but to be more than a stenographer. Instead of "Believe women," a more thoughtful posture would be "Listen to women," for it retains the presumption of innocence central to justice. Or as Emily Yoffe wrote, "If believing the woman is the beginning and the end of a search for the truth, then we have left the realm of justice for religion."

In Harvey's wake, it is common to see mashed together in the same basket all male miscreants who misbehaved but who, unlike Harvey, Bill Cosby, or Roger Ailes, did not commit the gravest and most egregious offenses. Even without verifiable proof, to be accused of sexual misbehavior is to risk execution by a Twitter mob. It is odd to talk to people who believe prisons should rehabilitate, but who don't believe a jerk who forced a kiss on a woman should be given a second chance. Debra Katz, who represented Christine Blasey Ford and other female victims of abuse, publicly told Jane Mayer, "All offensive behavior should be addressed, but not all offensive behavior warrants the most severe sanction."

The frenzied behavior of a Twitter mob can have dire consequences, as it did for David Bucci, fifty, chairman of the psychological and brain sciences department at Dartmouth College. A popular professor who female graduate students applauded after they confided in him, and he joined them in filing a complaint of sexual misconduct against three professors. Yet Bucci was aghast when seven female students filed a lawsuit against Dartmouth, accusing him of covering up sexual assaults and intimidating witnesses. He was deeply distressed, doubly so when the college advised him not to challenge the litigation, not because they thought him guilty but because they feared publicity would be harmful to Dartmouth. Bucci had suffered from depression earlier in his life, and as Anemona Hartocollis poignantly reported in *The New York Times*, he committed suicide.

In Harvey's wake, there have been salutary breakthroughs. Since his exposure in the fall of 2017 followed by #MeToo's amplified voice, reports Harvard's Institute for Sexual Wellness medical director, Dr. Renee Sorrentino, "We have seen referrals for behavior we have not seen before," with women more willing to come forward with complaints about sexual assaults. Prosecutors in New York and Los Angeles became more aggressive in filing charges in what in past years were considered problematic cases. A movement to curb the use of NDAs and to prevent them from being hidden from the public gained momentum in the U.S. and England, but reforms have been modest. Zelda Perkins, who has testified against NDAs before the British Parliament, says she plans "to launch an international campaign to demand the appropriate changes."

As 2017 came to an end, Harvey Weinstein was as reviled in Hollywood and the movie business as was the thuggish man he most hated being compared to, Harry Cohn. At Cohn's jam-packed funeral, Red Skelton cracked, "Well, it only proves what they always say—give the public something they want to see, and they'll come out for it."

THE SOUND IS
TURNED OFF

(2018–2019)

Harvey Weinstein was suicidal, or so he said. When he went to the sex addiction treatment center in Arizona in the fall of 2017, he composed a statement he planned to release publicly but never did:

> Three months ago I could never say the following words, nor even think them to myself:
>
> I'm an addict.
>
> I'm a sex addict.
>
> I'm an anger addict.
>
> To medicate, I comfort myself with bad food.
>
> My mind sees despair.
>
> My body has trauma.
>
> Vets tell me I have PTSD.
>
> Doctors tell me I'm lucky to be alive . . . but lucky is not how I feel.
>
> I have only despair. I have lost my family. I have daughters that will not talk to me. I have lost my wife. I have lost the respect

of my ex-wife and generally almost all of my friends. I have no company. I'm alone.

And I will be honest with you: I'm suicidal.

Those unconvinced of Harvey's sincerity could note that he sent two drafts of this statement for editing to Joe Polish, a marketing consultant. Whether or not the words were heartfelt, there's no denying Harvey's life was bleak. When he woke up alone in his vast Colonial in Westport, and later in a modest rented home in Westchester County, Harvey could not escape the crushing reality that he might face a criminal trial for rape that could send him to jail for the rest of his life. His company teetered near bankruptcy. Friends and colleagues had abandoned him. His only sibling and lifelong business partner, Bob Weinstein, after years of always striving to mollify and make peace with his big brother, now refused to speak to Harvey. His three adult daughters from his first marriage and his first wife also terminated all communication with him. His second wife would divorce him. His immense power in Hollywood and as a benefactor to presidents, senators, governors, and others, built up with assiduous attention over decades, vanished. His health was fragile: he contended with diabetes, high blood pressure, a steep cholesterol count, spinal stenosis from a back injury, which made him limp, and an eye condition requiring injections to stave off blindness. There were no assistants hovering to execute his orders; no cars with four televisions to screen films as he was whisked to another meeting or premiere. No one to carry the small Halliburton case locked with a passcode that was filled with prescription bottles of the twenty medications Harvey swallowed daily.

The Weinstein Company would enter a slow death spiral. Companies circled to buy its television assets, only to back off. Needing cash, the company sold some of its soon-to-be-released movies, and slashed one quarter of its payroll, from 120 full-time employees to 85. Quentin Tarantino moved to sell his ninth film—*Once Upon a Time in Hollywood*—to a Hollywood studio, the first time the Weinsteins would not distribute or produce a Tarantino film. Apple and Amazon Studios decided not to license Weinstein Company movies. Netflix and the A+E Networks would erase the company's logo from their TV shows. None of the company's assets could be sold.

In January 2018, the board fired David Glasser "for cause," claiming that the man who dutifully did Bob and Harvey's bidding, and who actually managed the business, was guilty of ignoring female sexual harassment complaints from the HR department and failed to share this information with the board. By late February, the company readied a bankruptcy filing. Although there were fitful buyer negotiations, they collapsed.

Harvey had not been charged with a crime, but he was already treated like a criminal. His company was sentenced to die. Choking on $520 million of debt and with only five hundred thousand dollars in cash on hand, in March 2018 the Weinstein Company finally declared bankruptcy. Among the creditors not paid were Harvey and Bob Weinstein's longtime lawyers, Bert Fields and David Boies. The company owed Fields's firm just under $10 million, and the Boies firm just over $10 million. Fields filed a lawsuit with what he said were low expectations of getting paid; Boies said he would not sue. A deep frustration of Lance Maerov's was that since Harvey and Bob had these two prominent lawyers represent both the company and them personally, including as mediators between the brothers, as a director he had no way of knowing what was a business and what was a personal expense. Maerov wondered whether some of Harvey's NDA payments to women were hidden in these enormous and opaque corporate legal bills, particularly to Boies.

Boies denied there were any hidden payments. And Boies insisted that neither he nor his firm ever negotiated an NDA for Harvey. When asked whether as Harvey's go-to attorney he enabled him, David Boies slowly pondered the question before answering. He finally said, "I think everybody who worked with him enabled him to do the affairs. But I don't think anybody who I know believed he was assaulting women."

What was striking about the Weinstein Company's bankruptcy,

observed Matthew Cantor, who worked for Lehman Brothers and spent many months after the collapse of the company officially reviewing the company's finances, was that from the day they filed for bankruptcy the Weinstein Company urgently pushed for the court to sell their assets. "That tells you the company thinks these are wasting assets, a melting ice cube."

The Weinstein Company would be sold in July 2018 to Lantern Capital Partners for $289 million, a company specializing in buying distressed assets; included in the purchase was the remaining library of 277 films. Days later, Bob Weinstein, Lance Maerov, Tarak Ben Ammar, and new member Frank Rainone were asked to step down; the one director asked to stay on was Ivona Smith, a specialist in corporate restructurings who had just joined the board. Bob Weinstein issued no public statement, exiting quietly. But he was enraged at his brother for his carelessness, for harming the lives of so many. And he was boiling at what he perceived as a personal injustice. Although Dimension had produced some lemons in later years, he had always made a profit at Dimension, always kept his costs low and his margins high, and in recent years had moved further away from his brother to run Dimension as a semiseparate company. Yet as was true throughout his life, Bob could not escape from the force field that was Harvey. Lance Maerov, who had drawn closer to Bob, thought back to October 2017 when they had voted together to terminate Harvey. He applauded Bob for doing the right thing and firing his brother. But he didn't think Bob fully comprehended what the impact of the Harvey scandal would be. "Bob did not fully realize that Dimension was also going down."

Late that winter, when Harvey's wife, Georgina Chapman, announced that she planned to divorce him, she granted an interview to her friend Anna Wintour's *Vogue* magazine in which she described her torment and shock at learning of Harvey's behavior. Asked whether she was ever suspicious, she responded, "Absolutely not. Never." She knew he traveled incessantly on business and attributed his absences and late nights out to work. Rare is the former member of Harvey's team who comprehends how Georgina, or Eve, could not have known Harvey cheated on them. After all, Georgina saw the headlines of her husband's alleged 2015 assault on Italian model Ambra Battilana Gutierrez that was being investigated by the Manhattan district attorney. And as one senior executive observed, "After every screening party, Harvey left his wife's table to sit with a table full of twentysomething young women, while Georgina went home." And a snapshot of the protocol "bible" compiled by staffers had very explicit directions on how to handle a call from Harvey's wife: "Be sensitive (how are you? Anything urgent? Can I tell him you called?) but be a gatekeeper (he's in a meeting.)"

"I do believe they're telling the truth," Bob Weinstein says of both Georgina and Eve, who claimed they did not know Harvey cheated. "When you live with people . . . like my brother who are expert at lying, they can convince those closest to them that they are devoted to them and their relationship."

Leaving Harvey, Georgina moved to Bedford Hills, in Westchester County. She kept a wary distance from him, though she did allow Harvey to spend time visiting his two young children, India Pearl, then seven, and Dashiell, four, which he did regularly. "She has decided that is the best route for the children," said a friend. Her gowns were not seen as often on the red carpet. Georgina and her founding partner at Marchesa split.

Harvey felt very much alone. "I don't know of anyone who is still in touch with him," said a former member of his inner circle. One exception was producer Paul Feldsher, whose consulting fee Harvey had once declined to pay, until in 2017 he did belatedly pay him sixty thousand of the ninety thousand dollars he was owed. Feldsher now talked to him regularly. "I was speaking to him partially because no one else was," Feldsher said. Feldsher became fiercely protective of Harvey, declining to grant personal interviews, dismissing critics as conformists sitting "atop Mt Moral High Ground."

The one person who remained a genuine intimate was not from his business life: Harvey's old SUNY Buffalo roommate, Dr. William Currao, a recently retired pediatrician.

Days for Harvey in the Bedford Hills rental were monotonous. He regularly visited his young son and daughter. Currao and his wife sometimes made a bed for Harvey at their Manhattan and Westport homes. He maintained a modest office above his friend Giuseppe Cipriani's restaurant on East Forty-Second Street, staffed by an assistant and a bookkeeper who ministered to Harvey's mounting bills. He was said to speak often by phone to a female psychologist at the Meadows. He read books, as he always had. He was rumored to be writing a movie script.

Always proactive, Harvey tried hard to convey his side of the story, but his public relations efforts did not go well. He had hired the firm of Sitrick and Company, but the person handling his account, Sallie Hofmeister, irritated many reporters with her robotic refrain that Harvey's accusers had to be lying because Harvey's extramarital sex was always "consensual." Months later, when asked if she really believed these claims, she said, "It's not my role to judge. You have to take what your client and the lawyers tell you."

Soon, Harvey was battling with the CEO of Sitrick and Company, Michael Sitrick, who declined to say why he dropped Weinstein as a client, but nonpayment was certainly an issue since Sitrick took their disagreement over money to arbitration. What Sitrick would say is, "If a client is not listening to us, they are wasting their money, and our time."

Sitrick was replaced that winter by Juda Engelmayer's New York firm, HeraldPR. Harvey feared mounting public rage and possible criminal charges from Manhattan district attorney Vance's office. He should have. The *New York Times* story "was a very big deal," said an official in Vance's office, and their reaction "was instantaneous." Unlike the Italian model case in 2015, they now had a list of alleged Harvey victims in New York City, and so the office began to explore a possible criminal case against Harvey.

Harvey was eager to shape a counternarrative. He phoned to spin his narrative to several journalists—author Michael Wolff, filmmaker Andrew Jarecki—offering to help them prove the women were not

telling the truth, that Harvey was truly a victim. None chose to participate. Harvey tried something else. With an assist from Engelmayer, he
produced a 48-page document challenging many of the claims lodged
against him. The plan had been to make the document available to the
press, but reporters who got an early look at the report portrayed it as
more PR spin from Harvey, so Engelmayer declined to widely distribute it.

The document begins by claiming that the legal case against Harvey
resulted from an avalanche of fevered press accounts. The "conclusions
in those articles are provably incomplete and inaccurate, but they painted
HW so negatively and so loudly that they provided a fertile ground for
individuals to come forward and cast their relationships with HW in
the same very negative light." One by one, the paper disputes the allegations made by various women, noting that "none of the accusers can
muster *any* objective data to support their claims." Nor could they deliver
a "third party witness," forensic evidence, or a police report. The paper cites prominent actresses—Meryl Streep, Jennifer Lawrence, Renée
Zellweger, Keira Knightley, Charlize Theron—who had said publicly
he was always a gentleman with them. The document admitted that he
misbehaved but claimed that "thirty-five of the women who allege that
he requested a massage or appeared nude in his robe all indicate that
HW stops when rebuffed." The document was silent about the much
larger number of women who said Harvey did not stop when rebuffed.
Although Ashley Judd asserted that he blackballed her after she rejected
his advances, the document noted that she worked in two subsequent
Miramax movies, *Frida* and *Crossing Over.* Gwyneth Paltrow starred in
eleven of his films after she said she rejected his sexual advances.

Knowing he might be indicted, Harvey scouted for a criminal lawyer and arranged to lunch with Ben Brafman at the Lambs Club
in Manhattan. Brafman, who is among the city's foremost criminal
attorneys, had never met Harvey Weinstein. But he held natural appeal

for Harvey. Born in Brooklyn to Holocaust survivors, Brafman, like Harvey, didn't graduate from prestigious schools and certainly qualified as a fellow "tough Jew." He was unafraid to take on unpopular clients, having represented another alleged sex offender, Dominique Strauss-Kahn, not to mention mobsters like Vincent "the Chin" Gigante and Salvatore "Sammy the Bull" Gravano.

As he waited at a discreet banquette, Brafman eyed Harvey as he walked in, his protruding stomach entering the restaurant before his short steps, a crisp, white linen shirt nicely draped over his girth. Sitting across from Harvey, Brafman noticed the dark shadows under his eyes, the deep lines chiseled into his round face, the patchy, unruly stubble.

Immediately, Brafman remembered, Harvey ordered a hamburger, a large order of fries, a separate bowl filled with ketchup, and a Diet Coke. Harvey did not wait for Brafman to begin eating his Nicoise salad before he attacked his burger, speaking as he chewed with an open mouth. Brafman, a fastidious man who wears dark, custom-tailored suits, worried he would be sprayed with food. This worry was soon replaced by revulsion as he watched Harvey hold a thick, oozing hamburger with one hand and with the other stab handfuls of fries, thrust them into the bowl of ketchup, and shove them into his mouth. Ketchup dripped from his fingers onto his white linen shirt, creating what looked like bloodstains. Soon a fry slathered in ketchup slipped down the un-buttoned top of his shirt and Harvey impatiently reached in to retrieve it.

"Harvey, you're ruining your shirt," Brafman exclaimed. He urged him to stand up. "The French fry will fall out of your untucked shirt."

Such an act would require patience. A man of raging impulses, Harvey had no time to peel open a cellophane package of cigarettes or lift the flip-top. Instead, he ripped off the whole top to grab a cigarette. Assistants often lined up three Diet Cokes for him in a row. When Ambra Gutierrez came to his office, he reached for her breasts like he was at an all-you-can-eat buffet.

It did not take Harvey long to decide to hire Ben Brafman. He did not like Brafman's steep fees—his hourly rate was fifteen hundred dollars—but he liked that *New York* magazine cited him as the city's "Best Criminal Defense Lawyer." Harvey would need him: on May 25, 2018, he was indicted for sexually assaulting three women and for raping one.

H arvey was ordered to surrender at the First Precinct station house in lower Manhattan at 7:25 a.m. He entered wearing a blue blazer and a powder blue V-neck over a white shirt, limping slightly and holding two books, one an autobiography of Elia Kazan. Questions were shouted at him by at least a hundred reporters and photographers who were fenced behind metal barricades. Harvey looked straight ahead, saying nothing as he entered.

Anyone indicted is required to be arraigned handcuffed. Harvey exited the police station with his hands cuffed behind his back, clasped at his elbows by two police officers in civilian clothes. He was whisked to the Criminal Court on Centre Street. In court he agreed to pay $1 million in cash bail, forfeit his passport, have his right ankle fastened with a metal brace to track his movements, and restrict his travel to just two states, New York and Connecticut. Waiting outside to witness Harvey's humiliation was ex-cop Glenn Cunningham, head of security for the Tribeca Film Center and the properties that housed Harvey's office and Robert De Niro's Greenwich Hotel. He could not resist visiting the courthouse to witness Harvey in handcuffs. "I hated that guy more than anything," he declared. "When I found out he was doing that shit, I walked over to make sure I saw him in fucking cuffs. I have a wife and triplet girls who are sixteen. Imagine if they were interning for this scumbag!"

To the assembled reporters, Brafman laid down a core defense argument: "Mr. Weinstein did not invent the casting couch in Hollywood," and "bad behavior" is not criminal behavior. In framing Harvey's defense, Brafman was willing to acknowledge that his client may have been morally deficient, but this was normal, certainly not criminal, behavior in the movie business. However, even if Brafman convinced a New York jury to exonerate Harvey in a criminal trial, awaiting him were possible criminal charges in Los Angeles, London, Dublin, and Toronto.

No less than thirteen civil lawsuits were also filed against him by women who claimed he had sexually abused them, with these cases requiring separate defense lawyers. And unlike a criminal case, where a jury convicts only if they believe the defendant is guilty "beyond a reasonable doubt," in a civil case proof of liability typically requires only a "preponderance of evidence." These thirteen cases included a wide array of claims under state and federal law, covering not just sexual assault, but fraud, defamation, and interference with a victim's economic livelihood. They included seven cases in which women asserted that Harvey had violated sex trafficking laws, and two cases in which women claimed that Harvey had violated the Racketeer Influenced and Corrupt Organizations act (RICO), a federal law initially targeting mobsters engaged in racketeering activity as part of a criminal enterprise. The claim was that Harvey's was a criminal enterprise organized to entrap women. Harvey also faced a possible defamation as well as a sexual harassment lawsuit brought by Ashley Judd, asserting that when she rejected his sexual advances he successfully lobbied producers and directors to deny her film roles. The civil cases would not be tried until Harvey's criminal trial concluded.

The attorney general of New York also filed a lawsuit against Harvey, Bob, and the Weinstein Company for failing to protect their employees, who lost their jobs due to their alleged unwillingness to police Harvey. Insurance companies filed at least four lawsuits arguing they should not be responsible for subsidizing Harvey and the company's legal costs. Targeted in many of these lawsuits were Bob Weinstein, the board of directors, and the Weinstein Company, all accused of covering up Harvey's crimes.

———

H arvey would have an excruciatingly long period in limbo as he
awaited trial. As he surveyed the business he once dominated, he
had reasons other than his public disgrace to be monumentally depressed. The movie business he loved was changing. Studios were hammered by their reliance on movie theater audiences: box office attendance
dropped 35 percent between 2002 and 2018. Adjusting for inflation,
box office revenues from movie theaters were greater in 1927 than in
2014, Tad Friend reported in *The New Yorker*. In an age of streaming
movies over the internet, movie theaters were imperiled, including those
small theaters that once welcomed independent films. Harvey and
Bob's beloved Mayfair Theater in Queens had switched from showing
foreign films to porn movies, and then Bollywood movies. In their
eagerness to tap quick revenues, studios and networks sold their movies
and TV shows to digital streaming companies like Netflix and Amazon, but in the process built up potent long-term competitors. Despite
the growing popularity of streaming movies in people's homes, the studios had long delayed insisting that movie theaters reduce the ninety-
day exclusive window the theaters demanded before studios could have
their movies appear elsewhere.

Emblematic of the times was Rupert Murdoch's announcement in
December 2017 that he was selling 21st Century Fox's film and TV
studios and its cable and satellite channels to Disney for $66 billion.
The sale was particularly shocking to those who long feared Murdoch's
power, for Murdoch was acknowledging that the worldwide media goliath he thought he had built was too puny to compete with companies
like Netflix. While Fox spent $2 billion annually to produce television
programs, Netflix spent five times as much. And the inflated stock
price of the digital giants now allowed them to outbid Murdoch on any
acquisition.

Still, Harvey continued to harbor a fervent hope that he could mount a comeback. His hopes appeared in a Cindy Adams column in the *New York Post*, sounding as if God, not Harvey, delivered the news:

> The question is, how is Harvey Weinstein.
>
> The answer is: He's coping.
>
> The man's watching his weight. Working out. Taking care of himself physically, feeling healthier, lessening the intake of medication. Staying in, out of any spotlight, not risking paparazzi . . . Playing the role of available dad, he's seeing the children regularly . . . he's getting signals from Europe. The realization is he'd be OK working abroad. Think fugitive Roman Polanski. Bum here/star there.

This hope was dashed when Harvey tested the waters in mid-2019, requesting that he travel to Italy to work on transforming his Best Foreign Language Film Oscar winner, *Cinema Paradiso*, into a play. In a pretrial hearing, the judge who would preside over his criminal trial, James M. Burke, forbade him to travel.

Harvey was despondent at Judge Burke's ruling, but even more so because of his own poor health. A man who once dominated rooms with his bluster and physical size, taking on the world, now walked with a limp and a cane. He would undergo an unsuccessful back operation in December 2019, and afterward was reliant on a walker. No doubt his decades of obesity and chain-smoking were catching up to him. For his various chronic health issues, he was under the care of five doctors.

With all these pressures weighing on him, Harvey began to look like an overweight vagrant, with pale skin and a pronounced limp. A man once feared for his power, he became a figure of scorn. *Saturday Night Live* cast member Michael Che joked about his facial hair, "He looks like chewed bubble gum rolled in cat hair!" When he ventured out to attend a monthly Actor's Hour at a downtown bar, comedian

Kelly Bachman, who had the floor, exclaimed, "I didn't know we had to bring our own mace and rape whistles to Actor's Hour, y'all." Audience members screeched at him, calling him "a fucking monster."

One thing did not change: the shouting. As he had always done, Harvey yelled at people, including Ben Brafman. But the prime target of Harvey's fury was Bob Weinstein. He blamed his brother for his termination from the company, and believed he was a primary source for Kantor and Twohey's revelations in *The New York Times*. Bob Weinstein vigorously denied he spoke with the reporters before their *Times* story was published; he acknowledged that he did speak to them, but only before they published their book. Facing multiple lawsuits, and seeking a new role in the film business on his own without his longtime partner, Bob Weinstein struggled to try to cleanse his name.

Harvey, said Juda Engelmayer, who spent enormous amounts of time with him, seemed obsessed by the fractured relationship with his brother. Among the books Harvey was seen carrying was *The Brothers Mankiewicz* by Sydney Ladensohn Stern. The Hollywood brothers were immensely talented. Herman Mankiewicz wrote the screenplay for *Citizen Kane*; brother Joe wrote *All About Eve*. They produced and directed many estimable films. Like the Weinstein brothers, they were talented and were not always allied; but their relationship was not defined by acrimony, as Harvey and Bob's now was. When associates asked Harvey why Bob was not involved with his pending trial and inquired about their relationship, Harvey was surprisingly discreet, telling them that he promised Miriam he would not speak ill of his brother. To those he was closer to, he privately railed against Bob. It did not take a great leap of imagination to know how upset Miriam Weinstein would have been that the brothers were estranged. What could she have done? Scream at them? Her sons were filled with too much bile to stand down, probably not even for their tiny, fierce mother.

If Harvey thought his brother was full of schadenfreude, he was mistaken. Like Harvey, Bob was also treated like an outcast. His phone calls were not returned, even by people who once worked for him. Agents ignored him. Hollywood executives told him it would be bad for business to partner with a Weinstein. Though Bob was a successful movie producer, he could find no work. Nor could he find a lawyer to rep him in Hollywood. "I have tried to refer him to a lawyer in the movie business," Bert Fields said. "They wouldn't do it. Crazy. Bob didn't do this. It's because his name is Weinstein." Bob announced a new production company, Watch This Entertainment, with the aim of making two or three films per year. Its initial movie would be an animated family film, *Endangered*, coproduced by actress Téa Leoni, who would be the voice of the principal character. The project never got off the ground, and the company faded away.

The brothers who had been together in business their entire adult lives were together again in unemployment. In the meantime, Harvey nervously awaited his trial.

17

THE LONG MARCH
TO TRIAL

(2019)

Initially, Harvey tried to manage his own criminal defense. Starting in the winter and spring of 2018, he would try to persuade Brafman: *Why can't we arrange a summit meeting with District Attorney Vance and my friend Governor Andrew Cuomo and make the indictment and trial disappear?* Harvey being Harvey, he did not take no for an answer when he wanted a yes, nor did he surrender when he seemed trapped. Hadn't history taught him that he could slip out of jams? Yes, Gwyneth Paltrow and Brad Pitt had confronted him, but they continued to appear in his movies. Agents buckled to his wishes. Hillary Clinton hosted the opening night of his movies. The president of the United States, Barack Obama, thanked him for hiring his daughter as an intern. When it looked like the police had cornered him for grabbing Gutierrez's breasts, he evaded punishment. Surely Harvey could escape prosecution now.

He kept telling Ben Brafman, *I can get off. The case can be made to disappear.*

You're living in a dream world, Brafman responded. *This case is too public to bury. The system is not corrupt. Even if it were, no one would be dumb enough to risk their career for a man who was a public ogre.* Brafman tried to reassure him: *Harvey, I can win this case if it goes to trial.* Yet over the coming months, according to three people who talked to Harvey directly about this, he continued to press for a summit meeting to make the case go away. Brafman was determined to focus his client on the reality of what lay ahead.

The prosecution of Harvey would be under the direction of Manhattan district attorney Cyrus R. Vance, Jr., sixty-six, a patrician figure, raised on the Upper East Side and schooled at Buckley, Groton, Yale. He was the son of Cyrus Vance, Sr., an esteemed former law partner at Simpson Thacher & Bartlett who served three presidents, concluding as President Jimmy Carter's secretary of state. A relative, John W. Davis, was the unsuccessful Democratic nominee for president in 1924, before going on to establish the white-shoe law firm Davis Polk & Wardwell.

After graduating from Georgetown Law in 1982, Cyrus Junior served for six years as an assistant district attorney in Manhattan under the legendary Robert Morgenthau. To establish his own identity, he moved to Seattle and cofounded a law firm, before returning to New York in 2004 to become a partner in another. Five years later, with the support of retiring D.A. Morgenthau and the political establishment, he was elected Manhattan district attorney.

Although Vance is personable, well liked, and has enjoyed successes, including a discreet, judicious approach to prosecutions and a major modernization and consolidation of bureaus, controversy has accompanied his three terms. His office initially granted convicted pedophile Jeffrey Epstein a less severe sex-offender status, and also agreed to a plea deal allowing Dr. Robert A. Hadden, the Columbia University gynecologist accused of sexual abuse by nineteen patients, to avoid prison. Critics wailed. As they did when Vance dropped the sex-crime prosecutions of Dominique Strauss-Kahn in 2011 and of Harvey himself in 2015, in both cases because Vance's office professed legitimate concerns about the credibility of the accusers.

To prosecute Harvey Weinstein, Vance was determined to win. He

bypassed the head of his sex crimes unit, Martha Bashford, who was not
an experienced trial lawyer. From the six hundred lawyers in his office,
he chose assistant district attorney Joan Illuzzi. A lifer in the Manhattan
D.A.'s office since she graduated from St. John's University's School of
Law in 1988, she had left her job only once, to run as the Republican
candidate for Staten Island district attorney, a race she lost. An experienced trial attorney, Illuzzi was known for questioning defense witnesses
by relentlessly drilling deep into their testimony. She gained courtroom
fame when she successfully prosecuted Pedro Hernandez for the kidnapping and murder forty years earlier of six-year-old Etan Patz.

In preparing for the trial, Illuzzi hoped to show a pattern of rapacious
sexual deviance, hidden for many years because none dared challenge
Harvey's power. It was true that several of the women who would testify
kept in touch with him after he assaulted them, but the prosecution
would seek to demonstrate the many reasons why women behaved as they
did after a sexual assault. Illuzzi planned to overcome juror doubts by
burrowing into the repellent details of Harvey's predations, overwhelming jurors with the searing tales of his victims. The prosecution was
emboldened when Bill Cosby was convicted for sexual assault and received a prison sentence in September 2018 of three to ten years.

Although they did not invoke this term publicly, in the trial the
prosecution would seek to demonstrate that Harvey was a sociopath.
The medical phrase for someone who treats women as Harvey did is
"antisocial personality disorder," commonly referred to as a sociopath.
As noted earlier, this usually means someone who checks off these three
boxes: is an extreme narcissist, lacks empathy or the ability to understand the feelings of others, and is not burdened by a guilty conscience.
To prevent Harvey and others from committing future assaults, the
prosecution claimed a guilty verdict would be an effective deterrent.

Harvey's life was to be in the hands of Ben Brafman, then seventy-
two, who portrayed himself in a courtroom as David against a government Goliath. An Orthodox Jew who strictly observed the Sabbath, he
was an assistant district attorney in Manhattan for three years before

starting his own law firm in 1980. Unlike Illuzzi, who often wore the same dark jacket or cardigan over a different blouse, Brafman favored an array of customized clothes. He commuted daily to Manhattan in a chauffeured Lincoln Continental from his home in Lawrence, Long Island. Standing five feet six inches tall, he was known for charming juries with this closing line: "The prosecution wants you to believe their side of the story. I wish I were taller. But we can't always get what we want."

Central to Harvey's defense was not to deny he had sex with these women but to prove the sex was consensual, demonstrated by the emails and continued relationships many of the alleged victims maintained long after they claimed to have been abused. Harvey would be portrayed as the true victim in this trial—which certainly aligned with Harvey's grievances—a man manipulated by ambitious wannabes, women eager to use his power to promote their careers. To succeed, the defense had to shred the women's credibility and offer the jury an alternative interpretation of the facts. A masterful storyteller, Brafman's plan was to create a narrative that would erode their credibility without being abusive to the women testifying. The defense was buoyed because the alleged crimes were never reported to the police, there were no corroborating witnesses, and there was no forensic or DNA evidence to demonstrate Harvey's guilt.

Presiding over the trial would be Judge James Burke, who had been chosen by lottery. Prior to his ascension to the bench, Burke had served for a dozen years as an assistant district attorney in Manhattan. A former colleague who was a member of the team that evaluated his performance described him as "a journeyman" prosecutor, neither a star nor a stumbler. He was first appointed as one of thirty-two judges on the Criminal Court by Mayor Rudy Giuliani in 2001, and twice reappointed by Mayor Michael Bloomberg to a court that handled misdemeanor cases. He was elevated in 2011 by the chief administrative judge to serve as acting justice of the State Supreme Court, with felony cases now his focus. He was one of 324 supreme court justices in the state, though this court was not supreme, as the name implies, for the Appellate Division of the State

Supreme Court can overturn its rulings. And in a stunning December 15, 2021, hearing, three of the five female justices questioned whether Judge Burke's rulings were "a pile on" that "inflamed the jury" by allowing the trial to pivot on Harvey Weinstein's "character" rather than his alleged crimes, which emboldened Harvey to believe the court might throw out his conviction. Even if the court did so in 2022, Harvey still faced a Los Angeles trial, a potential petition from the district attorneys to keep him in jail, and an appeal or a retrial in New York City. Also uncertain was whether the Appellate Court would impact the reappointment of Judge Burke by the the mayor in 2022.

After an initial wave of elation when Harvey was indicted in May 2018, for the remainder of 2018 the dominant mood among those who wanted to see him in jail seemed to be a gloomy belief that he would escape punishment. D.A. Vance's office reached out to many women and did not receive the expected outpouring of victims volunteering to testify against him. Only three women initially agreed to file charges. Many of the alleged crimes had not occurred in New York. Or the statute of limitations to file charges had expired. Perhaps the prospect of appearing on the witness stand was too daunting for some of the approximately one hundred women who had by now publicly stated or implied that Harvey molested them. In some cases, prosecutors decided their testimony would not persuade jurors. A headline in *The New York Times* captured the prevalent pessimism: IS THE CASE AGAINST HARVEY WEINSTEIN IN JEOPARDY?

Further gloom followed one of Harvey's first public court appearances. Before a trial commences, it is common for a judge to conduct hearings on major and minor trial issues. When he entered Judge Burke's marble, cathedral-ceilinged courtroom for an October 1, 2018, session, Harvey walked slowly, with a more noticeable limp, which Joan Illuzzi openly growled was fake. The sparsely attended hearing this day was to determine whether the court should remove a third woman from the May indictment, Lucia Evans, at the time of her alleged assault a college student who aspired to be an actress. The prosecution charged that Harvey forced her in 2004 to perform oral sex on him. Brafman had petitioned the court, claiming that he had evidence that a New York City detective failed to inform the district attorney that a friend of Evans had told the detective that Evans confided that she voluntarily performed oral sex in exchange for an acting role.

Judge Burke announced that he would remove Lucia Evans from the case, which brought a bright smile to Harvey's face. From his seat at the defense table, Harvey leaned over to offer an appreciative nod to Brafman.

The next month, Brafman produced evidence that the same detective, Nicholas DiGaudio, had coached Miriam Haleyi, one of the two remaining women in the indictment, to delete information from her cell phone revealing that she kept in touch with Harvey after he allegedly abused her. (Haleyi, thrust into public notoriety and besieged by people who searched Haleyi on Google and contacted her, and worried that employers and coworkers would pigeonhole her as Harvey's former girl-friend, decided to adopt a more common name, Haley, which was how she was now identified.) Brafman filed a motion asserting that, because of DiGaudio's coaching, the secret grand jury deliberation that led to the May indictment "was irreparably tainted by police misconduct," and due to this and other vulnerabilities in the prosecution case, all charges should be dismissed.

Before Judge Burke would issue a ruling, Brafman made another filing to buttress his argument for dismissal, asserting that Vance's office "unethically withheld" evidence of police misconduct from the grand jury. He added a second reason: Because "the two remaining complainants in this case"—Miriam Haley and Jessica Mann—wrote many emails to Harvey after his unproven crimes, demonstrating that for years afterward they "engaged in loving and often intimate conver-sations with a man they now claim to have sexually assaulted them," Brafman asserted that the case against Harvey should be thrown out.

By late November 2018, with the defense motion to dismiss the entire case pending before Judge Burke, a senior official in Vance's office did not sound optimistic. Speaking candidly on condition of not being identified or directly quoted, the source confided:

> *This is a hard-to-prove, tricky prosecution. Unlike a domestic abuse case where the wife has a broken arm, there is no physical evidence. Clearly, the indictment shows Weinstein took advantage of both his power and the women, but will a jury understand why the abused women kept in touch with him and wrote solicitous emails? And when asked on the witness stand why they did, would they be convincing? Our office is disappointed more women have not come forward, volunteering to testify. And those we spoke to had varied and depressing reasons for declining, including one woman who said she had never told her mother and didn't want her to know.*

Vance's office interviewed over one hundred women who were not part of the indictment but who also alleged abuse or knew of it, women who the judge might allow to testify to a pattern of Harvey's behavior. Vance and Illuzzi worried Judge Burke would not permit the prosecution to call such witnesses, known as Molineux witnesses. On occasion judges in New York and some other states permit witnesses to testify that the defendant committed similar acts against them, thus displaying what the Molineux ruling defines as a pattern of behavior. Many judges oppose the practice, fearing it violates one intent of the 1901 State Court of Appeals Molineux decision, which holds that the state "cannot prove against a defendant any crime not alleged in the indictment." That is to say, in Harvey's case, he could not be convicted of past assaults against a Molineux witness, although that witness's testimony could buttress the accounts of the women who had been able to press charges.

On December 20, 2018, Judge Burke held another hearing. Harvey entered the courtroom hopeful his appearance this day would be capped by a ruling to dismiss all criminal charges against him. Ben Brafman had filed thirteen motions or reasons to dismiss the case. Judge Burke disappointed them, issuing a 6-page ruling affirming the indictment. The core factors in his decision were that the DA's office "presented evidence in a fair manner," and the police misconduct was minor and if known would not have altered the grand jury indictment. The judge set a preliminary trial date for May 6, 2019. On the steps of the courthouse, Brafman did not try to spin defeat into victory: "We are obviously disappointed that the court did not dismiss the indictment. We remain confident in the outcome of the trial."

Harvey could not contain his rage as 2019 began. He was furious the judge refused to dismiss the indictment, liberating him from the looming possibility of prison. And the judge's decision he had thought was a victory, when the charges filed by Lucia Evans were dropped, Harvey now learned was really a victory that would cost him dearly. Because her claims dated to 2004, when Disney was Harvey's parent company, Disney insurance had been footing Harvey's entire legal bill from indictment to trial. But the claims of the two remaining women occurred post-Disney, and Harvey was now required to pay all legal costs from his own pocket. And the costs would be enormous. A storm of curses spat from Harvey's mouth when he learned.

This was not the first time Ben Brafman saw Harvey transformed into another person, a furious screamer. He and Harvey had been sparring for months. In one narrow sense, they had similar personalities: each was a controlling micromanager. Harvey kept telling Brafman he wanted to personally talk to reporters, spinning his side of the story. He insisted that he wanted "a skirt" added to his team, a woman who would help soften his image among jurors. He also pressed for a "dream team" of lawyers, as he said O. J. Simpson had.

Bullshit, Brafman countered. He said O. J. got off largely because he was Black and the jury was offended when a key prosecution witness admitted to using the N-word. He did not want Harvey talking to the press. And he was insulted by the thought that as a defense attorney he needed help. Ben Brafman was by now exhausted by Harvey. Harvey was unaccustomed to following instructions. His endless phone calls awakened Brafman at all hours of the night, with Harvey sometimes treating him like an assistant, and at other times like his psychiatrist. Then there was the money issue. Harvey often renegotiated the terms of a movie deal, even after the deal was set. He sometimes would stiff vendors. And now the money for this vendor—Ben Brafman—was coming from Harvey's own wallet. At a steep hourly rate, and with Harvey hogging Brafman's time with daily office visits and endless phone calls, the legal bills mounted.

Harvey wanted to renegotiate, moving from an hourly rate to a flat fee; he held up payment, and at one point even suggested, Brafman told friends, that he should represent Harvey for free because the publicity would attract more clients, as if one of the city's foremost criminal attorneys needed publicity.

In his legal career Ben Brafman had represented mobsters like John Gotti's right-hand man, "Sammy the Bull" Gravano, and a variety of murderers and embezzlers. But he placed Harvey in a singular category, confiding to a close friend: "Harvey's the worst person I've ever met."

Brafman wanted out, and in January 2019, he formally notified Judge Burke that he wished to step aside as Harvey's attorney. The request was granted. Both Brafman and Harvey issued insincere public statements praising the other and claiming the split was "amicable."

Although he hadn't decided who would replace Brafman, Harvey announced that he would soon reveal his new legal team.

Harvey's second set of lawyers wouldn't last six months. Searching for his dream team, he landed on lead attorneys Jose Baez, famous for his successful defense of Casey Anthony, accused of murdering her two-year-old daughter, and Ronald S. Sullivan, Jr., a Harvard law professor. Sullivan had teamed with Baez to acquit Aaron Hernandez, a former tight end for the New England Patriots, of a double murder charge, while Hernandez was already imprisoned for another murder. They were supported by Duncan Levin, a former federal prosecutor, Pamela Robillard Mackey, a Denver attorney who had successfully defended Kobe Bryant against rape charges, and Brooklyn-born Arthur Aidala and his firm, Aidala, Bertuna & Kamins. Brafman generally preferred to work solo, but Harvey, with an eye to a city jury, had put together a balanced legal ticket—Hispanic (Baez), Black (Sullivan), female (Mackey), Jewish (Levin), and Italian (Aidala).

Within weeks, Sullivan was gone. The first Black American to be appointed a Harvard faculty dean, Sullivan presided over Winthrop House, one of a dozen undergraduate residential houses. But protests flared over his defense of Weinstein, including sit-ins at the dormitory, with students and some faculty calling for his resignation as a faculty adviser to students. Sullivan countered, "Lawyers do law work, not the work of ideology. When I'm in my lawyer capacity, even one publicly vilified, it doesn't mean I'm supporting anything the client may have done."

Worried that students would not feel comfortable going to Sullivan for advice or support, Harvard caved, the administration announcing they were conducting what they described as a climate review of Winthrop House. Sullivan resigned from Weinstein's defense team, saying his heavy teaching obligations would intrude on his trial work. But Harvard then announced that Sullivan would not be reappointed a dean when his term ended on June 30, 2019. An overwhelming majority of the law faculty at Harvard defended Sullivan and the right of lawyers to represent clients who, however odious, should enjoy a presumption of innocence.

The first big test of Harvey's already depleted new legal team was on April 26, 2019, when Judge Burke scheduled a court session to hear a motion from prosecutors to have Molineux witnesses invited to testify that Harvey had also sexually abused them. This motion was strenuously opposed by Harvey's team. They were well aware that Bill Cosby's first trial ended in a hung jury, but after the judge in his second Pennsylvania trial allowed five women to testify as Molineux witnesses, testifying to a pattern of behavior, he was convicted. At this court session, Judge Burke announced that to allow Harvey's new lawyers to prepare, the start of the trial would be pushed from May to June 3.

Harvey's legal dream team was coming apart under his steady verbal assaults and his reluctance to pay his bills. Next to depart was Pamela Mackey. Like Brafman, she declined to reduce her legal fee. In June, he lost Jose Baez. Rebecca Rosenberg of the *New York Post*, who published a steady stream of Weinstein scoops, disclosed the contents of the scathing letter Baez sent to Judge Burke explaining that he and Weinstein no longer spoke, and that Harvey had threatened to sue his own lawyers:

> First, Mr. Weinstein has engaged in behavior that makes this representation unreasonably difficult to carry out effectively and has insisted upon taking actions with which I have fundamental disagreements. For example, he has engaged outside counsel to communicate with myself and my co-counsel and has decided to have another attorney threaten legal action against this Firm.
>
> Second, Mr. Weinstein has deliberately disregarded our fee agreement and has had outside counsel indicate that he intends to continue to do so.

Harvey was equally displeased. He thought the loss of Sullivan robbed the defense of perhaps its most brainy attorney, and that Baez was distracted by another trial. Harvey was also said to be unhappy that Baez did not know his way around a New York City courtroom, did not have an instinctive feel for, and knowledge of, Judge Burke and the court. While Duncan Levin was experienced and respected, he was part of Baez's team. Harvey had never played nice, and now that his life was on trial, he wasn't about to start. He decided to retain a supporting actor on Baez's team, Arthur Aidala, then fifty-one, the personable attorney who defended Anthony Weiner and Roger Ailes against sexual misconduct claims, who seemed to know the first names of even the dozen or so State Supreme Court cops who policed court appearances. Another bonus: he was Italian, from Brooklyn, which Harvey thought would play well with the jury.

By late June, Harvey had settled on his third set of lawyers. To allow them more time to prepare, Judge Burke pushed back the start of the trial three months, to September 9, 2019. Harvey had long wanted a skilled female attorney. He chose Chicago's Donna Rotunno, of Rotunno & Giralamo, whose specialty was defending men charged with sex crimes. A former Cook County prosecutor, Rotunno's vita boasted that in forty sex-crime cases, she'd lost only one. As a woman, Rotunno believed she had this advantage when cross-examining women: If a male attorney "goes at that woman with the same venom that I do, he looks like a bully. If I do it, nobody even bats an eyelash. And it is effective." Rotunno often tried cases with a close associate, fellow Chicagoan Damon Cheronis, a law school classmate whose small practice shared an office suite with hers. They planned to move into the quietly plush Four Seasons Hotel near Wall Street in August to prepare for Harvey's defense, aided by Aidala, whose office on Fifth Avenue and Forty-Fourth Street would serve as a central meeting place. They assured Judge Burke they would be ready for the start of the trial on September 9, 2019.

The new defense team and Harvey appeared before Judge Burke for the first time on July 11. In the courtroom, Jose Baez graciously introduced Harvey's new defense team, and then exited. In a conference with the judge, Harvey's new lawyers complained that the prosecution had failed to turn over the names of all the witnesses and trial documents. They were clearly angling for a later trial date to better prepare, though they dared not make such a request yet.

To reporters outside the courthouse, Rotunno cautioned that it was important to hold women to "personal accountability" for their actions. If women visited Weinstein's hotel suite, reporters needed to ask why.

Attorney Gloria Allred, the founding partner of Allred, Maroko & Goldberg, who represented three women who would testify in this criminal trial, followed Rotunno before the cameras and microphones. After a long career, Allred, seventy-eight, is probably the best-known female or male attorney in the United States for sexual misconduct cases, having represented women who brought sexual abuse claims against Donald Trump, Jeffrey Epstein, Michael Jackson, Arnold Schwarzenegger, Bill Cosby, and Anthony Weiner. Having been raped as a young woman, she was passionate on behalf of her female clients. To lawyers on the other side, like Donna Rotunno, Allred was an ambulance-chasing attorney, pursuing big civil trial or NDA settlement fees. She is controversial even among some crusaders against sexual harassment; she opposed a new statute in California that would have made the muzzling capacity of NDAs unlawful, saying that powerful men who sexually abuse women would refuse to make payments to their victims if these women were free to later speak out and expose them. To her critics, Allred was protecting her ability to collect 40 percent of her clients' potential civil trial damages.

Allred's only child, her daughter Lisa Bloom, was one of the lawyers on Harvey's crisis advisory team before the *New York Times* story broke, stepping down two days later. At the time, the ever-combative Allred had swiftly issued a statement saying, "While I would not represent Mr. Weinstein, I would consider representing anyone who accused Mr. Weinstein of sexual harassment, even if it meant that my daughter was the opposing counsel."

On the steps of the courthouse this day, Allred assailed Rotunno: "When a woman goes to a man's hotel room, it does not give him a license to rape and then blame the victim because she went to his hotel room." Nor, she said, should Rotunno assume that as a woman she could get away with more aggressively questioning females. "A bully is a bully, regardless of their gender." This would not be the last encounter between Allred and Rotunno during the trial.

A number of significant decisions were made in August 2019 that would impact the trial and its start. Early in the month, Judge Burke granted the prosecution request to allow Molineux witnesses. He would permit three, meaning that in addition to the two women whose claims led to the indictment, Miriam Haley and Jessica Mann, Harvey's defense would be required to assail the credibility of three other alleged victims. There were multiple reasons the three witnesses were not included in the indictment: some incidents with Harvey occurred in other states, or the statute of limitations expired, or there were personal reasons. Allred would represent one of the Molineux witnesses. The defense was outraged by this ruling, but the silver lining was that they knew if Harvey was convicted, their appeal to the higher court would assert that the ruling violated an intent of the original 1901 decision (the case of a serial poisoner) because it included witnesses who claimed harm that was not demonstrated in the indictment.

In a further blow to Harvey, District Attorney Vance's office went back to the grand jury and expanded the indictment, asserting that in "the winter season spanning 1993–1994" Weinstein raped actress Annabella Sciorra at her Gramercy Park apartment.

Sciorra's alleged attack occurred twenty-seven years earlier, and the statute of limitations for rape in New York was a mere five years. (Just a month after the expanded indictment, Governor Cuomo, spurred by the activists of Time's Up, including actresses Julianne Moore and Mira Sorvino, would extend the time frame to ten to twenty years, making New York rape laws among the strictest in the country.) By adding Sciorra to two of the five counts—predatory sexual assault against Miriam Haley (count one) and against Jessica Mann (count three)—prosecutors could legitimately call Sciorra to the stand to attest to a

pattern of behavior, bolstering all five counts in the indictment. After
being silent for almost three decades, Sciorra had been persuaded to tell
her story to the ever-persistent Ronan Farrow. Now she was eager to
testify against her tormentor. She, too, would be represented by Allred,
meaning Allred now represented three of Harvey's six accusers.

This also meant that the prosecution now had a celebrity witness.
The prosecution insisted Sciorra had a horrifying story to tell. The defense insisted the prosecution was trying to titillate jurors. Although
both sides publicly vied not to be blamed if the trial was delayed, they
each knew more pretrial preparation was needed. Judge Burke announced
that the trial start date would be moved one last time, to January 6, 2020.

There would be two other pretrial hearings. On August 26, when
Harvey appeared before the court to plead not guilty to the new Sciorra
charges, he arrived in court seemingly oblivious to courtroom rules
banning cell phone use. He pulled out his iPhone and bent over to use
it to text. Upset, Judge Burke barked, "Please refrain from doing that.
It's a court order."

Harvey tried to speak but Judge Burke snapped at him, "Don't talk
with me!"

Harvey's cell phone would return as an issue between Judge Burke
and Harvey. To those who thought Harvey defied all rules he did not
make, this was confirmation. To Harvey's defense team, it ominously
suggested that Judge Burke had it out for the defendant.

At the final December 11, 2019, pretrial hearing requested by the
prosecution, a little more than two years after the *Times* and *New Yorker*
stories broke, everyone but the judge was seated as Harvey slowly entered the courtroom with the assistance of two men holding him under
the arms of his baggy suit and ushered him to his chair at the defense
table. To rise and move from his chair, he needed assistance, and it did
not look like courtroom theater. He looked older, grayer, paler, frailer,
having lost in the past year at least seventy-five pounds, nearly one
quarter of his body weight. When the judge arrived at 9:30 a.m., defense attorney Aidala informed Judge Burke that Harvey was to be

operated on the next day to repair the condition in his back that caused his right foot to buckle when walking.

Okay, said Judge Burke, obviously wary that the defense was seeking to delay the trial. But if Mr. Weinstein was not in court on January 6, he warned, the trial would start without him.

Joan Illuzzi rose to explain why she wanted this hearing: she complained that Harvey's ankle monitor revealed he had fifty-seven violations over the past two months, when the monitor would suddenly go silent. Aidala rose to say these were merely "technical glitches."

"None of the device violations were accidental," Illuzzi shot back; she requested that Harvey be held in prison pending the outcome of the trial, a request Judge Burke denied.

With weeks to go before the official start of the trial, each side had a reasonable idea where they stood. Vance and Illuzzi knew the Molineux ruling was significant, doubling the number of women, from three to six, who would testify that Harvey abused them. But the names of these women—out of the many, many potential accusers—were not yet known to the defense. "When that Molineux ruling that these three unnamed women could come, that was a huge victory for the prosecution," Aidala conceded. At the heart of Rotunno's strategy for the defense, as it was for Brafman, was to acknowledge, Rotunno said, that Harvey was a sinner. "But there's a difference between sins and crimes, and I don't think he's a rapist."

While his lawyers were fighting for him in court, Harvey wanted to take the fight to a familiar battleground: the press. He had been itching to defend himself, to tout the good things he had done for women as a movie producer. He was deeply frustrated that his legacy would be defined by these dark headlines rather than the incandescent movies he brought to the screen. He embraced movies others wouldn't. He didn't produce the kind of "theme park movies" that diminished and transformed the movie business. Today people credit streaming services like Netflix for offering foreign and unusual films like *Roma*. Had they forgotten that Miramax—*ME, Harvey Weinstein*—was a pioneer?

After being largely silent for two years, Harvey could not contain his frustration. He was determined to finally offer his side of the story. Ben Brafman and Harvey had clashed over this, with his former lawyer telling him to keep his mouth zippered and not risk more damaging pretrial publicity. But in December 2019, just weeks before his trial, Harvey turned to the newspaper that had usually treated him generously, the *New York Post*. When, years before, he'd put *The New York Observer*'s Andrew Goldman in a headlock and dragged him out of a party, the *Post* had blamed the scuffle on "a couple of pushy reporters." For good reason, he considered them a friendly paper.

Without informing his lawyers, Harvey invited the *Post*'s Rebecca Rosenberg to his plush private hospital room a day after the three-hour spinal operation to relieve pressure on his vertebrae.

"I feel like the forgotten man," he told Rosenberg. "I made more movies directed by women and about women than any filmmaker, and I'm talking about thirty years ago. I'm not talking about now, when it's vogue. I did it first! I pioneered it!"

The ploy failed. The front-page headline of the December 16 *Post* roared: WHINE STEIN: HARVEY TELLS POST: I HAVE BEEN GREAT FOR WOMEN. The paper devoted its entire page four and five to what it bannered as an "exclusive," noting with relish the marble bathroom, Italian bed linens, and cucumber-infused water in this wing of the hospital reserved for VIPs. The photographs showed a somewhat dazed-looking Harvey in a T-shirt, shrunken inside the loose skin of someone who'd once been a huge physical presence, and zeroed in on the tubes draining his incision site.

The backlash to the interview was instantaneous. A statement released by twenty-three women who claimed they were sexually abused by Weinstein, including actresses Ashley Judd and Rosanna Arquette, declared that Harvey didn't "want to be forgotten. Well, he won't be. He will be remembered as an unrepentant abuser who took everything and deserves nothing." Rose McGowan tweeted, "I didn't forget you, Harvey. My body didn't forget you. I wish it could."

Whether out of narcissism, or because he resided in his own reality distortion field, or because he could not arrest his compulsions—or all three—Harvey couldn't resist responding when Chloe Melas of CNN emailed him eight questions. Two days before the start of his trial, CNN published his answers. Harvey wrote, "The past two years have been grueling and have presented me with a great opportunity for self-reflection. I realize now that I was consumed with my work, my company and my drive for success. This caused me to neglect my family, my relationships and to lash out at the people around me. I have been in rehab since October 2017, and have been involved in a 12-step program and meditation. I have learned to give up my need for control." Harvey was exaggerating his commitment to therapy. He did not explain how being "consumed" by work, or his "company," or "my drive for success," explained his compulsion for sex, either consensual or forced.

Reality was not always Harvey's friend. Prior to the start of the trial, as happened with Ben Brafman, Arthur Aidala said Harvey turned to him and, imagining he was the power broker he once was, urged him, "Why don't you go in and talk to Cy Vance one-on-one?"

"There is no one-on-one with the district attorney," Aidala explained to Harvey. Any meeting would be attended by assistant district attorneys, and the only way to avoid a criminal trial was to agree to a plea bargain.

Harvey was not easily deterred. He pressed his lawyers, as he had pressed Ben Brafman, to push for a summit meeting with Governor Cuomo. Harvey thought Cuomo might be amenable because Harvey had raised a total of $110,000 for Cuomo's campaigns, and because he had aided the career of the governor's longtime companion, Sandra Lee. Perhaps the governor could persuade D.A. Vance to drop the charges? Cuomo never met with Harvey, and would announce that he was returning all of Harvey's campaign contributions.

Harvey did not realize he was no longer Harvey.

COURTROOM 1530

(January 6–30, 2020)

On day one of his criminal trial, January 6, it was obvious the back operation three weeks earlier offered Harvey no relief. He entered the courtroom wearing black orthopedic shoes, on his metal walker with four tennis balls attached to its legs so he could slide to a front bench. Hunched over as he sat in the first row of the two visitor benches alongside his best friend, Dr. William Currao, he wore a baggy black suit, white shirt, and black tie. His skin was grayish and he looked as if he had been in a fistfight, with bulging red circles under his eyes.

The defense and prosecution lawyers waited quietly for the judge to arrive, and the contrast between the lead attorneys for the two teams was stark. Assistant district attorney Joan Illuzzi, fifty-seven, had on her standard dark suit jacket over a blouse, her brown hair in a blunt, shoulder-length cut. Courtroom sketch artists would highlight her broad shoulders and solid frame, often showing her ramrod straight and pointing an accusing finger at the defendant. She did not grant interviews, and usually sat at the prosecution table with her colleague, assistant district attorney Meghan Hast.

The lead defense attorney, Donna Rotunno, forty-four, was not shy about speaking to the press, freely offering her opinions. Rotunno was in all likelihood Harvey's final casting decision—Hollywood's image of the high-powered female defense attorney, all jawline and eyeliner, striding past the paparazzi every day in towering Jimmy Choo pumps, fashionable pussy-bow blouses, and expensive skirt suits from Dolce & Gabbana and Ferragamo. Over the next two months, she would not wear the same outfit to court twice. She told Maureen O'Connor, who covered the trial for *Vanity Fair*, that she brought eight suitcases from Chicago. Why? I asked. "I saw what the media did to Marcia Clark in the O. J. Simpson trial," she said. "Every day there was commentary on her appearance," most of it on how drab she looked. A stylish chain around her neck in gold letters read, "Not Guilty." Beside her at the defense table sat no fewer than five attorneys.

Courtroom 1530 contained eight rows of wooden benches with seat dividers, a carpeted aisle dividing the left and right sides, and two long benches pressed against the rear wall. The first two rows of benches had no dividers and were reserved for the defense and the prosecution. Most of the other six benches were occupied by reporters who waited to enter on a first-come, first-seated basis. After the press took their seats, spectators entered from their own line. With all the benches occupied, including the two against the rear wall, about 130 people could be crammed into this high-ceilinged space whose large overhead windows let in shafts of light that swept slowly over the courtroom during the long days of testimony, giving the court an imposing majesty that even the constantly wailing police sirens outside could not dispel. However, because of the marble surfaces and primitive acoustics, attendees strained to hear unless the speaker had a booming voice—which Illuzzi did, but not Rotunno—making it imperative for established press organizations to pay an exorbitant sum (from $4.40 to $5.40 per page for expedited delivery) to receive daily transcripts from the two court stenographers.

When Judge James Burke entered the courtroom at 9:30 a.m., Harvey was assisted from a front bench to his seat at the defense table. Judge Burke peeled off his dark suit jacket, placing it on the back of his tall leather chair, and slipped his black robe over his bland button-down shirt and tie. From his elevated platform he looked down on the defense and prosecution tables through large, square-framed black glasses that dominated a small face topped by neatly parted gray hair. By demeanor, Judge Burke conformed to stereotype: a sober, late-middle-aged white man of plain features and a steady gaze. He would prove to be a forceful, decisive judge.

Once the judge was in his seat and the court was called to order, the courtroom was hushed. Eight or so court officers who were members of the State Police patrolled the aisles, walking up and down, ordering conversations to cease and cell phones to be put away; the tapping of reporters on their laptops or iPads was permitted. The defense table was to the left side of the courtroom, and the prosecution, the wooden benches of the jury box, and the witness stand beside the judge was on the right.

Day one was dominated by procedural and scheduling questions—how Judge Burke planned to handle jury selection, the two months he expected the trial to last, among other issues. On day two, Judge Burke arrived angry. Court security officer Cheryl Ferguson had spotted Harvey texting on his iPhone and told him such cell phone use in the courtroom was banned and the judge had already admonished him. She was annoyed, she said, that only "eventually" did he stop, so she visited the judge's office off the courtroom to report Harvey's intransigence. Before calling the court to order, Judge Burke looked down at Harvey and exclaimed, "Is this really the way that you want to end up in jail for the rest of your life, by texting and violating a court order?"

Harvey started to respond, but Judge Burke cut him off. "Mr. Weinstein, I could not implore you more to not answer."

Perhaps not since Miriam Weinstein scolded her son in front of his classmates had Harvey been so publicly dressed down. Harvey had always escalated or deflected argument to shift a situation to his advantage. Now his ability to respond had been taken away by the basic rules of comportment in court, including a threat to be jailed for noncompliance, and he and his defense team were shocked by the tongue lashing.

What really happened was not an arrogant act, Harvey's public relations adviser, Juda Engelmayer, said. Engelmayer accompanied him to court most days. "Prior to the judge walking in I took his cell phone and shut it off—because Harvey doesn't know how to shut it off!—and I handed it to Donna. Harvey asked for the phone back to send a condolence note to businessman Ron Burkle, whose son died."

The defense felt Judge Burke had treated the phone incident as if it were a malevolent act and not a moment of forgetfulness, and they would add it to their swelling list of complaints about Burke's alleged bias against their client. An 8-page letter signed by Arthur Aidala was sent to Judge Burke that day requesting that he "recuse" himself and the case "be reassigned to another judge." The defense protested that the judge revealed his bias against Harvey Weinstein by refusing to allow them to call the police official who sympathetically coached three of the women who said Harvey assaulted them, and by refusing to allow the defense to call certain expert witnesses, among other claims. Judge Burke would reject this motion, the first of several that would be filed by the defense.

Although Bob Weinstein would never appear in this courtroom and still did not speak to his brother, sometimes when there was a story in the newspapers that suggested Harvey did not fare well, Bob would text a question to me, asking whether an incident, a piece of testimony, was good or bad for Harvey. He didn't ever say that he worried about his brother and the trial's outcome, but clearly he did. After all, they grew up together, talking about the Yankees and the Mets after lights-out; started their work life in Buffalo together as college dropouts; reinvented the business of independent filmmaking together. There had to be a huge hole in Bob's life now that his brother was no longer in it. Perhaps this is a reason Harvey, equally wounded at what he believed was Bob's betrayal, nevertheless lugged to the courtroom a copy of *The Brothers Mankiewicz*.

The next day and a half in court would be dominated by procedural issues, and by the news that the Los Angeles district attorney had indicted Harvey for sexually assaulting two yet-to-be-named women in 2013. A courtroom squabble over the L.A. indictment ensued, with Joan Illuzzi rising to say it increased the risk that Weinstein would flee. She again urged the court to remand him to custody, which Judge Burke again declined to do. Arthur Aidala rose for the defense and, citing the front-page headlines about the new indictments, cautioned that they would "taint" the jury. He called on the judge to observe "a cooling-off period" by delaying this trial, which Judge Burke also declined to do. Throughout, Harvey just stared straight ahead, impassively.

For the better part of the next two weeks, court days were consumed by the selection of the twelve-member jury and three alternative jurors. Each of about 2,000 potential jurors would file into the courtroom, 120 or so at a time. Once in the courtroom, the judge introduced prospective jurors to the defense and prosecution lawyers, and to the defendant, immediately creating a buzz among many potential jurors who swiveled their heads to whisper to their seatmates: *Holy shit, this is the Harvey Weinstein trial!*

The judge asked for a show of hands if anyone felt they could not be "impartial." Initially, only two hands tentatively rose, followed by silence. When the rest of the potential jury pool realized a raised hand was their pass to flee the trial, dozens of hands shot up; over the next two weeks, more than one third of the potential jurors would elevate their hand to this question from the judge, automatically eliminating them from the jury pool. Those who remained after another set of questions from the judge—Do you have a scheduling conflict? Do you have a work conflict? Do you have a health issue?—filled out a 16-page questionnaire. On the first afternoon of screening jurors, only 36 of 120 who entered the courtroom would be asked to fill out questionnaires.

Against Donna Rotunno's advice, Harvey insisted on hiring a jury consultant to help choose jurors; Rotunno was convinced that these consultants relied too much on preset formulas rather than instincts nurtured by years of defense work. Still, the legal team seemed reasonably harmonious, unlike Harvey's tempestuous relationship with his two previous lawyers.

Each side had a strategy for selecting jurors. The defense started out seeking older women and men who might be less judgmental than younger jurors. "Our goal throughout the selection process was individuals maybe a little older, with life experiences, and willing to put aside what they had read about Harvey Weinstein," said defense attorney Damon Cheronis. But during the prescreening, Aidala said, "When the judge asked who couldn't be impartial, there was no pattern. We realized we had to look at individuals." This excluded young women, who the defense strained to eliminate. It would be unreasonable to expect to find a potential juror that had never seen media coverage of Harvey Weinstein, Donna Rotunno often said, but what was vital was to locate jurors with "the courage" to stand up to what she saw as a convict-Harvey predilection.

The prosecution's aim was simpler: they sought young female jurors, women who may have once been raped or sexually harassed, who were likely to sympathize with presumed Harvey victims or to be horrified by the testimony, and more highly educated or informed jurors who might be more likely not to blame women who claimed to be sexual assault victims.

And yet the process of quizzing prospective jurors seemed too superficial even to establish these basic parameters. On the afternoon of January 16, when potential jurors filled every bench in the courtroom but one reserved in the back for a small press pool, Judge Burke defined the four essential questions for each if they got to voir dire, or final jury selection, as:

Where are you from?
Where do you live?
What is your occupation?
Can you be fair and impartial?

In order to whittle the number of jurors down to twelve and three alternates, Judge Burke decreed that twenty jurors at a time would be quizzed for a total of fifteen minutes, or an absurd average of just forty-five seconds each.

The defense and prosecution were each permitted the normal total of twelve vetoes or peremptory challenges. Judge Burke could, on his own, eliminate a juror who he felt might not be impartial. Spurred by the jury consultant, the defense exhausted their challenges to automatically eliminate younger white women or women who said they had been sexually assaulted or had friends who were. They had emptied their gun of its twelve bullets already, but Aidala said the juror he wished he had saved a bullet for was Amanda Brainerd, the author of a soon-to-be-published first novel, *Age of Consent*. According to Chris Francescani, a reporter for ABC News who wrote incisive daily memos to his news division and, despite the secrecy attached to juror names, managed to identify her, Brainerd's website described her novel as centering on young girls who encounter "predatory older men." She had also posted a favorable review of a recent book, *My Dark Vanessa*, which described "the repulsiveness of her predator, and her entrapment in the relationship." Now the harmony on the defense team cracked a bit, as Rotunno blamed the jury consultant for "removing people we need not have removed"—including a juror who she said had relatives in law enforcement and thus, she felt, might be inclined to want to punish Harvey. The defense bet Judge Burke would veto Brainerd for being unable to meet his "fair and impartial" test. But Judge Burke did not issue a challenge, and Brainerd became juror number 11; she also became part of a defense motion submitted that month to declare a mistrial, which was rejected by Judge Burke.

The final twelve selected jurors consisted of six white men, two white women, three Black women, and one Black man, who served as the jury foreman. There were three alternate jurors.

When the trial recessed daily at about 4:45 p.m., Harvey and his team got into their black SUVs and often gathered at Aidala's Fifth Avenue offices to review the day. Harvey did not dominate these sessions. Often he was passive, certainly not Harvey Scissorhands. "He's broken down physically," Aidala told me in one of the conversations we had as the trial progressed. "I feel the shaking. He's much more docile." At the end of the day, a subdued, seemingly depressed Harvey often retired to the office above his friend Giuseppe Cipriani's East 42nd Street restaurant, a lonely space occupied by just two staffers.

The jurors were tasked with weighing these five charges: Count one was predatory sexual assault against Miriam Haley and Annabella Sciorra, a count requiring the jury to find that Harvey Weinstein committed a serious sexual assault against two women. Count two was a criminal sexual act in the first degree against Miriam Haley, which required that the jury decide Harvey forcibly performed oral sex on her. Count three, like count one, was also a predatory sexual assault charge, but this time the two women were Jessica Mann and Annabella Sciorra. Count four was the most serious charge, rape in the first degree against Jessica Mann, which required that the jury decide Harvey used force or the threat of force. And count five was rape in the third degree against Jessica Mann, which only required proof that Jessica Mann did not consent.

The first day of the actual trial, January 22, began almost a half hour late because six of the twelve jurors got lost, wandering off to the wrong location. Cyrus Vance sat in the second of the two rows reserved for the prosecution, as he would for at least part of most days. For the district attorney to expend so much time in a courtroom was unusual, suggesting how important this case was to Vance and his reputation. Every seat in the eight rows of wooden benches in the courtroom was occupied; in the corridor outside, visitors and reporters waited in line to take any vacated seat.

Surprisingly, because the opening argument is usually made by each side's chief storyteller, Illuzzi turned the opening over to assistant D.A.

Meghan Hast, a tall, slender woman who stood at the lectern beside the jury box, reading from notes.

She opened by pointing to a frail Weinstein and saying, "The man seated on that side of the courtroom, despite what your eyes are looking at, is not a harmless old man." She clicked a remote-control button and a picture appeared on two large flat-screens on either side of the judge of a robust, smiling Weinstein with former president Bill Clinton in 2006. She described Weinstein as "a power broker in Hollywood" who was a sexual predator, "assaulting these women when they refused to comply with his desires and his orders."

This harsh description didn't seem to register with Harvey. He looked down at the defense table, and like on many other days when he was being scorched in court, wrote long sentences on a yellow legal pad, making you wonder whether he was purposely trying not to pay attention or if he was stubbornly masking a somber reality. Neither, Harvey later said in an email. He said he told his team he was writing a screenplay "to make them laugh. I was just taking notes to discuss with my legal team. I was so tired. Every book I read, everything I brought with me people were examining. So I finally said, 'I'm writing a screenplay,' and that kept everyone quiet."

Harvey kept staring at his yellow legal pad as Hast went on to describe in detail the various ways he sexually assaulted the six women who would testify as victims in this trial, clicking on pictures of each. Hast described the toll these violent acts had taken on them, and how even though they occurred over three decades, they established a pattern in which Weinstein "used his power in the entertainment business to ensure their silence." Hast was determined to inoculate the women from a major vulnerability of the prosecution case, explaining why many of Harvey's victims kept in touch with him afterward, writing him affectionate emails, seeking favors, sometimes having consensual sex with him. Hast said the prosecution would offer testimony from a forensic psychologist to explain why keeping in touch with a rapist was normal for victims. With no forensic evidence, or firsthand witnesses and police reports to support their claims, the prosecution had a huge obstacle to surmount, and the women they called to testify had to be impeccably convincing.

Hast gave the jury a brief description of some of those who worked for or with Harvey, asserting that Harvey used them to create an atmosphere of security for the women who would testify in this trial, setting them up for Harvey's assault: There was Bonnie Hung, who accompanied Molineux witness Dawn Dunning to a Manhattan hotel meeting with Harvey to discuss movie roles. As Hast related, Harvey opened the door in an open bathrobe. Horrified, Dunning looked at Bonnie Hung, who said nothing, leaving the impression that for her this was normal. After Hung left, Harvey pointed to a coffee table on which rested three contracts and told Dunning she could have all three parts. But sex was what he wanted in return. Then there was Claudia Salinas, who escorted twenty-two-year-old model Lauren Young, another Molineux witness, to his hotel suite, and allegedly blocked the door of the bathroom where Harvey assaulted her.

Hast sat down after a muted, paint-by-numbers presentation of one hour and forty-five minutes.

Like the prosecution, the defense did not choose to have its lead counsel, Donna Rotunno, make the opening argument. Damon Cheronis, unlike Hast, did not clamp his hands on a podium and look down at his notes. He strolled in front of the jury box, conversationally invoking the names of Weinstein's accusers. He emphasized the themes central to Harvey's defense. First, he insisted these were "consensual" relationships, proved by the solicitous emails to him from these women. Second, he said jurors should not convict Weinstein based on excited press accounts or an argument that all women must be believed. Don't be bullied, striving to do what's popular, he instructed. "Be strong. Be analytical. Use your common sense." And third, when they looked at these emails—here he clicked on a document on his laptop, which was connected to the big screen facing the jurors, and an email from Jessica Mann appeared: "Miss you big guy"—they should ask themselves if such a tender email could be from a woman who had been raped. Jurors, he said, had to hold women accountable for their behavior.

Focusing on what he contended were the women's vulnerabilities, Cheronis failed to acknowledge Harvey's. After all, to declare that what Harvey did was consensual is also to admit he possibly traded film roles for sex and cheated on his wife so compulsively that he established a pattern of habitual lying, and perhaps qualified as a sex addict, which would make him a menace to others. This was a striking potential weakness in the defense case. In addition, Cheronis and the entire defense, especially Donna Rotunno, who prided herself on her willingness to challenge women on the stand, had to perform a high-wire act, asking uncomfortable questions without being perceived as a badgering bully. A red line not to cross was demonstrated during the 2018 Bill Cosby trial, when his lawyers in open court came off as cruel, denouncing his main accuser for being "a con artist" and "a pathological liar." Cosby's lawyers even dismissed one Molineux witness as an "aged-out model" who "had slept with every single man on the planet." Cosby was then a guest of the state in the Collegeville, Pennsylvania, penitentiary, serving a term of three to ten years.

On the second day of the trial, Harvey seemed surprised when he heard Joan Illuzzi announce that the prosecution's first witness was Annabella Sciorra.

His eyes followed the dark-haired woman in the loose-fitting deep blue dress as she entered the courtroom, gliding past the defense table and settling into the witness chair between the judge and the jury. He never took his gaze off her. In the intensifying months before he was exposed, Sciorra was one of the women Harvey especially worried was sharing negative stories with the press. Now she was the third woman named in his indictment. The only time Sciorra, with a solemn face, looked at him was when Illuzzi asked her to identify the defendant, and she rose and with a stern *fuck you* expression pointed to Harvey. He seemed to nod at her, but she ignored the gesture, sat down, and kept her head craned toward the jurors.

Under gentle questioning by Illuzzi, Sciorra described what happened to her in late 1993 or early 1994, when she was thirty-three years old. She had starred in a Miramax movie, *The Night We Never Met*, which was filmed in 1992, and she had an amicable relationship with Harvey. When she got up to leave a Miramax dinner in New York with Weinstein and others, Harvey offered to drop her off at her Gramercy Park apartment. After she got ready for bed, she was jolted by a knock on her apartment door.

Never once in describing what happened would Sciorra, now fifty-nine, mention Harvey by name. Chomping on Mentos, which he kept popping into his mouth and chewing like bubble gum, his lips closed, his molars grinding away, Harvey stared at her.

What happened when you opened the door? Illuzzi asked.

Sciorra struggled to compose herself, and after a long pause said, "The defendant" pushed the door open and brushed past her to inspect each room to be sure no one else was there. He started to remove his shirt. He ignored her demand that he leave. He then shoved her on the bed. "I was punching him, I was kicking him," she remembers. To no avail; he outweighed her by more than 150 pounds. Harvey climbed on top of her and locked her hands and raped her. Her horror was paralyzing. Her body shut down.

When he was done, Harvey said, "This is for you." He then "put his mouth on my vagina."

"It was just so disgusting that my body started to shake in a way that was very unusual. . . . It was like a seizure or something." Harvey silently lifted himself from the bed and left the apartment.

Harvey, still looking at her, repeatedly shook his head no as she described that evening.

What did you do next? Illuzzi asked.

"I wanted to pretend it never happened," the witness said, describing how she refused to tell anyone. "I began to drink a lot. I began to cut myself." Blotting the blood with tissues, she pressed them against the walls of her apartment, staining them red. She said she became reclusive, addicted to Valium. She stopped working.

Some weeks after the rape, when her friend Meryl Poster invited her to a Miramax dinner, she went, hoping to verbally confront Harvey. When she approached him he bent down, and she testified that he warned her, "'This remains between you and me.' It was very menacing. His eyes went black." She was frightened, and thought he was going to hit her.

The jury paid rapt attention to her testimony. Unlike many subsequent witnesses, Sciorra did not wander off with wordy answers to the questions put to her. This would pose a challenge for Donna Rotunno's cross-examination, because it offered fewer targets.

Rotunno rose dramatically from the defense table, most eyes in the courtroom fastened on her handsome attire and her tall, thin heels, which were like stilts. She carried a thick black loose-leaf book containing documents, an array of facts, and her many questions. Walking to the lectern near the jury box facing the witness, she asked, *Why didn't you call the police?*

"At the time I didn't understand that was rape," Sciorra answered, explaining that she thought rape was something that happened in a back alley and was committed by a stranger.

Brooklyn-born Arthur Aidala jumped up and whispered in Rotunno's ear, urging her to ask Sciorra, "You grew up in South Brooklyn. How do you not know what rape is?"

Rotunno let it go, but continued to machine-gun Sciorra with questions.

Did you ask the doorman if he let Weinstein up?

No.

If the doorman didn't let him up, how did Harvey know your apartment number?

I don't know.

Did you complain to the building's co-op board?

No.

Did you call friends or family?

No.

How could you not know the date this rape occurred, vaguely saying it was either in late 1993 or early 1994?

I don't remember.

Isn't it true that years later you told your friend Paul Feldsher you had consensual sex with Harvey Weinstein?

No.

When Sciorra stepped down from the witness stand that same day and her exit from the courtroom took her past the defense table, she looked away from Harvey, whose eyes remained fixed on her.

One of Sciorra's friends—actress Rosie Perez—was the next witness and she described how Sciorra eventually told her on the telephone, "I think I was raped," though Sciorra refused to identify the culprit. After the prosecution got Perez to share her account of what Sciorra had told her, Damon Cheronis conducted the cross-examination. He bore in, asking why she didn't immediately go visit her friend or insist that she tell the police.

Perez said she phoned every day for a week, but no one answered. Since Sciorra declined to describe what happened, or who did it, Perez said, "I thought I was being respectful by leaving her alone." When she later guessed that the culprit was Weinstein, she encouraged Sciorra to report the crime.

"I can't, I can't," she said Sciorra told her. "He'll destroy my career."

Before concluding his cross, Cheronis ended with: *You were a close friend. A close friend should have rushed to her apartment.*

Perez answered that her friend made it clear to her that she wanted to be alone.

Next up was another Sciorra friend, model Carla Young. Aidala cross-examined her, asking a series of brutal postrape questions:

How bad was Sciorra's drug problem?

Her drinking?

Her self-destruction?

He hammered at her so hard, and so long, that Judge Burke ordered him to "sit down." At first Aidala resisted, insisting he had two more pages of questions. Young was excused, crying as she left the courtroom. Aidala was unhappy with the judge, convinced that Judge Burke, despite their many years' acquaintance, was personally hostile to him. Yet Aidala thought he had planted seeds of doubt in jurors' minds. And he said Harvey was pleased. "He told me at the end of the day, 'I really liked the way you fought for me in front of the judge. That's real New York. You got to teach Chicago that,'" presumably meaning Rotunno and Cheronis.

The next witness on January 27 was Miriam Haley, whose claims were a vital component of the charges leveled against Harvey. Just before she was summoned to the witness stand at 9:40 a.m., Juda Engelmayer placed two rolls of Mentos he purchased downstairs on the defense table beside Harvey, as he would most days. Like Sciorra, Haley did not look at Harvey as she passed him, or when seated in the witness box. She told the story of first meeting Harvey in 2004 at a film premiere in London, when she was twenty-seven. She ran into him again on a yacht docked at the Cannes Film Festival two years later, where Harvey invited her to his hotel suite. She asked for a job. He asked for a massage. She refused.

But he gave her his personal phone number, which she called several times, and she was hired as a production assistant under Barbara Schneeweiss, Harvey's close aide, on his TV fashion show, *Project Runway*. Months later, she testified, at the conclusion of her short-term employment, she wrote to thank him. He invited her to his SoHo loft apartment, where she said he tried to grab her, chased her into the bedroom, and pulled off her clothes. She told the courtroom that she screamed that she was menstruating, and he held her down, yanked out her tampon, and forced his tongue in her vagina. Her memory of the assault was so acute that she recalled the children's drawings on the wall of the room where it happened.

Jurors, their heads down, rapidly scribbled in the blue notebooks with their names on the covers as Haley described this assault. This incident was cited in two of the five charges in the indictment of Harvey.

The day of the assault, Haley said, she told a roommate what occurred, but refused to call the police. "She was a nobody on a visitor's visa who had no right even to work in the United States," assistant D.A. Hast told the jury. Despite this awful experience, when a month later Harvey invited her for drinks at the Tribeca Grand Hotel, she accepted. A Weinstein assistant met her at the bar, escorted her to Harvey's suite, and disappeared. Once in the room, she said, Harvey ordered her to undress and raped her. She lay there, she said, motionless, not fighting, feeling defeated.

Smartly anticipating how the defense would attack her testimony, Hast inquired, *Why did you keep in touch with Harvey?*

After the first incident, she answered, "I blamed myself." After the second time, "I was embarrassed. I just put it away in a box, as if it didn't happen." She was, Hast said, her eyes locked on the jury, trying to "almost normalize the situation." Sometimes victims blamed themselves, Hast said. Sometimes they were in denial that it had happened. Sometimes they feared Harvey would muddy their reputation. Or deny them the movie or television job they wanted. These were common reactions among rape victims, Hast said, promising that in coming days the prosecution would delve into the many reasons victims kept quiet.

In his rigorous cross-examination, Damon Cheronis treated what Hast had described as coping mechanisms as a confession. He began by declaring that Haley's relationship with Harvey was "consensual," not forced. Cheronis got Haley to acknowledge that even after Harvey allegedly raped her, weeks later, on July 26, 2006, she did have consensual sex with him. Methodically, Cheronis produced emails in which she asked for tickets to fly with Harvey to Cannes, for a trip to London, for a round-trip flight to Los Angeles to visit a friend, which Harvey paid for. She asked Harvey to review a TV pilot she wrote. She signed emails "Lots of love."

If he truly did these horrible things, Cheronis asked, *why did she keep in touch with him?*

"I needed a job. I wanted him to like me."

Therefore, Cheronis concluded, standing just inches away from the jury box, Harvey Weinstein wasn't the villain. He was the victim of ambitious women who manipulated him to advance their careers. "This is not predator and prey." Haley, not Harvey, was guilty. Rosanna Arquette had predicted this argument in her comments to Ronan Farrow: "They'll go after the girls. And suddenly the victims will be perpetrators."

"From the beginning, I was the most skeptical of the legal team," Arthur Aidala later said. "I was the one who said we should at least explore the possibility of a plea. But during the trial I grew more optimistic. I thought Damon was very effective against Mimi Haley. He brought out a lot of inconsistencies regarding her behavior. If someone sticks his face in your vagina, you go on an airplane with him after?"

Over the course of the trial, the prosecution would try to illustrate the jumble of thoughts—guilt, shame, fear, denial—that overwhelmed the witnesses. Aidala's remark may have been crude, but it demonstrated the strategy of Harvey's defense. They were not interested in delving into the psychology of a victim of sexual assault. They were interested in proving how the accusers' ambition drove them to cunningly seek to wring a career out of Harvey. The question for jurors would be: Was Miriam Haley or Harvey the victim?

On the seventh day of the trial the prosecution started to call the three Molineux witnesses. Each shared similar tales of Harvey's alleged abuse. Dawn Dunning, then thirty-four and an aspiring actress, met Harvey in 2004 when waitressing at a private lounge in New York. Harvey arranged a screen test for her. Days later, she said, he invited her to a meeting in his hotel suite. She was the only other person in the meeting. Harvey sat next to her on the couch and, she told the jury, he suddenly slipped his fingers under her skirt and inside her vagina. "I kind of froze," she said. "Then I stood up," crying.

From his defense table chair, with his head cupped in the palm of his right hand, Harvey slowly moved his head back and forth sideways, signaling that this was false.

She testified that he apologized and said, "It's not going to happen again." He then reverted to his role as powerful benefactor, promising to schedule acting auditions for her.

Did you tell anyone? Hast asked.

"No."

Why?

"I was embarrassed. I didn't want to be a victim."

She said Harvey's assistant called weeks later and asked her to meet him in the downstairs bar of a hotel to discuss film roles. She felt a crowded lobby bar was safe, so she agreed. When she arrived, his assistant was waiting and told her Harvey had meetings upstairs and please follow her. When Dunning entered the suite, she described what awaited: "He was wearing an open white bathrobe," and was naked.

She asked him to close the robe. She said he started to scream at her, "This is how the industry works!" Harvey, taking notes at the defense table, kept shaking his head no.

Before he began his cross-examination, Aidala consulted Harvey. At the lectern he asked, *At this second meeting, did Harvey ever place a hand on you?*

No.

Did he arrange a screen test for you?

Yes.

Did he invite you to company parties that you attended?

Yes.

Aidala hammered away: *Doesn't this suggest that yours was a consensual relationship?*

No, she insisted.

After Dunning was excused, Taralê Wulff took the stand in the afternoon. When she first encountered Harvey in 2005, she was twenty-eight, a tall and striking dark-haired model and aspiring actress working as a cocktail waitress at Cipriani's exclusive SoHo lounge. As she served him, Harvey inquired about her career ambitions and soon asked her to follow him upstairs to talk. In the secluded hallway he blocked her exit, and though she said she was so shocked that exact details were a blur, she did remember that he made her watch him masturbate. Afterward, she told no one. A week later, Harvey's office phoned to invite her to read for a part in a movie. She accepted and was waiting in an empty office when a Weinstein assistant came in to say he was detained at his SoHo apartment and a car was waiting downstairs to take her there. When she arrived, she told the jury, Harvey called for her to come in the bedroom, where he forcibly threw her on the bed and raped her.

"Don't worry," she said he told her. "I have a vasectomy," as if this excused rape. Like Miriam Haley, she said, "I froze." Dazed, she accepted a ride with Harvey back to his office.

Donna Rotunno in her cross-examination burrowed in: *Why didn't you report this to the police?*

"I just wanted it to go away," she answered, later adding, "I felt intimidated and scared."

Since you went to see him a second time and accepted a ride in his car to the office, wasn't this consensual sex, not rape?

Jurors were taking notes. Again, the defense was convinced they were demonstrating that the sex was volunteered.

Before inviting the third Molineux witness to take the stand, the prosecution called various witnesses to support the testimony of Dunning and Wulff. Then they invited Lauren Young, a model and aspiring actress when she met Harvey at a crowded 2013 Hollywood dinner. Attracted perhaps by a sweet face and short blond hair that made her appear even younger than twenty-three, Harvey sought her out. Displaying his ability to be charmingly inquisitive, he drew her out, and she told him she was writing a dark comedy. He took down her contact information. Not long after, Claudia Salinas, who knew Harvey and had met Young, was asked to invite her to the Montage Hotel in Beverly Hills to talk with Harvey about her dark comedy. Salinas was one of many women who worked for Harvey or were friendly with him who might be characterized as Harvey enablers, though the prosecution chose not to pound home this point.

Young was happy to accept the meeting invitation. "I put on my best dress and I was excited to network," she testified. She and Harvey and Salinas met in the bar. After listening to her description of her script, Harvey said he wasn't interested, but said she would be perfect to appear in *America's Next Top Model*. He invited both women to continue the conversation upstairs in his hotel suite.

Young followed Harvey as he entered the suite, with Salinas trailing behind. Before she knew it, they were in a large bathroom, with Harvey blocking one door to the suite and, she said, Salinas standing outside the bathroom and entrapping her by closing the other door. Harvey turned on the shower, shed his clothes, and began to masturbate, pinning her against a wall, unzipping her white lace dress, and pulling it down over her arms, exposing her breasts and limiting the movement of her arms. While the shower ran, he held one breast with his left hand and masturbated with his right hand. She blocked him when he reached for her vagina, screaming "No, no, no." He ejaculated into a towel and left the bathroom. She told friends but never called the police, she said.

Why? "Because he's got power."

The day after Young's encounter with Weinstein in the hotel bathroom in 2013, Barbara Schneeweiss reached out to her, Young said. They had a meeting, and Schneeweiss asked her about appearing on *America's Next Top Model*. Later, she said, Schneeweiss emailed to ask her for a headshot and a résumé. Had she pursued the opportunity, she assumed that Harvey would think it had smoothed things over. She never responded. "I didn't want anything to do with any of them," Young said.

Unlike the two other Molineux witnesses or Miriam Haley, Young and Sciorra did not continue to seek Harvey's favor after being molested. Rather than try to portray what happened with Harvey as consensual, the core of the defense accusation against Young and Sciorra was that they were lying.

Knowing that prosecutors rarely took on sex-crime cases in which victims kept in touch with perpetrators, and realizing that this was a huge vulnerability for the prosecution's case, Illuzzi invited to the stand Dr. Barbara Ziv, a forensic psychologist and Temple University professor who served as an expert witness in the Bill Cosby trial.

The defense attorneys wanted to counter Dr. Ziv and were enraged that Judge Burke refused to allow them to call their own experts. With the jury out of the courtroom, the judge ordered that defense experts could testify, but would not be permitted to address whether memories after a sexual encounter are accurate. If Harvey was found guilty, the defense planned to add this ruling to any appeal to overturn the verdict.

On the witness stand, Dr. Ziv said her job was to study evidence and be "objective" in the more than 1,000 rape cases she had probed and the roughly 250 times she had testified as an expert court witness. Contrary to popular belief, she said, "it is the norm" for sexual assault victims to keep in touch with their assailant and to have evolving memories of the horrifying experience they once tried to suppress. Citing statistics, she said it was a "rape myth" that sexual assaults are most common among strangers: 85 percent of the cases were among people who knew each other. As Haley's and Wulff's testimony seemed to confirm, only 20 to 40 percent of victims resisted. And as all six of these alleged victims illustrated, they rarely reported the crime.

And then Ziv came to the crux of what the prosecution hoped she would say. For "complex" reasons, most women continue to keep in touch with their assailants. "Contact can range from text messages to email exchanges to continuing in a relationship with them." Her experience and scholarly research confirmed, she continued, that victims are confused and terrified and there is no monolithic reason to explain why they react as they do. She cited the myriad reasons victims try to bury what happened, sometimes putting it in their words:

"I want to put it behind me.

"I don't want to ruin my reputation.

"I don't want to put my job in jeopardy.

"I feared retribution from the assailant.

"They feel like damaged goods. They can't believe it happened to them," so they pretend it didn't.

"They are ashamed," and blame themselves.

When Damon Cheronis conducted his cross-examination, he offered a more cynical explanation of why women had sex with powerful men like Harvey. Walking up to Dr. Ziv, Cheronis said she neglected to offer other important reasons:

These women wanted Harvey to advance their careers.

These women wanted to enrich themselves by filing a civil lawsuit.

The defense believed some of the witnesses planned to do so and was quick to note that Gloria Allred represented three of the six women who would testify—Haley, Sciorra, Young—and was in court most days. Douglas Wigdor represented Taralê Wulff and was also frequently in court.

Cheronis had another theory he presented to the jury: Perhaps these women now came forward to present themselves as victims because they wanted attention. They would be stars of their own movies.

Before he finished, Cheronis wondered: *You claim as a forensic psychologist that you seek evidence. Where's the DNA or police report evidence that Harvey physically abused these women?*

Evidence can be in the form of "corroborating witnesses," Ziv answered.

There's another explanation, Cheronis interrupted. *It's known as* "*relabeling,*" *meaning that individuals over time can reinterpret shameful incidents. Is this not true?*

This could be true, sometimes, Dr. Ziv responded.

The defense thought they scored some critical points against an expert witness. The prosecution thought Dr. Ziv effectively addressed the core vulnerability of the case against Harvey Weinstein.

Central to the outcome of this trial would be the next witness.

JESSICA MANN

(January 31–February 4, 2020)

I n any trial, the lawyers obsessively review the smallest details, script-
ing out their questions, their opening and closing arguments, their
legal maneuvers. The point of all that work is to tell a persuasive
story. Harvey proved his skill at that craft in the movie business. But
trials are not movies, shot under controlled conditions and subject to
revision in the editing room. They are live productions, dependent on
the chemistry of their participants, and not a little bit of luck. For all the
work the lawyers put in, it is the witnesses who do most of the talking,
who convey their stories to the jury, who supply the facts, the emotions,
and the drama. Sometimes, just one witness, even just one moment, defines the trial, and upends all the lawyers' carefully made plans.

That witness was Jessica Mann. The prosecution called her to the
stand on January 31. Mann was clearly the prosecution's most crucial
witness, for three of the five charges in the indictment pivoted on her
claims. Her importance would only increase over three days of emotional testimony.

She appeared at the end of the third week of the trial. Harvey entered the court early, at 9:10 a.m. on January 31, wearing a drab light-
gray suit and white shirt, its collar crumpled in the back; he seemed to

be in more of an upbeat mood than on previous court days. In the front row, on the right side of the court reserved for the prosecution, sat an unannounced guest, Paul Thompson, the deputy district attorney of Los Angeles, who was taking notes on Jessica Mann's testimony, as she would also be a witness in the expected L.A. trial. Cyrus Vance sat behind Thompson, chatting with him. When Vance attended the trial, which was most days, he was always trailed by a brawny bodyguard; he would not speak to reporters and paid intense attention to the witnesses as if his reputation was on trial, which in a sense it was.

Harvey looked up from the notes he was writing when Jessica Mann was summoned by the court clerk. She entered wearing a dark-gray skirt and black sweater, her long black hair flowing down her back, her face flawlessly made up, her lipstick understated. At thirty-four, she looked like a movie star, totally composed, confidently determined to share her story.

Joan Illuzzi began by inviting her to tell the jury about her early years. Mann described living in a trailer park on a dairy farm in the state of Washington. Hers was a strict Pentecostal Evangelical home, but her parents divorced when she was four, and her mother remarried twice. She moved in with her grandparents. She fled at sixteen to live with another family and became a licensed cosmetologist, but dreamed of becoming an actress, moving to Los Angeles when she was twenty-five. Sometime in late 2012 or early 2013, she and Talita Maia, another aspiring actress who was her roommate, went to a Hollywood party where she said she encountered an "old man" in a tuxedo outside who "seemed jolly." Harvey Weinstein was fifty-eight at the time.

"Do you know who I am?" he asked.

She had no idea.

"I'm Harvey Weinstein," and he mentioned some of the movies he brought to the big screen. She expressed real interest in learning more about Hollywood. At the end of the party, he came up to her outside, pulled her arm, and said, "I want to talk to you." He told her,

"I like how you look. I'm very interested in you as an actress." He took her number.

Someone from his office called a few days later and said Mr. Weinstein wanted to take her to Book Soup, a bookstore on Sunset Boulevard, so he could show her what books about Hollywood she should read. Cautious, she brought two friends. He was courtly and bought her four books. She was thrilled: "I thought God was blessing me."

He subsequently invited her to dinner at an Italian restaurant with Barbara Schneeweiss, the close associate who kept popping up in testimony. Schneeweiss had started working as one of Harvey's Miramax assistants in the latter half of the 1990s. Over the next twenty years, she rose to director of development at Miramax, supervisor of *Project Runway*, and vice president of productions and development for film and television at the Weinstein Company. Despite her elevated position, Schneeweiss remained very much in Harvey's personal orbit. Three of the six women at this trial who said Harvey abused them testified that Schneeweiss, who was based in L.A., was their point of contact. At dinner, Harvey told Mann that Schneeweiss would "plug" her "into his system."

Days after dinner, Harvey called and asked Mann to meet him at the Peninsula Hotel. She was impressed with how solicitous he was, asking about her family, when her parents divorced, where she grew up. "He asked a lot of personal questions. I was excited to talk about who I was." (This was the method Zelda Perkins had warned Rowena Chiu about.) They sat for dinner in the main dining room, and people there knew who he was. Since he shunned alcohol, he had his customary Diet Coke; she sipped a glass of wine. One man approached the table and bathed Harvey in compliments, lingering at the table too long. Irritated, Harvey summoned the waiter and declared, "We're going upstairs." He wanted the food delivered to the suite. She thought nothing of it, given the intrusion. But as soon as they entered his suite, he took off his shirt, walked into the bedroom, and said, "Let me give you a massage. Take off your shirt."

She refused. He persisted. "He was making me feel stupid, like I was making a big deal about nothing."

"Give me a massage," he demanded, handing her lotion as he lay face-down on the bed. Without removing her shirt, she granted his wish. "He had a lot of blackheads. The texture of that was uncomfortable," she said.

Every juror seemed to be furiously writing in their blue notebooks with their names on the covers, which the court officer handed them each morning and took away when court adjourned late in the afternoon.

Afterward, she said, "I'm not comfortable with something like this with someone I don't know." He tried to persuade her this was perfectly normal in Hollywood. He made no other advances this night.

Soon thereafter, an assistant in Harvey's office began inviting her and Talita Maia to parties, and once for late-night drinks at the Montage Hotel bar, where Harvey critiqued them, saying Mann needed to clear up her skin, and Maia needed to shed some pounds. Nevertheless, he said he wanted to cast them in a vampire film Dimension was producing, the presumption being that Harvey could cast Bob's movies. He invited them to his suite so he could share the script. It was a ruse, and given her previous experience, Mann said she was wary; Maia, who she had not told of the massage, was excited.

Upstairs, they sat on a couch. Harvey went into the bedroom, returning to stand in the doorway and bark, "Jessica, come here." Harvey slammed the bedroom door shut behind her and slathered her in kisses. The more she resisted, the more irate he became.

While jurors again took notes, Harvey at the defense table shook his head, cupping his forehead in his right hand and signaling frustration at not being able to respond.

Looking at Illuzzi, Mann said she tried to calm him with words. He was not to be denied, and he next spoke the silky words of someone about to do her a favor: "I'm not letting you leave until I do something for you." Her voice trembling, Mann described what happened next: "He went down on me. I started to fake an orgasm to get out of it."

Why did you do that? Illuzzi asked.

"I was nervous so I told him it was the best I ever had." She ran out and was surprised that Maia just sat there impassively, as if she had no idea what was going on in the bedroom despite the noise. Mann quickly told her what happened, and they left. Maia did not seem shocked. There were no scripts for the vampire movie in the suite. Mann said that Maia, equally ambitious to become an actress, urged her to stay in touch with Harvey. He was their meal ticket.

The jurors again were busily taking notes. Many reporters seemed stunned by this account, which was vivid, told in a voice at first measured but eventually vibrating with anguish.

At 11:15 a.m., Judge Burke ordered a ten-minute recess. Reporters buzzed in the hall, wondering if the prosecution would call Talita Maia to confirm this account. Damon Cheronis whispered that prosecutors would not dare call Maia because she would contradict Mann's testimony, which prosecutors later conceded was true. Talita Maia would testify for the defense.

When the jury returned at 11:25 a.m., from the lectern Illuzzi asked Mann, who for the moment remained composed and seemingly confident, *Were you in contact with Weinstein after this incident?*

"Yes, I made the decision to be in a relationship with him. . . . I entered into what I thought would be a real relationship then. It was extremely degrading. . . . He would talk very dirty to me." More than a few of the women who say they were abused by Harvey say he often boasted of the famous actresses he had sex with and the "kinky" things they did. Parading naked before Mann, he would say, "Do you like my big, fat Jewish dick?" She said he once urinated on her in the shower. She told of the time he wanted a threesome, and asked the other woman, Emanuela Postacchini, an aspiring actress he had chased, keeping her hopeful for an acting role, to undress and lie on the bed naked. She did, and Jessica said, "He told me, 'I want you to go down on her.'" This Mann refused to do. Postacchini was distressed by the encounter, Mann said, and when Mann curled up into a fetal position on the floor, sobbing, Postacchini tried to comfort her.

With his right arm on the back of his leather chair, Harvey just stared at Mann.

Illuzzi asked, *Did you have feelings for him?*

"I saw him the way I saw my father. . . . My dad had similar anger." While Mann's observations sounded authoritative and wise, and she was compellingly sympathetic, it was obvious to spectators in this courtroom that she was a wounded bird. It was impossible not to wonder if she would remain composed under cross-examination.

Jessica Mann was still in the comfort zone of Joan Illuzzi's questions. She was next asked, *How did Harvey Weinstein display anger?*

"If he heard the word 'no,' it was like a trigger for him," and "this monster would come out." Jessica went on to describe him, as others have, "like a Jekyll and Hyde. . . . He could be the most charming, informative person . . . and then behind closed doors it would be dependent upon if I gave him what he wanted."

It is interesting that this knee-jerk Jekyll and Hyde comparison was so common among victims and beleaguered staffers; it posits the notion that there were two distinct personalities contained within the same body. Harvey said as much in his offices when I'd been observing him for the *New Yorker* profile in 2002: *Do I be the good Harvey or the bad Harvey?* However, such cool-headed calculation suggested that at least some of the time Harvey was in command of his seemingly ungovernable temper, using a persona to achieve his goal.

Mann proceeded to shock the courtroom by offering a rough description of Harvey's anatomy—a big scar on his stomach; "he doesn't have testicles," a startling comment; he smelled "like poop, and he was just dirty." But she admitted her emotions were confused. "His approval meant so much to me."

Harvey blankly stared at her.

What did you like about him?

He was very successful, Mann answered, and he has "many likeable things when he was in his nice self."

Illuzzi sought to demonstrate that Jessica Mann was an ethical person.

Mann recounted for the jury how she refused to erase the emails and text messages in her mobile phone, which were personally embarrassing but provided powerful evidence against Harvey. And despite being desperately poor, when Harvey sent her an envelope containing one thousand dollars, she told him, "I would like to respectfully decline it."

Illuzzi asked her to describe a 2013 visit to New York City, her first. It was weeks after she and Harvey began a secret relationship. She flew with her agent, Thomas Richards, who paid for the trip, and with Talita Maia. They hoped Harvey had acting work for them. A breakfast with Harvey was scheduled at the Doubletree in Manhattan, the modest hotel where they were staying. Harvey surprised her by arriving very early. He met her in the lobby, where he booked a room. She forcefully told him not to, and they argued with raised voices. Enraged by this scene, he pulled her into the elevator, forced her into the room, and ordered her to undress. She tried to defy him, but he insisted. Afraid that her agent and Maia would learn of their ongoing sexual relationship if they came late together to breakfast, she followed orders, undressed, and got on the bed. He quickly disappeared into the bathroom for a moment, came out with an erection, got on top of her, and for the first time "put his penis inside of me." After it was over, she went into the bathroom and saw "a needle." She realized he had injected himself to induce an erection.

They went downstairs separately, and during breakfast Harvey cajoled them to stay another day to attend a Weinstein Company film premiere that night. Mann's hopes soared when Harvey arranged an audition for her and Maia for the Dimension vampire movie; only later did she learn that the parts were designed for teenagers. Joan Illuzzi produced emails from Barbara Schneeweiss inviting them to a February 2013 audition, although the roles had already been cast a month before.

Illuzzi did not pursue a line of inquiry many in the courtroom expected. Although Schneeweiss's name was invoked by Mann as well as by Haley, her reassuring emails to them shown on the courtroom's large screens, the prosecution chose not to summon her or others to testify under oath to what appeared to be their enabling role. Schneeweiss reported directly to Harvey as a vice president of the Weinstein Company, a member of its executive committee. She worked intimately with him for two decades. It was Schneeweiss who via email or phone arranged for Harvey's hotel assignations with a number of women who would later accuse him of assault. Harvey's emails revealed that he was obsessed with Jessica Mann, arranging to see her whenever in Los Angeles. Schneeweiss served as Harvey's soothing agent when Mann was agitated, inviting her to the office to pacify her, with Mann writing afterward:

> Barbara,
>   Thank you for making me feel so at ease yesterday when we met. You have an amazing bright personality and had me laughing.

Since she was not in the hotel suite with them, perhaps Schneeweiss did not know Harvey sexually assaulted Jessica Mann or Miriam Haley—although she was being sued by several women in the U.S. and Canada who believe she escorted them into rooms where she knew they would be assaulted.

No doubt, there were many who worked for Harvey who did not know of his assaults.

What we do know is that staff members escorted aspiring actresses to Harvey's hotel suites for meetings, then slipped out after several minutes. If Harvey shed his clothes and got into a bathrobe with an invited woman, staffers say they did not see this. If women were fleeing in tears, the staffers say they did not witness this. Yet at a minimum, they knew they were enabling Harvey to cheat on his wife and indulge his voracious sexual appetite. At the company, the female staffers who ferried women to Harvey's suite were known as "honeypots," since they made the visitors feel secure. Surely, some had to know. At a minimum, they embraced a corporate culture of silence.

Her acting career stalled, Jessica Mann continued to stay in touch with Harvey. He helped get her a job at the Peninsula as a hairdresser. They exchanged flattering emails.

Why did you send him sweet messages? Illuzzi asked. One email declared, "I love you, I always do. But I hate feeling like a booty call."

"His ego was so fragile," Mann explained. "And it would also make me feel safe. . . . I wanted to be perceived as innocent and naïve and not a threat." Harvey's odd behavior led her to believe, she said, that he was "autistic." Whether her description is accurate or not, it suggests that those who bumped up against Harvey's extreme behavior struggled to explain it.

The Harvey that Mann went on to describe was insecure, needy. "He loved to tell me Bill Clinton was his neighbor. He would talk about all the money that he would raise for big organizations," and of the celebrities he recruited to make political endorsements. These boasts—though they might have bolstered the fragile ego she described—also reminded her where the power in the relationship lay. If he was talking to presidents and raising money for important organizations, she feared, no one would "want to deal with someone crying rape." She would later tell the jury how Harvey would sometimes tell her, "People who are not my friends don't do well in this town."

They fell out of touch. When Mann was in financial trouble—living in her father's car, which she had inherited, and worried that it would be repossessed—she still felt she could turn to Harvey, and phoned Barbara Schneeweiss for help. "I didn't really know how to ask or what I really needed," she said. "I talked to Barbara a lot about the exact situation." Schneeweiss urged Weinstein to help, she said.

Illuzzi next asked Mann: "Did you begin a relationship with someone else?"

Yes, with an actor, she answered, which made her fret about Harvey's reaction. He had laid down rules for her to follow, and one was—she repeated his words—"You cannot date anyone in the industry. I won't have it. I find that disrespectful and unprofessional." It took her weeks but she worked up enough nerve to tell him. They met in his suite at the Peninsula. As she recounted in court telling Harvey that she cared for another person, Mann began to dissolve, her lips quivering, dabbing at her eyes with a tissue. She started to cry uncontrollably, prompting Illuzzi to ask Judge Burke if they could break for lunch.

At the start of the afternoon session, Illuzzi asked her again about the boyfriend. She recounted telling Harvey her boyfriend was an actor. He started screaming, "You owe me, you owe me one more time." He grabbed her arms and dragged her into the bedroom, threw her on the bed, demanded she remove her clothes. She begged him not to. He yanked off her pants, so violently that she said three prominent scratches were left on her legs. "He put his mouth on my vagina. Then he got on top of me and penetrated me." He made her get on her knees and "he shoved his penis in my mouth, and he had an orgasm." She retreated to the bathroom to clean up and wipe her wet eyes. He called for her and thanked her for his satisfaction, adding, "Now you can go and have your relationship, and what you can do is you can bring me other girls." He wanted her to be his procurer.

Mann sobbed, loudly, from the beginning to the end of telling this story.

Most of the jurors were vigorously writing in their notebooks. The defense team sat quietly at their table, aware they had a big task ahead.

From this point on, Mann said, she and Harvey rarely saw one another, though she did request additional favors, including asking him to write a letter of recommendation for her to become a member of the pricey Soho House in Los Angeles, which he did.

The prosecution was finished with its examination.

J udge Burke invited Donna Rotunno to begin her cross-examination at 3:00 p.m. Rotunno seemed eager to score a knockout, refusing to dance around her prey and flick light jabs.

Ms. Mann, you were manipulating Mr. Weinstein to get invited to fancy parties, correct?

"I was not manipulating him, but I was invited."

You didn't walk away from him, as you could have, when he asked for a massage or had oral sex, why?

"That could have been death to my attempt at a career."

By telling the jury you never wanted to have sex with Harvey Weinstein, you were lying to Harvey Weinstein, right?

"There were times where I did pretend to role-play with him."

When you told Harvey Weinstein his oral sex "was the best I ever had," you lied to him, right?

Harvey wanted to talk about it, so she did.

Rotunno cut her off with, *Did you lie to him?*

"Of course."

When you testified that Harvey assaulted you with oral sex at the Montage Hotel, Talita Maia was on the couch outside the bedroom. Why didn't you yell to her to come save you?

Shaking, Mann offered no coherent reason.

Although you say you resisted the threesome Weinstein requested, is it true you have engaged in threesomes with other women and men?

Yes, but with friends, she said, raising the eyebrows of more than a few spectators. Rotunno was succeeding at trashing Mann's credibility.

At 4:00 p.m., Judge Burke excused the jurors and the witness, asking Mann to return Monday for another round with Rotunno.

Entering court on Monday, Jessica Mann was simply dressed in a mock turtleneck, black pants, sans makeup. Whether deliberate or not, she looked less glamorous. She certainly knew she was in for a battle.

Rotunno continued her cross-examination by seeking to demonstrate that Mann was manipulating her client, and her flurry of punches would take a toll.

Rotunno displayed on the screen an email Mann wrote on April 12, 2013: "I appreciate all you do for me, it shows." She clicked on other emails revealing that Mann changed her phone number five times between 2013 and 2017.

Why did you, each time you changed your phone number, share it with Mr. Weinstein?

Why, if Weinstein was so abusive, did your emails regularly request things from him?

Mann's lack of clarity as to why she shared her phone numbers or wrote these emails left a clear impression of her dependency on Harvey as a benefactor.

You could have walked away from Harvey Weinstein and not ever seen him again, correct?

"Not from my point of view," she responded.

This was not a good moment for Jessica Mann. Jurors were, noticeably, staring down at their laps, or at Harvey.

Jessica Mann requested a time-out at 11:10 a.m., and the judge complied. In the hallway outside the courtroom, Juda Engelmayer, Harvey's public relations adviser, was ecstatic, whispering that Rotunno was demolishing Jessica Mann's credibility, and he added this sign of proof: "Did you see that the jury is not looking at her?"

District Attorney Vance observed the proceedings all morning. No doubt he was feeling some political heat. Within days, twelve members of the city council's Women's Caucus would call for his resignation for mishandling sexual assault cases. These council members and #MeToo advocates were still angry that his office failed to convict Dominique Strauss-Kahn and did not file charges against Harvey for assaulting Ambra Battilana Gutierrez.

Returning to the lectern after the recess, Rotunno pointed a finger at Mann, hammering her with questions. Despite the drama in this courtroom and in full view of the jury, which had a straight line of sight to the defense table, Harvey was battling to stay awake. At 12:32 p.m., his head dropped all the way to the table, only to quickly jolt up.

After lunch, Rotunno kept pummeling Mann with questions. While many were repetitive, Mann was on the ropes, her credibility weakened. She looked vulnerable. But had Rotunno crossed a line and been too savage?

Obviously, Rotunno did not think so. Before the afternoon session concluded, she seized on a letter Mann had written to her actor boyfriend on May 22, 2014. Mann was trying to explain to him her relationship with Harvey Weinstein and was upset her boyfriend didn't understand. She wrote to him, "I feel met with hate."

Throughout her cross-examination, Illuzzi would rise to object that Rotunno was, in effect, waterboarding the witness, and more often than not Judge Burke would sustain her objections to the wording or the low-blow intent of a Rotunno question. But Rotunno kept punching. She insisted that Jessica read the entire letter to her then boyfriend. Clearly shaken, she read slowly, tears sliding down her cheeks:

> Harvey [Weinstein] validated me. He always offered to help me in ways that my parents didn't. I felt approval to pursue the industry because he was encouraging. Harvey was my father's age and he gave me all the validation that I needed. . . . Sometimes I felt hopeless and should just be with an old man because I'm a lost cause. . . .

This letter, Rotunno said, was crucial; it suggested how confused, perhaps unstable, and certainly not credible the witness had been. At 3:30 p.m., in this vital moment of the cross-examination of a witness whose testimony could send him to jail for life, when Jessica Mann was openly sobbing on the witness stand, Harvey seemed unmoved. His eyes were closed, his head resting on his chest. Arthur Aidala rose from a nearby chair and gently poked him awake. A half minute later, Harvey's head again dropped.

Rotunno insisted that Mann continue reading the letter. When she reached the sentence where she confessed that she was sexually assaulted when very young, she started to hyperventilate, gasping for breath as she wailed. Judge Burke ordered a short break. Jessica Mann's tormented cries from the adjoining witness room penetrated the quiet courtroom, so loudly that jurors sequestered in the jury room could hear. This was, a prosecutor said later, for them maybe the worst moment of the trial, because they feared Jessica Mann "was so distraught she could not continue." Perhaps Rotunno had knocked out their central witness?

When she returned a few minutes later to the witness stand, Mann could not continue reading the letter. Between sobs, she couldn't catch her breath, placing a crumbled tissue over her mouth. Joan Illuzzi walked to the witness box. "Sit back," she urged, touching her arm. "Take a deep breath." Donna Rotunno, conveying sympathy, walked up to stand beside Illuzzi to offer a few soothing words. It fell to Judge Burke, acting as referee, to call an early recess, at 3:50 p.m. With a tissue pressed to her mouth, Jessica Mann walked past the defense table, Harvey's eyes following her all the way.

When he wheeled out of the courtroom to the corridor crowded with reporters lined up behind guardrails along both walls, Harvey for one of the few times in this trial turned to look at the reporters and offered a half smile and, "Hi guys." Clearly, he thought this was a good day for the defense. A reporter shouted, *Why did you fall asleep in court?*

"Oh, please," Harvey said, now upset and wheeling toward the elevators. Several steps behind, Arthur Aidala said Harvey's drowsiness was caused by his back medication. "I wasn't nodding off," Harvey later insisted in an email to me. "I just had a back operation after a car accident and I took Tramadol and Lyrica in the morning, and that somehow gives the impression that I look sleepy. I was in severe pain, severe back pain."

Jessica Mann returned the next day to complete her third and final day of testimony, and once again Harvey would struggle to stay awake. Once again she appeared sans makeup, wearing a plain gray turtleneck and black pants, her formerly blown-out hair in curls. She carried in one hand a small orange ball that she squeezed throughout the day to relieve anxiety. She seemed much more subdued, her voice hushed. She had gone from a self-possessed woman on day one, whose smart clothes and flowing hair matched her confidence, to a vulnerable, fragile woman on day three.

Donna Rotunno compelled her to finish reading the letter to her former boyfriend, and then reviewed a large volume of emails between her and Harvey Weinstein dating from June 2014 to February 2017, with Harvey arranging meetings, dinners, drinks, job referrals, offering sympathy when her dad died, recommending her for membership in Soho House. There were so many exchanges that one wondered how Harvey had time for Jessica Mann and his other dalliances while running a business and attending to his own family.

Rotunno called to the screen an April 27, 2016, email Jessica wrote four hours after having consensual sex with Harvey in his hotel suite: "I feel so fabulous and beautiful. Thank you for everything!"

By the afternoon, after the better part of three days on the witness stand for Jessica Mann, Judge Burke was eager to move on. Perhaps he was impatient with Rotunno, whose soliloquies he began to interrupt, urging her to frame a question. At one point, Rotunno noted that despite Mann's claims that she was extricating herself from Harvey, she had sex with him one last time in November 2016.

Yes, concurred Mann, and that was because of the death that month of Miriam Weinstein. Mann said she learned of Miriam Weinstein's death from Barbara Schneeweiss, who phoned to tell her, "Harvey wants to see you."

Looking for an out, Mann said, "What about his wife?" And Barbara said, "You're the only one he wants to see."

Feeling for him, Mann phoned Harvey. She said he cried. And she cried to hear him so upset. "He needed to be consoled for his grief and he wanted to talk to me because I understood grief."

When Mann arrived at his hotel suite, she was shocked and a little afraid. In a weak voice just above a whisper, she told the jury, "He's naked on the bed. All he wants to do is something sexual. . . . I think he masturbated in the mirror and then put himself in my mouth."

Rotunno stepped back from the podium, as if she had concluded her cross-examination. But she could not resist driving a final nail into Jessica Mann's credibility, so she stepped forward and attacked one more time: *Will you admit that your emails to Harvey are incriminating?*

Jessica Mann's answer seemed to rivet the attention of the jurors, for they looked directly at her, as she looked directly back at them. She began by candidly acknowledging she was not a perfect victim, having made questionable, even humiliating decisions. Then, her eyes dripping with tears and fixed on the jurors, she said slowly, forcefully, "I know the history of my relationship with him. I know it is complicated and different. But"—and here the volume of her voice rose—"it does not change the fact that he raped me."

This was a classic cross-examination mistake, asking one question too many, granting the witness a moment to get up from the canvas and throw a surprising knockout punch. And for the prosecution it was a knockout punch. Jessica Mann's comeback topped the prosecution's trial highlight reel. "Her raw frankness," a prosecutor later confided, "was a beautiful moment for any prosecution."

When Rotunno concluded at 3:17 p.m., the witness was excused, leaving the defense reeling. In a private moment at the end of this day, Harvey's usually ebullient lawyer, Arthur Aidala, seemed depressed. "My best hope from the jury," he admitted, "is a hung jury."

THE DEFENSE SPEAKS,
AND CLOSING ARGUMENTS

(February 6–14, 2020)

Those who knew Harvey Weinstein in his glory years were shocked by how old and frail he appeared in court. A bigger shock was how passive he seemed, a not terribly attentive spectator, similar to Monsieur Meursault in Albert Camus's novel *The Stranger*: detached, without remorse, only half listening at his own murder trial. In the courtroom, Camus writes, Meursault "wasn't even sure he was alive, because he was a living like a dead man . . . 'And I tried to listen again, because the prosecutor started talking about my soul.'"

Perhaps this emotional remove reflected an observation Rotunno once privately shared about her client: "It wouldn't surprise me if he fell somewhere on the spectrum," noting that she was surprised by "his ability to be removed" and his "social awkwardness." Perhaps it was a coping response to the humiliations this once powerful man had endured in this courtroom. Harvey listened mutely as various women described his body odor, his blubbery physique pimpled by blackheads and moles, his deformed genitals. Trying to spare him a conviction, Harvey's defense team acknowledged that he was, as one of his defense witnesses would testify, a sex addict. To demonstrate that the descriptions of his body by those who said he abused them were accurate, the prosecution had ordered him to pose naked and then used five of these photographs to share with the jury; these pictures seemed to repel jurors, for they winced and quickly passed them along when they were handed out as court exhibits by the prosecution.

On the afternoon of February 6, 2020, in the trial's sixth week, the defense began to call its own witnesses. It would call a total of only seven witnesses, in contrast to the twenty-eight called by the prosecution. This did not augur well for Harvey. "There was a problem getting people to come forward" on behalf of the defendant, admitted Damon Cheronis. The judge declined to allow one of their experts to testify. One prospective witness, TV and film producer Warren Leight, deliberately sabotaged plans to get him to testify by retweeting posts that endorsed prosecution claims against Weinstein. He was trying to make certain that he would not be summoned to speak on Harvey's behalf against his old friend Annabella Sciorra.

Other potential witnesses begged off, fearful of retribution. Members of Harvey's team said that after memory expert Dr. Elizabeth Loftus, their second defense witness, testified, she had two paid speeches cancelled. Among those who toiled for Harvey, there was a palpable sense that they were being chased by an angry mob.

The defense was weakened by a feeble start. Their first witness was Paul Feldsher, the former talent agent and current producer who was one of the small number of people who talked regularly to Harvey after he was first exposed as a sex fiend in October 2017. Feldsher had been a personal friend of Annabella Sciorra's. Fearing that Sciorra was a potent witness against Harvey, the defense summoned Feldsher in hopes of establishing that she lied in claiming Harvey raped her.

Under questioning by Donna Rotunno, Feldsher testified that Sciorra was once "one of my closest friends," and he recounted for the jury how soon after the alleged incident she told him "she'd done this crazy thing with Harvey." She wasn't traumatized, as she had claimed. She felt burdened by guilt for having consented to sex with Harvey.

Why did Sciorra claim she was raped? Rotunno asked.

"Well, the rape version got her a CAA agent!" Feldsher asserted with a big smile, insinuating that her public stance against Harvey might have been popular in Hollywood. He appeared cocky, someone who enjoyed performing for an audience.

Feldsher's boastfulness would vanish when Joan Illuzzi cross-examined him. Quoting from a text message he sent Harvey, she asked what he meant by describing Harvey's appetite for success and women as "voracious."

"What I meant by that was Harvey was very dogged in his pursuit of projects and material, et cetera, et cetera," he started to explain.

But what did you mean, Illuzzi interrupted, *when you texted that with "girls" he was "voracious"?*

"I meant that it was my understanding for a very long time that Harvey had a sex addiction and he dated a lot of women," he replied, provoking audible gasps in the courtroom and, later, a private admission from prosecutors that a defense witness admitting that Harvey was a sex addict was their favorite moment of the trial.

Illuzzi drilled deeper: "Then you go on to say, 'If a lot of these girls had been my daughter, I'd want to beat the shit out of you.' Is that correct?"

He acknowledged that it was correct, explaining, "I was trying to be a friend and to say 'I know the extremes of your personality. I know the extremes of your appetite.' But I did not believe that he was capable of the thing that he had been charged with."

"Did you say, sir, 'I think the dogpile of women who are suddenly bravely recalling repressed memories is hideous'?"

"I did," he replied.

Eager to lessen the harm Feldsher had done to his friend, in her redirect Donna Rotunno was able to elicit yes or no answers. She asked, *Did Harvey Weinstein ask you to testify?*

"No."

"You felt he deserved to have a friend?"

"Yes."

"In thirty years, did you ever see Harvey Weinstein treat women inappropriately?"

"No."

In her recross, Illuzzi noted that Feldsher assured the jury Harvey was never inappropriate with women, and she asked, *Were you ever alone in a hotel room with Weinstein and a woman?*

"No."

Feldsher was thanked for his testimony and the trial adjourned for the day. The headline in the next day's *New York Post* savaged Feldsher: DEFENSE WITNESS ENDS UP MAULING HARVEY.

The second defense witness, University of California, Irvine professor of cognitive psychology Dr. Elizabeth Loftus, was more effective. Her task was to demonstrate the unreliability of memory as time passes. She testified, "It doesn't take a PhD to know that memory fades over time."

Alluding to Annabella Sciorra's testimony, defense counsel Diana Fabi Samson asked, *What happens to memory after twenty-seven years?*

"That's an extraordinarily long period of time where there can be substantial fading of memory."

Was it possible, the counsel asked, *that a false memory could materialize when asked to testify in a criminal proceeding?*

One's memory becomes susceptible to "post-event information" that contaminates memory, Dr. Loftus answered. These include news accounts, trauma, therapy sessions, struggling to remember more, and "a great deal of emotion," including a desire to want to feel better about oneself after experiencing shame, which come together to create "false memories."

Again battling to stay awake, Harvey peeled off his suit jacket. The courtroom was warm, but no one else shed their jacket, including Cy Vance, who stayed most of the day.

In her cross-examination, Joan Illuzzi noted that the cognitive psychologist was speaking generally and was not offering an opinion on those who testified in this case. She couldn't, for Judge Burke ordered the defense expert not to discuss memories of sexual encounters. Some-what unkindly, Illuzzi asked the seventy-five-year-old memory expert, *Can you recall the exact dates you first spoke to the defense counsel?*

"I don't remember," she responded, eliciting giggles among jurors.

"Is that because of 'post-event information' that swayed your recol-lection?" Illuzzi countered, prompting the witness to smile.

The next set of defense witnesses bolstered Harvey's case. Nelson Lopez, the longtime superintendent of the Gramercy Park building Annabella Sciorra occupied, testified to a rigorous system in which doormen did not allow visitors to enter without buzzing for permission from the tenant. Therefore, he did not understand how Sciorra could have been surprised that a visitor knocked on her door. He said that over the thirty-one years he had worked in this building, never once had he known a doorman to violate this rule. When doormen needed a bathroom break, he said, a porter filled in, or they locked the front door. Lopez said the doorman on duty that night had since retired to Puerto Rico. It was surprising that the prosecution in its cross-examination failed to ask whether it was possible that the doorman saw Weinstein drop off Ms. Sciorra and thus remembered him when he came back several minutes later. Harvey's Miramax office knew her apartment number, the prosecution would show.

The next defense witness was Jessica Mann's former friend, Brazil-ian actress Talita Maia, who accompanied her to the Hollywood party where they met Harvey, was with her in the hotel when he allegedly first abused Mann, and went with her and an agent to see him in New York. She told the jury Mann never spoke to her of sexual abuse. In-stead, Mann told her Weinstein "was like her spiritual soul mate" and "the most wonderful person." Only once did Mann tell her she no lon-ger wished to see him. Contrary to the portrait painted by Mann, Maia said she was not personally eager to get work from Weinstein.

In her cross-examination, Illuzzi asked if it was true that she and Mann had "a very, very bitter falling out" in 2016.

"I don't dislike" Jessica Mann, she answered, though she admitted

Mann "did things in my life that impacted my life in a very negative way." But, she added, "I don't hate her or anything."

The next defense witness was Mexican actress and model Claudia Salinas, who Lauren Young accused of luring her to a hotel to meet Harvey and then blocking her exit from a bathroom as Harvey attacked Young. In a series of rapid-fire questions, Damon Cheronis asked: "Did you ever lure Lauren Young into a bathroom with Harvey Weinstein?"

"No."

"Did you ever lock Lauren Young in a bathroom with Harvey Weinstein?"

"It never happened."

"Did you ever stand outside a bathroom" as Harvey Weinstein assaulted anyone?

"If I had done that, I would remember that. I would never close the door on anybody."

Meghan Hast's cross-examination for the prosecution made Salinas somewhat defensive: *Did Harvey Weinstein ever hit on you?*

"He was flirtatious," Salinas answered. She said she was frustrated he never helped her professionally, though she acknowledged she regularly sought his help and received an invite to a Marchesa fashion event after she requested it.

"Did you introduce other women to Harvey Weinstein?"

"I didn't introduce other women. . . . He met some of my friends because I would always come with a friend. Harvey was always asking me to bring my better-looking friends."

Hast pressed on, noting that though Salinas had met Lauren Young only once before, she invited her to meet Harvey Weinstein at the Montage Hotel. "You did always bring your better-looking friends to . . . Harvey Weinstein?"

Salinas paused a moment before provoking laughter in the courtroom by answering, "All my friends are good-looking."

In his redirect of Salinas, Cheronis emphasized for the jury that she volunteered to testify, and he saluted her decision to come to New York without a lawyer because she was so certain of the truth.

The next day the seventh defense witness was Thomas Richards, the agent for Jessica Mann who flew with her to New York to meet Weinstein. Though witnesses like Richards offered no drama, Harvey was a more alert listener. In response to questions from Arthur Aidala, Richards said that at breakfast with Weinstein, Mann did not seem distressed. In fact, he said, she and Weinstein seemed friendly, and Mann told Richards she wanted to stay another day in New York because Weinstein had invited her to a film premiere. Throughout Aidala's questioning of Richards, Joan Illuzzi frequently objected to his questions as too opinionated or for leading the witness, and almost always Judge Burke instantly ruled, "Sustained." Yet when Illuzzi cross-examined Richards, she did not assail his claims. Obviously, the prosecution did not think his testimony was vulnerable, and he was excused after just forty-five minutes on the witness stand.

With the judge ordering a quick recess, Harvey and his lawyers huddled in a side room while a rumor raced through the press section that Harvey might testify in his own defense. It would be highly unusual in a criminal trial for the defendant to do so. In the two hundred or so criminal cases he's tried, Ben Brafman has had only four defendants testify. Before taking the stand, Harvey would have required days of rigorous rehearsals, including a mock trial with someone posing as Joan Illuzzi hurling hostile questions at him. Harvey had not had such rehearsals.

Yet Juda Engelmayer and members of Harvey's defense team whispered to reporters that they were arguing with Harvey that he should not testify. It appears that Harvey was engaged in a marketing ploy. This alleged debate over whether he should testify lasted for a half hour. Afterward, Arthur Aidala admitted, "The majority of time in that room was not about whether Harvey should testify." They appeared to be engaged in an effort to make Harvey Weinstein more sympathetic, to demonstrate his confidence. Prosecutors salivated at the prospect of cross-examining Harvey. "We were ready!" one confided.

When Harvey and his lawyers returned to the courtroom without the jury present, Judge Burke asked, *Does the defense have another witness?*

Harvey Weinstein does not wish to testify, replied Cheronis.

Leaning forward and looking down directly at him, Judge Burke asked, "Is that true, Mr. Weinstein?"

"Yes," the defendant replied, nodding.

Prior to the lunch hour, Judge Burke adjourned for the day, instructing both sides to offer their summations starting the next day, February 13. As reporters dashed from the courtroom hoping to catch Harvey with a question as he shuffled to the corridor, we were acutely aware that this daily drama was coming to a close. As he left the courtroom, reporters called out to Harvey, *Did you really want to testify?*

"I wanted to," he said.

To the assembled reporters outside, Arthur Aidala said the lawyers were united in opposition to their client testifying: "It wasn't necessary because our case was so strong." Press accounts took the bait and played up Harvey's spin. The *New York Times* headline blared, WEINSTEIN DECIDES NOT TO TAKE THE STAND, THOUGH HE SAYS HE "WANTED TO."

In truth, there was no way the defense would allow Harvey to testify. They believed Judge Burke violated Harvey's constitutional right to testify when he ruled before the start of the trial that if he testified the prosecution would be permitted to cross-examine him about dozens of his alleged but unproven bad acts over three decades. Prosecutors would be permitted to ask about Black Cube, about lies to his wives, his bullying of staff members and punching his brother Bob, his temper tantrums, his physical threats. Such a cross-examination, the defense reasonably concluded, would prejudice jurors.

Daily attendance by spectators had thinned out as the initial wave of interest crashed against the tedium of trial proceedings, but courtroom 1530 was packed on February 13 for the summations.

Harvey wore a somber black suit, white shirt, and dark tie. His face still looked as if it had been in a fistfight. District Attorney Vance arrived a few minutes late and a court officer found him a seat in the sixth row. Judge Burke, wearing a bright orange tie that pulsed from under his black robe, read his instructions to the jury.

The defense always leads off, so Judge Burke called on Donna Rotunno, who placed a black loose-leaf notebook on the lectern and called up a bullet-point slideshow on the big screens facing the jurors. She was acutely aware, as she would demonstrate, that the prosecution needed twelve jurors to agree, but the defense needed only one juror to dissent. Striding to about ten feet in front of the jury box, she framed her opening argument around the word *courage*, which she invoked twice in her first four sentences. "You promised during jury selection you would have the courage to make the right decision even if it was not the most popular. . . . The district attorney has failed to prove their case beyond a reasonable doubt. On behalf of Mr. Weinstein, we are imploring you to have the courage to tell that by saying not guilty on all the counts."

Rotunno spoke of the emotional argument she anticipated from the prosecution. "In a courtroom setting, you have to throw that gut feeling right out the window, because you have to evaluate evidence and never let your emotions cloud your intellect." They must, she instructed, pay no heed to "overzealous media" and prosecutors who demonized Harvey Weinstein. The false narrative the prosecution crafted, she continued, was predicated on the "offensive" notion that "women are not responsible for the parties they attend, the men they flirt with, the choices they make to further their own careers, the hotel room reservations, the plane tickets they accept, the jobs they ask for help to obtain. In their universe, they are not even responsible for sitting at their computers sending emails to someone across the country. In this script the powerful man is the villain."

Next, Rotunno chipped away at the damning spectacle of two witnesses—Haley and Mann—accusing Harvey of sexual assault in explicit detail, brushing aside the three Molineux witnesses and Sciorra, whose testimony was intended by the prosecution to buttress the primary accusers. "Your decision," Rotunno prompted, facing the jurors, "comes down to whether you believe two women, Miriam Haley and Jessica Mann." Rotunno set out to razor the claims made by each.

She cited Haley's warm, solicitous emails to Weinstein after he allegedly assaulted her. "If this were a kidnapping case and the alleged victim sent an email to her kidnapper saying, 'Thanks . . . had a great time, lots of love.' Would that be relevant to whether a kidnapping occurred?" At great length and with impressive recall of dates, she offered a timeline of Haley's relationship with Weinstein, and of the favors he bestowed, the consensual sex she granted. Haley was a persistent taker, Rotunno said, because she never reported her claims of sexual abuse from the time they met in 2004 to when the press reported in October 2017 that he was a predator. And what's the first step she took afterward? "The first thing she does is hire Gloria Allred," a civil lawyer "who sues people for money. Gloria has been here almost every day of this trial, sitting in the front row. She hasn't been paid. She doesn't sit here for her health." (As noted earlier, Allred represented two other witnesses, Annabella Sciorra and Lauren Young, and if her witnesses successfully brought civil charges against Harvey, Allred would receive a substantial portion of the settlement.)

Harvey was wide awake, listening intensely, often scanning the faces of the jurors.

Rotunno turned her fire on Jessica Mann, declaring, "She's lying about the circumstances of their relationship." She recited the many encounters Mann and Harvey had beginning in 2013. "We know that Jessica is not telling Harvey, 'I am using you for my career.' But we know that's exactly what she was doing. She was going to do anything she needed to do to have the career that she wanted to have." When Harvey knows she is visiting New York or in all his other emails to Jessica, Rotunno said, does he say, "'You must see me, you have no choice'?

None of that. Not once, not one time in 2012 to 2017 does Harvey Weinstein tell Jessica that she has to do anything."

Walking slowly before the jurors, Rotunno digressed for a moment to assail the prosecution and reassert Harvey's humanity: "In the alternative universe that the prosecutors have created for you, Harvey Weinstein is a monster, he's unattractive, he's overweight. They showed you naked pictures of him. Ask yourself, why? To do nothing more than shame him."

In the end, Rotunno portrayed Jessica Mann as a sad, confused, tormented soul who "could not keep anything straight. She could not keep a date straight. She broke down. I feel sorry for Jessica Mann. Jessica Mann is a victim of the prosecution that used her. Know how I know? They didn't even redirect her. After I was done, after two and one half days, the only witness they didn't ask another question to was Jessica Mann." (The reason why, the prosecution claimed, is because they worried that Jessica Mann was too distraught to continue.) The reason why, Rotunno told the jury, perhaps perilously crossing a line into brutality, was because of "all the symptoms she has." She dramatically paused, before identifying those symptoms as "borderline personality disorder."

Illuzzi swiftly objected, and Judge Burke sustained her, ordering the court stenographer to excise Rotunno's comment.

When the court broke for lunch at 12:50 p.m., Rotunno had already spoken for two hours and forty-five minutes.

When the summation resumed, Rotunno turned her attention to Annabella Sciorra, whom she dismissed as a superfluous witness. "Annabella was brought into this case for one reason and one reason only, she was brought in so there would be one witness who had star power. . . . Annabella makes claims in this courtroom that defy the statute of limitations, so the government cannot charge Mr. Weinstein with anything that they allege happened to Annabella." Her claims were twenty-seven years old. She couldn't remember if the incident took place in 1993 or

1994. She told her friend Paul Feldsher she did "a crazy thing" and had sex with Harvey.

Citing Dr. Loftus, Rotunno reminded jurors that memories can shift after so much time has passed: "There are resentments. There is a changed view of Harvey. There is a failed career. There is financial struggle. There is Ronan Farrow calling and . . . Ronan has a theory and if she fits into his theory, she becomes relevant and she can become a star again. And that's exactly what happened to Annabella."

The Molineux witnesses and others, like Rosie Perez, she claimed, were either "lying" or eager to make money using attorneys like Gloria Allred to bring civil lawsuits against Harvey.

Rotunno appeared to be wrapping up at last, but continued for another twenty minutes: "Justice demands a finding of not guilty, not because it is easy, and it shouldn't be, and not because it is popular, because it may not be, and not because the pendulum swings so far in one direction or another. Because the great thing about this system when it swings too far one way and swings back another, this system is the equalizer, this is the system that says they have to prove it." She concluded her four hour and thirty-five minute summation at 3:55 p.m.

Outside, a member of Harvey's team admitted he was depressed, confiding that Donna Rotunno was in many ways effective, "but went on too long." The defense now believed that if Harvey was convicted, Judge Burke would immediately remand him to custody. If he was found innocent, the Los Angeles district attorney "will bring him in handcuffs to L.A." to face another trial. And they dreaded Joan Illuzzi's closing argument the next day.

Joan Illuzzi arrived one hour before her February 14 summation. She didn't appear nervous; she was attired in her familiar black wool suit, worn over a white blouse. Harvey also arrived earlier than usual, 9:10 a.m., with D.A. Vance appearing a minute later. At 9:30 a.m., Illuzzi began by pushing the lectern away. Unlike Rotunno, she stood a foot or so from the jurors, without looking at the thick loose-leaf book in her hand. "What is this case about?" she said in a conversational voice. "It is about power, manipulation, and abuse . . . and it is additionally about the wanton lack of human empathy that most of us possess and take for granted in others." The defendant "was the master of his universe and the witnesses here were merely ants" who "were standing in line to get into his universe." Harvey did not look at Illuzzi. He listened intently but stared straight ahead.

Illuzzi discussed the women who testified, beginning with Annabella Sciorra, describing how the doorman probably recognized Harvey and allowed him upstairs, and how a man casing the apartment to see if anyone else was there was not consistent with a consensual tryst. Why did Annabella keep quiet? Illuzzi quoted Dr. Ziv, who said women "want to get on with their lives," forget it happened, spare their reputation, not jeopardize careers.

"Let's talk about Paul Feldsher," she segued, wondering: Why is it believable that his memory was precise about a conversation with Sciorra that was not traumatic for him and took place twenty-seven years ago? Are we to believe the same man who described women who claimed to be victims of Weinstein as a "dogpile of actresses," or when he asserts that Sciorra confessed to him she had sex with Harvey? Here is a witness, a friend of Weinstein's, who "wants to make you not believe Annabella Sciorra, but on the witness stand describes Weinstein as 'a sex addict.'"

You want to know what kind of a person Harvey Weinstein is? Illuzzi continued. Go back to October 2017, when Ronan Farrow asked Harvey's public relations adviser, Sallie Hofmeister: Was it true he raped Annabella Sciorra? Harvey Weinstein told Hofmeister, in an email jurors saw, to tell reporters: "We are going to say it was consensual or deny it." Well, Illuzzi declared, "'consensual or deny it' are the polar opposite of each other."

Lies were commonplace in Harvey's business career, she asserted. His willingness to lie extended to his accusers in this case, the women she said Weinstein thought of as "disposables." One was Miriam Haley. When Haley had an appointment at Harvey's hotel for what she thought was a job discussion, he asked for a massage, which she declined. She departed soon after. No job discussion. "How does Miriam say she felt? Humiliated and stupid. How many times have you heard that from the complainants in this case?" That's exactly the way Weinstein wanted them to feel. "If you feel stupid and belittled, belittled, stupid people do not complain." Afterward, Miriam Haley went to Harvey Weinstein's apartment for a meeting because "she is still trying to keep a good relationship with him."

Is that consent to have sex?

Is it a blurred line?

There are no blurred lines here. This is a crime.

Yes, Miriam Haley did months later stop resisting when she met him at the Tribeca Grand. But by now the defendant was jobless, she said, and felt like a broken woman, her shoes old and worn, her pocketbook bare. She was desperate for work. She considered herself, as Dr. Ziv testified about many victims, "damaged goods."

Illuzzi briefly discussed the three Molineux witnesses. Dawn Dunning? She was brought to Weinstein's suite for a business meeting by one of his assistants—"always an assistant"—and suddenly she is alone sitting next to him and "he sticks his finger right up her skirt and into her vagina." She screams. *What does Weinstein do? He makes her "feel belittled and stupid" by saying, Don't make a big deal about this.*

Taralê Wulff? It doesn't matter if she doesn't recall exact details of how he trapped her into watching him masturbate at Cipriani's. *What matters is that he brutally raped her in his apartment.*

Lauren Young? Weinstein assaulted her in a bathroom, pulled her top over her arms, reached for her vagina. She managed to escape being raped. *All you need to do to gauge whether Young is telling the truth is to use your common sense: Was Lauren Young believable?*

Illuzzi chose to spend most of her summation discussing the six female victims. "There are two things you got to know about Jessica

Mann to properly evaluate her testimony," Illuzzi began. One was that despite being crushingly poor at twenty-seven and sleeping in her late father's car, when Weinstein sends her an envelope containing one thousand dollars, what does she do? She told him, "I would like to respectfully decline it." The second thing is she took "the moral high ground" and, though cautioned by a detective to delete personally embarrassing emails and text messages, she turned over everything in her mobile phones, "and that is why you are seeing what you are seeing in this courtroom. . . . So that is how we have independent proof of Jessica Mann's morality."

Illuzzi boldly conceded the defense claim that Jessica Mann engaged in a "transactional" relationship with Harvey. But transactional means "you give something and you get something that you believe is fair in return." Echoing the powerful words Jessica Mann offered with tears in her eyes near the end of her almost three days of testimony, Illuzzi said, Yes, she made mistakes. It doesn't matter whether she was in love with Harvey Weinstein, or "had his name tattooed on her arm," or was married to him. "But all that, if all that were true, it still wouldn't make a difference. He still would not be allowed to rape her on March 18, 2013."

Concluding her nearly three-hour summation just prior to the lunch break, Illuzzi said the women who testified "came to be heard. They sacrificed their dignity, their privacy and their peace for the prospect of having that voice and their voices would be enough for justice. Based upon the evidence in this case, we are asking you to find Harvey Weinstein guilty."

Rotunno and Illuzzi painted two very different portraits of Harvey Weinstein, nicely summed up by Brent Lang and Elizabeth Wagmeister in the opening lines of their next day's account in *Variety*: "Predator or prey? Victimizer or victim? Rapist or philanderer?"

Nevertheless, courtroom skeptics were dubious about the optimism expressed by many, including Harvey's alleged victims, at the start of this trial. On day one, actress Rosanna Arquette proclaimed, "Time's

up on sexual harassment in all workplaces. Time's up on blaming survivors. Time's up on empty apologies without consequences. And time's
up on the pervasive culture of silence that has enabled abusers like
Weinstein."

The hard reality, however, was that it would take just a single dis-
senting juror to declare Harvey Weinstein innocent.

21

THE VERDICT

(February 18–24, 2020)

Among the twelve members of the jury, juror number 11 was a lightning rod. Amanda Brainerd was, at fifty-two, a successful real estate agent and also a first-time novelist whose book centered on prep school girls and their entanglements with rapacious older men. She was the very juror the defense did not want in the jury box—a well-educated feminist and, based on her own words, a past victim of sexual abuse. A magna cum laude graduate from Harvard with a master's degree in architecture from Columbia, she was the wife of an architect, the mother of three children, and an affluent resident of the Upper East Side. Throughout this trial, Harvey's defense team groused that she was the equivalent of a subversive fifth column embedded in the jury, someone secretly committed to taking Harvey down. Her soon to be published novel, *Age of Consent*, centers on two young women and older men. The defense argued that it was autobiographical, citing the text she wrote to a friend stating that in the book she struggled to "tell *my* deeply personal story, albeit in novel form."

A woman with dark shoulder-length hair who dressed casually, often wearing jeans, she did not stand out from the other jurors silently entering the courtroom each day in a single file in the order in which they were seated. Brainerd was in the back row. Knowing she was being watched, she never once flashed a facial expression—an eye roll, a nod, a shake of her head—that betrayed an opinion about what any witness said. But since she wrote about sexual abusers, Harvey's team was convinced she would strive to sway the jury to convict him. They planned to petition the judge first thing on the morning of February 18 to disqualify her before deliberations began.

Harvey arrived at 9:15 a.m. Instead of his usual head-down approach as he pushed his walker toward the front door, he said "Good morning" to the press line along his path. He looked sharper this day, his scraggly half beard more neatly trimmed. D.A. Vance was already in the courtroom when Harvey entered, though they never once acknowledged each other. Judge Burke appeared promptly at 9:30, ready for his first task: to define for jurors the law they must follow, and to explain the five counts lodged against Harvey Weinstein.

But before Judge Burke could invite the jury to enter, Damon Cheronis stood up to announce in a stern voice that the defense was resuming its protest against empowering juror number 11 and was submitting documents to the court about her. He explained that she wasn't impartial because she was soon to publish her first novel, a book about older men who were sex perverts. And, Cheronis added, she failed to disclose this in her paperwork or her jury selection interview. Cheronis offered what the defense considered additional damning evidence: juror number 11 recently reviewed *My Dark Vanessa*, a "book about the same subject." (Actually, it's about a woman reassessing her passionate teenage love affair with a teacher.) He also said she was reading and would review a memoir by a woman preyed upon by an older man when she was thirteen.

Facing the judge from the defense table, Cheronis asked that juror number 11 be discharged and replaced by an alternate juror. In a loud voice, Illuzzi challenged Cheronis, claiming that in her spare time from her work as a real estate agent juror number 11 wrote and reviewed books and "has done nothing to make herself grossly unqualified" in reviewing a book about child abuse, which is "completely unrelated to the charges" in this case.

Judge Burke decided to ask juror number 11 to enter the courtroom alone so he could question her in open court. *Was it true she was reviewing books online?* he asked.

In a quiet voice—because of the courtroom's antiquated sound system, many voices were barely audible—she said she was not reviewing books online.

Was it true she was reviewing My Dark Vanessa?

No, she answered, she was in the middle of reading it on Goodreads, a website where "you put up the book you are reading."

Almost instantly, without probing further, Judge Burke denied the defense motion to dismiss juror number 11.

The defense lawyers were deeply unhappy, convinced that Judge Burke's decision was more evidence that he was biased. In the hallway later that morning they promised that their request to dismiss juror number 11 would be added to any appeal they made to either the State Appellate Division or the state's highest court, the Court of Appeals, to overturn a potential guilty verdict.

After the jury was seated at 10:40, Judge Burke reminded them that they "are the exclusive judges of the facts. I'm the exclusive judge of the law," and he proceeded, in a neutral way, much like a referee, to school them as to the law, starting with an explanation of "the presumption of innocence." The burden of proof rested with the prosecution. The "defendant is not required to prove or disprove anything." Nor should any inferences be drawn when a defendant declines to testify. He further cautioned: "It is not sufficient to prove that a defendant is probably guilty. In a criminal case, the proof of guilt must be stronger than that, it must be beyond a reasonable doubt." The five charges were outlined for the jury. Count one was predatory sexual assault against Miriam Haley and Annabella Sciorra; such a charge required evidence of assaults against at least two victims, thus establishing a pattern, hence Sciorra's addition to the original indictment.

Count two was a criminal sexual act in the first degree against Miriam Haley when Harvey allegedly forcibly performed oral sex on her. Count three, like count one, was also a predatory sexual assault charge, but this time against Jessica Mann and Annabella Sciorra. Count four was the most serious charge, rape in the first degree against Jessica Mann, if Harvey used force or the threat of force. And Count five was "Rape in the Third Degree" against Jessica Mann, if she did not consent. Three of the five counts pivoted on Jessica Mann.

Judge Burke reminded the jurors that on each count to find Harvey Weinstein guilty they must be unanimous. They could refer to their notebooks, but what they had written was not a substitute for the trial transcript. If during their deliberations they wanted to review the transcript of what a witness said or of a court exhibit, or if they had questions, a note to the judge needed to come from the jury foreman, juror number 1. The foreman was instructed to communicate by notes to the judge on behalf of his fellow jurors, and to announce the jury verdict. The jurors' cell phones would be collected by a court officer and held while they were sequestered around a long wooden conference table with a large whiteboard in a narrow, forty-foot-long jury room. They would be in this cramped, two-windowed room from 9:30 a.m. through the late afternoon, until they reached a verdict. What role the jury foreman was to play in their deliberations, if any, was not defined. Jurors would be allowed to return home at night but were admonished not to discuss the case.

The jury was released at 11:30 to begin deliberating.

While the jury convened in the room off the courtroom, the defense, the prosecution, the judge, the court officers, and the press waited. Sometimes we waited on the hard benches in the courtroom; sometimes we congregated in the corridor. Sometimes the judge slipped into his nearby office, and the defense waited in a tiny office just outside the courtroom. Most days everyone sat in the courtroom chatting or pecking away on their laptops, which is permitted even when the court is in session. Or we stared at Harvey.

Nothing happened on day one of jury deliberation. Fixated on the damage juror number 11 might do to the defense's case, on day two the first thing Damon Cheronis did when the judge took his seat at 9:30 a.m. was to reissue his motion to dismiss her. Politely, Judge Burke announced, "My finding is that she just hasn't done anything wrong."

While the jury deliberated, we resumed our wait. We did not have to wait long, for at 9:50 the shrill jury buzzer went off, and Judge Burke read a request for the transcript of Miriam Haley's testimony, as well as all emails between her and Mr. Weinstein, plus a request for the judge to reread and explain to them counts one and two. When the jurors filed in, one of the court stenographers read to them Haley's graphic testimony in the same drone he might use in reading a telephone book aloud, though the testimony concerned forced oral sex and rape. Harvey listened intently, slipping Mentos into his mouth. He shook his head no twice when Haley was quoted saying the intercourse wasn't consensual.

The court wait resumed through the morning and past the lunch break, with the buzzer again going off at 3:25 p.m. This time the jury wanted to be read the testimony of Rosie Perez and Paul Feldsher about Annabella Sciorra.

The next day, Thursday, no buzzer rang all morning. The jury labored away; they had posted the five charges with a black marker on a whiteboard and consumed regular takeout orders from Dunkin' Donuts and lunch from a deli. After lunch, at 3:00 p.m., D.A. Vance appeared and conferred with Illuzzi. He had also waited in court the day before, reading memos, scanning an iPhone, anxiously waiting, like Harvey. The jury buzzer went off just after 4:00, with a request to hear Annabella Sciorra's testimony. Since it would take at least two hours to read the many dozens of pages, the judge postponed the reading for the next day.

The next day, Arthur Aidala was feeling glum. Privately, he confided that he feared the jury's request to rehear Sciorra's testimony suggested to him that they had already decided to convict on at least two counts. He still had hopes that one or two jurors would resist, but these hopes were waning. It was Friday, and he said most juries hate recessing for a weekend without a verdict, thus he fretted that jurors would be stampeded by family pressures to reach a guilty verdict today. If they didn't, his confidence that there would be a hung jury would rise.

The buzzer went off at 2:15, and the note to Judge Burke asked if it was OK if they were hung on counts one and three but were unanimous on the others. Counts one and three were the two predatory sexual assault charges, one against Miriam Haley, the other against Jessica Mann, and required jurors to believe not only their claims against Harvey but also Annabella Sciorra's. The note, which set off a furor in the courtroom, seemed to indicate that the jurors might have doubts about Sciorra's testimony.

Judge Burke polled both sides. The prosecution said they wanted the jury to keep working to resolve their deadlock. The defense huddled with Harvey. The defense team knew the jury deadlock was not a good sign, guessing that it meant they were in agreement to convict Harvey on three of the five counts. At this moment, Harvey was no longer a passive, seemingly detached observer. He animatedly told his lawyers he wanted the jury to continue deliberating. Judge Burke summoned both sides to assemble before the bench. When the jurors reentered he instructed them "to continue their deliberations." The jury had by now pondered the case for a total of twenty-four and a half hours, and when the jury went back to their room, Judge Burke asked both sides if before today's adjournment he should grant the jury twenty more minutes to try to end their deadlock.

Harvey shook his head no. He wanted what might be his last weekend of freedom. The judge adjourned for the day. Harvey looked downcast as he grimly wheeled past a throng of reporters. D.A. Vance smiled widely as he strode past the press without stopping to speak.

At 9:30 Monday morning, February 24, Harvey entered the court wearing a handsome navy-blue suit, accompanied by his best friend, Dr. William Currao.

At 11:30, the jury buzzer rang. The judge received note number 12 from the jury and read it aloud: "We the jury have reached a verdict."

Within minutes, D.A. Vance arrived from his nearby office behind the courthouse at 1 Hogan Place, as did an extra contingent of armed Supreme Court officers in bulletproof vests, who populated the three aisles and stood a discreet distance behind the defendant in case he needed to be restrained. At 11:40 the jury entered, and as was their daily routine, they didn't look at Harvey as they filed past him on the way to the jury box. Harvey, leaning forward slightly, stared straight ahead. Over the weekend, he had confided on the phone to a longtime associate that he believed the jury would convict him.

Jury foreman Bernard Cody, an always colorfully dressed Black man with a neatly trimmed beard—today he wore a dark dress shirt with a vibrant red bow tie—rose to announce their verdicts:

Count one, predatory sexual assault: "Not guilty."

Count two, a criminal sexual act in the first degree: "Guilty."

Count three, predatory sexual assault: "Not Guilty."

Count four, rape in the first degree: "Not Guilty."

Count five, rape in the third degree: "Guilty."

The court clerk, in a commanding voice, slowly polled each juror by number, 1 through 12, to ask how they voted on each individual count. Each juror, without displaying emotion, confirmed their guilty verdict. Harvey, hands clasped, head slightly bowed while looking straight ahead, seemed not to notice the four armed court officers who quickly moved to stand directly behind him, presumably to restrain him. All we could see of Harvey was his motionless back.

Meanwhile, reporters turned to one another to note their shock that the jury seemed to discount the testimony of Annabella Sciorra, since the jury acquitted Harvey on counts one and three, where she was essential to the predatory sexual assault charges requiring two victims plus a pattern of sexual assault. Because the rape occurred three decades ago and Sciorra was unsure whether it took place in 1993 or 1994, jurors presumably wondered whether her memory was clouded. Furthermore, they were perplexed that the attack, a rape in her own home, didn't conform to Harvey's MO of hotel/bathrobe/massage—an unfortunate result of the DA's lack of success in getting more women to come forward, for there were other examples of Harvey allegedly barging into women's homes and assaulting them, or trying to. Lysette Anthony claimed she was raped in the vestibule of her London house. Mira Sorvino said that Harvey showed up at her apartment door, having somehow talked his way past the doorman, though she evaded assault by claiming her boyfriend was on his way. But two anonymous jurors later confided to *The New York Times* that however credible Sciorra's testimony, it did not meet the "beyond a reasonable doubt" threshold.

Judge Burke thanked the jurors for their service and dismissed them. He then asked if either side wished to make an application to the court. "Yes, Your Honor," Illuzzi responded. "We are asking that the defendant be remanded at this point to await sentencing," taken immediately into custody. The penalty for the two guilty counts could total twenty-nine years and remanding him presumably would reduce the risk that Harvey would flee or commit suicide.

Rotunno asked that her client's bail and monitoring terms remain the same. Looking at Harvey, who was seated next to her at the defense table, she said, "He has significant medical issues. I have letters from all his doctors, Judge. He's under the care of five doctors currently. He's dealing with the remnants of his back operation, which was not successful. He's in need of a walker. He takes a list of different medicines. Judge, he's currently receiving shots in his eyes so he does not go blind." Rotunno urged the judge to place Harvey under house arrest until sentencing.

"Thank you," Judge Burke said. "I don't doubt the severity of his medical conditions. How is Wednesday, March 11, for sentence?"

Both sides approved the date, about three weeks away, and with that the judge abruptly ordered that Harvey be remanded and recommended that he be admitted to the medical facility at the prison.

Lieutenant Michael McKee, the amiable officer who politely supervised the officers and courtroom seating and its waiting lines, leaned over and told Harvey his men would now handcuff him in front of his body and lift him under his arms from the chair and take him upstairs to Corrections on the sixteenth floor, before he was transported to the prison on Rikers Island.

Lifted from his seat, seemingly in shock, Harvey looked to his lawyers and in a low voice exclaimed, "But I'm innocent. I'm innocent. I'm innocent. How could this happen in America?"

22

THE CONVICT

(February 24, 2020, to 2021)

Cyrus Vance and Joan Illuzzi looked like they had won the lottery. Minutes after Harvey was convicted, they strode from the courtroom, big smiles brightening their faces. At the other end of the corridor from the courtroom, Vance conducted a brief press conference, his first of the trial, thanking Illuzzi and Hast and the women who testified and "changed the course of history in the fight against sexual violence."

On the courthouse steps a moment later, also smiling was attorney Debra Katz, who represents many female victims of sexual assault, including Dr. Christine Blasey Ford, who had told the Senate that as a young woman she was assaulted by future Supreme Court justice Brett Kavanaugh. Katz was elated. "This was a watershed verdict," she said. "The jury repudiated the argument Weinstein's lawyers made that this was transactional. The jury understood that he was a sexual beast. Because of this verdict, prosecutors will be less reluctant to take on a hard case." Like others, she praised Cyrus Vance for daring to take on this case.

The public reaction was swift. Mira Sorvino tweeted, "I literally cried tears of amazement, gratitude that the justice system has worked on behalf of all of his victims today." Ashley Judd tweeted, "For the women who testified in this case, and walked through traumatic hell, you did a public service to girls and women everywhere." A fusillade of tweets hailed the three extraordinary journalists who first stripped Harvey of his invincible shield—Jodi Kantor, Megan Twohey, and Ronan Farrow. Tarana Burke, the founder of #MeToo, praised "the silence breakers in and outside of the courtroom." But she added a warning to the euphoria found on Twitter: "And, though today a man has been found guilty, we have to wonder whether anyone will care about the rest of us tomorrow. This is why we say MeToo."

After being taken in handcuffs from the courtroom to the Corrections office, Harvey Weinstein was seized by chest pains; his blood pressure shot up. He was rushed by ambulance to a prisoner section at the Bellevue Medical Center, where a stent was inserted into a coronary artery to avert blockages. He remained in Bellevue until transferred a week later to join the other seven thousand prisoners on Rikers Island.

Harvey returned to the courtroom for sentencing on March 11, just before New York was placed on lockdown because of the coronavirus. It could not have been a happy sight for Harvey when he was rolled into the courtroom in a wheelchair, passing the first row on the right reserved for the prosecution, where a Mount Rushmore of his victims— Jessica Mann, Miriam Haley, Annabella Sciorra, Taralê Wulff, Dawn Dunning, and Lauren Young—sat side by side. They were joined in the same row by Cyrus Vance, Rosie Perez, and Gloria Allred.

Just the day before, Taralê Wulff published a poignant statement describing the pain and shame she and these women suffered and explaining why they did not come forward earlier:

> After I was raped by Weinstein in 2005, I was confused. Why didn't I scream? Why didn't I fight? I thought I was stronger and I hated myself for being weak. That self-hate turned into shame

and guilt. Shame that I never should have felt and guilt that was not mine to own. I didn't know that at the time. I didn't realize it for 12 more years.

Harvey stole a part of my self-worth, treating me like I was nothing and I became fearful and mistrustful, not only of others but of myself.

Sitting at the defense table among his lawyers while waiting for Judge Burke to arrive, Harvey was possibly more alone than he had ever been. The letters he had requested from former associates and his two ex-wives urging Judge Burke to impose a lenient sentence on a good man were never written. And if he glanced around the packed courtroom, Harvey would not see in court this day, or any other day throughout the trial, his brother, Bob Weinstein, his three adult daughters, any of his former employees, or the array of actors and directors he had championed.

Prosecutor Illuzzi, as is customary, was invited to speak first about the sentence Harvey should receive. The presumption in a criminal trial is that the judge has probably decided the sentence he will impose before the prosecution or the defense pleads. Illuzzi began by thanking Judge Burke for the "fair and judicious manner" in which he presided. She turned to look at Harvey and described the "dream" many share to be part of the Hollywood entertainment world. The defendant had that dream come true. He made movies, he got to go to all the parties, he walked the red carpet and mingled with the stars. He enjoyed the wealth, and he had the power to make or break careers.

"How did he use that power?" she asked in a booming but controlled voice. "He got drunk on the power. He saw no authority over him. No limit to what he could take, no desire he could not grant himself. The young, struggling dreamers were not even people to him."

She urged Judge Burke to "sentence this defendant to the maximum"—twenty-nine years—"or near maximum." Then she stepped back and requested that Miriam Haley and Jessica Mann be allowed to read personal statements to the court.

Miriam Haley spoke of Harvey's vindictiveness. "I've lived in fear and paranoia on a daily basis—in fear of retaliation, paranoid my every move was being tracked and monitored, having learned of the methods Harvey Weinstein has used to intimidate and silence people. Having had a friend tell me his private investigator showed up at their door, asking questions about me. I've had panic attacks and nightmares. I've feared for my life."

Jessica Mann spoke next. Harvey stared straight ahead. "The day my uncontrollable screams were heard from the witness room was the day my full voice came back into my power," she said. She ended her brief statement by urging the judge to give Harvey "a maximum sentence. . . . I ask to be given the gift of knowing exactly where Harvey is at all times, so that I can truly live" free of fear.

Arthur Aidala was to be the first speaker for the defense. Because the defense perceived for reasons they did not comprehend that Judge Burke was personally hostile to Aidala, even though they had known each other for three decades, his role in cross-examining witnesses was scaled back. This day Aidala had something to prove. He was intent on boxing in Judge Burke by addressing what he saw as the judge's bias, thus making him vulnerable to being reversed by the appeals court if, among other reasons, he imposed on Harvey a more draconian sentence than he had imposed on others charged with similar crimes. In New York State, Aidala said, the mean sentence for those convicted of the same two felonies as Harvey Weinstein is just eight and a half years, not the maximum of twenty-nine years Judge Burke could impose. And unlike Harvey, many of these defendants had prior criminal records. Aidala cited a similar sexual abuse case Judge Burke himself tried in August 2018, one in which the defendant pled guilty to three counts, including the more serious rape in the first degree, and yet Judge Burke sentenced that defendant to only seven and a half years. Based on this evidence, Aidala urged Judge Burke to impose a five-year sentence.

Donna Rotunno was next; she sought to engender sympathy for Harvey. She cited "the eighty-plus Oscars that he is responsible for," the heartbreak of three daughters from his first marriage who no longer speak to him, the two young children from his second marriage whom he saw daily and who should not be deprived of their father for many years, and Harvey's perilous health. "At his age, I think, no matter what this court does, we're really looking at a de facto life sentence. And, Judge, frankly, even if the court gives the minimum five years that we think is a more than adequate sentence . . . it is very possible that Mr. Weinstein, given his health, doesn't live to see the end of that sentence."

Next came a surprise. There was an audible gasp in the courtroom when Rotunno announced that her client wished to speak. Judge Burke awarded the floor to Harvey.

From his wheelchair, Harvey began humbly, in a conciliatory vein, though, oddly, he referred to the good times he'd shared with his accusers. "First of all, to all the women who testified, we may have different truths, but I have great remorse for all of you. . . . I can't help looking at Jessica and Mimi and hope that something of our old friendship in me could emerge. . . . I'm not going to say these aren't great people. I had wonderful times with these people, you know."

Suddenly, Harvey switched from sympathy to victimhood: "I'm totally confused and I think men are confused about all these issues." What Harvey meant by confusion was confusing, for it did not center on ambiguity in sexual mores. Rather it centered on "men and women who are losing due process." A #MeToo lynch mob was responsible for his confusion, he suggested. What he worried about—and here he shifted from speaking on behalf of men to speaking for himself—was "a repeat of the blacklist there was in the 1950s when lots of men like myself, Dalton Trumbo [a screenwriter who had refused to testify before the House Un-American Activities Committee] . . . did not work, went to jail because people thought they were communists. You know, there was a scare . . . and I think that is what is happening now all over this country." A new form of McCarthyism aimed to destroy Harvey Weinstein, he seemed to be suggesting.

He challenged the prosecution's assertion that he possessed immense power: "I had no great power in this industry. Miramax at the height of its fame was a smaller company by far than any Walt Disney, any Sony, Paramount. I could not blackball anybody."

Then he switched modes again, seeking to convey that he had changed: "If I had to do a lot of things over, I would care less about the movies and care more about my children, family, and other people and friends." He offered a self-portrait of a man whose "empathy has grown over the last two and a half years. I can look at everybody there, you know"—he turned to look at the six women in the first row who testified against him—"and just say, you know, I understand things, I empathize, I feel things, and I was not that person until this crisis started." This stilted language was similar to the vow Harvey had made to live a kinder, calmer life, more centered around family and "human things," when I'd profiled him almost twenty years before. It was jolting to contemplate how such a gifted producer, who could anticipate what an audience would be moved by in a script or on the screen, could struggle to find ways to convincingly express his sense that other people existed. He seemed blind to the feelings of the women before him. Blind to the likelihood of the public's blistering reaction to another self-involved statement. Blind to the stern-faced judge who would sentence him.

Twice during Harvey's address to the court, attorney Arthur Aidala rose in an apparent attempt to get him to cut it short. "OK, let's take a deep breath," he whispered the first time. But Harvey continued, as he would after the second Aidala interruption.

Looking up at Judge Burke, Harvey insisted he fervently wanted to testify but was held back by his attorneys. Then he switched subjects again, now emphasizing his humanity. He described his many years of philanthropy and the money he said he had raised—the $100 million for the 9/11 victims' families and first responders, the $77 million raised for those victimized by Hurricane Sandy, the $2.5 billion he helped galvanize for Robin Hood's mission to assist our poorest citizens, and the $170 million for amfAR's AIDS work.

He then concluded: "I feel emotional . . . really caring and really trying to be a better person. Thank you, Your Honor, for the time."

Press accounts did not treat his statement kindly. It was, the Bloomberg News reporters wrote, "a disjointed rant."

Judge Burke briskly thanked Mr. Weinstein and the attorneys, then looked down at the defendant and grimly declared: "Although this is a first conviction, it is not a first offense."

Harvey could anticipate what came next. To strengthen the prosecution's argument for a stiff sentence, on March 6 D.A. Vance had given Judge Burke a detailed report containing accounts of the many dozens of times Harvey allegedly sexually molested women. In deciding a sentence, the judge said he took into consideration the "evidence before me of other incidents of sexual assault involving a number of women, all of which are legitimate considerations for sentence." Staring directly at the defendant, Judge Burke imposed a severe sentence: twenty years for criminal sexual assault (count two) and three years for third degree rape (count five).

"Court stands adjourned," Judge Burke brusquely concluded. "Officer, take charge."

Outside the courtroom, Harvey's lawyers called the sentence a craven political surrender by Judge Burke to a mob, presumably to give a boost to Burke's own election in 2022. Rotunno vented, "This severe sentence was obscene," and reflected "the Court's animus toward the Defendant."

"Please shut up Donna Rotunno," Rosanna Arquette tweeted, "the only obscene person here is you. He got what he deserved because he's a rapist."

On March 16, Harvey returned to Buffalo, the place where he first gained both notoriety and fame, where Harvey the Queens nerd became Harvey the impresario. He was now imprisoned at the Wende Correctional Facility, a fifteen-acre maximum security prison twenty miles east of Buffalo. With about a thousand male prisoners, Wende is one of five New York State prisons with a long-term medical care unit; moving about in a wheelchair or walking with a cane, Harvey shared a hospital ward with a handful of prisoners. He was locked in a cell. He had no internet access or daily access to news, save for postal deliveries and what the few preapproved individuals shared with him on the few telephone calls he was permitted. He spoke regularly by phone to his young son and daughter from his second marriage, and twice weekly with Aidala. Because of the COVID-19 pandemic, the prison permitted no visitors from March to early August 2020. Subsequently, his best friend, William Currao, paid visits, and Aidala recruited a Buffalo lawyer to drop in and serve as an intermediary. Harvey was also reportedly visited by actress Alexandra Vino, twenty-seven, an outspoken critic of his accusers, who was said to be his girlfriend.

When Harvey once spent a weekend at Camp David as the guest of President Bill Clinton, he went hungry for two days because he couldn't abide the processed-ham sandwiches in the Navy mess and called Jeffrey Katzenberg for help. Katzenberg told him about a Wendy's nearby, and Weinstein directed a Navy driver to take him there. Now he ate in a mess with the inmates from the hospital ward, though apart from the general prison population, which included Mark David Chapman, who murdered John Lennon. He consumed large amounts of processed cold cuts, bread, potatoes, and pasta, which explained why his weight had again ballooned. The man who once stayed in $3,500-per-night hotel suites and who casually chartered private jets, was allowed out of his cell three hours per day, had access to a sparse prison library, and was given a tablet without internet access. His trial was over, but Harvey's legal difficulties mounted.

Meanwhile, the district attorney of Los Angeles, Jackie Lacey, announced the beginning of "the process of extraditing defendant Weinstein to California" to face felony charges. COVID-19 would severely delay her plans. In the summer of 2020, she filed a court request to extradite Harvey to L.A., a request that awaited an extradition hearing. In October 2020, the D.A. added six new charges, bringing the total to eleven sexual assault claims by five women in Los Angeles between 2004 and 2013. In November, district attorney Lacey was defeated for reelection, but her successor pledged to prosecute Harvey. In the summer of 2021, a New York judge approved Harvey's extradition to L.A. for a trial, and in July 2021 Harvey was flown to Los Angeles to be tried in the fall or winter. If convicted of all charges, the maximum sentence would be 140 years, to be served after he is returned to New York to complete his twenty-three-year sentence.

A plethora of civil cases brought by women who claimed he abused them were pending against Harvey in New York and California. They included the lawsuit filed by former assistants Sandeep Rehal and Michelle Franklin, who charged that he expected them to purchase his erectile dysfunction drugs and to clean up afterward by wiping his semen off couches and retrieving his used condoms. Their lawsuit asserted, in seeming contradiction of the many claims from staff that they were unaware of his abuse, "Harvey Weinstein's sexual abuse and conduct, and his use of the office, TWC [The Weinstein Co] and staff to enable it, was common knowledge in the office."

Many of the civil cases await the resolution of the Los Angeles criminal trial, as they earlier awaited the New York criminal trial. In early 2021, a global agreement settled many of the civil cases, including lawsuits brought against Harvey by the New York State Attorney General, with $17 million awarded as compensation to the women. Since insurance companies paid this amount, it outrages critics that Harvey escaped paying a dime. But the global agreement did not bar other victims from pursuing their own claims, and at the end of 2021, several individual plaintiff lawsuits remained pending, awaiting the resolution of his California criminal trial.

In addition, a sexual assault case seemed to be moving forward in England. Even what seemed like momentary good news for Harvey turned bad. He was momentarily happy when the New York State attorney general agreed in the summer of 2020 to settle two major civil lawsuits against Harvey and his board for $25 million, with none of the targets accepting guilt and with much of the money earmarked for the lawyers. But this was contested by some of the women and their attorneys, and a federal judge ruled that the agreement was unjust to the women and that the legal fees paid to the lawyers, including Harvey Weinstein's lawyers, were "obnoxious," keeping the lawsuits alive.

Harvey had not given up hope he could elude his prison sentence by overturning his criminal conviction with an appeal to the Appellate Division of the State Supreme Court. To orchestrate an appeal, Harvey decided to bypass his Chicago lawyers and to rely on Barry Kamins, a partner in Aidala, Bertuna & Kamins and a retired State Supreme Court judge and former administrative judge of the Criminal Court of New York City, who knew many judges on the appellate court. The appeal was filed April 5, 2021, and hinged on these four basic claims, each relying on an assertion of judicial bias: First, because of juror number 11, Harvey was "denied his constitutional right to be tried by an impartial jury." Second, Judge Burke's Molineux ruling "violated his Sixth Amendment right to be tried only upon charges brought by a Grand Jury." Third, he was denied a fair trial when the judge rejected the defense request to have experts testify on the same subject matter as the prosecution's experts. Four, he "received a sentence that was harsh and excessive."

On December 15, 2021, the appellate court heard Harvey's appeal. The five female justices asked withering questions of the prosecuting attorney, giving Harvey and his team hope his appeal might succeed. Even if it did, for him there would be no sunlight. As early as the spring of 2020, Harvey was desperate for money. In secret, worried about Harvey's ability to satisfy the child support terms of his divorces, in April 2020 his two ex-wives separately successfully petitioned two different judges to freeze a total of $6 million of Harvey's liquid assets.

Many of Harvey's bills went unpaid. That spring, his jury consultant sued him for nonpayment of $166,000; in June, Donna Rotunno admitted that while Harvey had honored the first part of their flat-fee contract, he had "not fully taken care of" the remainder; his public relations adviser, Juda Engelmayer, admitted Harvey was "one month short" in paying him. By July 2020, it was three months short. By November, attorney Charles Harder, who had threatened a lawsuit against *The New York Times* and *The New Yorker* on behalf of Harvey in the fall of 2017, filed a lawsuit claiming that Harvey owed him $180,000. The reason Harvey's appeal wasn't filed until April 2021 was because Harvey's financial woes stalled Aidala's law firm from working on an appeal. "He doesn't have access to any cash and has to sell assets," Juda Engelmayer explained in late 2020. In May 2021, Harvey filed a lawsuit against Jose Baez, his second criminal attorney, demanding he return $1 million in legal fees because Baez was "regularly preoccupied with other matters" and thus was inattentive. By suing his former lawyer, Baez's attorney, Joe Tacopina, said Harvey had waived attorney-client privilege, allowing Tacopina on Baez's behalf to denounce Harvey as "a vile fiend" and a "rapist."

Harvey's finances were a mystery. Over the years he had made at least several hundred million dollars. Many expenses were chalked up to the company. The sale of his many homes swelled his bank account. Even sharing the proceeds with two former wives, that presumably left him ample funds. He retained a Buffalo attorney, and a New York City attorney to replace Charles Harder. A prominent Los Angeles attorney, Mark Werksman, was recruited to serve as his defense counsel for the Los Angeles trial. He retained lawyers to defend him against both an array of civil lawsuits and potential prosecution in England, Ireland, and Toronto. And by late 2021, Juda Engelmayer still served as his paid public relations adviser. Yet his brother Bob believed Harvey's wallet was nearly empty.

Bob had reason to believe this. In the past, Harvey's solution to a cash crunch had often been to seduce a potential investor. Who, though, would listen to a pitch from a man in prison? A brother, perhaps. Bob Weinstein said Harvey reached out to him after two months at Wende, a claim Harvey denies. "Absolutely not," Harvey emailed from prison.

In self-defense, Bob shared the text message Harvey sent him from prison on May 15, 2020, via his close friend William Currao, who conveyed Harvey's thoughts, since prisoners are not permitted email:

> I am writing what he has said to me. First of all, he wants to apologize to you. He has said this repeatedly to me. But he does need your help. Georgina and Eve are after him and they are relentless. He has already given Eve over 40 million and Georgina over 15 million. Harvey's net worth now is total debt. His appeal is coming up and his lawyers are very confident they can reverse this. . . . He acknowledges his infidelity to his wives, but he swears there was never any crime on his part. He completely denies any rape. He is very sad about his behavior toward you, your family, and his family. He would like you to seriously consider buying the rights to *Dogma* from him, and to patch up your relationship with Kevin Smith. He would like to get 3-3.5 million for the film, but he feels it could easily bring over 5 million in global rights, Netflix, AT&T, etc. He would like to talk to you about this. . . . He also sends his best to you and your family. He would be very happy to speak to you and hear about your life.

With the clarity Bob now had about his older brother, he looked upon this proposal as just another Harvey con. "Harvey proposed that if we re-released this film for streaming it would be worth five million dollars. The truth is, it is probably worth closer to fifty thousand, if that. He was completely lying. He said that he would like me to give him three and a half million towards the fictitious five million that this picture was worth. My reaction to reading that Harvey said he felt 'horrible' for the pain he caused me and his entire family was that it was complete bullshit. The only thing he cared about was trying to convince me to give him three and a half million dollars. I did not respond."

Harvey's money woes were matched by fears for his legacy. The Silence Breakers, two dozen of Harvey's accusers, including Ashley Judd, Rosanna Arquette, and Rose McGowan, issued a public statement after he was sentenced, announcing, "Harvey Weinstein's legacy will always be that he's a convicted rapist." He was now, his lawyers' brief to the Court of Appeals conceded, "treated as a pariah."

Chased from his legacy, he feared being reduced to an asterisk were the outstanding films he introduced, the Oscars he won. Former employees who once came to work at Miramax certain they were changing the cinema world now confessed to being "embarrassed to say we worked there." Eric Robinson, who started as Harvey's assistant and rose over ten years to a major executive role, said, "People ask what was your last position, and you don't want to say. It's sad to have a ten-year chapter of your career redacted."

Who would listen to former employees who extolled what he'd built? He would have ranted at Amy Israel for daring to help expose him to Jodi Kantor and Megan Twohey of the *Times*, but Harvey would also have taken pleasure to hear what the former head of acquisitions for Miramax, who used to keep him in his seat during screenings by feeding him cookies, said about his contribution to film history: "I think that Miramax was one of the most groundbreaking film studios that ever was. It changed the nature of the film business. Miramax made and distributed visionary movies that were subversive and noisy and created a cultural conversation around them through ingenious, disruptive marketing, which has had a deep impact on the film and television industry today. Miramax acquired foreign language films that may never have seen the light of day, and marketed them in such a bold, innovative way that it helped them win Academy Awards and introduced them to a worldwide audience. There is no way that a movie like *Roma* would thrive in the way it did without the legacy of Harvey and Bob."

Peter Biskind, author of an important early book about the transformation Miramax wrought, commented after Harvey's disgrace: "He broke out of the art film ghetto and put independent films in theaters in suburbia. He got Oscars for independent films. He transformed Oscar campaigning. He had a real knack for identifying films no one wanted and making a lot of money with them." But Biskind added, "there was a downside to it, too." When Harvey started outbidding everyone with Disney money, his competition had to overspend as well, and creativity suffered. "You become more conservative . . . instead of looking for new talent or taking risks. I think that contributed to the decline of independent film. . . . He developed it and then he broke it to some degree."

Prison allowed Harvey too much time to think about his legacy. As the summer of 2020 gave way to fall, then to 2021, as Harvey counted the days until March 11, 2043, the end of his New York sentence, he was looking at a total of 81,223 days behind bars, assuming no additional sentences and that he lived that long, a very big if.

23

ROSEBUD?

Only a few jurors spoke to the press after the verdict. The one who spoke most often and in detail, on television and to print reporters, was jury foreman Bernard Cody. In a lengthy interview with Jean Casarez of CNN, he said that at first the jury was deadlocked nine to three after four days, and eleven to one on the morning of the fifth and final day. He said three events were critical to achieve a unanimous guilty verdict. First, defense witness Paul Feldsher's claim that his friend Harvey "had a sex addiction and that he dated a lot of women . . . That's how we really decided on the verdict, kind of more on his testimony." Second, Cody blamed Harvey's appearance in court. "Even when the witnesses were talking, he was, like, in and out, not paying attention to what they were saying." And third, although the judge cautioned not to be swayed by whether the defendant testified or not, Cody said the jury wanted not only to hear from more than the seven defense witnesses; they wanted to hear from Harvey Weinstein. "If you're on trial for your life, no matter what the circumstance is, if you believe in your heart that you didn't do it, then just go on the witness stand." Two anonymous jurors agreed, telling *The New York Times* that the failure of Harvey to testify troubled them.

They also wondered why his only brother, his lifelong business partner, did not appear to vouch for him on the witness stand.

It's striking that the male foreman cited the testimony or behavior of two men as being crucial to the jury's decision, not the testimony of, say, Jessica Mann, Miriam Haley, Annabella Sciorra, or the other women who testified, suggesting that "believe women" may face a steep uphill climb.

Jurors reported that the trial and deliberations took a heavy psychological toll, and several fell ill, they believed from the stress. Afterward, we were all left to wonder: When Harvey Weinstein placed his head on a pillow at night after raping Jessica Mann, or forcibly performing oral sex on Miriam Haley, or entrapping Taralê Wulff to watch him masturbate, how did he explain to himself what he had done?

Did Harvey truly believe he never raped or sexually abused the roughly one hundred women who say he did? Did he feel remorse? Did he suffer from "cognitive distortion," convincing himself, as one of his victims, Rowena Chiu, has said, that he was a Don Juan and women really wanted him? Because of his power and narcissism, did he feel entitled? Did he believe this was a fair trade, sex for career assistance, even if some of the women showed signs of extreme distress—weeping, screaming, running away? Was it normal for him to deny what he had done because he was only human and didn't want to think of himself as a rapist? The six-paragraph statement he issued after being terminated by the Weinstein Company included three sentences that blamed his behavior not on himself, but on his times: "I came of age in the 60's and 70's, when all the rules about behavior and workplaces were different. That was the culture then. I have since learned it's not an excuse."

Or was Harvey Weinstein a sociopath, unable to comprehend the suffering of others, or to distinguish right from wrong?

How do students of such behavior explain it?

They don't. Experts are quick to caution that they don't know Harvey Weinstein. They usually also concede that the causes of sexual abuse cannot be described empirically.

Even if one assumes Harvey did not know that what he did was wrong, his efforts to hide what he did confirm that he feared being exposed. "There's a difference between knowing it is wrong, morally, and knowing it is wrong 'because I would be punished,'" observes Dr. James Cantor, a professor at the University of Toronto and director of the Toronto Sexuality Center.

If you conclude that Harvey is a sociopath, you're left with another question: What's the cause?

It would be too glib to suggest that one experience or person in Harvey's life defined him. But several factors converge to point a finger at Harvey's Queens home. Screaming, denigration, and a persistent cyclone of emotional turbulence was as common in the Weinstein home as it would become in the offices of Harvey and Bob. One of Harvey's closest childhood friends, Alan Brewer, believes Harvey's "assaulting of women has less to do with sex than with control, dominance."

Dr. Meg Kaplan of Columbia believes there may be a link between verbal brutality and sexual brutality. Someone who enjoys verbally savaging people, she says, often enjoys sexually humiliating women. But Bob, who grew up in the same household, did not become a serial sex offender. The sinister flowering of Harvey's more violent impulses is a mystery that may never be fully understood.

For his part, Bob Weinstein says he sees much of Miriam Weinstein in Harvey. Why?

"Harvey exhibited the same dual traits that my mother had. Parents often say, 'Try telling your children they did something wrong. Don't tell them they're a bad person.' Miriam's nature was to say, 'You're no good.' Harvey picked up on that. He would often tell people, 'You're no good.'"

As the lawyer for the Weinsteins, David Boies knew Miriam, but not well. However, he had many conversations with Harvey and Bob about her, and said, "The picture I have of Miriam is of someone who was very strong and not a gentle person. I think they were hurt by what she said about them. They grew up in an environment where their mother acted in a way that hurt them." Their father, Max, "was not a dominant person." Boies knew Harvey and Bob were angry, perennially, whether or not there was cause. "I think they felt diminished, unsuccessful, not measuring up." Miriam was "very proud" of their success at Miramax. "But it was too late. Everything that happens after you're eighteen is too late."

One among the many who have served as an attorney to Harvey, and who publicly asserted his innocence, nevertheless describes him this way: "Harvey is a sociopath. He is not someone who thinks he did anything wrong and is burdened by a heavy conscience. He believes that if a woman wants something from him, even if he pins her down and rapes her, he thinks it is a consensual act." He is making a trade: what he wants in return for what she wants.

Those who worked closely with Harvey have thought long and hard about the hole in his psyche they believe he was desperate to fill. They could see it in the way he ate, so excessively that he became obese and eventually diabetic, in the way he chain-smoked cigarettes, in the way he spent money, so heedlessly that he burned through a billion dollars of investors' money at the Weinstein Company, but especially in the way he pursued women as prey. Mark Gill, the former president of Miramax in Hollywood, described Harvey as someone who lunged at everything, and linked this to his incessant need for more: "You'd see it in Harvey's physique. But you'd see it in everything he did. He was always wanting more. More press. More sales. More good reviews. More movies. More stars. More parties. More, more, more."

Former Weinstein Company vice president of production Abby Ex, as noted earlier, observed, "I thought Harvey was a man who had impulse control problems. It spanned across all areas—in greed, food, power, awards, money, and in women."

Problems controlling hunger, and a hunger for control—this was the Möbius strip of Harvey's appetites. "Having someone in their control is arousing," observes Dr. Meg Kaplan of the hundreds of cases of psychosexual disorder she's witnessed. "They objectify women as objects, not as real people."

No evidence has surfaced of Harvey's sexual abuse in high school or college. It began when he gained power as a music promoter in Buffalo.

Harvey's sense of his own power was obviously a factor in shaping his behavior. Harvey saw himself as the "fucking sheriff of this fucking lawless piece-of-shit town." A sheriff is the law. "It's all part of a power trip," Zelda Perkins, his former assistant, once said. "I don't think he's a sex addict. He's a power addict. . . . He put an enormous amount of energy into humiliating men and an enormous amount of energy into getting women to submit."

Looking back on Harvey's life, it's worth digesting the thoughts of the person who presumably knew Harvey best. In an attempt to understand his brother, Bob Weinstein said that in recent years he had reached out to medical professionals who studied sexual abuse. These professionals told him they could not make a diagnosis without seeing a patient, but they indicated that the person Bob was describing exhibited sociopathic tendencies. While on the telephone with me, Bob googled the definition of a sociopath. The words that marched down his screen were:

Lack of empathy.
Narcissism.
Difficult relationships.
Manipulative.
Deceitful.
Callousness.
Hostility.
Irresponsibility.
Impulsive.
Lack of guilt.

Bob read these out loud. Each of these descriptions, he told me, applied to his brother. No longer did Bob Weinstein believe his brother was merely a sex addict. Months earlier, I had asked, "You know Harvey better than anyone. How do you explain why Harvey committed such foul acts?"

"I didn't know him better than anyone," Bob responded. "You're missing something big."

"I'm all ears."

"He's doing this thing that you and I can't imagine, and you're applying logic to something that is illogical. Pathologies like his seem to be illogical. You're looking for a Rosebud clue why Harvey did all he did. You'll never get that." Bob Weinstein's conclusion: "Does it really matter? He should just be judged on his actions. Which is what the jury did."

Nevertheless, Bob was still Harvey's younger brother, who had shared a Queens bedroom with him and stayed up late to listen to Yankee games on the radio, who went with him to Saturday matinees, where they fell in love with movies together, who followed him to college outside Buffalo, who as a partner jointly forged Miramax and delivered some wonderful movies to the big screen. No matter how bitter Bob was that his brother's sexual perversions had sentenced him to career purgatory, soon after Harvey was sentenced to twenty-three years in prison, sympathy and memories and brotherly concern quenched Bob's anger.

Soon after Harvey was sentenced to prison in 2020, Bob recalls, "I read in the papers that Harvey was placed in isolation because he has the coronavirus. I reached out to my lawyer, who reached out to Bill Currao, and I asked, 'Does my brother have it?' I worried that my brother could die without my having had a conversation with him. I wanted a conversation, to be able to say good-bye." In any event, it turned out the reports were false. Harvey did test positive for the virus, but he had no debilitating symptoms.

Harvey denied to me that his brother ever reached out to him:

"Bob has been antagonistic since this all happened. Nothing but antagonistic," Harvey declared in a dictated email from prison. "I tried to reach out to him, and he's not receptive. I just got cursed at and dismissed."

Bob Weinstein insisted that Harvey, once again, was not telling the truth. He described a March 27, 2020, phone call from Harvey's best friend: "Bill Currao called me and said, 'Bob, you probably wonder why I'm calling you.' My first thought was, 'Perhaps he's calling to tell me my brother died?' Instead, what he said was, 'Harvey heard that you reached out and wanted to speak to him. He asked me to find out, What is it Bob wants?'"

To Bob, Harvey was displaying the same emotional opacity he'd revealed at the Four Seasons lunch years before, where Bob hoped David Boies could help Harvey comprehend the transformative power of gratitude and pride. After Boies finished, Harvey had said, *I don't get it. What are you trying to say?* Bob now understood at last, after years of trying, that it wasn't a question of finding the right way to reach his brother.

"When I heard that Harvey asked, 'What is it Bob wants?' even though I should not have been surprised, it still shocked me," Bob told me. "Harvey was treating his brother, me, as if I was bothering him, as if he were in a meeting in his office. *What was it I wanted to disturb him about?*

"It was a reminder for me: there is no Harvey, no real human being there."

Author's Note

A word of explanation about my interactions with Harvey Weinstein and the presence of his voice in this book: Many of his recollections here, specifically many of those referencing his childhood through to 2002, are taken from the twelve or so hours of taped interviews we did in 2002 for a twenty-thousand-word *New Yorker* profile. Harvey was displeased by that profile. Before and during his criminal trial, which I attended daily, he declined my interview requests. When I introduced myself during the trial to his best friend, William Currao, and started to walk with him from the courtroom during a break, Harvey suddenly turned from his chair ten feet away and barked, "Bill, don't talk to him."

After Harvey was convicted, I asked his public relations representative, Juda Engelmayer, for permission to interview Harvey in prison, not expecting that Harvey would comply. Late in the spring of 2020, at Engelmayer's suggestion, I emailed a long list of questions, which he promised to forward to Harvey in prison. I expected no reply, and months went by without one. Then, on September 14, 2020, Engelmayer forwarded Harvey's dictated responses to my questions via email. His answers were usually short, sometimes cryptic; I've incorporated many of them. This process was repeated in May 2021; Harvey usually responded only to factual questions.

Harvey denied every single meaningful allegation. I asked him: "Over 100 women have come forward claiming you sexually assaulted them. Are they all lying?"

He responded: "Give us the list of the 100 women who claimed they were sexually assaulted and we will give you direct responses."

Then, in November 2020, one of Harvey's lawyers, Robert Hantman, dispatched a letter to Carolyn K. Foley, an associate general counsel at Penguin Random House, insisting that his client wanted to be able to respond to every single allegation made against him in the book, and requested that I also name my sources. He announced that I could interview Harvey, but the interview would be limited to just factual questions. This was an easy offer to reject; journalists rarely allow the subject to restrict the topics to be discussed in an interview, and sharing all sources with the subject of a book is a nonstarter.

In December 2020, an email from Juda Engelmayer to me reopened the discussion. He said that Harvey wanted an "opportunity to respond to all allegations" made against him (sexual or otherwise) in the book. Harvey would consent to a not-in-person interview, he said. Since no internet is permitted for inmates, it was obvious there could be no Zoom interview. And since I insisted on a live interview, email responses were off the table. But I would agree to multiple phone interviews, which would contain dozens of questions of my choosing, including:

- After you were exposed as a predator in October 2017, you told reporters you knew you needed help and would attend an Arizona treatment center to get help. What did you think you needed help for?
- When you placed your head on a pillow at night, how did you explain to yourself what you did that night with a young woman? Did you feel any guilt?

I next heard from Harvey's team on January 12, 2021, when Hantman emailed Penguin's Carolyn Foley claiming that since I use the word *Monster* in the title of my book, this "title makes clear" the book will be a "one-sided and biased portrayal of Mr. Weinstein." Therefore, he demanded: "Mr. Weinstein seeks the names and contact information for each person to be included in the book, as well as their specific allegations, to afford him an opportunity to appropriately respond." The request, he said, was reasonable under the First Amendment because without this I would be revealing my "malice" and "reckless disregard for truth."

I emailed Juda Engelmayer that Hantman's letter was ridiculous, and in the first instance was wrong in claiming that "I use the word 'Monster' in the title for my book." I wrote: "For the record, we have not even had a discussion about the title for this book." I learned that it was Harvey who assured his team that *Monster* was the title of my book. I laid out my ground rules for an interview with Harvey:

1. I agreed to ask Harvey to respond to sexual or other claims made against him that he has not responded to already.
2. The interview would be taped and on the record.
3. He would be expected to agree to field other questions I would ask.
4. Considering that prison authorities may limit his time on the phone, and because I have so many questions to cover, I would expect him to agree to multiple interviews.
5. I would share no questions in advance of the interviews.

Over the next few months Harvey's posture toward this interview changed like the weather. At first he told Engelmayer he would answer no general questions. Then he switched to say that as long as he could respond to claims made against him, he would agree to my interview terms—if I agreed there would be no release of the actual taped interview before publication of the book. I agreed, having no interest in cannibalizing my book. As long as I remained free to use the recorded interview as I pleased in the book and after it was published, I was satisfied. There followed weeks of silence. On March 1, 2021, I emailed asking when we might schedule the first interview. Harvey and his team now wanted to change the ground rules: Engelmayer emailed to ask if I would do the interview in his lawyer's office without recording it.

No, I responded. Since I don't take stenography and would miss many words, I record my interviews. This assures accuracy. An almost comical series of email exchanges followed. Engelmayer said Harvey's lawyer had an assistant who could transcribe the interview. No, I responded, a journalist couldn't rely on Harvey's team to produce the text of the interview. If my answer was no, Engelmayer wrote back, then there would be no interview. Should Harvey be willing to return to the terms he originally agreed to, I replied, I'd be happy to proceed. Otherwise, we're done.

Within days, Engelmayer emailed that Harvey would agree if instead of recording the interview I brought my own stenographer. I don't have a stenographer, and even if I did this would not guarantee accuracy. A recording assures accuracy and also frees the interviewer to listen more closely. "To decline a recorded interview is a dealbreaker for me," I emailed. Harvey's team came back with an offer to have their own stenographer provide a transcript and also record the interview, allowing me to check but not take the recording. Unacceptable, I said.

Two weeks later, Harvey consented to a single interview that I would record in his lawyer's New York City office. The day before the scheduled April 14, 2021, interview, Harvey's Los Angeles attorney, Mark Werksman, phoned to say that with a Los Angeles trial likely to be scheduled in the fall of 2021, he and Harvey agreed that such an interview could put Harvey in legal jeopardy. He thought my book was scheduled to be published in the fall of 2021, around the time of an expected L.A. trial. I said the book would not be published until sometime in 2022. Let me discuss that and get back to you, he responded.

He never got back to me.

Acknowledgments

I n writing about Harvey, I struggled to convey that he was more
than a monster. He had obvious talents, and one task was to explore
this talent, his virtues as well as vices. There is, of course, no way
to escape brutal arguments over whether monstrous behavior nullifies
brilliant work. Since Caravaggio was a murderer, should we dismiss—
or at least diminish—his art? Was Ezra Pound not a good poet because
he was a fascist? Since Picasso treated women so miserably, does this
mean we should discount *Guernica* and other sublime paintings? Harvey Weinstein does not belong in this first rank of artists. However, he
did produce and distribute many extraordinary movies, brilliantly promoted them, and was an independent film pioneer. Do we erase the
successes in his career because of his beastly sexual behavior and brutality? Obviously, the Bad Harvey outweighs the Good Harvey in these
pages. But I hope readers will see more than a stick figure.

In reporting this book, I am indebted to the many people who gifted
me their time and attention as I sought to understand Harvey Weinstein. In all, I conducted several hundred interviews, the majority of
them on the record. I was surprised at how many people who worked
for Harvey were willing to allow their names to accompany their

thoughts. Others who worked for Harvey were proud that they toiled to advance movies the Hollywood studios shunned, yet didn't want their names married to Harvey's, fearful it would be a black mark on their résumé. Or that readers would assume that they must have known Harvey sexually abused women. "Harvey earned his black mark," a ranking former Miramax executive said. "I didn't."

Among the many who shared their time and insights, I owe a special thanks to Bob Weinstein, who opened himself to a near stranger for many hours of conversation. I am sure he will say "ouch" more than once if he reads this book. But he has my gratitude. As an independent director of the Weinstein Company, Lance Maerov displayed the courage to consistently challenge Harvey, and then devoted many hours to helping me understand the drama of the Weinstein Company. David Boies is someone I've known and covered over many years. Although he knew he would be compelled to answer some uncomfortable questions, thankfully he cooperated.

This biography is a very different book than those written by Ronan Farrow, Jodi Kantor, and Megan Twohey. Nevertheless, I stand on their shoulders. They did extraordinary digging to expose Harvey's abuses. As someone who tried, and failed, in earlier years to persuade his victims to go on the record, I marvel at their feat. They displayed enough human empathy to make understandably vulnerable women comfortable enough to talk. I am indebted to Peter Biskind, whose microscopic and telescopic reporting on Harvey and Miramax's early years and the movie business in general was invaluable.

In writing this book, I owe special thanks to my friend Courtney Hodell, who carefully read and commented on the manuscript. Courtney helped make this a better book. And her life partner, Nathan Rostron, helped me solve a vexing potential problem: how to be sure that page notes for sources in the manuscript stay the same for the repaginated pages of a finished book.

I am indebted to my close friend Richard Cohen, who undertook a forensic rather than a casual read of the manuscript, making invaluable suggestions. Jason Stavers, a lawyer who was in a graduate writing program at NYU and volunteered for a mentor program where he was expected to devote five hours per week to fact-checking, and in exchange I was to read his work and offer mentoring advice. In the end, Jason mentored me when I later hired him to fact-check the book. His memos were lucid and well-written and the equal of his careful fact-checking. In the early stages of this book, Ben Kalin performed invaluable fact-checking feats. Obviously, if there are mistakes in this book, unlike Harvey, I take responsibility. The photographs in this book were gathered by Crary Pullen, who was a pleasure to work with.

Several of the interviews from my 2002 profile of Weinstein are not dated in the page notes because I no longer have all the interview dates. However, each interview was recorded and fact-checked by *The New Yorker*. I retained the recorded Harvey Weinstein interviews from 2002, and the dates of each are cited, as are his recent emailed responses from prison to my questions. A paragraph or sentence here and there was extracted from my 2002 *New Yorker* profile of Harvey. I owe a special note of gratitude to David Remnick, editor of the magazine, who approved the original Harvey profile and was my stalwart partner, as was the magazine's amazing team of editors, fact-checkers, copy editors, and lawyers. What has always been special about *The New Yorker* since I wrote my maiden piece in 1978 is the absence of sharp elbows and the gratifying sense that all are rowing together to make your work better.

This is my fifth book with the same editor, Scott Moyers, and I still marvel at the careful way Scott reads and edits a book. I have friends who complain that their editors too often offer superficial commentaries on their manuscripts, taking too long to respond, pulling their punches. Scott is the opposite. Deeply engaged, willing to offer tough love—sometimes a verbal shove, sometimes a pat on the back. I was blessed to have the legendary Jason Epstein as my editor for my first eight books. I fretted that I would not see his like again. I have.

In addition to Scott Moyers, once again the team at Penguin led by my my friend Ann Godoff performed admirably. Mia Council in Scott's office kept the train running on time; she was assisted by Natalie Coleman. Once again, copy editor Jane Cavolina was at her brilliant best; Sarah Hutson's public relations team under Gail Brussel would labor long and hard on my behalf; Carolyn Foley subjected me to a rigorous legal cross-examination; Aly D'Amato, Danielle Plafsky, Alicia Cooper, Christopher King, and Amanda Dewey are also owed special thanks.

My ICM agent, Sloan Harris, has been a stalwart, combining the true qualities you want in an agent: business manager, protector, alert reader, challenger, and friend.

No one invests more perspiration in my books than Amanda "Binky" Urban, my better half. I have the bruises to prove she reacts to every word. The idea to do this book belongs to her, as does my gratitude.

Notes

PROLOGUE: THE GRAY CONCRETE CARPET

2 **An elevator whisked Harvey:** I attended court daily throughout the trial, and for each of Weinstein's court dates starting in 2018. Therefore, I will not provide an endnote for each reference to the pretrial or actual trial days.

5 **"We used to say of his home":** Author interview with Amanda Lundberg, March 13, 2019.

6 **Kane, as being burdened by:** Orson Welles quoted in Frank Brady, *Citizen Welles* (New York: NY Creative Publishing, 2015) and requoted in Simon Callow, *Orson Welles: The Road to Xanadu* (New York: Viking, 1995).

CHAPTER ONE: YOUNG WEINSTEIN

8 **"In a good year":** Author interview with Harvey Weinstein, June 27, 2002, for his *New Yorker* profile of Harvey Weinstein, "Beauty and the Beast," which was published December 16, 2002.

8 **"wanted his sons to be close":** Author interview with Bob Weinstein about his father, May 6, 2019.

8 **"I want to be a somebody":** Author interview with Bob Weinstein about Max Weinstein, September 14, 2018.

9 **"Harvey called her 'Momma Portnoy'":** Author interview with Alan Brewer about Miriam Weinstein, October 10, 2019.

9 **"point a bread knife at my heart?":** Philip Roth, *Portnoy's Complaint* (New York: Random House, 1967).

9 **"quintessential Jewish mommy":** Author interview with Harvey Weinstein about Miriam Weinstein, June 27, 2002, for *New Yorker* profile.

9 **"fancy magazines, like *Vogue*":** Author interview with Bob Weinstein about Miriam Weinstein's style, and her influence on Harvey Weinstein, September 14, 2018.

10 **"You always have to be loyal":** Author interview with Harvey Weinstein about Max Weinstein and the Kennedy brothers, June 27, 2002, for *New Yorker* profile.

10 **"I promise I'll take the blame":** Bob Weinstein, "Bob Weinstein's Love Letter to Brother Harvey," *Hollywood Reporter*, February 18, 2015.

11 **"the love of reading started":** Author interview with Harvey Weinstein about his eye accident and reading, June 27, 2002, for *New Yorker* profile.

11 **door-to-door selling:** Harvey's Boy Scout adventure in the seventh grade reported by Scott Johnson and Stephen Galloway, "Young Harvey Weinstein: The Making of a Monster," *Hollywood Reporter*, February 28, 2018.

11 **"There was magic in the theater":** Author interview with Bob Weinstein about their father taking them to the movies, September 14, 2018.

12 **"exactly what I was feeling":** Author interview with Harvey Weinstein about *The 400 Blows*, and falling in love with movies, June 27, 2002, for *New Yorker* profile.

12 **"my eyes were falling out of my head":** Author interviews with Harvey Weinstein about Truffaut influence, June 27, 2002, and October 9, 2002, for *New Yorker* profile.

13 **"I knew that it was Sergei Bondarchuk":** Author interview with Harvey Weinstein about developing an encyclopedic knowledge of movies, June 27, 2002, for *New Yorker* profile.

13 **"not part of the in-crowd":** Author interview with Harvey Weinstein about high school, June 27, 2002, for *New Yorker* profile.

13 **"Harvey was not particularly attractive":** Author interview with Michael Ellenberg about Harvey dating in high school, April 4, 2019.

13 **remembered him as "sullen":** Author interview with Cari Best about Harvey in high school, April 8, 2019.

14 **"He never seemed to be interested":** Author interview with Margaret Bishop about Harvey in high school, April 8, 2019.

14 **insisted that Harvey had a girlfriend:** Author interview with Bob Weinstein about Harvey's high school girlfriend, October 8, 2019.

14 **"not somebody you'd think":** Author interview with Harvey's classmate Michael Fox, April 23, 2019.

14 **"he had the idea to be an organizer":** Author interviews with Alan Brewer, September 11, 2019, and October 10, 2019.

14 **"Harvey arranged that":** Author interview with Peter Adler about Harvey arranging for Padraic Colum to come to class, May 24, 2019.

15 **"He was afraid of her":** Author interview with Peter Adler about Miriam Weinstein, May 24, 2019.

15 **"always comparing Harvey":** Author interview with Alan Brewer, October 10, 2019.

15 **wrote of a trip:** Bob Weinstein, "All Thanks to Max," *Vanity Fair*, April 2003.

16 **"she could turn on you":** Author interview with Bob Weinstein about Miriam Weinstein, June 11, 2020.

16 **"In the home, one of the things":** Author interview with Dr. Glen Gabbard on verbally abusive parents, May 13, 2019.

16 **"She could have been Sheryl":** Phoebe Eaton, "The Making of a Predator, Part I," *Air Mail*, June 13, 2020.

16 **"I see my mother in my brother":** Author interview with Bob Weinstein about his mother, September 14, 2018.

16 **"a real sense of integrity":** Author interview with Bob Weinstein about his father, May 6, 2019.

16 **Harvey tried his best to craft:** Author interview with Harvey Weinstein about his father with the Jewish underground, June 27, 2002, for *New Yorker* profile.

17 **he offered free credit:** Author interview with Bob Weinstein about Uncle Shimmy, June 16, 2021.

17 **like a classic Shimmy hustle:** Author interview with Peter Adler about Uncle Shimmy's influence, May 24, 2019.

CHAPTER TWO: BECOMING HARVEY

18 **he could take courses:** Author interview with Harvey Weinstein on why he chose Buffalo, June 27, 2002, for *New Yorker* profile of Harvey Weinstein, "Beauty and the Beast," published December 16, 2002.

19 **"the 'Berkeley of the East'":** Howard Kurtz email to author, September 21, 2019.

19 **"Harvey was outside selling flowers":** Corky Burger quoted in Andrew Z. Galarneau and Nicole Peradotto, "He's Harvey Weinstein—And You're Not Not," *Buffalo News*, March 22, 1997.

19 **"Denny the Hustler":** Harvey Weinstein and Horace "Corky" Burger, "Patchwork," *The Spectrum*, February 22, 1971.

19 **Corky denied writing "one word":** About Denny the Hustler to Benjamin Blanchet, *The Spectrum*, October 19, 2017.

20 **"under-the-table payments":** Author interview with Christina Metzler, September 5, 2019.

20 **The "one word" that sums up:** Author interview with Jo-Ann Armao, who confirms Metzler account, September 5, 2019.

20 **"no one was giving up anything":** Harvey Weinstein email dictated to his public relations adviser, Juda Engelmayer, from prison and sent to author, denying claims that he and Corky were terminated by *The Spectrum*, September 14, 2020.

20 **"The idea of calling these guys pigs":** Author interview with Harvey Weinstein on his Buffalo friends, June 27, 2002, for *New Yorker* profile.

21 **Harvey playing football:** Author interview with Eugene Fahey, 2002, for *New Yorker* profile. (There will be several endnotes like this one that refer to my 2002 profile of Harvey Weinstein but that don't specify dates. That is because though I do retain the Weinstein tapes and dates, I no longer retain the dates of some of these interviews. Every interview was rigorously fact-checked by *The New Yorker* before publication.)

21 **"Did you brush your teeth'":** Author interview with Harvey Weinstein describing when a limousine picked him up in Queens, June 27, 2002, for *New Yorker* profile.

22 **"There was a lot of resistance":** Author interview with Beryl Handler, 2002, for *New Yorker* profile.

23 **"Harvey seemed to be able":** Author interview with Mickey Osterreicher, February 26, 2019.

23 **"people in Buffalo knew Harvey":** Author interview with Jo-Ann Armao about their fame, September 5, 2019.

23 **"He made a reputation":** Author interview with Dave Channon about how Harvey was changed by success, April 18, 2019.

24 **"If he was bad to you"**: John Wolf quoted in Galarneau and Peradotto, "He's Harvey Weinstein."

24 **Corky "was very calm"**: Author interview with Mickey Osterreicher describing Harvey and Corky, February 26, 2019.

24 **"I never saw Harvey with a woman"**: Author interview with Mickey Osterreicher, February 26, 2019.

25 **he did have "a girlfriend"**: Author interview with Hope d'Amore, September 17, 2019.

25 **"I had many steady girlfriends"**: Harvey Weinstein email dictated to his public relations adviser, Juda Engelmayer, from prison and sent to author, stating that he had girlfriends in Buffalo, September 14, 2020.

25 **"don't be alone with Harvey Weinstein"**: Monica Hesse and Dan Zak, "Violence. Threats. Becoming. Harvey Weinstein's 30-Year Pattern of Abuse in Hollywood," *Washington Post*, October 14, 2017.

25 **"Bob kept to himself"**: Author interview with Hope d'Amore about Bob Weinstein, September 17, 2019.

27 **"Listen, you fuckers"**: Author interview with Harvey Weinstein about the showing of the Claude Lelouch film, July 9, 2002, for *New Yorker* profile; and Galarneau and Peradotto, "He's Harvey Weinstein."

27 **"is how Miramax started"**: Author interview with Harvey Weinstein about the seed planted for Miramax, July 9, 2002, for *New Yorker* profile.

28 **"never came to any concerts"**: Author interview with Bob Weinstein, April 23, 2021.

28 **Max was felled by a massive:** Bob Weinstein, "All Thanks to Max," *Vanity Fair*, April 2003.

29 **"I'm going to be this rich"**: Author interview with Peter Adler about Harvey's boast, and his insistence on playing quarterback, May 24, 2019.

29 **"I grew up in the Rock-n-Roll culture"**: Harvey Weinstein 3-page unpublished essay in which he explains how the concert business shaped his attitude toward sexual consent is contained in court documents released on March 11, 2020, as part of his criminal trial in New York.

30 **"Complete and utter nonsense"**: Harvey Weinstein email dictated to his public relations adviser, Juda Engelmayer, from prison and sent to author, denying Wende Walsh assault claim, September 14, 2020.

31 **"sometimes you have to put the rat"**: Author interview with Harvey Weinstein about Arthur Manson's speech, July 9, 2002, for *New Yorker* profile.

31 **the first movie the brothers distributed:** Author interview with Bob Weinstein on how they got the *Genesis* movie, November 1, 2019; and Bob Weinstein, "All Thanks to Max."

31 **"we would rent out big music halls"**: Author interview with Harvey Weinstein about the *Genesis* movie, July 9, 2002, for *New Yorker* profile.

32 **Harvey was a good listener:** Author interview with Hope d'Amore about conversations with Harvey Weinstein, September 17, 2019.

33 **She tried to push him away:** Author interview with Hope d'Amore about being raped, September 17, 2019.

33 **"Another event that never"**: Harvey Weinstein email dictated to his public relations adviser, Juda Engelmayer, from prison and sent to author, denying that he raped Hope d'Amore, September 14, 2020.

34 **normal in show business:** Accounts of Buffalo women claiming to be abused by Harvey reported by Maki Becker, "Another Buffalo Woman Accuses Harvey Weinstein of Sexual Assault," *Buffalo News*, November 4, 2017.

34 **"Another urban legend"**: Harvey Weinstein email dictated to his public relations adviser, Juda Engelmayer, from prison and sent to author, denying Paula Wachowiak potential assault claim, September 14, 2020.

34 **A study of ninety-two rape victims:** Dr. Ann Wolbert Burgess and Dr. Lynda Lytle Holmstrom, "Rape Trauma Syndrome," *American Journal of Psychiatry* 131 (September 1974).

34 **years of trauma:** Author interview with Hope d'Amore, September 17, 2019.

35 **Then she called Jodi Kantor:** Hope d'Amore interview in BBC documentary *Untouchable*, 2019; and author interview with d'Amore, September 17, 2019.

CHAPTER THREE: THE BOTTOM-FEEDERS

36 **"It was the ultimate compliment"**: Miriam Weinstein reaction to the name Miramax, in Jesse Green, "The Mother of All Independents," *New York Times*, November 16, 1997.

37 **"You fucked me!"**: The Jonathan Taplin confrontation reported by Peter Biskind, *Down and Dirty Pictures* (New York: Simon & Schuster, 2004).

38 **"*Spartacus* was one"**: Author interview with Harvey Weinstein about Hollywood studios, October 9, 2002, for *New Yorker* profile of Harvey Weinstein, "Beauty and the Beast," published December 16, 2002.

38 **a perfect row of capped white teeth:** Harvey was a patient of celebrity cosmetic dentist Dr. Larry Rosenthal, in Ellen Tien, "Whose Teeth Are You Wearing?," *New York Times*, July 20, 2003.

38 **"It was perhaps the last time"**: Peter Bart quoted, as is Biskind, in Peter Biskind, *Easy Riders, Raging Bulls: How the Sex-Drugs-and-Rock 'n' Roll Generation Saved Hollywood* (New York: Simon & Schuster, 1998).

39 **"Teenagers became the biggest"**: Mike Medavoy with Josh Young, *You're Only as Good as Your Next One: 100 Great Films, 100 Good Films, and 100 for Which I Should Be Shot* (New York: Pocket Books, 2002).

39 **"you were merely a cog":** Author interview with Barry Diller about changing studio corporate ownership, September 19, 2018.

40 **an "ill-tempered Jewish monomaniac":** Owen Gleiberman review of Ira Deutchman's documentary, *Searching for Mr. Rugoff*, "An Enthralling Movie-Love Doc," *Variety*, November 23, 2019.

40 **"You could buy a small movie":** Author interview on July 15, 2002, with Tom Bernard about the art film business for *New Yorker* profile.

40 **they felt an arctic blast:** Author interview with Harvey Weinstein about their first visit to Cannes and their financial plan, October 9, 2002, for *New Yorker* profile.

41 **he spoke for "the Oral Majority":** Author interview with Harvey Weinstein about *The Secret Policeman's Other Ball*, July 9, 2002, for *New Yorker* profile; and Peter Biskind writes about Martin Lewis's marketing role in *Easy Riders, Raging Bulls*.

42 **the company was barely profitable:** Author interview with Bob Weinstein about how marginally profitable Miramax was in the first ten years, November 1, 2019.

42 **cost less than $2 million:** Box office from *New York Times*, March 31, 2019.

42 **"John Eastman explained":** Author interview with Bob Weinstein on John Eastman, November 1, 2019.

43 **if you knock them down:** Author interview with John Eastman about his advice to Harvey Weinstein, July 1, 2019.

43 **he made a bad trade:** Accounts of Harvey and Corky's co-ownership of Miramax and falling out from Andrew Z. Galarneau and Nicole Peradotto, "He's Harvey Weinstein—And You're Not Not," *Buffalo News*, March 22, 1997; from a rare Corky Burger interview by Charity Vogel and Jane Kwiatkowski, "Corky's Quirky Career After the Breakup," *Buffalo News*, January 15, 2000; and from author interview with Harvey Weinstein, July 9, 2002, for *New Yorker* profile. Repeated attempts of the author by phone and email to speak with Corky Burger were unsuccessful.

43 **Corky admitted that:** Vogel and Kwiatkowski, "Corky's Quirky Career."

44 **"Bob was the kind of guy":** Author interview with Donald Rosenfeld describing the differences between the Weinstein brothers, September 25, 2018.

44 **"I thought he was like Mr. Wolf":** Author interview with Tom Freston about Bob Weinstein, September 10, 2018.

44 **"It was hard to get between":** Author interview with Robert Newman about the bond between the brothers, January 28, 2019.

44 **"an alliance that cannot be broken":** Bob Weinstein, "All Thanks to Max," *Vanity Fair*, April 2003.

45 **"He forced her on the bed":** Author interviews with Alan Brewer about what happened while making *Playing for Keeps*, September 11, 2019, and October 10, 2019; and Alan Brewer interviews in Scott Johnson and Stephen Galloway, "Young Harvey Weinstein: The Making of a Monster," *Hollywood Reporter*, February 28, 2018, and Monica Hesse and Dan Zak, "Violence. Threats. Becoming. Harvey Weinstein's 30-Year Pattern of Abuse in Hollywood," *Washington Post*, October 14, 2017.

46 **"Harvey just attacked me":** Mark Lipsky interview, Amelia Gentleman and Holly Watt, "It Was Like Tending to a Disgusting Baby: Life as a Harvey Weinstein Employee," *The Guardian*, September 29, 2018.

46 **"He would completely emasculate a man":** Author interview with Cynthia Swartz about Harvey's volatility, December 13, 2019.

46 **the brothers as "the Kray-zies":** Biskind, *Down and Dirty Pictures*, 74.

47 **"at that point they owned you":** Mark Lipsky interview, Gentleman and Watt, "It Was Like Tending."

47 **"feels a bit ridiculous now":** Anonymous female employee at Miramax describing her two interviews with Harvey in Gentleman and Watt, "It Was Like Tending."

48 **pushing her head down:** Cynthia Burr interview about being sexually assaulted by Harvey Weinstein, in Ellen Gabler, Megan Twohey, and Jodi Kantor, "New Accusers Expand Harvey Weinstein Sexual Assault Claims Back to '70s," *New York Times*, October 30, 2017.

48 **"the diametric opposite of Harvey":** Author interview with Mark Gill describing difference between Eve and Harvey Weinstein, December 5, 2018.

48 **"something of Kay Corleone in Eve":** Biskind, *Down and Dirty Pictures*.

49 **"in a polo shirt with food":** Author interview with John Schmidt about seeing Harvey Weinstein on the Vineyard, February 5, 2019.

50 **"Harvey was devoted":** Author interview with Bob Weinstein about Harvey Weinstein as a father and uncle, and devotion to Miriam, May 4, 2021.

50 **"He pushed me inside":** Lysette Anthony rape allegation reported by Nardine Saad, "Harvey Weinstein's Accusers: List Includes Fledgling Actresses and Hollywood Royalty," *Los Angeles Times*, May 25, 2018; and Jon Lockett, "I Have Nightmares," *The Sun*, December 20, 2019.

51 **"we didn't know whether the paychecks":** Author interview with Harvey Weinstein about Miramax financial difficulties, July 9, 2002, for *New Yorker* profile.

51 **"What if they refuse?"**: Author interview with John Schmidt about Harvey Weinstein refusing to pay bills, February 5, 2019.

52 **"'Let's give it another year'"**: Author interview with Bob Weinstein about agreeing not to give up on Miramax, November 1, 2019.

52 **"No one had ever heard"**: Author interview with Amanda Lundberg about low recognition of Miramax, March 13, 2019.

52 **"Phase One. We were a boutique"**: Author interview with Bob Weinstein about Miramax's Phase One, November 1, 2019.

CHAPTER FOUR: THE BARNUM AND BAILEY OF THE MOVIE BUSINESS

54 **"*Scandal* received an X rating"**: Kevin Sandler, *The Naked Truth: Why Hollywood Doesn't Make X-Rated Movies* (New Brunswick, NJ: Rutgers University Press, 2007).

54 **"We showed theaters"**: Author interview with Bob Weinstein about the movie *Scandal*, November 1, 2019.

55 **"Are these guys nuts?"**: Author interview with Steven Soderbergh on July 17, 2002, about why he chose to align with Miramax, for *New Yorker* profile of Harvey Weinstein, "Beauty and the Beast," published December 16, 2002.

55 **"No, it's gonna gross more'"**: Author interview with Harvey Weinstein about *Sex, Lies, and Videotape*, July 9, 2002, for *New Yorker* profile.

56 **"the big bang of the modern indie film"**: Peter Biskind on the impact of *Sex, Lies, and Videotape* in *Down and Dirty Pictures* (New York: Simon & Schuster, 2004).

58 **"This guy was making the kind"**: Author interview with Gwyneth Paltrow on meeting Harvey Weinstein in Toronto, August 2, 2019.

58 **"Harvey had a safecracker's feel"**: Author interview with John Eastman on Harvey Weinstein's talent, July 11, 2019.

58 **The moniker was:** The origin of "Harvey Scissorhands," popularized by Elliott Stein in *The Village Voice* in 1990 and described in Biskind, *Down and Dirty Pictures*.

59 **"The film we admired"**: Louis Malle quoted in Biskind, *Down and Dirty Pictures*.

60 **"he refused to take no"**: Author interview with HBO's Henry McGee about his dealings with Harvey Weinstein, September 24, 2018.

61 **after a screaming match with Harvey:** Tom Tykwer to Biskind, *Down and Dirty Pictures*.

61 **"I had a grudging respect"**: Author interview with Bob Shaye about Harvey Weinstein, December 17, 2018.

61 **"'We're going to bury you'"**: Author interview with Ira Deutchman about fearsome Bob Weinstein, October 11, 2018.

61 **"I might have said"**: Author interview with Bob Weinstein about Ira Deutchman, June 16, 2021.

61 **"when you stiff a filmmaker"**: Author interview with John Schmidt about Harvey Weinstein not paying bills, February 5, 2019.

62 **"missed the last third entirely"**: Interview with James Ivory about dealing with Harvey Weinstein, Iain Blair, *The Wrap*, April 24, 2010.

62 **Out to the street they marched:** Account of conflict between Harvey and Merchant Ivory from author interview with former Merchant Ivory president Donald Rosenfeld, September 25, 2018; from Tim Teeman, "James Ivory on Sex with Peaches, Oscars, Fighting Harvey Weinstein, and 50 Years of Moviemaking," *Daily Beast*, February 20, 2018; and from Biskind, *Down and Dirty Pictures*.

62 **"both a genius and an asshole"**: James Ivory quoted in David Carr, "The Emperor Miramaximus," *New York* magazine, December 3, 2001.

63 **"The wall just shook"**: Author interview with Donna Gigliotti about Harvey Weinstein throwing things, 2002, for *New Yorker* profile.

63 **"I am a moron"**: Author interview with Mark Gill describing Harvey's temper, December 5, 2018.

63 **among the worst bosses:** "America's Toughest Bosses," *Fortune*, October 18, 1993.

63 **"I think I was a bad boss"**: Author interview with Harvey Weinstein on how he was personally reforming, July 9, 2002, for *New Yorker* profile.

64 **a plate of freshly baked cookies:** Author interview with Amy Israel about keeping Harvey Weinstein at a screening, February 15, 2019.

64 **"learned how to think outside the box"**: Author interview with Amy Israel on the entrepreneurial culture Harvey Weinstein created, November 18, 2020.

65 **"I was corunning a department"**: Author interview with Amy Israel about Miramax meritocracy, February 15, 2019.

65 **"I admired their relentlessness"**: Author interview with Gina Gardini about Harvey's refusal to take no for an answer, October 29, 2019.

66 **"self-love and self-hatred contend"**: Biskind describes some Harvey personality traits, *Down and Dirty Pictures.*

66 **"He's a good man"**: Author interview with Harvey Weinstein's driver, Sayed Khorshed, June 6, 2019.

67 **On her frequent visits**: A rare interview and description of Miriam Weinstein visiting Miramax, Jesse Green, "The Mother of All Independents," *New York Times,* November 16, 1997.

67 **"How did this kindly woman"**: Author interview with John Schmidt about Miriam Weinstein, February 5, 2019.

67 **"never short with her"**: Author interview with Gina Gardini about Miriam Weinstein, October 29, 2019.

67 **"a momma's boy"**: Author interview with Vicki Gordon about Miriam Weinstein, September 17, 2018.

67 **"'where's the next one?'"**: Ivana Lowell quoted in Phoebe Eaton, "The Making of a Predator, Part II," *Air Mail,* June 13, 2020.

68 **"'I'd like you to do this for me'"**: Author interview with Jonathan Gordon about Miriam Weinstein, January 25, 2019.

68 **"She didn't realize"**: Author interview with Amanda Lundberg about Miriam Weinstein, March 13, 2019.

69 **needed a massage**: Laura Madden's description of Harvey Weinstein in a Dublin hotel reported in *Irish Central,* September 20, 2019; in Olivia Blair, "Weinstein Accusers Unmasked: Meet the British Women Who Risked It All to Change Hollywood," *Elle,* March 12, 2019; and in Jodi Kantor and Megan Twohey, *She Said: Breaking the Sexual Harassment Story That Helped Ignite a Movement* (New York: Penguin Press, 2019).

69 **He emerged from the bathroom naked**: Katherine Kendall interview on PBS *NewsHour,* October 18, 2017.

70 **"'No one is going to care'"**: Account of why Katherine Kendall kept quiet contained in Monica Hesse and Dan Zak, "Violence. Threats. Becoming. Harvey Weinstein's 30-Year Pattern of Abuse in Hollywood," *Washington Post,* October 14, 2017.

70 **was "a one-off"**: Author interview with John Schmidt about Harvey Weinstein abusing a young woman, February 5, 2019.

70 **"I did not leave immediately"**: Author interview with John Schmidt about why he finally quit, February 5, 2019.

71 **"it's really not pretty"**: Sean Young interviewed in a PBS *Frontline* documentary, *Weinstein,* March 2, 2018.

71 **Harvey punished her**: Sean Young complaint about Hollywood reported by Rebecca Rubin, "Actress Sean Young Alleges Harvey Weinstein Exposed Himself to Her," *Variety,* October 20, 2017.

71 **Arquette stormed out**: BBC documentary *Untouchable,* 2019, includes the testimony of Rosanna Arquette; account also contained in Ronan Farrow, *Catch and Kill: Lies, Spies, and a Conspiracy to Protect Predators* (New York: Little, Brown and Company, 2019).

71 **he'd be willing to take**: Harvey Weinstein email dictated to his public relations adviser, Juda Engelmayer, from prison and sent to author, containing denial of Arquette's claims, January 29, 2021.

72 **"I love violent movies"**: Scene of Tarantino at Sundance screening of *Reservoir Dogs* reported in Biskind, *Down and Dirty Pictures.*

72 **"first-rate new American" directors**: Review of Quentin Tarantino's *Reservoir Dogs,* Vincent Canby, "A Caper Goes Wrong Resoundingly, *New York Times,* October 23, 1992.

73 **Harvey "was the opposite of a bully"**: Author interview with Quentin Tarantino about *Reservoir Dogs,* October 9, 2002, for *New Yorker* profile.

73 **"an uncontrolled spender"**: Author interview with John Schmidt on Harvey Weinstein's spending, February 5, 2019.

73 **"The hardest part of my job"**: Author interview with Agnès Mentre on Harvey Weinstein's impulsive spending, September 5, 2019.

74 **"Felix can call someone"**: Author interview with Steven Rattner on troubled Miramax, May 22, 2019.

74 **"Harvey was brilliant"**: Author interview with Ira Deutchman on Harvey Weinstein and *The Crying Game,* October 11, 2018.

75 **Harvey called the editor**: Weinstein's appeal to the Associated Press reported in Robert W. Welkos, "The Secret of 'The Crying Game': Don't Read Any Further If You Haven't Seen This Film," *Los Angeles Times,* February 18, 1993.

75 **"Harvey was clearly the Barnum"**: Author interview with Mark Gill describing Harvey Weinstein as a marketer, December 5, 1998.

75 **One third of the 1993 nominations**: Independent movie Oscar nominations from "Modest Movies Are Big-Time Oscar Nominees," *New York Times,* February 8, 1993.

76 **"the only brand"**: Author interview with Michael Eisner on the value of the Miramax brand, December 4, 2018.

77 **the perils that defeated Max**: Bob Weinstein, "All Thanks to Max," *Vanity Fair,* April 2003.

77 **"he also lacked a partner"**: Author interview with Bob Weinstein about why his father's independent business failed, May 6, 2019.

77 **still a relatively small company:** Miramax 1993 revenues and profits from Disney document shared with the author.

78 **"It broke my heart":** Author interview with Harvey Weinstein on losing Jim Sheridan, July 9, 2002, for *New Yorker* profile.

79 **"I spent a lot of time alone":** Annabella Sciorra testimony against Harvey Weinstein in his 2020 New York criminal trial, which the author attended daily; her rape was first reported by Ronan Farrow in *Catch and Kill*.

79 **He would stalk her for years:** Sciorra interview with Ronan Farrow in *Catch and Kill*.

CHAPTER FIVE: THE CULTURE OF SILENCE

80 **"I wanted to buy his company":** Author interview with Jeffrey Katzenberg on why Disney acquired Miramax, March 7, 2019.

80 **"The question we had":** Author interview with Peter Murphy about Disney's concerns, February 21, 2019.

81 **they promised bonuses:** Reported in Peter Biskind, *Down and Dirty Pictures* (New York: Simon & Schuster, 2004).

81 **"only they would get rich":** Author interview with Amanda Lundberg about the staff not sharing the financial benefits of the sale to Disney, March 13, 2019.

82 **To fire either Weinstein:** Copy of Disney employment contract with the Weinsteins, April 1993.

82 **"Harvey wanted to believe":** Author interview with Peter Murphy on how Harvey Weinstein didn't think he reported to anyone, February 21, 2019.

82 **"He made a great pitch":** Author interview with Jeffrey Katzenberg on the Tarantino movie, March 7, 2019.

83 **joined by his screenwriter buddy:** Relationship between Tarantino and Avary described in Biskind, *Down and Dirty Pictures*, 167.

83 **"We're making this movie":** Mark Seal, "Cinema Tarantino: The Making of *Pulp Fiction*," *Vanity Fair*, February 13, 2013.

84 **Tarantino was dazzled:** Author interview with Quentin Tarantino, October 9, 2002, for *New Yorker* profile of Harvey Weinstein, "Beauty and the Beast," published December 16, 2002.

85 **his favorite Chinese movies:** Author interview with Harvey Weinstein about Quentin Tarantino's Chinese movie recommendations, July 9, 2002, for *New Yorker* profile.

85 **"Nobody else in town":** Author interview with Quentin Tarantino on why he admired the Weinsteins, October 9, 2002, parts of which appeared in author's *New Yorker* profile.

85 **his company "the house":** Biskind, *Down and Dirty Pictures*.

86 **"He trusted no one":** Author interview with Jonathan Gordon about Harvey Weinstein's mistrustful nature, January 25, 2019.

86 **a reminder that personal factors:** The author extensively reported on the Eisner/Katzenberg rupture in "The Human Factor," *New Yorker*, September 26, 1994.

86 **"I saw the good Harvey":** Author interview with Jeffrey Katzenberg on his rapport with Harvey Weinstein, March 7, 2019.

87 **"They were paranoid about me":** Author interview with Joe Roth about his New York meeting with Harvey and Bob, 2002, for *New Yorker* profile.

87 **Harvey phoned and screamed:** Author interview with Peter Murphy describing Harvey on the phone, February 21, 2019.

88 **"Harvey became more of the crown prince":** Author interview with Bob Shaye on Miramax becoming a juggernaut, December 17, 2018.

88 **"It was always bullying":** Jack Foley quoted in Biskind, *Down and Dirty Pictures*, 157.

88 **"I'm not giving it up":** Harvey Weinstein's devotion to *Sling Blade* and the marketing of it reported in Biskind, *Down and Dirty Pictures*.

88 **his eye for a good script:** Author interview with Abby Ex on Harvey's storytelling talent, January 15, 2019.

89 **"He knew *The Piano*":** Author interview with Meryl Poster on Harvey Weinstein's script talent, November 30, 2018.

89 **Roger Ebert described:** Roger Ebert review of *The Piano*, November 19, 1993, https://www.rogerebert.com/reviews/the-piano-1993.

90 **"Polanski directed it":** Author interview with Harvey Weinstein about the importance of a script, June 27, 2002, for *New Yorker* profile.

90 *My Name Is Modesty*: Harvey Weinstein editing movie reported and fact-checked in author's *New Yorker* profile.

90 **"is unheard of":** Author interview with Harvey denying he bossed around directors, August 7, 2002, for *New Yorker* profile.

90 **Bernardo Bertolucci would dismiss:** Biskind, *Down and Dirty Pictures.*

91 **"he came up with the entire":** Author interview with Amy Israel about Harvey Weinstein and *Il Postino*, February 15, 2019.

92 **Roger Ebert wrote:** Roger Ebert review of *The Crow*, May 13, 2004, https://www.rogerebert.com/reviews /the-crow-1994.

92 **"It gave me my own thing":** Author interview with Bob Weinstein on expansion of Dimension, September 14, 2019.

94 **"one of the greatest calls":** The blow-by-blow account of the making of *Scream* is told by Peter Biskind, "The Weinstein Way," *Vanity Fair*, February 5, 2011.

94 **Bob defied convention:** Bob Weinstein email to author about the long-term impact of *Scream*, August 20, 2020.

95 **"He loved that":** Author interview with Marcy Granata about Bob Weinstein and being hired by Harvey Weinstein, October 19, 2018.

95 **Bob Weinstein had real talent:** Author interview with Marcy Granata about her encounter with Bob Weinstein, and her discussion with Miriam Weinstein about Bob's talent, October 19, 2018.

96 **the more successful Bob was:** Author interview with David Boies about the relationship between Bob and Harvey Weinstein, November 27, 2018.

96 **"Bob was more prudent":** Author interview with Mark Gill on Bob Weinstein's financial discipline, December 5, 2018.

96 **"His ability to fix a script":** Author interview with Meryl Poster on Bob Weinstein's talent, October 19, 2018.

96 **"He has peaks and valleys":** B. J. Rack quoted in Biskind, *Down and Dirty Pictures*, 267.

97 **"I had to duck":** Author interview with Mark Gill describing Harvey Weinstein's behavior and the ten-pound urn Harvey threw at him, November 17, 2020.

97 **"threw me up against the wall":** Author interview with Eric Robinson about what staff feared, January 23, 2019.

97 **"You never knew when he would explode":** Author interview with Abby Ex on fear of Harvey Weinstein in office, January 15, 2019.

97 **"inseparable from his dark side":** Author interview with Mark Gill about Harvey Weinstein's genius and his abuse, December 5, 2018.

98 **"terrified of Harvey":** Author interview with Agnès Mentre on how employees feared Harvey and Bob Weinstein, September 5, 2019.

98 **"She's fifty percent right":** Author interview with Bob Weinstein, June 16, 2021.

98 **"'Talk to my brother'":** Author interview with Jason Blum on how Miramax was a family company, December 18, 2018.

99 **wearing matching T-shirts:** Megan Twohey, Jodi Kantor, Susan Dominus, Jim Rutenberg, and Steve Eder, "Weinstein's Complicity Machine," *New York Times*, December 5, 2017.

99 **"He doesn't stay on the same floor":** Author interview with Jonathan Gordon about traveling with Harvey Weinstein, January 25, 2019.

100 **Male executives privately advised:** Author interview with Mark Gill on how everyone knew Harvey Weinstein chased women around the couch, December 5, 2018.

102 **"people who enabled his behavior?":** Author interview with Hillary Silver on how she was warned not to take a job, in order to avoid Harvey's sexual assaults, March 20, 2020.

102 **"I find that hard to believe":** Author interview with Amy Israel on those who deny they knew, February 15, 2019.

103 **"Go fuck yourself":** Amy Israel described Harvey hitting on her to Jodi Kantor and Megan Twohey, *She Said: Breaking the Sexual Harassment Story That Helped Ignite a Movement* (New York: Penguin Press, 2019).

103 **"I did know":** Paul Webster interviewed in PBS *Frontline* documentary, *Weinstein*, March 2, 2018.

104 **"Walking behind me":** Rose McGowan describes being raped in *Brave* (New York: HarperOne, 2018).

104 **Harvey got McGowan:** Rose McGowan to Ronan Farrow, *Catch and Kill: Lies, Spies, and a Conspiracy to Protect Predators* (New York: Little, Brown and Company, 2019).

105 **"After the rape, he won":** Asia Argento to Farrow, *Catch and Kill.*

105 **the vast majority don't report:** Testimony of Dr. Barbara Ziv at Harvey Weinstein's criminal trial, January 30, 2020.

105 **"I said no, a lot of ways":** Ashley Judd on spurning Harvey Weinstein in interview with Ramin Satoodeh, "How Women in Hollywood Are Finally Taking a Stand Against Sexism," *Variety*, October 6, 2015.

105 **"When I win an Academy Award":** Ashley Judd joke shared with Kantor and Twohey, *She Said*, 32.

105 **"I'll let you out of that deal":** Harvey's offer to Judd reported by Satoodeh, "How Women in Hollywood."

106 **"the Miramax smear campaign":** Molly Redden, "Peter Jackson: I Blacklisted Ashley Judd and Mira Sorvino Under Pressure from Weinstein," *The Guardian*, December 16, 2017.

106 **Actress Kate Beckinsale chimed in:** Accounts of various women allegedly abused by Harvey Weinstein, including Kate Beckinsale, contained in voluminous report by Nardine Saad, "Harvey Weinstein's Accusers: List Includes Fledgling Actresses and Hollywood Royalty," *Los Angeles Times*, May 25, 2018, and in abuse claims many women shared in Kantor and Twohey, *She Said*, and Farrow, *Catch and Kill*.

106 **"I'll give you that if":** Author interview with Gwyneth Paltrow on Harvey Weinstein's quid pro quos, August 2, 2019.

107 **"I'll kill you":** Gwyneth Paltrow on how Brad Pitt confronted Harvey Weinstein, from Becky Freeth, "Gwyneth Paltrow Claims Harvey Weinstein Was 'Scared' of Brad Pitt and Wanted to 'Keep the Actor on Side' after Making Her Feel Uncomfortable," *Metro*, October 4, 2018.

107 **She managed to mollify him:** Gwyneth Paltrow describing Harvey Weinstein's attempted assault contained in Kantor and Twohey, *She Said*, and in Brad Pitt interview with Marla Pasquini, *Sunday Times* (London), July 29, 2019.

107 **"We all knew he was":** Author interview with Gwyneth Paltrow on her eye rolls, August 2, 2019.

CHAPTER SIX: THE MOGUL

108 **"Miramax itself was being Disneyized":** Peter Biskind, *Down and Dirty Pictures* (New York: Simon & Schuster, 2004).

108 **Harvey began to ignore:** Author interview with Michael Eisner about Harvey Weinstein violating his contract, December 4, 2018.

109 **"Get the fuck out of the car!'":** Author interview with Daniel Murray about serving as Harvey Weinstein's assistant, December 18, 2018.

110 **"I always thought it would":** Author interview with Harvey Weinstein about *Talk* and Tina Brown, August 7, 2002, for *New Yorker* profile of Harvey Weinstein, "Beauty and the Beast," published December 16, 2002.

110 **He dangled extravagant salaries:** Author interview with Vicki Gordon about her *Talk* job offer, September 17, 2018.

110 **"What magazine?" he asked:** Author interview with Michael Eisner about *Talk*, December 4, 2018.

111 **offered extravagant book contracts:** Author interview with Talk Books editor Jonathan Burnham about Harvey Weinstein's book promises, May 31, 2019.

111 **"Bob thought we were sucking":** Author interview with Burnham about Bob Weinstein's attitude, May 31, 2019.

112 **"It was the only time":** Author interview with Burnham about Harvey Weinstein's talent, May 31, 2019.

112 **"irrational bouts of anger":** Author interview with Burnham about Harvey Weinstein's temper, May 31, 2019.

112 **"a little scary":** Author interview with Susan Mercandetti about Harvey Weinstein and Talk Books, March 8, 2019.

112 **Talk published about eighty books:** Jonathan Burnham email, May 27, 2020.

112 **At lunch Harvey pitched Boies:** Author interview with David Boies about Harvey Weinstein and his book contract, November 27, 2018.

114 **"I don't understand that blow-job scene":** This is one of the versions Harvey Weinstein has related; transcript of Howard Stern interview with Weinstein about *Good Will Hunting*, January 15, 2014, in *Howard Stern Comes Again* (New York: Simon & Schuster, 2019).

115 **"That's the worst thing":** Author interview with Harvey Weinstein about Harry Cohn, August 7, 2002, for *New Yorker* profile.

115 **"he used the lie as an assault weapon":** Megan Twohey, Jodi Kantor, Susan Dominus, Jim Rutenberg, and Steve Eder report on Harvey's boasting about actresses he's slept with, "Weinstein's Complicity Machine," *New York Times*, December 5, 2017.

116 **"Harvey had to find a way":** Author interview with Eric Robinson on how Harvey Weinstein flew to Milan to applaud Russell Crowe, January 23, 2019.

117 **Miramax actually lost money:** Author interviews with Saul Zaentz, Anthony Minghella, and Harvey Weinstein about the true financial returns of *The English Patient*, 2002, from his fact-checked *New Yorker* profile of Weinstein.

117 **"men who have power":** Author interview with Susan Lyne about Hollywood culture and women, September 14, 2018.

118 **Harvey would sometimes take two suites:** Phoebe Eaton, "The Making of a Predator, Part II," *Air Mail*, June 13, 2020.

118 **"'You do not like me because I'm fat'":** Zoe Brock interviewed in PBS *Frontline* documentary, *Weinstein*, March 2, 2018.

118 **"No girl looked at me":** Harvey Weinstein interview with Taki Theodoracopulos in *The Spectator*, July 13, 2018. (The original column is no longer on *The Spectator*'s website, but this next-day story recounts the interview.)

119 **"a cost-benefit analysis":** Barbara Bradley Hagerty quotes Deborah Tuerkheimer in "The Weinstein Conviction Shows Why Rape Convictions Are So Rare," *The Atlantic*, February 24, 2020.

119 **Daryl Hannah was one of Harvey's targets:** Hannah's claims reported by Molly Redden, "Peter Jackson: I Blacklisted Ashley Judd and Mira Sorvino Under Pressure from Weinstein," *The Guardian*, December 16, 2017.

119 **"we are not believed":** Daryl Hannah interview with Ronan Farrow on why she did not report Harvey Weinstein, Ronan Farrow, *Catch and Kill: Lies, Spies, and a Conspiracy to Protect Predators* (New York: Little, Brown and Company, 2019).

119 **their CAA agents, who did nothing:** Mia Kirshner's and Gwyneth Paltrow's claims that they reported Weinstein's licentious behavior to their CAA agents and they did nothing is contained in the civil lawsuit filed by ten of his alleged victims against Harvey Weinstein, the company's board, and its executives before the U.S. District Court of the Southern District, October 31, 2018.

119 **"We apologize to":** CAA apology reported in Dawn C. Chmielewski, "NYT Report Details Harvey Weinstein Enablers; CAA Issues Apology 'To Any Person the Agency Let Down,'" *Deadline*, December 5, 2017.

119 **"I knew enough to do more":** Quentin Tarantino admits he should have done more, Jodi Kantor and Annie Brown, "Listen: Why This Actress Returned to Weinstein's Hotel Room," *New York Times*, October 19, 2017.

120 **"You're like an animal wriggling away":** Maureen Dowd, "This Is Why Uma Thurman Is Angry," *New York Times*, February 3, 2018.

121 **"he wanted strong women around him":** Author interview with Zelda Perkins about her life and coming to work for Miramax, July 17, 2019.

121 **"To be around someone so powerful":** Author interview with Zelda Perkins on Harvey Weinstein's charisma, July 16, 2019; Perkins also spoke of this in interview with Emily Maitlis and Lucinda Day, "Harvey Weinstein: Ex-Assistant Criticises Gagging Orders," BBC Newsnight, December 19, 2017.

122 **"Power does strange things to people":** Author interview with Zelda Perkins on Harvey Weinstein's corrupting power, July 17, 2019.

122 **"Harvey always had a girlfriend":** Perkins describes buying condoms for Harvey in an October 21, 2019, email to author.

122 **"to normalize" his weird behavior:** Perkins describes Harvey Weinstein in Jodi Kantor and Megan Twohey, *She Said: Breaking the Sexual Harassment Story That Helped Ignite a Movement* (New York: Penguin Press, 2019).

123 **she copied and shared these admonitions:** Author interview with Zelda Perkins on what to do to avoid Harvey Weinstein assaults, July 30, 2019, and how Harvey "normalized" abnormal behavior, July 17, 2019.

124 **"Sit the fuck down!":** Rowena Chiu, "Harvey Weinstein Told Me He Liked Chinese Girls," *New York Times*, October 5, 2019.

124 **"I think he looked for weakness":** Author's separate interviews in London with Zelda Perkins on July 17, 2019, and Rowena Chiu on July 16, 2019, and with Perkins and Chiu together on July 16, 2019. Perkins also described Weinstein's behavior in PBS *Frontline* documentary, *Weinstein*, March 2, 2018; in Maitlis and Day, "Ex-Assistant Criticises Gagging Orders"; and in BBC documentary *Untouchable*, 2019.

125 **"Wear two pairs of tights":** Author interview with Zelda Perkins for advice to Rowena Chiu and her own motivations and analysis of Harvey Weinstein's behavior, July 16, 2019.

126 **Harvey was now in full seduction mode:** Chiu, "Harvey Weinstein Told Me."

126 **He cornered her on the bed:** Kantor and Twohey, *She Said*, 64.

127 **Chiu managed to slide off the bed:** Ticktock of what happened between Harvey Weinstein and Rowena Chiu at the Excelsior on September 6, 1998, based on author interviews with Rowena Chiu on July 16, 2019, and June 13, 2019, and with Chiu and Zelda Perkins together on July 16, 2019. Less detailed accounts of that evening were reported in Chiu, "Harvey Weinstein Told Me," and in Kantor and Twohey, *She Said*.

128 **"it's like she was my parent":** Author interview with Rowena Chiu on how she looked up to Zelda Perkins, July 16, 2019.

128 **peeled off all his clothes:** Author interview with Zelda Perkins on how Harvey Weinstein normalized abnormal behavior, July 16, 2019.

129 **"I know you're fucking lying":** Author interview with Zelda Perkins on how she interrupted Harvey Weinstein's lunch with Martin Scorsese, July 16, 2019.

129 **"a one-woman Erin Brockovich":** Author interview with Rowena Chiu comparing Zelda Perkins to Erin Brockovich, July 16, 2019.

129 **He lived in his own:** Author interview with Harvey Weinstein on how he had found "peace" under Disney, July 9, 2002, for *New Yorker* profile.

130 **yanked the smoke detector:** Author interview with Michael Eisner about Harvey Weinstein's rage, December 4, 2018.

130 **"a little bit of Dr. Jekyll and Mr. Hyde":** Author interview with Peter Murphy about Harvey Weinstein's dual personalities, February 21, 2019.

130 **a terrifying "top-down" company:** Author interview with Eric Robinson on Miramax culture, January 23, 2019.

130 **The "genius" was linked:** Author interview with Mark Gill on Harvey Weinstein's genius and anger, December 5, 2018.

CHAPTER SEVEN: THE ART OF THE NDA

131 **it was America's dominant:** Author interview with Mark Gill, in which he claims Miramax had 80 percent market share of independent movies, December 5, 2018.

133 **"Write me, Will":** Author interview with Mark Gill about crafting the ending of *Shakespeare in Love*, November 17, 2020.

133 **dismissed as "complete bullshit":** Mark Gill on Harvey Weinstein's claim that he took a leave of absence to produce contained in Scott Feinberg, "Spielberg and the Oral History of the Nastiest Oscar Campaign Ever," *Hollywood Reporter*, February 20, 2019.

133 **"the kind of arty gem":** Lael Loewenstein review of *Shakespeare in Love* in *Variety*, December 6, 1998.

133 **"He bet," said Mark Gill:** Author interview with Mark Gill about shrewd way Miramax targeted actors to win Best Picture, December 5, 2018.

134 **For only twelve thousand dollars:** Author interview with Meryl Poster about sending DVDs to Academy voters, November 30, 2018.

134 **a 'whisper campaign' against":** Terry Press about the harm Harvey Weinstein's campaign against *Saving Private Ryan* did to his reputation, quoted in Feinberg, "Spielberg and the Oral History."

134 **"It's the greatest opening'":** Author interview with Mark Gill on how Harvey bad-mouthed *Saving Private Ryan*, November 17, 2020.

135 **"I knew we won":** Author interview with Bob Weinstein describing Harrison Ford opening the Oscar envelope, December 3, 2019.

135 **"The threat was implicit":** Author Zoom interview with Donna Gigliotti about Harvey Weinstein insisting he must speak if *Shakespeare in Love* won Best Picture, June 18, 2020.

136 **Harvey lingered until 4:30 a.m.:** Description of Weinstein at the after-parties, Frank DiGiacomo, "A Tense Best-Picture Victory for the Miramax Mogul Who Stormed Oscar Beach," *New York Observer*, March 28, 1999.

136 **"he didn't yell at me":** Author interview with Mark Gill about Oscar night, December 5, 2018.

136 **Harvey Weinstein was barreling:** Author interview with Peggy Siegal about Spielberg's table, October 22, 2018.

136 **"Harvey came in like a drill sergeant":** Author interview with Marcy Granata on Harvey Weinstein's instructions the morning after the Academy Awards, October 19, 2018.

137 **"whole 'blame Miramax'":** Author interview with Harvey Weinstein on attacks on Miramax, August 7, 2002, for *New Yorker* profile of Harvey Weinstein, "Beauty and the Beast," published December 16, 2002.

137 **now was a target of fierce Hollywood:** Criticism of Harvey Weinstein and Miramax in Bernard Weinraub, "Mogul in Love . . . with Winning; Monday Morning Quarterbacking After Miramax's Big Night," *New York Times*, March 23, 1999.

138 **"You better get yourself a lawyer":** Author interview with Zelda Perkins on confiding in Donna Gigliotti, July 16, 2019.

139 **"Absolutely, she helped me":** A 7-page email to author from Donna Gigliotti offering what she did to help Zelda Perkins and Rowena Chiu, June 9, 2020, and a subsequent Zoom interview, June 18, 2020.

139 **"she continued working for Harvey":** Author interview with Rowena Chiu criticizing Donna Gigliotti, June 13, 2019.

139 **Needing health insurance:** Donna Gigliotti email to author explaining her subsequent work for Harvey Weinstein, June 9, 2020.

140 **She said she confronted him:** Author interview with Donna Gigliotti about what Harvey told her about Rowena Chiu, December 4, 2019,

141 **"I want to make you guys happy":** Zelda Perkins retained Harvey Weinstein's phone messages and played them for the author on July 17, 2019.

141 **"How can I not think"**: Author interview with Rowena Chiu about staff members as enablers, June 13, 2019.

141 **"a huge system of enablement"**: Author interview with Rowena Chiu defining three types of enablers, June 13, 2019.

142 **business affairs executive Steve Hutensky**: Author interview with Katrina Wolfe about her old boss, April 2, 2019.

142 **The NDA sessions**: Zelda Perkins interview about NDA negotiations, Amelia Gentleman and Holly Watt, "It Was Like Tending to a Disgusting Baby: Life as a Harvey Weinstein Employee," *The Guardian*, September 29, 2018.

142 **accept Harvey's terms**: Copy of October 23, 1998, NDA provided to the author by Zelda Perkins.

143 **They issued their own demands**: What Perkins and Chiu demanded in NDA, October 23, 1998, NDA.

143 **"he was very much the aggressive lead"**: Zelda Perkins email to author describing Steven Hutensky's active role in the NDA negotiations, June 20, 2020.

144 **NDA document mentions Hutensky twice**: Zelda Perkins email, June 20, 2020.

144 **he knows the NDA's**: Author email to Steven Hutensky asking him about his role in the 1998 NDA negotiations, June 20, 2020. These are the questions emailed to him:

> 1) Did you attend the NDA discussions, particularly the long session prior to its signing? 2) Did you initial the pages of the NDA? 3) Did you witness Harvey's apology and confession? 4) Why isn't the NDA signed by Harvey an admission of guilt, particularly since he agreed to seek therapy and agreed he would be terminated if he sexually misbehaved and he agreed to overhaul Miramax's HR policies?

> Hutensky responded with an angry email he insisted was off the record but declined to answer the questions.

144 **what Harvey said**: Zelda Perkins essay on the signing of their NDA and Harvey's words appears in the "Sometimes Don't Know When It's Consensual," *Tortoise Media*, February 25, 2020.

145 **"an atomic bomb"**: Description of the negotiations and Harvey's admission in the London law office from author's joint interview with Zelda Perkins and Rowena Chiu in London, July 6, 2020, and from Gentleman and Watt, "It Was Like Tending."

146 **"We were excited"**: Author interview with ex-*Premiere* editor Susan Lyne about John Connolly, September 14, 2018.

146 **Connolly did sign such a book contract**: Author interviews with John Connolly about his reporting on Harvey Weinstein and Rowena Chiu, his meeting with Weinstein, and his confirmation of Talk Books contract, May 9, 2019.

147 **"I have kept this woman's secret"**: John Connolly email to author about keeping Rowena Chiu's secret, September 9, 2019.

147 **she never spoke to Connolly**: Author interview with Rowena Chiu stating that she has never spoken to Connolly, June 13, 2019.

CHAPTER EIGHT: "I'M THE FUCKING SHERIFF OF THIS FUCKING LAWLESS PIECE-OF-SHIT TOWN"

148 **According to internal Disney documents**: Author was able to read and take notes on internal Disney documents, but not permitted to copy them or to disclose the person who shared them.

150 **Eisner fumed, but outwardly**: Author interview with Michael Eisner on Harvey Weinstein exceeding spending limits for movies, December 4, 2018.

150 **Dimension's profits helped**: Author interview with Bob Weinstein, who confirms Dimension profits, September 14, 2018.

150 **"every filmmaker wanted to sell"**: Author interview with Agnès Mentre on filmmakers chasing Harvey Weinstein, September 5, 2019.

150 **describe Harvey's power**: Author interview with Michael Eisner describing four components of Harvey Weinstein's power, December 4, 2018.

150 **Eisner, too, trod cautiously**: Author interview with Michael Eisner on his caution in battling Harvey Weinstein, December 4, 2018.

150 **likened Harvey to a bull**: Author interview with Anthony Minghella on Harvey Weinstein, 2002, for *New Yorker* profile of Harvey Weinstein, "Beauty and the Beast," published December 16, 2002.

151 **"Would you like to meet"**: Author interview with Meryl Streep describing Harvey Weinstein asking her to say hi, November 16, 2019.

151 **He had the hubris**: Author interview with Paramount studio chief Tony Vinciquerra about a Harvey Weinstein phone call insisting they speak at 2:00 p.m., November 13, 2018.

151 **to actress Ashley Judd**: Ashley Judd agreed to perform in two additional Miramax movies, Jodi Kantor and Megan Twohey, "Harvey Weinstein Paid Off Sexual Harassment Accusers for Decades," *New York Times*, October 5, 2017.

151 **Joseph Ravitch, a well-connected:** Author interview with Joseph Ravitch describing Harvey's powerful press relationships, June 5, 2019.

152 **seeking to buy their favor:** Accounts of Harvey Weinstein's courting reporters from my fact-checked 2002 *New Yorker* profile of Weinstein.

152 **Roger Friedman, a prolific:** Author interview with Roger Friedman claiming he never took a cent from Harvey Weinstein, then acknowledging that Harvey financed his documentary, January 24, 2019.

152 **Cindy Adams said:** Author interview with Cindy Adams, 2002, for *New Yorker* profile.

152 **When Mitchell Fink:** Author interview with Mitchell Fink about Harvey Weinstein as a source, May 21, 2019.

152 **for *Premiere* magazine:** Peter Biskind, *Down and Dirty Pictures* (New York: Simon & Schuster, 2004).

153 **"He was always available":** Author interview with Lloyd Grove on Harvey and the press, January 28, 2019.

153 **What role did a lax press play:** Although numerous accounts of Harvey Weinstein's abuse of women are reported in various places and occasional warnings, they are gathered in one place, the Wikipedia page entitled "Harvey Weinstein Sexual Abuse Allegations."

153 **In her memoir, Ivana:** Ivana Lowell on Harvey's sexual appetite, *Why Not Say What Happened?: A Memoir* (New York: Bloomsbury Publishing, 2010).

154 **Phoebe Eaton, a reporter:** Phoebe Eaton's report on Harvey's alleged Fournier gangrene infection in "The Making of a Predator, Part II," *Air Mail*, June 13, 2020.

154 **he once gently rebuked his brother:** Bob Weinstein, "Bob Weinstein's Love Letter to Brother Harvey," *Hollywood Reporter*, February 18, 2015.

156 **"the same people who criticize me":** Harvey Weinstein explaining that what he does in Hollywood is no different than what Spielberg does is from author interview with Weinstein, 2002, for *New Yorker* profile.

156 **He was unusually "mistrustful":** Author interview with Jonathan Gordon about Harvey Weinstein's cynicism, January 25, 2019.

156 **thought of himself as a confidant:** Marcy Granata email to author, October 31, 2018.

157 **Clinton told me:** Author interview on September 19, 2002, with Bill Clinton, for 2002 *New Yorker* profile.

157 **He sprinkled his money:** Author interview with Harvey Weinstein on his political giving, October 9, 2002, for *New Yorker* profile.

157 **Harvey insisted on doing a run-through:** Author interview with James Naughton, 2002, for *New Yorker* profile.

157 **"Harvey became Tony Soprano":** Nathan Lane describes Harvey acting like Tony Soprano on *Late Night with Seth Meyers*, March 6, 2018.

158 **Roseland event, "was insane":** Author interview with Jane Rosenthal on Roseland scene, June 24, 2019.

158 **Republicans would pummel Hillary:** Author interview with Harvey Weinstein, October 9, 2002, for *New Yorker* profile.

158 **when Hillary Clinton's aides:** An account of Clinton's staff ignoring warnings about Harvey Weinstein is reported in Ronan Farrow, *Catch and Kill: Lies, Spies, and a Conspiracy to Protect Predators* (New York: Little, Brown and Company, 2019).

158 **"He was forcing executives":** Author interview with Michael Eisner about Harvey's political pressure, December 4, 2018.

158 **called "Citizen Harvey":** Marcy Granata email to author about Harvey getting "very full of himself," October 31, 2018.

159 **"'Harvey, you're becoming a one-name person'":** Author interview with Bob Weinstein about Harvey's self-promotion, September 14, 2018.

159 **the *Observer*, Andrew Goldman:** Andrew Goldman's articles in *The New York Observer* that angered Weinstein: "Broadway's Not-So-Wild Party," June 12, 2000, and "Harvey's P.R. Angels Fly the Coop," August 14, 2000.

160 **grabbing him in a headlock:** Account of Weinstein's confrontation with Rebecca Traister and Andrew Goldman was reported in author's *New Yorker* profile, and more fully reported in Traister's *Good and Mad: The Revolutionary Power of Women's Anger* (New York: Simon & Schuster, 2018).

160 **placed the blame on:** Page Six account describing pictureless account of the scene, "Journo Feels Harvey's Heave-Ho," *New York Post*, November 8, 2000.

160 **"I swear on my kids' life!":** Author email exchanges with Marcy Granata about Harvey Weinstein's lie that he never used the C-word, July 16 and July 24, 2020.

161 **At a Los Angeles event:** Graydon Carter and Kurt Anderson interviewed by David Carr of *New York Times* at the New York Public Library on the twentieth anniversary of *Spy* magazine, November 3, 2006.

161 **Carter thought they would:** The exchange between Graydon Carter and Harvey Weinstein based on interviews with both, and fact-checked for *New Yorker* profile.

162 **"like going into a lion's cage"**: Author interview with Charles Layton about Miramax's culture, January 12, 2019.

162 **"Harvey's assistants were as powerful"**: Author interview with Jason Blum about culture of Miramax, December 18, 2018.

162 **Harvey chartered a plane**: Author interview with Jonathan Gordon about how Harvey flew Gordon's parents back to L.A., January 25, 2019.

162 **"We were a tribe"**: Author interview with Katrina Wolfe about tribal culture of Miramax, April 2, 2019.

163 **"the company runs best"**: Anonymous Miramax staffer interviewed in Amelia Gentleman and Holly Watt, "It Was Like Tending to a Disgusting Baby: Life as a Harvey Weinstein Employee," *The Guardian*, September 29, 2018.

164 **he was a fearsome sight**: Author interview with Stacey Snider about her encounter with Harvey Weinstein, 2002, for *New Yorker* profile.

164 **"You are a bully"**: Author interviews with Barry Diller about clash with Harvey Weinstein, on June 18, 2002, and September 19, 2018; and the account of Weinstein's confrontations with Stacey Snider and Barry Diller were reported and fact-checked in *New Yorker* profile.

165 **"Why do I have to keep fighting?"**: Harvey Weinstein's thoughts on these encounters were reported in *New Yorker* profile from October 9, 2002, interview.

165 **"The thing I hate most about myself"**: Author interview with Harvey Weinstein about his temper and pledge to donate $100,000 to the Hole in the Wall Gang camp each time he erupted in public, October 9, 2002, for *New Yorker* profile.

165 **Now that he had turned fifty**: Author interview with Harvey Weinstein about his longing for more family time, June 27, 2002, for *New Yorker* profile.

166 **"We always whispered"**: Author interview with Katrina Wolfe, April 2, 2019.

166 **"She got on the phone"**: Author interview with Marcy Granata about Miriam Weinstein, October 19, 2018, and author email exchange with Granata confirming details, May 28, 2020.

167 **"She created these monsters"**: Author interview with Meryl Poster about Miriam Weinstein, November 30, 2018.

167 **she described Harvey as "my monster"**: Salma Hayek op-ed describing Harvey Weinstein's behavior and how her body cried, "Harvey Weinstein Is My Monster Too," *New York Times*, December 12, 2017.

168 **at a test screening**: Accounts of Harvey's confrontation with Julie Taymor reported in *New Yorker* profile.

169 **she stopped trying**: Jodi Kantor and Megan Twohey talk to Zelda Perkins about Harvey ignoring terms of the NDA in *She Said: Breaking the Sexual Harassment Story That Helped Ignite a Movement* (New York: Penguin Press, 2019).

169 **"I know you want to get Harvey"**: Author interview with Zelda Perkins describing a telephone call from Donna Gigliotti, June 13, 2019.

169 **"Zelda became angry"**: Donna Gigliotti email to author describing her phone conversation with Zelda Perkins in Guatemala, June 8, 2020; and Zelda Perkins email to author on June 29, 2020, describing the phone conversation.

170 **"it was not my story to tell"**: Donna Gigliotti email to author explaining why she could not go public with information about Harvey's abuse of Rowena Chiu without violating Zelda Perkins's admonition, June 8, 2020.

170 **she had to leave the industry**: Author interview with Zelda Perkins on how prospective employers assumed she offered sex to Harvey Weinstein, July 16, 2019.

171 **move to Hong Kong**: Rowena Chiu, "Harvey Weinstein Told Me He Liked Chinese Girls," *New York Times*, October 5, 2019.

171 **"tried to commit suicide"**: Author interview with Rowena Chiu on her life after Venice, June 13, 2019.

173 **"they close ranks"**: Author interview with Michael Eisner about Harvey and Bob for his 2002 *New Yorker* profile.

CHAPTER NINE: TWO DIVORCES

175 **downplayed the audit**: Author interview with Michael Eisner was fact-checked for *New Yorker* profile of Harvey Weinstein, "Beauty and the Beast," published December 16, 2002.

175 **"they weren't true"**: Author interview with Michael Eisner about Harvey Weinstein false profit claims, December 4, 2018, and internal Disney memo shared with author to take notes but not to copy them or to disclose the person who shared them.

176 **concluded was excessive spending**: Author's notes from internal Disney memo sent to Michael Eisner about Miramax spending, May 4, 2001.

176 **It galled him that Disney**: Howard Stern interview with Harvey Weinstein about *The Lord of the Rings*, January 15, 2014, reprinted in *Howard Stern Comes Again* (New York: Simon & Schuster, 2019).

176 **New Line's profit:** Author interview with Bob Shaye on *Lord of the Rings* profits, December 17, 2018.

176 **"a colossal mistake" by Disney:** Author interview with Harvey Weinstein on missed opportunity by Disney, August 7, 2002.

177 **"it wasn't worth the risk":** Author email exchange with Michael Eisner on *Lord of the Rings*, June 8, 2020.

177 **Those who departed:** Names of executives who left Miramax between 2000 and 2002 found in Peter Biskind, *Down and Dirty Pictures* (New York: Simon & Schuster, 2004).

177 **personal tension between Harvey and Bob:** Bob Weinstein, "Bob Weinstein's Love Letter to Brother Harvey," *Hollywood Reporter*, February 18, 2015.

178 **"The less I saw him":** Author interview with Bob Weinstein about growing estrangement between the brothers, December 3, 2019.

178 **Bob again erupted:** Accounts of my interview with Bob Weinstein and Harvey Weinstein's attempt to mollify his brother are in the fact-checked *New Yorker* profile.

179 **The brothers had other differences:** Author interview with Bob Weinstein about his frustrations with Harvey Weinstein, December 3, 2019.

181 **"Do I argue to fix the movie?":** The battle with Scott Rudin and the scenes in Harvey Weinstein's conference room attended by author; interviews with Rudin on July 9, 2002, and Weinstein and others are from author's *New Yorker* profile.

183 **"makes me look like Mary Poppins":** Author interviews with Harvey Weinstein about Scott Rudin, June 27 and August 7, 2002, for *New Yorker* profile.

183 **"good but not great":** Author interview with Harvey Weinstein about Jay Cocks screenplay, August 7, 2002, for *New Yorker* profile.

184 **an "awful" experience:** Author interview with Jay Cocks on Scorsese's work with Harvey Weinstein, June 20, 2002, for *New Yorker* profile.

185 **had mirrors installed:** Martin Scorsese's mirrors reported in Biskind, *Down and Dirty Pictures*.

185 **"I don't like to be told anything":** Author interview with Martin Scorsese on June 14, 2002, for *New Yorker* profile.

185 **"I saw eighty films":** Author interview with Harvey Weinstein, July 9, 2002, for *New Yorker* profile.

185 **as exceeding budgets:** Disney memo to Michael Eisner from strategic planning on cost of *Gangs of New York*, May 4, 2001.

185 **Miramax losses were offset:** Disney strategic planning memo on *Gangs of New York* losses and *Chicago*'s profits, April 20, 2004.

186 **bonuses totaling $162 million:** Disney and Michael Eisner claims that Miramax overstated its profits and reaped huge bonuses reported by Laura M. Holson, "How the Tumultuous Marriage of Miramax and Disney Failed," *New York Times*, March 6, 2005.

186 **Disney's contentions deserve:** Strategic planning memo to Michael Eisner and Robert Iger on Miramax's true 2002 profits of $43 million, December 19, 2003.

186 **take Law to England:** Author interviews with Anthony Minghella about working with Harvey Weinstein, for author's 2002 *New Yorker* profile.

187 **"Ask Jeffrey Katzenberg":** Author interview with Harvey Weinstein, August 7, 2002, for *New Yorker* profile.

187 **"I win, and you lose":** Author interview with Peter Murphy claiming Harvey was not a good businessman, February 21, 2019.

187 **that Jeffrey Epstein:** Harvey Weinstein's partnership with Epstein to try to buy *New York* magazine was reported by Adam K. Raymond and Matt Stieb, "Jeffrey Epstein's Rolodex," *New York* magazine, July 10, 2019.

187 **"Miramax overspent its approved":** Strategic planning memo to Michael Eisner and Robert Iger on Miramax exceeding its 2003 production budget, December 19, 2003.

188 **"argue with each other like a cartoon":** Author interview with Peter Murphy about Harvey and Bob Weinstein, February 21, 2019.

188 **"We own it!":** Author interview with Michael Eisner about Michael Moore's *Fahrenheit 9/11*, December 4, 2018.

189 **"I told Harvey to sell it":** Author interview with Michael Eisner about ordering Harvey Weinstein to sell Michael Moore's *Fahrenheit 9/11*, December 4, 2018.

190 **"let's ask these people what":** Author interview with Harvey Weinstein about *Chocolat* and scene with *USA Today* critic, July 2, 2002.

191 **"his secretary call my office":** Author interview with Skip Brittenham about dealing with Harvey Weinstein, January 8, 2019.

191 **British-born clothing designer:** Author interview with Gina Gardini about the time Harvey Weinstein was spending in Europe, and falling in love with Georgina Chapman, October 29, 2019.

192 **under the name Postel:** Author interview with Sayed Khorshed about hotel booking for Georgina Chapman, June 6, 2019.

192 **"It boggled our minds":** Author interview with Eric Robinson about Eve Chilton and Harvey's philandering, January 23, 2019.

192 **It was a tense weekend:** Author interview with Jonathan Burnham about weekend in Capri, May 31, 2019.

193 **tool of conflict, an NDA:** The May 20, 2004, separation agreement between Harvey Weinstein and Eve Chilton filed with New York State Supreme Court.

193 **"generated a twenty-two percent":** Author interviews with Joseph Ravitch on Bob Weinstein's huge profits at Dimension, June 5, 2019, and January 27, 2021.

193 **he rejected it:** Author interview with Bob Weinstein, who discusses his refusal to be separated from Harvey Weinstein, December 3, 2019.

193 **"terminate their services":** Internal Disney memo recounting chronology of proposed divorce from Miramax, September 15, 2004.

193 **"It's my parents' name!":** Author interview with Joseph Ravitch on Disney insisting on retaining the Miramax name, June 5, 2019.

193 **It killed Miriam:** Author interview with Michael Eisner on why he kept the Miramax name, December 4, 2018.

194 **They had delivered the quality movies:** Miramax box office and Oscar nominations and wins reported in Holson, "How the Tumultuous Marriage."

194 **"I always made money":** Harvey Weinstein email responding to author's questions and criticizing Peter Murphy was dictated to Weinstein's public relations adviser, Juda Engelmayer, from prison and sent to author, September 14, 2020.

194 **Harvey threw another smoke bomb:** Harvey Weinstein tells Sharon Waxman he and Bob were not fired by Disney, "Harvey Weinstein Grilled: 'I'm Loving Playing Inside the Box,'" *The Wrap*, January 4, 2011.

195 **"No event or person":** Bob Weinstein on the bonds between the brothers reported in Holson, "How the Tumultuous Marriage."

CHAPTER TEN: "WE CAN TALK ANYBODY INTO ANYTHING"

197 **"the Weinsteins were bad partners":** Author interview with Peter Murphy about warning Goldman Sachs not to do business with the Weinsteins, February 21, 2019.

197 **a sweetheart contract:** Terms of Harvey and Bob Weinstein's contract with the Weinstein Company, dated September 2005, and contained in the 257-page federal class action complaint filed in the U.S. District Court of the Southern District of New York on October 31, 2018.

199 **under the name Max Postel:** Author interview with Glenn Cunningham, vice president and security director of the Greenwich Hotel, on how much Harvey Weinstein spent on hotel suites, July 10, 2019.

199 **Haleyi said, Harvey:** The author was present when Miriam Haleyi testified on January 27, 2020.

200 **"You have to wear":** Jennifer Aniston interviewed about rejecting Marchesa dresses in Kenzie Bryant, "Jennifer Aniston Says Harvey Weinstein Pressured Her to Wear Marchesa," *Vanity Fair*, October 9, 2019.

201 **a "corporate wedding":** Author interviews with Bob Weinstein discussing Harvey's wedding to Georgina Chapman, February 17, 2020, and June 16, 2021.

201 **"The fashion business was also a cover":** Daniel Miller, Meg James, and Kim Christensen, "How Harvey Weinstein Used His Fashion Business as a Pipeline to Models," *Los Angeles Times*, October 21, 2017.

202 **Grey Goose vodka:** Author interview with Joseph Ravitch about Harvey's fascination with branding, June 5, 2019.

203 **not acquiring Marvel:** Author interviews with Joseph Ravitch about Harvey's business mistakes, June 5, 2019, and January 27 and 29, 2021.

203 **the idea wasn't "locked up":** Harvey Weinstein email dictated to his public relations adviser, Juda Engelmayer, from prison and sent to author, responding to question about Marvel, May 19, 2021.

204 **the end of Blockbuster:** Account of Netflix proposed sale to Blockbuster in Reed Hastings and Erin Meyer, *No Rules Rules: Netflix and the Culture of Reinvention* (New York: Penguin Press, 2020); and Greg Satell, "A Look Back at Why Blockbuster Really Failed and Why It Didn't Have To," *Forbes*, September 5, 2014.

205 **Weinstein Company board meetings:** Author interview with Lance Maerov on screaming at board meetings, August 30, 2019.

205 **Bob Weinstein acknowledged:** Author interview with Bob Weinstein confirming fights with Harvey at board meetings, February 17, 2020.

206 **"deteriorated into personal attacks":** Author interview with Lance Maerov about how Harvey Weinstein did most of the screaming at board meetings, May 29, 2020.

206 **"We never knew if":** Author interview with Abby Ex on the Weinstein Company's dire financial situation in 2008, January 15, 2019.

206 **Bob Weinstein was alarmed:** Author interview with Bob Weinstein on Harvey's fleeting attention span, February 17, 2020.

208 **"Harvey was the Trump":** Larry Hackett interview about Harvey Weinstein and *People* magazine in Monica Hesse and Dan Zak, "Violence. Threats. Becoming. Harvey Weinstein's 30-Year Pattern of Abuse in Hollywood," *Washington Post*, October 14, 2017.

208 **"we can talk anybody into anything":** Author interview with Quentin Tarantino about how persuasive he and Harvey Weinstein were, October 9, 2002, for *New Yorker* profile of Harvey Weinstein, "Beauty and the Beast," published December 16, 2002.

CHAPTER ELEVEN: BLOOD, BROTHERS

209 **"Harvey pressed to renegotiate":** Author interviews with Joseph Ravitch about Disney's sale of the Miramax library, June 5, 2019, and January 27, 2021.

209 **two different versions:** Harvey Weinstein email dictated to his public relations adviser, Juda Engelmayer, from prison and sent to author, blaming Ron Burkle's lower bid for the collapse of negotiations to buy back the Miramax film library, May 19, 2021.

210 **Harvey blamed Disney:** Harvey Weinstein email dictated to his public relations adviser, Juda Engelmayer, from prison and sent to author, claiming that Disney was "spiteful," and that the $660 million Disney sale of Miramax demonstrated he built value as a businessman, September 14, 2020.

210 **Greenwich Hotel suites:** Author interview with Glenn Cunningham, vice president and security director of the Greenwich Hotel, on how much Harvey spent on hotel suites, July 10, 2019.

210 **Lucia Evans, who would appear:** Interview with Ronan Farrow, *Catch and Kill: Lies, Spies, and a Conspiracy to Protect Predators* (New York: Little, Brown and Company, 2019).

210 **Jessica Mann, a twenty-five-year-old:** Author was present at Harvey Weinstein's criminal trial on January 31, 2020, when Jessica Mann described under oath what occurred at the Montage Hotel.

211 **"impulse control problems":** Author interview with Abby Ex on how Weinstein used hotel suites to prey on women, January 15, 2019.

211 **a civil suit alleging:** Sandeep Rehal's civil lawsuit filed by ten alleged victims against Harvey Weinstein, the company's board, and its executives before the U.S. District Court of the Southern District, October 31, 2018.

212 **Quentin Tarantino admitted:** Quentin Tarantino admits he knew of Harvey's sexual abuse in PBS *Frontline* documentary, *Weinstein*, March 2, 2018.

212 **"Stop doing bad shit":** Account of Irwin Reiter email to Harvey Weinstein reported in Jodi Kantor and Megan Twohey, *She Said: Breaking the Sexual Harassment Story That Helped Ignite a Movement* (New York: Penguin Press, 2019).

212 **"I decide if you graduate":** Jodi Kantor interview with Sandeep Rehal in Kantor and Twohey, *She Said*.

213 **"it doesn't work that way":** Howard Stern interview with Harvey Weinstein in *Howard Stern Comes Again* (New York: Simon & Schuster, 2019).

213 **"This is not a guy who":** Howard Stern to John Carucci, "In New Book, Stern Talks Regret," AP News, May 14, 2019.

214 **"Am I allowed to flirt with you?":** Melissa Thompson video encounter with Harvey Weinstein can be located via a Google search. It is found by searching Sky News interview with Melissa Thompson about Harvey Weinstein, and includes an interview with Thompson on September 16, 2018; Melissa Thompson's emails to a friend can be found on the same search.

216 **he was shocked by:** Author interview with Lance Maerov on what a weak business the Weinstein Company was, and that Dimension was a better business, August 30, 2019.

217 **was "incredibly unsophisticated":** Author interview with Lance Maerov about Harvey Weinstein's lack of business knowledge, March 13, 2019.

217 **"He would spend more money":** Author interview with Bob Weinstein about Harvey Weinstein's thirst to spend, February 17, 2020.

217 **"'Find your voice'":** Author interview with Peggy Siegal about how Harvey Weinstein marketed *The King's Speech*, October 22, 2018.

218 **"'What the fuck was he thinking?'":** Author interview with Abby Ex about Harvey's reaction to *The Artist*, January 15, 2019.

218 **confidence in his brother's movie taste:** Author interview with Bob Weinstein about how Harvey Weinstein relied on his own gut to decide what movies he liked, February 17, 2020.

219 **"He's a genius":** Author interview with Abby Ex on toll from Harvey Weinstein's verbal abuse, and what she learned working for him, January 15, 2019.

219 **"an aging prime minister":** Author interview with Meryl Streep on Harvey Weinstein's attempting to boss around the *Iron Lady* director, November 16, 2019.

220 **"If I called Quentin Tarantino":** Tom Barrack, Jr., explaining to Mike Fleming, Jr., why he made a deal with Harvey Weinstein to exploit the Miramax film library, "Miramax TWC Linkup Homecoming Means

'Shakespeare in Love' and 'Rounders' Sequels, and 'Good Will Hunting' Series," *Deadline Hollywood*, December 16, 2013.

220 **sounding like Don Corleone:** Barry Avrich, *Moguls, Monsters and Madmen: An Uncensored Life in Show Business* (Toronto: ECW Press, 2016); Don Corleone quote from script of opening scene from *The Godfather*.

221 **"I want to talk to the pope":** Author interview with Gina Gardini about Harvey thinking of himself as a head of state, October 29, 2019.

221 **"this has to be done!":** Author interview with Joel Klein about phone call with Harvey Weinstein, March 2, 2020.

221 **Harvey's version: "Nonsense":** Harvey Weinstein email dictated to his public relations adviser, Juda Engelmayer, from prison and sent to author, denying that he threatened schools chancellor Joel Klein, September 14, 2020.

222 **David Boies, Harvey's attorney:** Author interview with David Boies about how Harvey Weinstein condescended to Bob, June 18, 2019.

222 **"he wasn't very charming with me":** Author interview with Bob Weinstein about Harvey treating him as the younger brother, December 3, 2019.

223 **"The brothers were not talking":** Author interview with Meryl Poster about Bob Weinstein and about the estrangement between the Weinstein brothers, November 30, 2018.

223 **At lunch Boies set out:** Author interview with Bob Weinstein about lunch with Harvey and David Boies, May 6, 2019.

224 **"You're a liar":** Author interview with Bob Weinstein about Harvey punching him, September 14, 2018; the first brief mention of this incident that I'm aware of was in Kantor and Twohey, *She Said*.

225 **"After Bob pushed me":** Harvey Weinstein email dictated to his public relations adviser, Juda Engelmayer, from prison and sent to author, in response to author's questions and blaming Bob Weinstein for starting their physical fight by pushing him, September 14, 2020.

225 **"there was blood on the floor":** Author interview with Abby Ex about Harvey Weinstein punching Bob, May 6, 2019.

225 **"a real breaking point for me":** Author interview with Bob Weinstein about reasons for his deteriorating relationship with his brother, and turning to David Glasser, February 17, 2020.

225 **Harry and Jack Warner:** Relationship between the Warner brothers described in Neal Gabler, *Empire of Their Own: How the Jews Invented Hollywood* (New York: Crown, 1988).

225 **"Over time my relationship":** Author interview with Bob Weinstein about his deteriorating relationship with his brother, February 17, 2020.

225 **but Bob's jealousy:** Harvey Weinstein email dictated to his public relations adviser, Juda Engelmayer, from prison and sent to author, answering question about whether his spending was the crucial source of tension with Bob, September 14, 2020.

226 **"They were mediators":** Author interview with Bob Weinstein on mediating role of David Boies and Bert Fields, February 17, 2020.

226 **dividing the company in two:** Bob Weinstein wanting to split the company and Harvey resisting is from Kantor and Twohey, *She Said*.

226 **"You're making a lot of good points'":** Author interview with Lance Maerov on how Bob Weinstein and he seemed to be more allied, August 30, 2019.

CHAPTER TWELVE: "I'M THE CHAIRMAN OF THIS COMPANY!"

227 **he seemed even less particular:** Several women who claim Harvey sexually assaulted them, including Melissa Thompson and Jessica Mann, have described his stubble and hygiene.

229 **The police had their confession:** The fullest account of what happened between Ambra Gutierrez and Harvey Weinstein is reported in Ronan Farrow, *Catch and Kill: Lies, Spies, and a Conspiracy to Protect Predators* (New York: Little, Brown and Company, 2019). Farrow was the first to retrieve a copy of the police tape of Weinstein confirming he groped her breasts, which Farrow disclosed in *The New Yorker*.

229 **"I know Bill Bratton":** Author interview with former New York City chief of detectives Robert Boyce, February 13, 2020.

231 **He emailed his buddy:** Harvey Weinstein email to James Dolan asking his help to tamp down *Daily News* coverage of Ambra Gutierrez's sexual assault claims against him, April 1, 2015.

232 **"hold hands and jump":** Jennifer Senior, tweet, March 30, 2015.

233 **In exchange for $1 million:** Copy of Ambra Battilana Gutierrez affidavit, signed and notarized on April 20, 2015.

234 **"never turned a profit":** Emails and text messages between the author and Lance Maerov about the company never turning a profit in ten years, September 5, 2020.

235 **"It was clear to me":** Author interview with David Boies about Harvey's personnel file, August 3, 2020.

235 **"the loss of Bob Weinstein":** Bert Fields letter to Lance Maerov, July 31, 2015.

235 **a volley of five emails:** Emails exchanged rapidly between Harvey Weinstein and Lance Maerov regarding a new contract, May 12, 2015; and author interview with Lance Maerov on Weinstein Company losses, February 19, 2019.

236 **sentimental personal essays:** Bob Weinstein, "Bob Weinstein's Love Letter to Brother Harvey," *Hollywood Reporter*, February 18, 2015.

237 *listen to me:* The June 2, 2015, conference call was recorded, and the author has a recording of the call between Harvey Weinstein, David Glasser, and board members Lance Maerov, Tarak Ben Ammar, and Jeffrey Sackman.

237 **Maerov and the others thought:** Author interview with Lance Maerov on his thoughts about the June 2 conference call, August 26, 2020.

240 **If David Glasser:** David Glasser declined to be interviewed.

243 **"Not true. HW wanted":** Harvey Weinstein email dictated to his public relations adviser, Juda Engelmayer, from prison and sent to author, in answer to question about why he wanted Bob Weinstein demoted, May 19, 2021.

243 **sent him threatening letters:** Author interview with Lance Maerov about letters from the lawyers, March 15, 2019.

244 **"I'm gonna kill you!":** Author interview with Lance Maerov describing Harvey Weinstein threatening him in the movie theater, March 15, 2019.

244 **"review Harvey's personnel file":** David Boies email to Lance Maerov and Weinstein Company attorney Philip Richter, July 21, 2015.

244 **Realizing this was the best:** Author interview with Lance Maerov about seeking access to Harvey Weinstein's personnel file, and how H. Rodgin Cohen was retained to investigate file, March 15, 2019.

244 **H. Rodgin Cohen reported:** H. Rodgin Cohen letter to Weinstein Company law firm asserting that Harvey Weinstein's personnel file exonerates him, September 4, 2015.

245 **Anxious, he followed up:** A copy of Cohen's September 4, 2015, handwritten note to Philip Richter, a partner of the Weinstein Company's law firm, Fried, Frank, Harris, Shriver & Jacobson.

CHAPTER THIRTEEN: NO MORE "BOBBY" WEINSTEIN

246 **made a peace pact:** Author interview with Lance Maerov on why Bob and Harvey made peace, April 13, 2021.

246 *There have been instances:* Bob Weinstein letter to Harvey, quoted in Jodi Kantor and Megan Twohey, *She Said: Breaking the Sexual Harassment Story That Helped Ignite a Movement* (New York: Penguin Press, 2019).

247 **Harvey's "numerous affairs":** Author interview with Bob Weinstein about Harvey's "misbehaviors," June 16, 2021.

247 **he was resigning:** David Glasser email to independent directors and others, including Harvey and Bob Weinstein, July 28, 2015.

247 **came to believe Glasser:** Harvey Weinstein email dictated to his public relations adviser, Juda Engelmayer, from prison and sent to author, acknowledging that he came to see Glasser as duplicitous, September 14, 2020; confirmation of this view from author interview with Bob Weinstein, April 9, 2021.

248 **advised, "Call Miriam":** Author interview with Sayed Khorshed about Miriam Weinstein as peacemaker, June 6, 2019.

248 **Code of Conduct for its executives:** Copy of revised terms of Harvey and Bob Weinstein's contract, October 20, 2015.

248 **"He wanted to make peace":** Author interview with David Boies about why Harvey Weinstein agreed to new contract in 2015, June 18, 2019.

248 **"Bob seemed to make a deal":** Author interview with Lance Maerov, who learned Bob Weinstein would support Harvey if Harvey got help for his sex addiction, March 15, 2019.

249 *"this is utterly fantastic":* Copy of Bob Weinstein email to Harvey about his ITV negotiations, August 6, 2015.

249 **"toll on Bob's self confidence":** Author interview with Lance Maerov about relationship between the Weinstein brothers, August 30, 2019.

249 **"He beat everyone down":** Author interview with Bob Weinstein on how Harvey "wore" people down, February 17, 2020.

249 **"he was constantly in a panic":** Author interview with Jules Kroll about Harvey Weinstein's panic, March 28, 2019.

250 **"I told him what the piece was about":** Author interview with Gina Gardini about *New York* magazine investigation of Harvey Weinstein, October 29, 2019.

250 **The balance of power is me:** Lauren O'Connor memo circulated to Weinstein Company executives, November 3, 2015, and reported in Kantor and Twohey, *She Said.*

251   **he "went ballistic":** Author interview with David Boies on Bob Weinstein's reaction to Lauren O'Connor memo, June 18, 2019; and author interview with Bob Weinstein about his reaction to O'Connor memo, July 22, 2020.

252   **prosecutor Linda Fairstein:** Harvey Weinstein 3-page unpublished essay in which he says he turned to Linda Fairstein to probe Lauren O'Connor sexual claims, contained in court documents released on March 11, 2020, as part of his criminal trial in New York.

252   **Boies insists he did not:** Author email exchange with David Boies in which he says neither he nor his firm ever negotiated an NDA for Harvey Weinstein, July 22 and 23, 2020.

252   **"she did not withdraw":** Author interview with Lance Maerov about what David Boies said about the O'Connor NDA, August 30, 2019.

253   **his amateur band:** Mark Schneider, "MSG's James Dolan Opens for Eagles, Pens Songs About Eliot Spitzer and Trayvon Martin," *Billboard*, September 12, 2014.

255   **"Weinstein was a gatekeeper":** Ben Thompson on Harvey Weinstein's power, "Goodbye Gatekeepers," *Stratechery* (blog), October 16, 2017.

255   **"I didn't want to hurt":** Bob Weinstein, "Bob Weinstein's Love Letter to Brother Harvey," *Hollywood Reporter*, February 18, 2015.

255   **desecrating Miriam's memory:** Author interview with Meryl Poster about Miriam Weinstein's memorial service, November 30, 2018.

256   **event was "quite fake":** Author interview with Agnès Mentre about Miriam Weinstein's memorial service, September 5, 2019.

256   **"kill his brother Fredo":** Author interview with David Boies about the impact of Miriam Weinstein's death on her sons, November 27, 2018.

256   **"My mother was a strong person":** Harvey Weinstein email dictated to his public relations adviser, Juda Engelmayer, from prison and sent to author, acknowledging that the death of Miriam Weinstein removed a vital bridge between the brothers, September 14, 2020.

256   **Upon arriving at his hotel:** Transcript from Harvey Weinstein's 2020 New York criminal trial, describing trading his grief over his mother's death for sex with Jessica Mann, February 3, 2020.

256   **More than once Bob had:** Author interview with Glenn Cunningham describing insults he witnessed Harvey Weinstein hurling at Bob, July 10, 2019.

257   **Harvey traveled outside:** In an attempt to show the jury in Weinstein's 2020 New York criminal trial that he was paying too much attention to chasing women, the prosecution called to the witness stand Daniel Rothman, an executive with the U.S. Customs and Border Protection agency, which keeps records on when people leave and return to the U.S. Rothman recited the 243 days Harvey was out of the U.S.

257   **charged it to the company:** Author interviews with Lance Maerov on Harvey's misuse of corporate funds, February 19, 2019 and March 15, 2019.

257   **Harvey's lawyer, Philip Richter:** Philip Richter later acknowledged in his December 11 and December 15, 2014, letters to the board that Harvey Weinstein did use corporate funds for personal expenses, but insisted that Harvey reimbursed the company.

257   **2004 hit, *Finding Neverland*:** The first press disclosures of Harvey Weinstein's machinations on behalf of amfAR and himself were reported by Megan Twohey, "Tumult After AIDS Fund-Raiser Supports Harvey Weinstein Production," *New York Times*, September 23, 2017.

258   **"Weinstein recouped all":** A sharp analysis of Harvey Weinstein's behavior in William D. Cohan, "'Nothing About This Deal Feels Right to Me'": Inside Harvey Weinstein's Other Nightmare," *Vanity Fair*, December 20, 2017. Yashar Ali also wrote a vivid account of what he described as "a shady deal" in "How Harvey Weinstein and Kenneth Cole Covered Up a Shady Deal," *Huffington Post*, October 27, 2017.

258   **"They divided the employees":** Author interview with David Boies describing effort to split the company into two parts, one run by Bob Weinstein, the other by Harvey, November 6, 2018.

258   **But the detailed plan:** Author interview with Bob Weinstein about effort to split Dimension from the Weinstein Company, February 17, 2020.

259   **"But, no bullshit":** Harvey boasted in an interview with Gregg Kilday that the company was in great financial shape, "Harvey Weinstein Addresses Executive Exits: Company Is in 'Great Shape,'" *Hollywood Reporter*, August 12, 2015.

CHAPTER FOURTEEN: THE DAM OF SILENCE COLLAPSES

260   **Harvey's instinctive default posture:** Author interview with Jonathan Gordon on how mistrustful Harvey was, January 25, 2019.

260   **"lacked the money":** Author interview with David Boies confirming loss of over $1 billion, June 18, 2019.

262   **had probed his behavior toward women:** Author interview with Thomas Ajamie about Harvey Weinstein's behavior, July 11, 2019.

262 **he demanded, and got:** NDAs from the amfAR board but not from Ajamie, reported by Megan Twohey, "Tumult After AIDS Fund-Raiser Supports Harvey Weinstein Production," *New York Times*, September 23, 2017.

262 **admitted he and McGowan had sex:** Author interview with David Boies about Harvey Weinstein insisting sex was consensual, June 18, 2019.

262 **"I have a naked picture of her":** Author interview with Meryl Poster about Harvey Weinstein's claim that he possessed a naked picture of Rose McGowan, May 28, 2020.

263 **"I always felt like your kid sister":** Susan Jeanne Slonaker "heads-up" email to Harvey Weinstein, June 23, 2017.

263 **she attacked Harvey's potential accusers:** Lisa Bloom's role for Weinstein is reported in Jodi Kantor and Megan Twohey, *She Said: Breaking the Sexual Harassment Story That Helped Ignite a Movement* (New York: Penguin Press, 2019).

263 **"This is great stuff":** Harvey Weinstein email to Lanny Davis, July 25, 2017, forwarding Susan Jeanne Slonaker's email, and Lanny Davis's same-day emailed reply.

263 **call *Times* editor:** Author interview with David Boies about Harvey Weinstein's concern about Rose McGowan, June 18, 2019.

264 **"He was calling every book agent":** Author interview with Jonathan Burnham about Rose McGowan's book, May 31, 2019.

264 **via Black Cube:** The 5-page Black Cube contract with Weinstein's law firm, Boies Schiller & Flexner LLP, dated July 11, 2017, was an exhibit in his 2020 New York criminal trial. A brilliant exposure of Black Cube's role on behalf of Weinstein, including menacing reporters, was reported in Ronan Farrow, *Catch and Kill: Lies, Spies, and a Conspiracy to Protect Predators* (New York: Little, Brown and Company, 2019); *Daily Mail* also deeply probed Black Cube's role in reporting by Alana Goodman, "The SPY Who Duped Rose McGowan UNMASKED!," November 8, 2017. The estimated $2 million paid to Black Cube comes from adding together what was reported by Ronan Farrow and Alana Goodman.

264 **was Seth Freedman:** Adam Luck and Ben Lazarus exposed the machinations of Black Cube operatives, "'How I Was Hired by Harvey Weinstein to Dig Dirt on His Accusers,'" *Daily Mail*, November 30, 2019.

264 **the nameless "Monster":** Rose McGowan, *Brave* (New York: HarperOne, 2018).

265 **told Ben Affleck:** Harvey Weinstein response to criticism over the years contained in a 48-page document, "The Proper Narrative for Addressing the Harvey Weinstein Case," that his public relations firm, Herald PR, produced, and which quotes Ben Affleck, December 2, 2019.

265 **she has been photographed with Harvey:** Photographs of Harvey Weinstein and Rose McGowan together can be seen at https://www.google.com/search?q=Harvey+Weinstein+and+Rose+McGowan&client=safari& rls=en&source=lnms&tbm=isch&sa=X&ved=2ahUKEwjdiqz488XyAhUuF1kFIIYXuCssQ_AUoAnoEC AEQBA&biw=1847&bih=961.

265 **Farrow's interest was ignited:** The Rose McGowan tweet and George Pataki's phone call to Weinstein reported in Farrow, *Catch and Kill*.

266 **Harvey had already stopped:** Author interview with David Boies about Weinstein being told by NBC executives in July 2017 that the Ronan Farrow investigation was dead, June 18, 2019.

267 **all say they repeatedly refused:** A detailed account of Harvey Weinstein's attempted or actual contacts with NBC News executives is contained in a lengthy September 3, 2018, memo and fact sheet sent to employees by NBC News chairman Andrew Lack, defending why the News division rejected Ronan Farrow's reporting.

267 **"this women's issue":** Account of Harvey Weinstein pressing Lanny Davis on Rose McGowan reported in Farrow, *Catch and Kill*.

268 **described the encounter:** Author interviews with Lanny Davis about his visit to Noah Oppenheim at NBC, May 10 and 11, 2020.

268 **Davis had reassured Harvey:** Lanny Davis email to Harvey Weinstein stating that he had "a great record treating women well," July 25, 2017.

268 **described his meeting with Davis:** Author email exchange with Noah Oppenheim, who describes his meeting with Lanny Davis, June 9, 2020.

268 **"is a lie":** Author interviews with Lanny Davis denying Oppenheim's claim, May 11 and June 9, 2020.

269 **NBC can't dodge this incriminating fact:** Ronan Farrow's detailed chronology of when and how he was told by NBC News that his Weinstein story was killed is contained in a June 19, 2020, email to the author, and in Farrow, *Catch and Kill*.

269 **claiming Farrow had "not a single victim":** NBC News chairman Andrew Lack's September 3, 2018, memo and fact sheet claims that Ronan Farrow failed to produce while reporting for MSNBC any victims or witnesses "to misconduct by Weinstein."

269 **vehemently refuted these claims:** Ronan Farrow response to NBC contained in Jeremy Barr's account of the battle, "NBC News Chief Andy Lack Attacks 'Baseless Speculation' on Ronan Farrow Relationship," *Hollywood Reporter*, September 3, 2018.

270 **what evidence Farrow first shared:** Author phone interview with Deirdre Foley-Mendelssohn to confirm what facts Ronan Farrow brought to *The New Yorker* in August 2017, June 28, 2018. This information was double-checked and confirmed in a February 28, 2020, email exchange with her.

271 **"Bella. Meryl Poster asked me":** Text message from Paul Feldsher to Annabella Sciorra introduced as a court exhibit in the 2020 New York criminal trial of Harvey Weinstein, and Feldsher testimony at trial on February 6, 2020.

271 **Poster flatly denies this:** Meryl Poster email to author explaining why she asked for Annabella Sciorra's phone number, May 27, 2020.

271 **Hi Ms. Sciorra, it's Seth:** Seth Freedman of Black Cube left this message for Annabella Sciorra on August 17, 2017, which was introduced as evidence at Weinstein's criminal trial.

272 *Please send $60K*: Harvey Weinstein email to Bob Peck and David Hutkin instructing them to wire money to Paul Feldsher, April 4, 2017, submitted as evidence during Harvey's 2020 New York criminal trial.

272 **why Harvey agreed to pay personally:** Emails were introduced at Harvey's 2020 New York criminal trial documenting that his company owed Feldsher ninety thousand dollars for his producing work, and Harvey's email to his staff to immediately pay Feldsher sixty thousand dollars out of his personal account and that the company could later reimburse him.

273 **dozens of red-flagged names:** The "red flags" emails were introduced as court exhibits in Harvey Weinstein's 2020 New York criminal trial.

273 **"something very different from":** Pamela Lubell interview with Ronan Farrow about the calls Harvey asked her to make to women is reported in Farrow's *New Yorker* piece "Harvey Weinstein's Army of Spies," November 6, 2017.

273 **would be sent to Black Cube:** Reported in Farrow, *Catch and Kill*.

274 **Madden refused to:** Account of the Pamela Lubell phone call to Laura Madden in Kantor and Twohey, *She Said*.

274 **"That is absolutely not true":** Email exchange with Pamela Lubell conducted by author's fact-checker, Jason Stavers, March 29, 2020; and Lubell response to author in email exchange, May 10, 2020.

274 **"'Whose side are you on?'":** Author interview with Lanny Davis about Harvey Weinstein's paranoia, May 10, 2019.

275 *I have an idea*: Author interview with Kim Masters, April 8, 2019, and copy of Harvey Weinstein email to Masters, June 29, 2017.

275 **Meryl Poster sharing an email:** Meryl Poster email alerting Harvey Weinstein to Ronan Farrow, September 26, 2017, and Harvey Weinstein email to Black Cube, September 27, 2017.

275 **Alexandra Canosa, who would say:** Civil lawsuit filed in the New York State Supreme Court by Alexandra Canosa against Harvey Weinstein and the board of the Weinstein Company, April 30, 2018.

276 **"I never called":** Author interview with Jane Rosenthal about Harvey Weinstein's request that she call Jodi Kantor, June 24, 2019.

276 **Rattner ended the call:** Author interview with Steven Rattner about Harvey Weinstein's request that he call Arthur Sulzberger, May 22, 2019.

276 **He attended, he insisted:** Harvey Weinstein email dictated to his public relations adviser, Juda Engelmayer, from prison and sent to author, in which he said he was invited to speak at Gwyneth Paltrow's summer of 2017 party for Jake Paltrow, September 14, 2020.

277 **"This guy is completely pathological":** Gwyneth Paltrow email to author explaining what happened with Harvey Weinstein at her party, November 19, 2020.

277 **Boies would later acknowledge:** David Boies's explanation of his work with Black Cube contained in Farrow, "Harvey Weinstein's Army."

278 **"Sorry, Harvey, the board":** Author interviews with Lance Maerov about when he learned *The New York Times* was going to expose Harvey Weinstein and what steps he took, February 19, 2019, and August 30, 2019.

278 **Harvey declared, "is disgusting":** Description of Harvey Weinstein threatening to reveal letter written by Lance Maerov, in Kantor and Twohey, *She Said*.

278 **he would sell six homes:** Candace Taylor, "Harvey Weinstein Started Selling His Real Estate About Six Months Before His Downfall," *Wall Street Journal*, August 9, 2019.

279 **ignoring the First Amendment censorship:** Charles Harder letter to *New Yorker* disclosed in Farrow, *Catch and Kill*.

279 **Bob Weinstein was strangely quiet:** Dialogue at board meetings from author interviews with Lance Maerov, March 15, 2019; David Boies, June 18, 2019; and Bob Weinstein, February 17, 2020.

280 **Kim Masters and Chris Gardner:** Kim Masters and Chris Gardner, "Harvey Weinstein Lawyers Battling N.Y. Times, New Yorker Over Potentially Explosive Stories," *Hollywood Reporter,* October 4, 2017.

280 **"He was in a panic":** Lubell quoted in Farrow, "Harvey Weinstein's Army."

280 **a tiny glass-walled conference room:** Harvey's visit to *The New York Times* in Kantor and Twohey, *She Said.*

281 **offering an apology, sort of:** Harvey Weinstein's response to Jodi Kantor and Megan Twohey's exposé, "Harvey Weinstein Paid Off Sexual Harassment Accusers for Decades," *New York Times,* October 5, 2017.

282 **urging her to please shut up:** Email correspondence between Lisa Bloom and the board, October 5, 2017, and email responses from Lance Maerov and Bob Weinstein, October 6, 2017.

283 **"I'm coming back":** Description of shouting at October 5, 2017, board meeting from author interview with Lance Maerov, June 1, 2020

283 **law firm of Debevoise & Plimpton:** Compromise reached at board described in author interview with Lance Maerov, June 1, 2020.

283 **"ran for the hills":** Shawn Tully wrote an excellent ticktock about the Weinstein board's role, in which he quotes Ben Ammar and describes the board, "How a Handful of Billionaires Kept Their Friend Harvey Weinstein in Power," *Fortune,* November 19, 2017.

283 **"I love you," he wrote:** Paul Tudor Jones note to his friend Harvey Weinstein contained in class action complaint filed in U.S. District Court of the Southern District of New York on October 31, 2018, against the Weinstein Company board by his alleged victims.

283 **"I made my decisions":** Dirk Ziff email to Harvey Weinstein, October 5, 2017, telling him he resigned from the board before *New York Times* revelations. Ziff declined to speak to author.

284 **to his board. None did:** Copies of letter Harvey Weinstein sent to prominent friends pleading with them to write to his board contained in criminal court document, People of the State of New York against Harvey Weinstein, December 19, 2019, exhibits 1010–0034.

284 **"I had the veto vote":** Author interview with Bob Weinstein in which he says he fired his brother, February 17, 2020.

284 **the Weinstein Company did not operate:** Author interview with David Boies about Lance Maerov, June 18, 2019.

285 **sent a scathing email:** Bob Weinstein email to Harvey Weinstein, November 1, 2017, contained in a motion filed in December 2019 by Harvey Weinstein's defense team to the State Supreme Court to preclude these documents from being used in the criminal trial.

285 **"I didn't know any of that":** Author interview with Bob Weinstein, in which he says he had no prior knowledge of his brother's sexual abuse, September 14, 2018.

286 **Sixteen former and current:** Ronan Farrow's first report in *New Yorker* exposing Weinstein's sexual predations and his enablers, October 10, 2017.

286 **"We did not know":** Letter from thirty anonymous staffers claiming they did not know Weinstein was a "serial sexual predator" reported by Brian Stelter, CNN, October 19, 2017.

286 **"an ounce of remorse":** Bob Weinstein tells *Hollywood Reporter* that his brother is a "predator," Matthew Belloni and Gregg Kilday, "Bob Weinstein Gets Emotional on 'Depraved' Harvey," October 14, 2017.

286 **He now credited him:** Author interview with Bob Weinstein praising Lance Maerov, February 17, 2020.

286 **"maybe something could have changed":** Author interview with Bob Weinstein about his own complicity, July 22, 2020.

287 **a tone-deaf statement:** Harvey Weinstein tells *New York Times* he will wage war against the National Rifle Association, October 5, 2017. The full 6-paragraph statement is printed in the class action complaint filed in the U.S. District Court of the Southern District of New York on October 31, 2018, against the Weinstein Company board by his alleged victims.

CHAPTER FIFTEEN: THE VICTIM

288 **enrolled in Gentle Path:** Description of program in Julie Miller, "Harvey Weinstein Reportedly Failed to Complete Inpatient Sex Rehab," Vanityfair.com, March 9, 2018.

289 **likens sex addiction to:** Dr. Patrick Carnes, *Out of the Shadows: Understanding Sexual Addiction* (Center City, MN: Hazelden Publishing, 1994).

289 **they "might be seeking attachment":** Erica Sarr's explanation of the program is found on https://www.themeadows.com/about/locations/gentle-path-at-the-meadows/.

289 **"Healing starts the moment":** The website of the Gentle Path at the Meadows describes their philosophy, themeadowsbhc.com.

289 **"I got off the elevator":** Author interview with Bob Weinstein about his alcoholism, December 3, 2019.

289 **"falling on deaf ears":** Author interview with Bob Weinstein about how Harvey could not get proper treatment from "the comfort of a hotel room," September 14, 2018.

290 **how they describe their behavior:** Dr. Glen Gabbard, *Boundaries and Boundary Violations in Psychoanalysis* (New York: Basic Books, 1995).

290 **"As narcissists, they believe":** Author interview with Dr. Glen Gabbard describing what sociopaths think of what they have done, May 13, 2019.

290 **"she's really saying yes":** Author interview with Dr. Richard B. Krueger and Dr. Meg S. Kaplan, October 9, 2018.

290 **rampant narcissism and an absence:** Author interview with Dr. Elizabeth Jeglic, July 22, 2019.

291 **There appear to be two Harvey Weinsteins:** Matthew Belloni and Kim Masters, "Jeffrey Katzenberg Shares His Email to Harvey Weinstein," *Hollywood Reporter*, October 10, 2017.

291 **none would comment:** Sam Levin and Julie Carrie Wong, "Hollywood Men Silent over Weinstein Allegations as Women Speak Out," *The Guardian*, October 10, 2017.

292 **American Media Inc.:** Ronan Farrow, "Harvey Weinstein's Army of Spies," *New Yorker*, November 6, 2017.

292 **"he asked me if he tried":** Kate Beckinsale discussing Harvey Weinstein with Seth Kelley, "'He Couldn't Remember If He Had Assaulted Me,'" *Variety*, October 12, 2017.

293 **"very quid pro quo":** Gwyneth Paltrow described being propositioned by Harvey Weinstein and their relationship in Taffy Brodesser-Akner, "The Big Business of Being Gwyneth Paltrow," *New York Times Magazine*, July 29, 2018.

293 **became a pivotal source:** Gwyneth Paltrow role in exposing Harvey Weinstein is reported in Jodi Kantor and Megan Twohey, *She Said: Breaking the Sexual Harassment Story That Helped Ignite a Movement* (New York: Penguin Press, 2019).

293 **primitive view of women:** Elia Kazan, *A Life* (New York: Alfred A. Knopf, 1988).

294 **"Do I want to fuck her?":** Elia Kazan on female casting test in Hollywood, *A Life*.

294 **"a male-dominated enterprise":** Manohla Dargis, "Harvey Weinstein Is Gone. But Hollywood Still Has a Problem," *New York Times*, October 11, 2017.

295 **lost their government positions:** Georgetown study conducted by law professor Jamillah Bowman Williams reported the number of elected and appointed officials who lost their jobs, Haley Britzky, "#MeToo Gets Results: 75% of Officials Accused Will Be Gone by 2019," *Axios*, November 9, 2018.

295 **"a desire for power":** Rebecca Traister, *Good and Mad: The Revolutionary Power of Women's Anger* (New York: Simon & Schuster, 2018).

295 **Sweeping antiharassment legislation:** Restriction on NDAs imposed by states reported by Jodi Kantor, "Weinstein Is Convicted. Where Does #MeToo Go from Here?," *New York Times*, February 26, 2020.

296 **"it won't continue":** Author interview with Tony Vinciquerra about impact of #MeToo, November 13, 2018.

296 **it does continue:** "Sexism Still Rife in Hollywood Despite #MeToo Uproar, Survey Finds," Reuters, December 16, 2020.

296 **Instead of "Believe women":** Emily Yoffe, "Understanding Harvey" *Huffington Post*, June 26, 2018; and Bari Weiss, "The Limits of 'Believe All Women,'" *New York Times*, November 28, 2017.

297 **"not all offensive behavior warrants":** Debra Katz quoted in Jane Mayer, "The Case of Al Franken," *New Yorker*, July 29, 2019.

297 **David Bucci, fifty, chairman:** Anemona Hartocollis, "He Was Accused of Enabling Abuse. Then Came A Downward Spiral," *The New York Times*, January 4, 2020.

297 **women more willing to come forward:** Author interview with Dr. Renee Sorrentino about burst of new referrals to her clinic, August 1, 2019.

297 **"to launch an international campaign":** Zelda Perkins email to author about her plans to launch campaign to end NDAs, May 14, 2021.

297 **"give the public something":** Red Skelton remark about Harry Cohn's funeral from Neal Gabler, *An Empire of Their Own: How the Jews Invented Hollywood* (New York: Crown, 1988).

CHAPTER SIXTEEN: THE SOUND IS TURNED OFF

298 **I have only despair:** Draft of Harvey Weinstein December 21, 2017, statement was an email he sent to marketing consultant Joe Polish; this email and the consultant's response were among many Weinstein emails released during his 2020 New York criminal trial.

299 **he sent two drafts:** Joe Polish's website describes his marketing business and goals.

299 **His health was fragile:** Harvey Weinstein's medical ailments were cited by his counsel, Donna Rotunno, to Judge James Burke on the day the criminal trial jury delivered its verdict, February 24, 2020, and in Weinstein's April 5, 2021, appeal of his conviction.

299 **a slow death spiral:** Cutbacks and cancelled contracts with the Weinstein Company are described in the legal filing made by the company's chief restructuring officer, Robert Del Genio, to the U.S. Bankruptcy Court for the District of Delaware, March 20, 2018.

300 **the board fired David Glasser:** After telling the author on the phone he would be happy to be interviewed, Glasser declined to return phone calls.

300 **finally declared bankruptcy:** Debts and cash of the Weinstein Company from filing by chief restructuring officer, Robert Del Genio, to the U.S. Bankruptcy Court for the District of Delaware, March 20, 2018.

300 **opaque corporate legal bills:** Lance Maerov email to author expressing his frustration with the legal bills from David Boies and Bert Fields, July 1, 2020.

300 **"I don't think anybody":** Author interview with David Boies about how he was aware Harvey had affairs but that's all, June 18, 2019.

301 **"a melting ice cube":** Author interview with bankruptcy attorney Matthew Cantor, October 9, 2017.

301 **"Bob did not fully realize":** Author interview with Lance Maerov about Bob Weinstein, August 30, 2019.

301 **Asked whether she was ever suspicious:** Jonathan Van Meter, "Georgina Chapman on Life After Harvey Weinstein," *Vogue*, May 10, 2018.

302 **how to handle a call from Harvey's wife:** Harvey Weinstein's staff instructions reported by Megan Twohey, Jodi Kantor, Susan Dominus, Jim Rutenberg, and Steve Eder, "Weinstein's Complicity Machine," *New York Times*, December 5, 2017.

302 **"When you live with people":** Author interview with Bob Weinstein, June 21, 2021.

302 **Feldsher now talked to him regularly:** Paul Feldsher testified as a defense witness at Harvey Weinstein's criminal trial on February 6, 2020, and described their relationship and how his old friend, Annabella Sciorra, lied when she claimed she was raped.

302 **dismissing critics as conformists:** Paul Feldsher email exchanges with author, December 19, 2018, and June 10, 2019.

303 **"It's not my role to judge":** Author interview with Sallie Hofmeister, June 7, 2019.

303 **"If a client is not listening to us":** Author interview with Michael Sitrick about why his firm parted with Harvey Weinstein, June 7, 2019.

304 **48-page document:** Essay prepared by Harvey's team disputing allegations and defending his career accomplishments, 2019.

305 **"you're ruining your shirt":** Author interview with Ben Brafman, who said he was free to describe this first lunch with Harvey Weinstein since the lunch occurred before he signed on as his attorney, January 25, 2021.

306 **"Best Criminal Defense Lawyer":** *New York* magazine cites Benjamin Brafman as city's best criminal attorney, April 15, 1996.

306 **"I hated that guy":** Author interview with Glenn Cunningham about seeing Harvey Weinstein in handcuffs, July 10, 2019.

308 **box office attendance dropped:** Statistics and analysis of decline in movie theater attendance in Matthew Ball, "The Absurdities of 'Franchise Fatigue' and 'Sequelitis' (Or, What Is Happening to the Box Office?!)," *REDEF*, August 4, 2019.

308 **Tad Friend reported:** Reports on shrinking movie theater revenues, "The Mogul in the Middle," *New Yorker*, January 4, 2016.

309 **The question is, how is Harvey Weinstein:** Cindy Adams, "Harvey Ponders Life Abroad," *New York Post*, September 18, 2019.

309 **chronic health issues:** Harvey Weinstein's five doctors and unsuccessful back operation were cited in a plea for leniency by his counsel, Donna Rotunno, to Judge James Burke on the day the criminal trial jury delivered its verdict, February 24, 2020, and in Harvey's April 5, 2021, legal appeal of his conviction.

309 **"bubble gum rolled in cat hair":** *Saturday Night Live* skit on Harvey Weinstein, November 2, 2019.

310 **calling him "a fucking monster":** Accounts of what occurred with Harvey Weinstein at the Actor's Hour reported by Yohana Desta, "Harvey Weinstein Makes a Chaotic Return at New York Actors Showcase," VanityFair.com, October 25, 2019, and by Tracy Connor, "Actors Hour Apologizes for Letting Harvey Weinstein Attend NYC Performance," *Daily Beast*, October 25, 2019.

310 **Weinstein vigorously denied:** Author interview with Bob Weinstein denying he spoke to the two *New York Times* reporters for their October 5, 2017, exposé of Harvey Weinstein, June 20, 2020.

310 **seemed obsessed by:** Author interview with Juda Engelmayer about the bile between Harvey and Bob Weinstein, January 14, 2019.

310 **he promised Miriam:** Author interview with Juda Engelmayer about Harvey Weinstein promising Miriam not to speak ill of Bob, January 14, 2019.

311 **"It's because his name is Weinstein":** Author interview with Bert Fields about people shunning Bob Weinstein, May 31, 2019.

311 **The project never got off the ground:** Nicholas Sperling, "A Weinstein Is Returning to Hollywood," *New York Times*, October 14, 2019.

CHAPTER SEVENTEEN: THE LONG MARCH TO TRIAL

315 **"I wish I were taller"**: Brafman quip to jury about his height from Eric Sullivan profile of Brafman, "'I'm Not the Morality Police': Inside Benjamin Brafman's Defense of Harvey Weinstein," *Esquire*, January 14, 2019.

316 **the prevalent pessimism**: Jan Ransom, "Is the Case Against Harvey Weinstein in Jeopardy?," *New York Times*, October 29, 2018.

317 **remove Lucia Evans**: The author attended this October 11, 2018, hearing in Judge James Burke's courtroom and all the hearings described in this chapter.

317 **DiGaudio's coaching**: Supplemental Notice of Motion filed by Benjamin Brafman to dismiss all charges against Harvey Weinstein, November 5, 2018.

317 **"the two remaining complainants"**: Benjamin Brafman's 3-page letter to Judge James Burke claiming that D.A. Vance and his office withheld evidence, December 12, 2018.

318 **1901 State Court of Appeals**: Original Molineux ruling, *People v. Molineux*, 168 N.Y. 264 (1901).

319 **"We are obviously disappointed"**: Author present for Ben Brafman's press statement after December 20, 2018, hearing.

321 **But protests flared over**: Ronald Sullivan interview conducted by Catherine Elton for *Boston* magazine, August 14, 2019.

322 **Mr. Weinstein has deliberately disregarded**: Jose Baez letter to Judge James Burke reported by Rebecca Rosenberg, "Harvey Weinstein's Lawyer Jose Baez Wants Off the Case," *New York Post*, June 17, 2019.

323 **"nobody even bats an eyelash"**: Donna Rotunno discusses her advantage in a sex-crime trial in Bryan Smith profile, "The Defender," *Chicago* magazine, January 23, 2018.

324 **Attorney Gloria Allred**: Gloria Allred's opposition to eliminating NDAs reported in Jodi Kantor and Megan Twohey, *She Said: Breaking the Sexual Harassment Story That Helped Ignite a Movement* (New York: Penguin Press, 2019).

325 **among the strictest**: Natasha Bach, "New York's Rape Laws Are Now Some of the Toughest in the Country," *Fortune*, September 20, 2019.

327 **"a huge victory for the prosecution"**: Author interview with Arthur Aidala about Molineux ruling, January 8, 2020.

327 **"a difference between sins and crimes"**: Donna Rotunno says Harvey Weinstein is not a rapist, "Harvey's Lawyer Says He's a Sinner, Not a Rapist," *USA Today*, September 17, 2019.

328 **the December 16 *Post* roared**: Rebecca Rosenberg Harvey Weinstein exclusive, "Whine Stein: Harvey Tells Post: I Have Been Great for Women," *New York Post*, December 16, 2019.

329 **"My body didn't forget you"**: Alan Feuer, "Weinstein Interview Infuriates Accusers," including Rose McGowan, *New York Times*, December 17, 2019.

329 **"my need for control"**: Harvey Weinstein email quoted in Chloe Melas, "Harvey Weinstein Addresses His Pending Criminal Trial," CNN, January 4, 2020.

329 **"There is no one-on-one"**: Author interview with Arthur Aidala describing Weinstein's proposal to work it out with Cyrus Vance, January 8, 2020.

329 **summit meeting with Governor Cuomo**: Total of $110,000 contributed by Harvey Weinstein to Andrew Cuomo campaigns reported by Jesse McKinley, "Reversing Course, Cuomo Will Return Weinstein's Money," *New York Times*, October 12, 2017.

CHAPTER EIGHTEEN: COURTROOM 1530

331 **"I saw what the media"**: Author interview with Donna Rotunno about her clothes and Marcia Clark, June 8, 2020.

332 **Harvey texting on his iPhone**: Author interview with Officer Cheryl Ferguson, January 16, 2020.

332 **Harvey started to respond**: The entire account of testimony and behavior in court—including confrontation between Harvey Weinstein and Judge James Burke over iPhone use, January 7, 2020—was observed by the author. Since author was in the courtroom daily, there will be no further endnotes regarding author's observations in court.

333 **The defense protested**: Letter from Arthur Aidala urging Judge Burke to recuse himself, January 8, 2020.

334 **hiring a jury consultant**: Author interview with Donna Rotunno about a jury consultant, June 8, 2020.

335 **"Our goal throughout"**: Author interview with Damon Cheronis about jury selection, May 6, 2020.

335 **"we had to look at individuals"**: Author interview with Arthur Aidala about jury selection, January 28, 2020.

335 **locate jurors with "the courage"**: Donna Rotunno seeks "courage" from a prospective juror, interview with NBC reporter Stephanie Gosk, *Today* show, January 5, 2020.

336 **described her novel**: Chris Francescani, ABC memo, "The Saga of Juror 11," February 23, 2020.

336 **the harmony on the defense team:** Author interview with Donna Rotunno about her disagreements with their jury consultant, June 8, 2020.

337 **"He's much more docile":** Author interview with Arthur Aidala about Harvey Weinstein's role on the defense, January 28, 2020.

337 **The first day:** Lucian Chalfen, the court's director of public information, told author court session started late because six jurors got lost, January 22, 2020.

338 **"'I'm writing a screenplay'":** Harvey Weinstein email dictated to his public relations adviser, Juda Engelmayer, from prison and sent to author, denying he was writing a screenplay, September 14, 2020.

340 **Cosby's lawyers even dismissed:** Chris Francescani covered the Bill Cosby trial and wrote for ABC online, "How Bill Cosby's Defense Team's Vicious Strategy Backfired: Analysis," April 28, 2018.

342 **"How do you not know what rape is?":** Arthur Aidala shares with the author advice he whispered in Donna Rotunno's ear, January 24, 2020.

344 **"That's real New York":** Arthur Aidala tells author what Harvey Weinstein said to him after he questioned Rosie Perez, January 28, 2020.

344 **Her memory of the assault:** Haley testimony and children's drawings recalled by a juror in Jan Ransom, Sharon Otterman, and Laura Dimon, "Why the Weinstein Jury Decided to Convict," *New York Times*, March 2, 2020.

346 **"the victims will be perpetrators":** Ronan Farrow, *Catch and Kill: Lies, Spies, and a Conspiracy to Protect Predators* (New York: Little, Brown and Company, 2019).

346 **"Damon was very effective":** Arthur Aidala had wanted to explore a plea bargain, and praises Damon Cheronis to author, April 10, 2020.

CHAPTER NINETEEN: JESSICA MANN

357 **prosecutors would not dare call:** Author discussion with Damon Cheronis about why prosecution would not dare summon Talita Maia to testify, January 31, 2020.

360 *Thank you for making me:* Schneeweiss did not respond to several emails. Her lawyer, Robert M. Barta, responded for her, saying, "Regrettably, litigation currently pending against her" makes it "impossible" for her to speak freely. When later asked if the emails released at the trial suggested Schneeweiss was an enabler, Barta replied, "Your assertion that emails introduced by the Prosecutor suggested that Ms. Schneeweiss enabled Weinstein's behavior is nonsense. No reasonable interpretation of those emails would suggest anything other than my client doing her legitimate job duties. Neither Ms. Schneeweiss, nor any other assistant employed by Weinstein is a mind reader." Barbara Schneeweiss emails dated February 20, 27, and 28, 2013, released at Weinstein's criminal trial, and Jessica Mann email, February 27, 2013. The two email responses from Schneeweiss's lawyer, Robert M. Barta, to author were dated January 17, 2019, and April 3, 2020.

360 **she escorted them:** Gene Maddaus, Elizabeth Wagmeister, and Brent Lange probe enablers in "Harvey Weinstein Is Behind Bars, but Has the Culture in Hollywood Really Changed?," *Variety*, February 6, 2020.

364 **"the jury is not looking at her?":** Author conversation with Juda Engelmayer, who was confident the defense was shredding Mann's testimony, February 3, 2020.

364 **he was feeling some political heat:** A dozen female members of the city council call for Vance's resignation, *New York Post*, February 7, 2020.

366 **"the impression that I look sleepy":** Harvey Weinstein email dictated to his public relations adviser, Juda Engelmayer, from prison and sent to author, denying he had trouble staying awake and describing his "severe back pain," September 14, 2020.

368 **"My best hope":** Author interview with Arthur Aidala assessing the trial after Jessica Mann testimony, January 28, 2020.

CHAPTER TWENTY: THE DEFENSE SPEAKS, AND CLOSING ARGUMENTS

369 **how passive he seemed:** Damon Cheronis email response to author's question: Did Harvey often pepper his lawyers with suggestions? He did not, said Cheronis, September 22, 2020.

369 **his "social awkwardness":** Author interview with Donna Rotunno about Harvey Weinstein being on "the spectrum," June 8, 2020.

370 **"There was a problem":** Author interview with Damon Cheronis on why only seven defense witnesses, May 6, 2020.

372 DEFENSE WITNESS ENDS UP: *New York Post* headline about Harvey Weinstein's first defense witness, February 7, 2020.

375 **"The majority of time in that room":** Author interview with Arthur Aidala about whether the lawyers had a lengthy discussion with Harvey Weinstein about him testifying, February 12, 2020.

376 WEINSTEIN DECIDES NOT TO: *New York Times* headline claiming Harvey Weinstein wanted to testify, February 12, 2020.

376 **Such a cross-examination:** The defense explanation of why Harvey could not testify is contained in their April 5, 2021, brief to the State Court of Appeals asking it to overrule the verdict in this trial.

383 **two very different portraits:** Predator or prey analysis by Brent Lang and Elizabeth Wagmeister, "Attorneys Draw Starkly Different Portraits of Harvey Weinstein in Closing Arguments," *Variety*, February 14, 2020.

384 **"pervasive culture of silence":** Rosanna Arquette quote from first day of trial reported in Lang and Wagmeister, "Attorneys Draw Starkly."

CHAPTER TWENTY-ONE: THE VERDICT

385 **someone secretly committed:** Amanda Brainerd, *Age of Consent* (New York: Viking, 2020).

385 **"*my deeply personal story*":** Amanda Brainerd text message to her friend Deborah Copaken, published in "The Glorious, Messy Life of Liz Wurtzel," *The Atlantic*, January 7, 2020, about their mutual friend Elizabeth Wurtzel.

389 **lunch from a deli:** A description of the jury room and the food provided appeared in Jan Ransom, Sharon Otterman, and Laura Dimon, "Why the Weinstein Jury Decided to Convict," *New York Times*, March 2, 2020.

390 **most juries hate recessing:** Author interview with Arthur Aidala expressing his concern over the potential jury verdict, February 21, 2020.

390 **might have doubts about Sciorra's:** Explanation of complexity of counts, Alan Feuer and Jan Ransom, "What Note from Jury Could Mean as Weinstein Deliberations Resume," *New York Times*, February 21, 2020, updated February 24, 2020.

392 **talked his way past the doorman:** As described by Mira Sorvino in Ronan Farrow, *Catch and Kill: Lies, Spies, and a Conspiracy to Protect Predators* (New York: Little, Brown and Company, 2019).

392 **"reasonable doubt" threshold:** A description from two anonymous jurors why they had doubts about whether Harvey Weinstein raped Annabella Sciorra in Ransom, Otterman, and Dimon, "Why the Weinstein Jury."

CHAPTER TWENTY-TWO: THE CONVICT

394 **"Because of this verdict":** Author interview with attorney Debra Katz after the Weinstein verdict, February 24, 2020.

394 **"I literally cried":** Reaction of people in Hollywood to the stiff sentence given Harvey Weinstein, Ted Johnson, "Hollywood Reacts to Harvey Weinstein Sentencing," *Deadline*, March 11, 2020.

395 **"This is why we say MeToo":** Tarana Burke reaction to guilty verdict, Ella Alexander, "Hollywood Reacts to Harvey Weinstein Verdict: 'This Is Taking Out the Trash,'" *Harpers Bazaar*, February 24, 2020.

395 **After I was raped:** Essay written by Taralê Wulff, "Harvey Weinstein's Prison Sentence Can Never Heal Me. But It's a Start," *Medium*, March 10, 2020.

396 **urging Judge Burke to impose:** Weinstein's two ex-wives and others decline to write letters to Judge James Burke, Rebecca Rosenberg, "Harvey Weinstein's Ex-Wives Refused to Vouch for Him to Judge," *New York Post*, March 11, 2020.

399 **to get him to cut it short:** Arthur Aidala described to ABC News's Chris Francescani his attempt to curtail Weinstein's speech in court; it was reported in Francescani's memo to ABC, March 11, 2020.

400 **Press accounts did not:** Description of Weinstein's "rant" reported by Olivia Raimonde and Patricia Hurtado, "Harvey Weinstein Stunned Courtroom with Bizarre Rant Before Sentencing," *Bloomberg News*, March 11, 2020.

400 **To strengthen the prosecution's:** Letter from District Attorney Vance's office delineating the many alleged sexual abuses committed by Harvey Weinstein, March 6, 2020.

400 **"Please shut up Donna":** Rosanna Arquette tweets about Donna Rotunno reported in Johnson, "Hollywood Reacts."

401 **He spoke regularly:** Author interview with Arthur Aidala on speaking to Harvey Weinstein in prison and recruiting a Buffalo lawyer, December 5, 2020.

401 **said to be his girlfriend:** Report of Alexandra Vino visit to Harvey Weinstein in prison, Martin Gould, "Disgraced Movie Mogul Harvey Weinstein, 68, Was Paid a Special Visit in Jail," *Daily Mail*, December 4, 2020.

401 **Harvey's legal difficulties mounted:** Press release by Los Angeles district attorney Jackie Lacey, March 11, 2020. Her successors pledged to pursue the case and ultimately plan to extradite Harvey to L.A.

402 **Their lawsuit asserted:** Sandeep Rehal's civil lawsuit filed by ten alleged victims against Harvey Weinstein, the company's board, and its executives before the U.S. District Court of the Southern District of New York, October 31, 2018.

403 **"obnoxious," keeping the lawsuits:** Federal judge upends $25 million civil lawsuit, Jodi Kantor and Megan Twohey, "Judge, Expressing Skepticism, Upends $25 Million Harvey Weinstein Settlement," *New York Times*, July 14, 2020.

403 **"harsh and excessive":** Appeal filed by Aidala, Bertuna & Kamins, PC, April 5, 2021, Appellate Case No.: 2020-00590.

403 **Harvey's liquid assets:** ABC News first reported on July 10, 2020, that Harvey's two ex-wives successfully petitioned the court to freeze $6 million of his liquid assets.

403 **bills went unpaid:** Jury consultant suing Harvey Weinstein reported by Gene Maddaus, "Harvey Weinstein's Jury Consultant Sues Over Unpaid $166K Bill," *Variety*, May 27, 2020.

403 **"not fully taken care of":** Author interview with Donna Rotunno about Harvey's nonpayment of second half of their fee, June 8, 2020.

404 **"one month short":** Author interview with Juda Engelmayer saying Harvey Weinstein is "one month short" in payment, June 10, 2020, and email confirming short a third month but insisting it will be solved, July 24, 2020.

404 **Harvey owed him:** Charles Harder sues Harvey Weinstein for unpaid legal bills, Ashley Cullins, "Charles Harder Takes Harvey Weinstein to Court Over $180,000 in Unpaid Legal Fees," *Hollywood Reporter*, November 25, 2020.

404 **"has to sell assets":** Author interview with Juda Engelmayer on how lack of dollars slowed Harvey Weinstein's appeal, December 1, 2020.

404 **"a vile fiend":** Harvey Weinstein sues ex-lawyer for $1 million and ex-lawyer responds, Gene Maddaus, "Harvey Weinstein Seeks to Recoup $1 Million from Ex-Lawyer Jose Baez," *Variety*, May 5, 2021.

404 **a claim Harvey denies:** Harvey Weinstein email dictated to his public relations adviser, Juda Engelmayer, from prison and sent to author, denying he reached out to his brother for financial help, September 14, 2020.

405 **he does need your help:** Harvey Weinstein (via Bill Currao) to Bob Weinstein, May 15, 2020.

405 **"I did not respond":** Author interview with Bob Weinstein explaining that Harvey asked him for $3.5 million to cover his legal costs, June 11, 2020.

406 **"a convicted rapist":** Statement by the Silence Breakers about Harvey's legacy in Johnson, "Hollywood Reacts."

406 **"It's sad to have":** Author interview with Eric Robinson about Harvey Weinstein's legacy, January 23, 2019.

406 **"It changed the nature":** Author interview with Amy Israel about Miramax legacy, February 15, 2019.

406 **"the art film ghetto":** Peter Biskind interviewed by Isaac Chotiner, "You Heard Stories About Hanky Panky," *Slate*, October 12, 2017.

CHAPTER TWENTY-THREE: ROSEBUD?

408 **"That's how we really decided":** Jury Foreman Bernard Cody interviewed by CNN's Jean Casarez and Lauren Del Valle, March 13, 2020.

408 **failure of Harvey to testify:** Two anonymous jurors say Harvey Weinstein's failure to testify, or to have his brother vouch for him, was important to the jury, Jan Ransom, Sharon Otterman, and Laura Dimon, "Why the Weinstein Jury Decided to Convict," *New York Times*, March 3, 2020.

409 **"That was the culture then":** The full 6-paragraph statement is printed in the class action complaint filed in the U.S. District Court of the Southern District of New York on October 31, 2018, against the Weinstein Company board by his alleged victims.

410 **Dr. James Cantor, a professor:** Author interview with Dr. James Cantor on the difference between knowing behavior is wrong and knowing exposure would be harmful, May 21, 2019.

410 **"less to do with sex":** Author interviews with Alan Brewer about Harvey Weinstein's need to dominate, September 11, 2019, and October 10, 2019.

410 **Someone who enjoys:** Author interview with Dr. Meg S. Kaplan on the connection between verbal and sexual violence, October 9, 2018.

410 **"You're no good'":** Author interview with Bob Weinstein about Miriam, June 11, 2020.

411 **"after you're eighteen is too late":** Author interview with David Boies about Miriam Weinstein, November 27, 2018.

411 **"He was always wanting more":** Mark Gill interview in BBC documentary *Untouchable*, 2019.

411 **"Harvey was a man":** Author interview with Abby Ex, January 15, 2019.

412 **"They objectify women":** Author interview with Dr. Meg S. Kaplan on men aroused when women are in their control, October 9, 2018.

412 **"getting women to submit":** Zelda Perkins interviewed about Harvey "as a power addict," Emily Maitlis and Lucinda Day, "Harvey Weinstein: Ex-Assistant Criticises Gagging Orders," BBC Newsnight, December 19, 2017.

412 **Bob googled the definition:** Author interview with Bob Weinstein matching the definition of a sociopath to his brother, May 25, 2020.

412 **The words that marched:** Google search for the definition of a sociopath reveals Rosie McCall, "9 Ways to Spot a Sociopath," Health.com, and various professional profiles of sociopaths.

413 **"You're missing something big":** Author interviews with Bob Weinstein about the illogic of his brother's behavior, September 14, 2018, and June 11, 2020.

414 **"I just got cursed at":** Harvey Weinstein email dictated to his public relations adviser, Juda Engelmayer, from prison and sent to author, denying that Bob reached out to him, September 14, 2020.

414 **"there is no Harvey":** Author interview with Bob Weinstein about reaching out to Harvey in prison, Harvey's response via William Currao, and Bob's final impression, June 11, 2020.

IMAGE CREDITS

p. 9, bottom: Ken McKay/ITV/Shutterstock

p. 10: Brian Cahn/ZUMA Press, Inc./Alamy Stock Photo

p. 11, top: Katy Winn/ Getty Images Entertainment via Getty Images

p. 11, bottom: Ilya S. Savenok/Getty Images Entertainment via Getty Images

p. 12, top: Mathew Imaging/WireImage via Getty Images

p. 12, center: Jamie McCarthy/Getty Images Entertainment via Getty Images

p. 12, bottom: Theo Wargo via Getty Images

p. 13, top: Martin Schoeller/August

p. 13, bottom: Andrew Lih/Wikimedia Commons

p. 14, top: Lucas Jackson/Reuters/Alamy Stock Photo

p. 14, bottom: © Starmax/Newscom via Zuma Press

p. 15, top: Lucas Jackson/Reuters/Alamy Stock Photo

p. 15, bottom: Seth Wenig/AP/Shutterstock

p. 16, top: Richard Drew/AP/Shutterstock

p. 16, center: Sam Wong/Getty Images Entertainment via Getty Images

p. 16, bottom: Uncredited/AP/Shutterstock

INDEX